0123431

0715613901

THE ENGLISH VICE

Beating, Sex and Shame in
Victorian England and After

IAN GIBSON

DUCKWORTH

Third impression 1992
Second impression 1979
First published in 1978 by
Gerald Duckworth & Co. Ltd.
The Old Piano Factory
48 Hoxton Square, London N1 6PB
© 1978 by Ian Gibson

Paper   ISBN 0 7156 13901

Photoset in Great Britain by
Specialised Offset Services Ltd., Liverpool
and printed and bound by
REDWOOD PRESS LIMITED
Melksham, Wiltshire

CONTENTS

List of Illustrations   vii

Preface   ix

1. Knowledge and Warnings about Sexual Flagellation before Freud   1

2. Home and School Beating in Nineteenth-century England and Later   48

3. Eton, the Birch and Swinburne   99

4. Judicial, Prison, Army and Naval Flogging in Britain   144

5. The Flagellant Correspondence Column in Nineteenth-century England   194

6. Flagellant Prostitution in Victorian England and After   233

7. The Flagellant Fantasy   265

8. Towards an Understanding of Sexual Flagellation   284

9. 'It Never Did *Me* Any Harm'   310

Appendices

A. French text of quotations from Rousseau's *Confessions*   316

B. The use of corporal punishment in schools outside the United Kingdom (as at July 1977)   318

C. Two flagellant poems published by Swinburne in *The Pearl*   320

Bibliography   329

Index   348

England ... das gelobte Land, die Hochburg des Flagellantismus.

Alfred Eulenburg, *Sadismus und Masochismus*, 1911

The first time a school-master ordered me to take my trousers down I knew it was not from any doubt that he could punish me efficiently enough with them up.

Sir Laurence Olivier, letter to *The Observer*, 21 November 1965.

No other activity of man (or woman) as a sexual being raises so many questions as flagellation.

Ronald Pearsall, *The Worm in the Bud*, 1969

ILLUSTRATIONS

Between pages 148 and 149

1. Action in an early-eighteenth-century flagellant brothel.
2. The frontispiece of Paullini's *Flagellum Salutis* (1698).
3. Early fifteenth-century Flagellation of Christ, attributed to the Catalan painter Luis Borrassá.
4. Fanny Hill applies the Meibomian rod to Mr Barville.
5. Title page of *The Children's Petition* (1669).
6. Picture from the family magazine *Home Chat* in 1903.
7. A flagellant hoax advertisement in *Punch* (1863).
8. A flagellant advertisement in the religious weekly *The Guardian* (1876).
9. A nineteenth-century French comment on the English Vice.
10. An article in *Home Chat*.
11. A bit of modern English fun from the weekly comic *Smash*.
12. The Eton rod.
13. The 'Library' at Eton, where Upper School birchings were administered.
14. Swinburne's tutor, the Rev. James Leigh Joynes, Lower Master of Eton 1878-1887.
15. Birching at Eton in the good old days.
16. An anti-birching cartoon published in *The Humanitarian*, November 1909.
17. The birch for Irish rebels.
18. The mayor of Cork on the Etonian block, with Gladstone in the guise of headmaster.
19. A mother birching her son on a French mediaeval misericord.

20. 'Lower discipline' Spanish-style, from a mediaeval misericord in Zamora Cathedral.
21. Plate 3 of Hogarth's *A Harlot's Progress*.
22. The scopophobic Englishman, from Hector France's *La pudique Albion* (1885).
23. Arthur Horner's view of the English Vice.
24. Flagellant advertisements from *Society* 1900.
25. More flagellant advertisements from *Society*.
26. Theresa Berkley's celebrated *chevalet*.
27. Lady Termagant Flaybum prepares to excoriate her stepson.
28. A birching scene attributed to H.F. Gravelot.

PREFACE

The idea of writing this book first occurred to me ten years ago, in Granada, while I was working on Lorca. Before arriving in Spain I had read with fascination Mario Praz's great work, *La carne, la morte e il diavolo nella letteratura romantica*, translated by Angus Davidson into English, in 1933, under the unaccountable title *The Romantic Agony*. Praz's appendix, 'Swinburne and "Le Vice Anglais"' had interested me: not only did the Italian scholar state that 'it seems to be an assured fact that sexual flagellation has been practised in England with greater frequency than elsewhere', but he provided a considerable amount of information, new to me, in support of this unusual contention. The stress in Praz's appendix was on English sadism and its literary repercussions, especially in France. Here for the first time I heard of W.T. Stead's 'The Maiden Tribute of Modern Babylon'; of the perversity of Swinburne; and of the widespread reputation for refined cruelty enjoyed by the English aristocracy in *fin de siècle* French literature. Among other French authors, Praz quoted from Péladan's chapter 'Le vice anglais' in *La Vertu suprême* (*c*. 1896):

> Swinburne a chanté le sadisme et toujours l'Anglo-Saxon incarnera la honte humaine: la race qui ensanglante la volupté, qui cache le couteau de l'assassin dans le lit de l'amour.*
>
> (Praz, 1960, p.474)

It seemed to me, reading Praz, that the French decadents had perhaps assumed too readily that 'the English Vice' was sadism rather than masochism. Might these foreigners not have got hold of the wrong end of the stick, as it were? Other reading before I knew Praz's work had in fact suggested to me that, if Englishmen of the middle and upper classes were interested in the admixture of pain and pleasure, it was more as passive than as active partners.

---

* 'Swinburne sang of sadism, and the Anglo-Saxon will always represent human depravation – the race which stains pleasure with blood, which conceals an assassin's knife in the bed of love.'

In Granada an American hispanist friend, Sanford Sheperd, made me the generous gift of a copy of Randolph Hughes's edition of Swinburne's *Lesbia Brandon*. Hughes's commentary and notes, along with the evidence of the text itself, showed beyond any doubt that Swinburne's obsession with flagellation was as much masochistic as sadistic. About him, at any rate, the French seemed to be wrong.

Over the following years my reading turned up more and more references to the English predilection for the rod. I became gradually convinced that 'the English Vice' was not simply sadism but flagellomania, and my belief was confirmed when I read the three great bibliographies of erotica published in the late Victorian period by Pisanus Fraxi (Henry Spencer Ashbee). There seemed to be no question about it: flagellomania, while almost totally absent in France, Spain and Italy, was widespread in Britain, especially in England. Was it not a fact that flogging with the cat o' nine tails and the birch had only been abolished in English prisons in 1967? That birching still existed in the Isle of Man? That caning was still common in schools, particularly at the public schools? That every so often scandals involving flagellant prostitution hit the headlines, as during the Ward case in 1958? It seemed to me that a book must be written to explain such an odd proclivity.

When I decided to investigate the subject I did not realise that the roots of the English Vice struck so deep.

A word about the organisation of the book. I have tried as far as possible to avoid theoretical considerations in the first six chapters, and to limit myself to documenting different manifestations of the English beating mania, mainly in the nineteenth century. I have sought to let the material presented speak for itself, although of course it has not been possible for me entirely to avoid shaping that material or guiding the reader's response to it. My hope is that, by Chapter Seven, the reader will feel that he knows enough about the flagellant phenomenon to enable him to consider with some insight the views put forward by psychoanalysts and other investigators. Without the former, certainly, we would not be in a position to understand sexual flagellation, to look beneath its surface and try to fathom what it is about.

I must express my indebtedness to three outstanding books which, along with Praz's, have helped me greatly during my research. Without Ronald Pearsall's *The Worm in the Bud: The World of Victorian Sexuality* (1969) and Steven Marcus's *The Other Victorians: A Study of Sexuality and Pornography in Mid-Nineteenth Century England* (1964), indeed, it is doubtful if I would have taken the decision to embark on this book at all; while Jonathan Gathorne-Hardy's *The Rise and Fall of the British Nanny* (1972), which I read late in my investigation, opened up unsuspected vistas and suggested some new lines of approach. Cecil Lang's magnificent edition of *The Swinburne Letters* (1959-62) – a model of scholarship – was also indispensable.

My publisher and I are grateful to the following for permission to quote copyright material: Corinna Adam and the *New Statesman* ('Beating in Britain'); Miss Felicity Ashbee and the Provost and Scholars of King's College, Cambridge (the C.R. Ashbee diaries); David Benedictus and Blond Briggs (*The Fourth of June*); the British Library Board (Swinburne's *The Flogging-Block*; letters to Swinburne from Richard Monckton Milnes and Mary Leith; communication from Frederick Hankey to H.S. Ashbee); the Keeper of the Brotherton Collection, University of Leeds (letter from George Powell to Swinburne); The Controller of Her Majesty's Stationery Office (HMSO publications); J.M. Cohen and Penguin Books (English translation of passages from Rousseau's *Confessions*); André Deutsch (Cyril Connolly, *Enemies of Promise*); Éditions Gallimard (Rousseau's *Confessions*); Geoffrey Gorer and Barrie and Jenkins (*Exploring English Character*); The Hamlyn Publishing Group Ltd. (Winston Churchill, *My Early Life*); The Hogarth Press Ltd. (*Standard Edition of the Complete Psychological Works of Sigmund Freud*, translated and edited by James Strachey); Graham Kalton and Longman Group Ltd. (*The Public Schools: A Factual Survey of Headmasters' Conference Schools in England and Wales*); Prof. Cecil Lang and Yale University Press (*The Swinburne Letters*); Macmillan of London and Basingstoke (Ralph Nevill, *Floreat Etona*); Desmond Morris and Jonathan Cape Ltd. (*The Naked Ape*); David Niven, Hamish Hamilton Ltd. and Coronet Books (*The Moon's a Balloon*); W.W. Norton and Company, Inc. (Otto Fenichel, *The Psychoanalytic Theory of Neurosis* and Erik Erikson, *Childhood and Society*); Lord Olivier (letter to *The Observer*); G.P. Putnam's Sons (Krafft-Ebing, *Psychopathia Sexualis*, translated by Harry E. Wedeck); Anthony Storr (*Sexual Deviation*); Tavistock Publications Ltd. (D.W. Winnicott, *The Child and the Family* and *The Child and the Outside World*); The Master and Fellows of Trinity College, Cambridge (quotations from the commonplace books of Richard Monckton Milnes; letters to Milnes from Sir Richard Burton); the Literary Estate of Virginia Woolf and The Hogarth Press Ltd. (*Roger Fry: A Biography*); 'Y' and Paul Elek Ltd. (*The Autobiography of an Englishman*).

Several friends and acquaintances helped me to write this book by providing bibliographical information or sending me cuttings from the British press relevant to my subject: in this category it is a pleasure to thank Dr James Dickie, Professors Anthony Watson and James

Cummins, Dr Roger Walker, Mr Ronald Pearsall, Mr Timothy d'Arch Smith, Mr Neville Hilary, Ms Marion Stern, Mr and Mrs David Rowlands and Mr Richard Brinkley. Mr Ian Todd was indefatigable in obtaining, and sending me, books published in America. Prof. Steven Marcus kindly sent me an off-print of an article on Sacher-Masoch by Ms Gertrud Lenzer. Ms Gene Adams and Mr Colin Bagnall of STOPP (The Society of Teachers Opposed to Physical Punishment) replied with generous alacrity to my last-minute requests for up-to-date information on school beating in Britain. Dr Nigel Dennis sent me photocopies of the letters from Richard Burton to Lord Houghton preserved in Trinity College Library, Cambridge. Dr Louis Doat took the trouble to make enquiries on my behalf concerning the abolition of corporal punishment in French schools. The staffs at the London Library, Wellcome Medical Library, University of London Library and British Library were unfailingly helpful, and I must thank particularly Dr David Clements and Ms Margaret Johnson of the latter institution. Mrs Angela Proud did me many a good turn. Mr John S. Mayfield sent me some useful Swinburne information, as did Mr Patrick Strong of Eton College. I owe a special debt of thanks to the present headmaster of Eton, Mr Michael McCrum, who answered my questions about beating at that establishment with frankness. Finally, I am indebted once again to my wife Carole, for her forbearance, criticisms and help at every stage of my research.

Les Playes (Var)
July 1977   I.G.

1

Knowledge and Warnings about Sexual Flagellation before Freud

Meibom and his influence

The first coherent attempt to explain flagellation as a sexual stimulant seems to have been that made by the German doctor Johann Heinrich Meibom (1590-1655), often known by his Latin name Meibomius, in his remarkable treatise *De Flagrorum Usu in Re Veneria & Lumborum Renumque Officio* ('On the Use of Rods in Venereal Matters and in the Office of the Loins and Reins'). This work was first published at Leyden in 1629 and went through numerous editions. It was translated into German, French and English. The British Library has a copy of the 47-page fourth Latin edition, published at Leyden in 1643, and of several subsequent editions in that language, including one published at London in 1770;[1] it also has English and French translations, but these are kept in the Private Case. It used to be impossible to consult them without special permission, but the situation has recently changed. Perhaps it was felt that Latin scholars are less likely than the rest of literate mankind to be corrupted by the perusal of Meibom's work.

Over the years additions were made to the treatise, notably by the Danish doctor Thomas Bartholinus (1619-1680), whose letter to Meibom's son Heinrich (1638-1700) and the latter's reply were included in several editions (Meibom junior, also a distinguished doctor, gave his name to certain sebaceous glands of the eyelid). In some editions the title underwent modification and the treatise was ascribed to Bartholinus and not Meibom. Mercier's French translation of 1792 contained an introduction, notes and bibliography, and was reprinted frequently during the nineteenth century. The quotations that follow are taken from the 1718 London

---

[1] The Wellcome Medical Library, London, has copies of the Leyden 1643 and Frankfurt 1669 and 1670 editions of Meibom's work.

edition.

Meibom's treatise is a serious attempt (1) to establish as a fact that flogging can indeed act as a stimulus to erection in the 'victim' and (2) to essay an explanation of such a weird phenomenon. It is written in the form of an epistle to Meibom's friend Christianus Cassius who, as the title-page shows, was Counsellor to the Bishop of Lübeck and the Duke of Holstein. It appears that, over wine, Cassius had expressed his disbelief that flagellation could cure many ailments, including impotence:

> But what you could not so readily believe upon my Affirmation, was that there are Persons who are stimulated to *Venery by Strokes of Rods, and worked up into a Flame of Lust by Blows*; and that the *Part*, which distinguishes us to be *Men*, should be raised by the Charm of invigorating Lashes. But I will convince you, my Friend *Cassius*, that it is so. (pp. 5-6)

Meibom begins by appealing to a wide range of authorities in support of his argument. Madness, melancholy caused by unhappy love, 'erotic mania', skinniness and bodily weakness – these and other disorders respond to flagellation or urtication (rubbing or beating with stinging nettles). But the most curious case is undoubtedly that of sexual impotence in the male. Meibom recounts some contemporary examples of flagellant activity in Germany (culled from the law courts) and refers Cassius to those authors, beginning with Petronius, who have treated of the subject. In the *Satyricon*, he reminds his friend, Oenothea, the priestess of Priapus, undertakes to render Encolpius's temporarily flagging member 'as stiff as a horn' (*fascinum tam rigidum reddituram, ut cornu*) by whipping his belly and navel with green nettles. And had not Otto Brunfels recorded more recently in his *Onomastikon Medicinae* (1534) that some men are impotent unless they are flogged first, and 'that at Munich, the Seat of the Duke of Bavaria, there lived a Man who never could enjoy his Wife, if he was not soundly flogged to it before he made his Attempts'? (pp. 10-11). Among those who have written on sexual flagellation, however, Meibom has no doubt that the most important is the great Italian humanist, Pico della Mirandola (1463-94) who, in his *Disputationes Adversus Astrologiam Divinatricem* (1502), Ch. 27, has given us a racy account of a kinky acquaintance:

> There is now alive, says he, a Man of a prodigious, and almost unheard of kind of Lechery: For he is never inflamed to Pleasure, but when he is whipt; and yet he is so intent on the Act, and longs for the Strokes with such an Earnestness, that he blames the Flogger that uses him gently, and is never thoroughly Master of his Wishes unless the Blood starts, and the

Whip rages smartly o'er the wicked Limbs of the Monster. This Creature begs this Favour of the Woman he is to enjoy, brings her a Rod himself, soak'd and harden'd in Vinegar a Day before for the same Purpose, and intreats the Blessing of a Whipping from the Harlot on his Knees; and the more smartly he is whipt, he rages the more eagerly, and goes the same Pace both to Pleasure and Pain. A singular Instance of one who finds a Delight in the Midst of Torment; and as he is not a Man very vicious in other Respects, he acknowledges his Distemper, and abhors it. (pp. 7-9)

Pico was fascinated, not surprisingly, by this man's strange behaviour and, refusing to accept that it was astrologically conditioned, asked him if he himself could explain it. The answer might have been taken from one of Krafft-Ebing's case histories published 400 years later:

When I seriously enquir'd of him the Cause of this uncommon Plague, his Reply was, I have used my self to it from a Boy. And upon repeating the Question to him, he added, That he was educated with a Number of wicked Boys, who set up this Trade of Whipping among themselves, and purchased of each other these infamous stripes at the expence of their Modesty.[2] (pp. 13-14)

The case of this unfortunate flagellant became well known and was cited by many writers, including the Italian doctor Ludovicus Coelius Richerius or Rhodiginus (1450-1525) in his famous *Lectionum Antiquarum* (Loudun, 1562, vol. II, bk. XI, ch. XV, pp. 49-50). Coelius follows Pico's account almost word for word, and agrees that the case proves that bad habits contracted in childhood can become permanent:

by the Force of a vicious Habit gaining ground upon him, he practis'd a Vice he disapprov'd. But it grew more obstinate and rooted in his Nature,

---

[2] Vivit adhuc homo mihi notus, prodigiosae libidinis et inauditae: nam ad Venerem numquam accenditur nisi vapulet, et tamen scelus id ita cogitat, saevientes ita plagas desiderat, ut increpet verberantem, si cum eo lentius egerit, haud compos plene voti nisi eruperit sanguis, et innocentis artus hominis nocentissimi violentior scutica disseruerit. Efflagitat ille miser hanc operam summis precibus ab ea semper femina quam adivit, praebetque flagellum, pridie sibi ad id officii aceti infusione duratum, et supplex a meretrice verberari postulat, a qua quanto caeditur durius eo ferventius incalescit et pari passu ad voluptatem doloremque contendit, unus inventus homo qui corporeas delicias inter cruciatum inveniat. Is, cum non alioquin pessimus sit, morbum suum agnoscit et odit, quoniamque mihi familiaris multis iam retro annis, quid pateretur libere patefecit; a quo diligenter tam insolitae pestis causam cum sciscitarer, ≪ a puero, inquit, sic assuevi ≫. Et me rursus consuetudinis causam interrogante, educatum se cum pueris scelestissimis, inter quos convenisset hac caedendi licentia, quasi pretio quodam, mutuum sibi vendere flagitiosa alternatione pudorem. Pico della Mirandola, *Disputationes adversus astrologiam divinatricem* (Florence, 1946), I, p.412.

from his using it from a Child, when a reciprocal Frication among his
School-Fellows used to be provoked by the Titulation of Stripes. A strange
Instance what a Power the force of Education has in grafting inveterate ill
Habits on our Morals. (Meibom, pp. 14-15)

Meibom, however, is not happy about this explanation and feels
certain that there must be another cause which makes the
establishment of such an extraordinary habit possible. Cutting
through the quotations and learned references with which his treatise
is larded, it is not difficult to isolate the basic components of his
theory.

The first point is that, for Meibom, the semen is elaborated, not in
the testicles but in two seminal vesicles or vessels (Latin *vas*,
receptacle) which are located close to the kidneys. This whole
vaguely-defined area he terms the *lombes* (the lumbar region, the
'loins' of the Bible, defined by the OED as 'the seat of strength and of
generative power'); the *renes* ('reins') are 'a Part of the *Loins* and ...
administer to Generation' (p.27). When the seminal fluid is excited
and *hot*, it descends from this region via a system of seminal veins and
arteries (*seminaria vena, arteria seminaria*) to the respective testicles (the
contents of the left *vas* to the left testicle, that of the right to the right).
Discharge follows, either through involuntary nocturnal emissions
(*nocturnas in somno pollutiones*) or through intercourse. Oddly, Meibom
does not mention masturbation.

What has happened to those men who need the remedy of
flagellation to rouse their dormant sexuality is that the internal organs
of the lumbar region have, for some reason, become, literally, *cold*. It
follows, given Meibom's anatomical scheme, that flagellation applied
to the lower back and buttocks will serve to 'warm up' the affected
area lying behind them; that the heat thereby generated will be
communicated to the sperm-producing organs (those erstwhile *partes
refrigeratas*); and that the reinvigorated, heated semen will descend to
the testicles and stimulate erection. It is all very straightforward, very
mechanical, a simple matter of hot and cold. Meibom also holds that,
on the principle of *ubi stimulus ibi affluxus* ('where the stimulus there the
flow of blood'), the general heating of the beaten area helps to arouse
the sexual appetite:

I further conclude, that *Strokes* upon the *Back* and *Loins*, as Parts
appropriated for the Generating of the Seed, and carrying it to the
Genitals, warm and inflame those Parts, and contribute very much to the
irritation of *Lechery*. From all which, it is no wonder that such shameless
Wretches, Victims of a detested Appetite, such as we have mention'd, or
others exhausted by too frequent a Repetition, the *Loins* and their Vessels

being drain'd have sought for a Remedy by FLOGGING. For 'tis very
probable, that the refrigerated Parts grow warm by such Stripes, and
excite a Heat in the Seminal Matter, and that more particularly from the
Pain of the *flogg'd* Parts, which is the Reason that the Blood and Spirits are
attracted in a greater Quantity, 'till the Heat is communicated to the
Organs of Generation, and the perverse and frenzical Appetite is satisfied,
and Nature, tho' unwilling drawn beyond the Stretch of her common
Power, to the Commission of such an abominable Crime. (pp. 50-1)

Despite his anatomical inaccuracy, Meibom established beyond
doubt that flagellation is related to impotence and practised by men
who cannot achieve erection without it; and he showed that sexual
beating is always applied to the buttocks. Moreover, the account given
by Pico and Coelius, which Meibom quotes, indicates that the passive
flagellant (Meibom is not aware of the active variety) is ashamed of
having to indulge in such a ceremony in order to become sexually
excited. Thus, as a result of the publication of Meibom's treatise,
several basic components of the flagellant phenomenon had been
accurately isolated.

Meibom's work made an undoubted impact on the medical world,
and his theory of the mechanics of sexual flagellation was accepted
more or less uncritically by his professional successors. During the
seventeenth century his material was rehashed in several popular
volumes of medical divulgation, among them the famous
Geneanthropeiae (1642) by Giovanni Sinibaldi, a professor of medicine
at Rome. This book was an incredible hotchpotch of sexual fact and
fiction and, where flagellation was concerned, Sinibaldi repeated the
accounts given by Pico and Coelius, and provided information about
some other similar cases. In 1658 a bowdlerised English version of the
Geneanthropeiae appeared, entitled *Rare Verities. The Cabinet of Venus
Unlocked*. In this the author, referring to the aphrodisiac virtues of
beating, remarks: 'Dear God, what have we here? A Prodigy? that
pleasure should come from pain, sweet from bitter, lust from bloody
wounds? Does the same road lead to torment and to delight?' (quoted
by Comfort, 1968, p.30).

At about the same time there appeared what Havelock Ellis called
'the earliest definitely described case of sadistic pleasure in the sight of
active whipping which I have myself come across' (1942, p.132). This
occurred in a letter, dated 24 February 1672, from the celebrated
doctor Johann Matthias Nesterus to his friend Christian Friedrich
Garmann:

I have known intimately a very learned man, whose name I shall omit for
honour's sake, who, whenever in school or elsewhere he sees a boy

punished, unbreeched and beaten, and hears his cries, at once ejaculates semen copiously without any tension or erection of the penis but with such mental confusion that he could almost swoon, and the same thing happens to him frequently in sleep when he dreams of this subject.[3]

Ellis evidently did not know the early fifteenth century Flagellation attributed to the Catalan painter Luis Borrassá (see Plate 3), in which the sadistic element in beating is made surprisingly explicit. And, despite his wide knowledge of Spanish literature, he seems not to have noticed that in the thirteenth century epic, the *Poema de Myo Cid*, there is a beating scene (in the 'Afrenta de Corpes' incident) with strongly sadistic overtones. In a recent article on this passage, Roger Walker (1977) has shown that it almost certainly derives from a similar scene in the French *Chanson de Florence de Rome*. A remarkable aspect of the French poem, as Walker notes, is the poet's intuition that there is a connection between sadism and sexual impotence.

By the end of the seventeenth century, Meibom's ideas were well known to the educated men of Europe, including the theologians. That the Roman Catholic Church was aware of his treatise can be seen from the Abbé Boileau's *Historia Flagellantium, de recto et perverso flagrorum usu apud Christianos* ('The History of the Flagellants, and of the Correct and Perverse Use of Rods Among Christians') (Paris, 1700), and the bitter controversy that followed its publication. This curious work, the first edition of which appeared anonymously, was published in a French translation at Amsterdam in 1701, apparently without Boileau's approval. A second edition of the translation appeared in 1732, and it is to this that I shall refer here.

Boileau's book is not simply, as its title perhaps suggests, a history of the ideas and practices of the sects of religious flagellants who roamed Europe between the thirteenth and sixteenth centuries. It is essentially an attempt to prove that the everyday use of 'voluntary discipline', that is, self-flagellation, in convents and monasteries is a recent innovation unattested in the Early Church, and that the practice is contrary to the Divine Will. Boileau shows that two forms of ecclesiastical discipline were current at the time – *sursum disciplina* or 'upper discipline' (applied to the shoulders, usually naked) and *deorsum disciplina* or 'lower discipline' (applied to the naked buttocks

---

[3] *L. Christiani Friderici Garmanni a Alior. Viror. Clarissimor. Epistolarum Centuria*, etc., Rostock and Leipzig, 1714: 'Novi Virum doctissimum mihique familiarissimum, quem honoris ergo nominare omittam, qui quoties in Schola vel alibi puerum quendam castigare, braccas detrahere ac ferulis caedere videt, illumque plorantem audit, toties sine membri virilis tensione atque tentigine semen copiosissime ejaculare cogitur, tanta animi commotione, ac si in lipothymiam incidere deberet, quod etiam ei dormienti saepius accidit, quando hac de re somniat' (*Epistola* 88, p.365).

and thighs). Boileau is not opposed to the mortification of the flesh as such, since in various forms this is a well-established practice in the Church, but only to the obsessive infliction of self-flagellation in isolation from other forms of penance. He maintains that the references in the Bible to flagellation, chastisement with rods, etc., are intended to be taken metaphorically and not literally (an opposite view to that of the English floggers whom we shall meet in the next chapter).

Boileau holds that the 'lower discipline' is particularly dangerous, and in the last chapter of his book explains why. This chapter is little more than a summary of Meibom, and Boileau acknowledges his source. After a quick run through the physiology of the spine (with details from Thomas Bartholinus), Boileau refers to the *physical* dangers attendant upon the practice of 'upper discipline'. It is because of these dangers (especially to the eyes) that the Capucins and many nuns have abandoned 'upper discipline' in favour of the 'lower' variety. But in doing so, alas, they may have fallen out of the frying pan into the fire or, as Boileau puts it, quoting a Latin proverb, 'they should be careful lest ... in their desire to avoid *Scylla* they fall into *Charybdis*' (p.293). For flagellation of the loins is 'all the more dangerous since the ills of the soul are more to be feared than those of the body'.[4]

Boileau explains that the loins are closely linked by internal and external muscular connections to the buttocks; that the latter in turn are connected to the pubis (*os pubis*); and that, this being so, it follows that when flagellation is applied to the buttocks 'the animal spirits are forced back violently towards the *os pubis* and that they excite lascivious movements on account of the proximity of the genitals' (pp. 294-5).[5] Boileau's explanation, as the reader can see, is not quite so fantastic as that given by Meibom, although it derives from it. Experience, maintains Boileau, shows that this response to flagellation of the buttocks is frequent, and doctors, 'who probe into the most hidden recesses of nature' (p.295), know that there are many lecherous men who, in order to put themselves in fettle for sexual intercourse, have themselves beaten. Boileau takes his examples straight from Meibom (Frankfurt edition, 1670), and reproduces yet again the case of the flagellant given originally by Pico della Mirandola. He also cites Meibom's account, derived from two close

---

[4] 'Il faut prendre garde que ... dans le désir qu'ils ont d'éviter *Scylla*, ils ne tombent en *Charybde* ... d'autant plus dangereuse, que les maladies de l'esprit sont plus à craindre que celles du corps.'

[5] 'Les esprits animaux soient repoussez vers l'os *pubis*, et qu'ils excitent des mouvemens impudiques à cause de la proximité des parties génitales.'

friends, of a recent event that occurred at Lübeck, where a wife confessed in court that her husband could not get an erection unless he had been birched first: 'She said, moreover, that having done his duty, he was incapable of recommencing unless he were beaten on his buttocks all over again' (p.301).[6] Let everyone reflect on these grave matters, then, concludes Boileau 'and I flatter myself that they will agree that lower discipline has almost always been considered, not only a modern and pointless usage, but also a bad, vile and disreputable one' (p.306).[7]

Boileau's insinuations attracted the wrath of many churchmen, among them Jean-Baptiste Thiers, 'Docteur en Théologie et Curé de Vibraye', who published his riposte, *Critique de l'Histoire des Flagellans*, at Paris in 1703. It is not necessary to burden the reader with a detailed account of the arguments and evidence put forward by Thiers in defence of 'voluntary discipline'. Thiers's principal aim is to establish that self-flagellation was, contrary to Boileau's view, practised by the Early Church and that its modern usage is legitimate. Unlike Boileau, Thiers takes the Biblical references to divine castigation literally. Moreover he insists that Christ Himself was the first exponent of voluntary flagellation (of the 'upper' variety), arguing that He could have prevented His flagellation had He wished to do so. Thiers wishes to make it clear that those who flagellate themselves, including those with a preference for 'lower discipline', are motivated by the purest intentions, seeking at once to 'repress the disordered movements of the flesh' (*reprimer les mouvemens déreglés de la chair*) (p.412) and to imitate the flagellation of Christ. He points out repeatedly that many monastic orders have enjoined their members to meditate on His flagellation while they undergo their own fustigation for His sake. How dare Boileau impugn the purity of these people?

> What greater insult could one offer to the holy men and women who apply lower discipline to themselves than to say that they are superstitious idolaters, that they possess neither common sense nor shame, that they are in ignorance and error; in a word, that they are dishonest? (p.101)[8]

[6] 'Elle disait de plus, qu'après avoir fait son devoir, il était incapable de recommencer à moins qu'être fessé tout de nouveau.'

[7] 'Et je me flatte qu'ils tomberont d'accord, que la Discipline d'enbas a presque toujours passé, non seulement pour un usage moderne et inutile, mais aussi pour un exercice mauvais, vilain et infâme.'

[8] 'Mais quelle plus grande injure peut-on faire aux Saints et aux Saintes qui se disciplinent par en bas, que de dire qu'ils sont des idolâtres et des superstitieux, qu'ils n'ont ni sens commun ni pudeur, qu'ils sont dans l'ignorance et dans l'erreur; en un mot qu'ils sont faux?'

Worse still, Boileau – far from listening to his critics – has written a *Historia Flagellantium Vindicata*, which Thiers has seen in an unpublished manuscript. In this work the sexual aspects of the subject are evidently dealt with even more fully, to judge from the remarks made by the learned parish priest of Vibraye. All this, he maintains, would be very well for a Doctor, Anatomist or Surgeon, but not for a Priest and Doctor of Theology, who should not even mention such things lest he arouse, albeit unintentionally, impure thoughts in the reader. For 'experience teaches us that often it is better not to explain in detail what is forbidden, in order not to suggest the possibility of doing it – for we are as a rule drawn to what is forbidden' (pp. 77-8).[9] And aware that he too is perhaps transgressing by even mentioning these matters, Thiers hastens to bring to a close this section of his *Critique*.

Thiers, in short, makes no attempt to disprove Meibom's thesis as expounded by Boileau. Indeed he accepts tacitly that there may be a connection between 'lower discipline' and the sexual instinct, but refuses to discuss the matter, with the excuse that to do so would be morally dangerous. We shall meet with a similar attitude to the sexual implications of beating in Victorian England.

It can be seen from the Boileau-Thiers debate that Meibom's ideas about sexual flagellation were well-known in France at the beginning of the eighteenth century, though perhaps not many people had actually seen an edition of the German doctor's treatise. Further fuel was added to the polemic by Boileau's more famous brother, Nicolas Boileau Despréaux (1636-1711), theorist of French classicism and distinguished poet, who lent his fraternal aid and produced a mordant satire against that 'false piety'

> Qui, sous couleur d'éteindre en nous la volupté,
> Par l'austérité même et par la pénitence
> Sait allumer le feu de la lubricité.[10] (1969, p.161)

In the midst of the Boileau-Thiers debate, Martin Schurig discussed sexual flagellation in his celebrated *Spermatologia* (Frankfurt, 1720), quoted directly from Meibom's treatise (ascribing it to Thomas Bartholinus) and added some new cases of his own. Schurig's explanation of the flagellant phenomenon follows the mechanical, *ubi*

[9] 'L'expérience nous fait voir que souvent il vaut mieux ne pas expliquer en particulier ce qui est défendu, afin de ne pas donner occasion de le faire, parce qu'on se porte ordinairement aux choses défendues.'

[10] 'Which, under the pretence of extinguishing our voluptuousness, by that very austerity and by penance knows how to ignite the flame of lubricity.'

stimulus ibi affluxus formation. 'Psychology' had still not made its
début, and Schurig seems unaware of 'sadistic' beating.[11]

The contents of Boileau's book, and of Thiers's commentary upon
it, became widely known in England as the result of the publication of
a volume ascribed to John Lois Delolme: *The History of the Flagellants:
Otherwise, of Religious Flagellations among Different Nations, and Especially
among Christians. Being a Paraphrase and Commentary on the Historia
Flagellantium of the Abbé Boileau, Doctor of the Sorbonne, Canon of the Holy
Chapel, etc. By One who is not a Doctor of the Sorbonne* (London, 1777).
There were several subsequent editions of this work.[12]

Nor were Boileau and Thiers completely forgotten in England
during the nineteenth century. The erudite journal *Notes and Queries*,
as we shall see, specialised in flagellant communications. Among
them appeared this one, published on 9 September 1876:

> Some time since a correspondent said that the history of flagellants had
> still to be written; I forget in allusion to what he made the remark. But I
> would bring to his notice, if perchance he may not already have them, two
> works upon that subject: *Histoire des Flagellans*, by l'Abbé Boileau (my
> edition of this was printed at Amsterdam, 1701), and *Critique de l'Histoire
> des Flagellans*, by Thiers, edition printed at Paris, 1703.
>
> H.A.W. (p.215)

A few weeks later, amidst a discussion of topics related to corporal
punishment, another learned correspondent chipped in (30
September 1876):

> THE BIRCH ROD (5th S.vi.133,215.) – To the list of works on this
> subject add –
>   'Historia Flagellantium, de recto et perverso flagrorum usu apud
> Christianos.' Paris, 1700.
>
> H. FISHWICK, F.S.A. (p.277)

Between 1718 and 1898 there were at least four English translations
of Meibom's treatise, and probably several more. As has been said,
there were also French and German translations, not to mention the
many Latin editions. So there can be no doubt that the German
doctor's ideas on the subject of sexual flagellation were well known in
England.

As an example of this we might look at a curious exchange
concerning Meibom that took place in *The Gentleman's Magazine* in

[11] Schurig, *Spermatologia*, Ch.5 'De coitu', pp. 253-7.
[12] See Pisanus Fraxi, *Centuria Librorum Absconditorum*, p.495; Speculator Morum,
Bibliotheca Arcana, no.17, p.4.

1780. A letter to the editor ('Mr Urban') from 'A.B.', a New College, Oxford, man (October 1780, pp. 462-3) had deplored the cruel floggings daily inflicted in the schools of England by the 'birch-en-scepter'd monarchs', as he calls the schoolmasters. For 'A.B.' 'the severe, shameful and indelicate' beatings administered by 'these cloistered Dionysii' to 'the defenceless nudities' of their charges are 'an obscene custom', 'a humiliating treatment'. 'The indecency of whipping youths who have reached seventeen or eighteen years of age,' 'A.B.' insists, 'is too notorious to need representation.' Children have a right to rebel against a system that flouts 'the laws of decency' and seeks to scourge them 'into loss of spirit'. Indeed, a good retaliatory whipping administered to 'a pampered sacerdotal rump' would not go amiss. Finally, 'A.B.' insinuates that, if schoolmasters were to find a more humane way of disciplining their pupils, they 'might escape suspicion of deriving their attachment to the rod for motives which are best explained by writers like *Bartholinus De usu flagrorum*' (sic).

That such a forthright comment could have been published in a respectable and widely-read journal in 1780 prompts one to marvel at the hypocrisy of the Victorian age that was to follow some fifty years later. For 'A.B.' clearly had no doubt about what nowadays we would call the 'sadistic' element in whipping. Nor had he any doubt about the part of the body on which the flagellant obsession focusses.

'A.B.' 's letter provoked an angry reply from 'D.B.' in the December 1780 issue of the journal. The 'poor pedagogues', we learn, are in fact decent chaps doing a difficult job, and it was 'unmanly and illiberal' of 'A.B.' to compare them to gaolers, butchers and hangmen. 'D.B.' 'will not hesitate' to own himself a schoolmaster, and feels that 'to prevent a total degeneracy in the boys' the rod must be preserved – 'for when all subordination is destroyed, anarchy and confusion will necessarily ensue'. He has been particularly outraged by 'A.B.' 's reference to Meibom:

> His introduction of Bartholinus's book, *De Usu Flagellorum* [sic], is so gross an affront upon the taste of Mr Urban and his friends, that the bare mention of it cannot fail to create in them the most ineffable contempt towards the letter writer, who, whilst he is contending for purity of sentiment, endeavours to obtrude upon them a work, teeming in every page with the grossest obscenity. (p.618)

In other words, bottoms must be whipped so that order may be maintained; but no one must think that there is any lubricity involved in the practice. To suggest that schoolmasters could actually enjoy whipping! To dare to mention Meibom! As we shall see, the schoolmasters of England have habitually refused to admit the sexual element in beating, and that can be as true today as it was in the eighteenth century.

Sir John Davies, 'The Virtuoso' (1676) and 'Fanny Hill' (1748 or 1749)

If the sexual element in flagellation was known to the doctors it was no secret either to English literary men. Thus Sir John Davies (1569-1626), the Elizabethan poet, published an epigram – often attributed to Marlowe – which shows that he was aware of the connection between flagellation and impotence (quoted by Pisanus Fraxi, *Centuria Librorum Absconditorum*). Perhaps Davies had been awakened to the sexual implications of flogging while a pupil at Winchester:

> When Francis comes to solace with his whore,
> He sends for rods and strips himself stark naked;
> For his lust sleeps, and will not rise before
> By whipping of the wench it be awaked.
> I envy him not, but wish I had the power
> To make myself his wench but one half hour.

A notorious scene in Thomas Shadwell's comedy *The Virtuoso* (1676) shows that he recognised the dangerous influence of school floggings. In Act III, scene ii, we find the old libertine Snarl in dalliance with a prostitute, Mrs Figgup. They are in a brothel, and Snarl is in heat:

Snarl. Ah poor little rogue. In sadness, I'll bite thee by the lip, i'faith I will. Thou has incens't me strangely; thou hast fir'd my blood; I can bear it no longer, i'faith I cannot. Where are the instruments of our pleasure? Nay, prithee do not frown; by the mass, thou shalt do't now.

Mrs Figgup. I wonder that should please you so much that pleases me so little.

Snarl. I was so us'd to 't at Westminster School I could never leave it off since.

Mrs Figgup. Well, look under the carpet then if I must.

Snarl. Very well, my dear rogue. But dost hear, thou art too gentle. Do not spare thy pains. I love castigation mightily. So here's good provision.

Pulls the carpet; three or four great rods fall down. (1966, p.67)

The scene is interrupted by Mrs Figgup's brother before the flogging can get under way.

John Cleland (1707-89), author of the famous erotic novel *Memoirs of a Woman of Pleasure* (1748 or 1749), better known as *Fanny Hill*, had been a pupil at Westminster School, and no doubt appreciated Shadwell's reference to its reputation as a great flogging institution (Dr Busby, one of the school's headmasters in the seventeenth century, has been regarded by flagellants as perhaps the finest expert with the rod that England_has ever known). Perhaps Cleland had direct experience of the Westminster birch. At all events he certainly understood sexual flagellation, for the beating scene in *Fanny Hill* is remarkable for its psychological perception.

The scene in question takes place towards the end of Fanny's memoirs, in the establishment of Mrs Cole, the worldly-wise yet gentle madame to whom Fanny has confided her fortunes. Mr Barville, just arrived in town, is, poor fellow, 'under the tyranny of a cruel taste' and can only achieve erection after the reception and application of the birch. Fanny, to whom all this is new, is surprised to find a penchant for flagellation in one so youthful (Barville is only 23) and gives the impression that she has been reading Meibom:

> But what yet increased the oddity of this strange fancy was the gentleman being young; whereas it generally attacks, it seems, such as are, through age, obliged to have recourse to this experiment, for quickening the circulation of their sluggish juices, and determining a conflux of the spirits of pleasure towards those flagging, shrively parts, that rise to life only by virtue of those titillating ardours created by the discipline of their opposites, with which they have so surprising a consent. (1974, p.173)

A surprising consent, indeed, and one which Fanny is at a loss to explain.

Mrs Cole advises Fanny how to proceed. The 'transaction' will be cloaked in secrecy (although Madame herself will be watching how things go from a hidden vantage point) and thereby preserved 'from the ridicule that otherwise vulgarly attended it' (p.174). Mrs Cole is aware, that is, of the shame component in flagellation. She believes that in life pleasure is all that matters, and that how we arrive there is immaterial provided that no one is harmed on the way. Moreover, she is rather sorry for the Barvilles of the world, for whom pleasure comes so hard and 'who are under a subjection they cannot shake off, to those arbitrary tastes that rule their appetites of pleasure with an unaccountable control' (p.174).

Mrs Cole has received Barville's instructions concerning the details of the forthcoming ceremony, and in accordance with them decks Fanny out all in white, virginal, 'like a victim led to sacrifice' (p.174).

Fanny is introduced to her tormentor. He is rather podgy, looks even younger than he is. Cleland's description of his expression is superb: his 'round, plump, fresh colour'd face gave him greatly the look of a *Bacchus*, had not an air of austerity, not to say sternness, very unsuitable even to the shape of face, dash'd that character of joy, necessary to complete the resemblance' (p.175).

The sensitive Fanny realises that Barville's tense outward expression reveals the inner state of turmoil in which he is forced by his eccentricity to live:

> As soon as Mrs Cole was gone, he seated me near him, when now his face turned upon me into an expression of the most pleasing sweetness and good humour, the more remarkable for its sudden shift from the other extreme, which, I found afterwards, when I knew more of his character, was owing to a habitual state of conflict with and dislike of himself for being enslaved to so peculiar a taste, by the fatality of a constitutional ascendant, that rendr'd him incapable of receiving any pleasure till he submitted to these extraordinary means of procuring it at the hands of pain, whilst the constancy of this repining consciousness stamp'd at length that cast of sourness and severity on his features: which was, in fact, very foreign to the natural sweetness of his temper. (p.175)

It is a brilliantly perceptive vignette. Despite Fanny's reference to 'the fatality of a constitutional ascendant', there can be no doubt that we have entered the realm of 'psychology' in this passage. Cleland has seen clearly the conflict (his word, amazingly) that lies at the heart of the deviation; and, in his description of Barville's shifting facial expression, has anticipated by more than 200 years Theodor Reik's reference to the 'Janus face' of masochism, 'one half of which is distorted by anxiety, the other entranced with pleasure' (1962, p.133).

What now takes place is foreseeable: Barville apologises for his odd tastes, begs Fanny to go through her 'part' with spirit, prescribes the details of the ceremony. Birch rods are fetched (very much as in *The Virtuoso*), a bench is produced, and Barville's preliminary divestment gets under way:

> I led him then to the bench, and according to my cue, play'd at forcing him to lie down; which, after some little show of reluctance, for form's sake, he submitted to; he was straightaway extended flat upon his belly, on the bench, with a pillow under his face; and as he thus tamely lay, I tied him tightly, hand and foot, to the legs of it; which done, his shirt remaining truss'd up over the small of his back, I drew his breeches quite down to his knees. (p.176)

This, too, is perceptive. Cleland, who does not have our modern notion of the 'acting out' of a fantasy, nonetheless sees the ceremonial, theatrical nature of the scene ('cue', 'play'd', 'some small show of reluctance'); whatever Barville is up to it is clear that he is enacting a role. In a later chapter I shall return to this aspect of the subject.

The reader can be spared the details of Barville's fustigation. Fanny is 'mov'd at the piteous sight' of the bloody ravages she has wrought on the man's chubby bottom, but is totally unexcited sexually by the proceedings. She is no sadist. And anyway, Barville 'seem'd no more concern'd, or to mind them, than a lobster would a flea-bite' (p.176). Eventually the treatment begins to produce the desired effect (see Plate 4). Fanny has a look, and finds that Barville's previously minute penis has grown 'not only to a prodigious stiffness of erection, but to a size that frighted even me' (p.177). At last Barville ejaculates, after three bundles of birch have been 'fairly worn out' (p.178). So far there has been no question of copulation.

It is now poor Fanny's turn. Barville, it turns out, is more of a 'sado-masochist' than a masochist (psychoanalysis has shown that most flagellants in fact display a combination of active and passive elements). A ceremonial revelation of the girl's buttocks gets under way, attended with intense pleasure by Barville. Fanny's bottom receives passionate kisses – followed by a growing crescendo of stripes. Finally blood is fetched. As Barville becomes increasingly excited he loses his apparent repugnance for the female genitals and directs the rod towards 'the province of pleasure':

> But still I bore everything without crying out: when presently, giving me another pause, he rush'd, as it were, on that part whose lips, and round-about, had felt this cruelty, and by way of reparation, glues his own to them; then he opened, shut, squeez'd them, pluck'd softly the overgrowing moss, and all this in a style of wild passionate rapture and enthusiasm, that express'd excess of pleasure. (p.180)

Despite Barville's excitement the couple do not yet attempt copulation: Cleland shows that the impotent Barville has to be absolutely sure that he is fully erect before he will risk intercourse for, like all flagellants, he is terrified of failure.

Fanny and Barville now make a splendid supper together. Her pain begins to subside under the benign influence of wine and food, and suddenly, being a lusty lady, she starts to feel sexually aroused. Barville tries to help, but finds that he is not erect:

> for as he was unbuttoned to me, and tried to provoke and rouse to action his unactive torpid machine, he blushingly own'd that no good was to be

expected from it, unless I took it in hand to re-excite its languid loitering powers, by just refreshing the smart of the yet recent blood-drawn cuts, seeing it could, no more than a boy's top, keep up without lashing. (p.181)

Fanny does the needful, and soon her client is back in form. Despite their smarting posteriors the couple have a satisfactory bout of intercourse, and the evening ends with smiles all round.

Reflecting on this experience, which she resolves shall be the last of its kind, Fanny concludes that flagellation acts 'somewhat in the manner of a dose of Spanish flies, with more pain perhaps, but less danger' (p.183). She does not realise that this explanation fails to take into account the active variety of the phenomenon.

Was this Cleland's view as well as Fanny's? We cannot be sure, I think. What is certain is that Cleland is feeling his way towards a psychological interpretation of what was by the middle of the eighteenth century recognised as a common sexual deviation. His description of Fanny's painful adventure with Barville has a ring of authenticity that places it far above the sort of flagellant pornography that would flood the market in the Victorian period; and, in identifying the 'habitual state of conflict' in which Barville is forced by his peculiarity to live, the author made a perceptive contribution to the understanding of the problem.

Fanny Hill, of course, was always in trouble with the British censor – until her liberation a few years ago. The first edition was almost immediately suppressed. 'Pisanus Fraxi' (Henry Spencer Ashbee) lists twenty editions which appeared between 1749 and 1845 to back up his assertion that *Fanny Hill* was 'the best known of all English erotic novels' (*Catena Librorum Tacendorum*, p.62). As Ashbee shows, it was also widely translated, especially into French, in which language there were numerous editions, and there can be no doubt that the book helped to spread abroad the belief, largely justified in point of fact, that the English Gentleman was obsessed by flagellation.

'Les Coutumes théâtrales ou Scènes secrètes des foyers' (1743)

According to Iwan Bloch (1903, p.384), this work, which I have not seen, treats freely of the relation between impotence and sexual flagellation. As we shall see, the French have been far more prepared than the English to accept, recognise and talk about this connection and, as a result, to forbid the use of 'lower discipline' in schools. Bloch quotes the following verse spoken by a courtesan to her client in this book:

Apprends, cher bon ami, que les coups vigoureux
Te rendront plus sensible aux plaisirs amoureux.
Ceux dont la nature trop lente
Ne peut satisfaire une amante
Par quelques coups de verge appliqués fortement
Se portent au combat plus vigoureusement.[13]

Voltaire: Dictionnaire philosophique (1769)

Voltaire, as one would expect, was both aware of the sexual implications of gluteal flagellation[14] and an enemy of those teachers who practised it. In his article 'Verge. Baguette divinatoire' ('Rod. Divining Rod') in the famous *Dictionnaire philosophique*, he had this to say on the subject:

> It is shameful and abominable that such a punishment should be administered to the buttocks of young boys and girls. It used to be the punishment of slaves. In our colleges I have seen barbarians strip children almost naked and a brute, often drunk, lacerate their flesh with long rods, which made their groins bleed and swell fearfully. The two nerves which join the sphincter to the pubis being irritated, emissions were produced; and this has often happened to young girls.[15] (1819, p.464)

Jean-Jacques Rousseau's 'Confessions' (1782)

The first part of Rousseau's *Confessions* appeared in 1782, four years after his death. The book immediately became famous throughout Europe. Intended by Rousseau to be the most honest autobiography ever written, it certainly gave the world the first authentic account of what it felt like to be addicted to beating fantasies of the passive variety.

Rousseau's flagellant confession comes at the beginning of his memoir, and it is clear that he had to overcome enormous inner

[13] 'Learn, dear friend, that vigorous blows will render you more apt for amorous pleasures. Those whose too sluggish nature cannot satisfy a lover take themselves to the combat with more energy after they have undergone some strongly applied lashes of the rod.'

[14] Glutaeus, gluteal, from the Greek word for buttocks.

[15] 'Il est honteux et abominable qu'on inflige un pareil châtiment sur les fesses à de jeunes garçons et à de jeunes filles. C'était autrefois le supplice des esclaves. J'ai vu dans des collèges, des barbares qui fesaient dépouiller les enfans presque entièrement; une espèce de bourreau, souvent ivre, les déchirait avec de longues verges, qui mettaient en sang leurs aines et les fesaient enfler démesurément. D'autres les fesaient frapper avec douceur, et il en naissait un autre inconvénient. Les deux nerfs qui vont du sphincter au pubis étant irrités, causaient des pollutions; c'est ce qui est arrivé souvent à de jeunes filles.'

resistance before he could bring himself to tell the truth about his
secret longings – for secret they were; clear, too, that the very notion of
'confessing' who he really was related to the intense shame he felt
about what he calls his 'goût bizarre'. One can positively share his
relief when he gets the terrible confession off his chest:[16]

> Now I have made the first and most painful step in the dark and miry
> maze of my confessions. It is the ridiculous and the shameful, not one's
> criminal actions, that it is hardest to confess. But henceforth I am certain
> of myself; after what I have just had the courage to say, nothing else will
> defeat me. (1954, p.28)[17]

The shame that Rousseau felt about his flagellant obsession
accompanied him throughout his life, and made him awkward and
embarrassed in company. Once he has unburdened himself of his
initial confession, he does not return overtly to the subject again.

Jean-Jacques explains the origin of his obsession as follows. His
mother died bringing him into the world, and his early years were
spent in the company of a loving father and a group of indulgent
relatives and family friends. When his father got into trouble with the
Geneva authorities and had to flee the country, Rousseau was sent
with his cousin to a little country school at Bossey, about four miles
from Geneva; this was run by an amiable Protestant clergyman, M.
Lambercier, and his unmarried sister. Rousseau adored the
Lamberciers and wanted only to please them; well-behaved, he was
extremely sensitive to criticism and suffered already from a crippling
sense of shame.

Mlle Lambercier could be severe, though never cruel, and
Rousseau, plucking up his courage, prepares to tell us all. This
passage is a *locus classicus* in the annals of 'sado-masochism' and must
be quoted pretty fully:

> Since Mlle Lambercier treated us with a mother's love, she had also a
> mother's authority, which she exercised sometimes by inflicting on us
> such childish chastisements as we had earned. For a long while she
> confined herself to threats, and the threat of a punishment entirely
> unknown to me frightened me sufficiently. But when in the end I was

[16] The translation of this and subsequent passages is taken from J.M. Cohen's
rendering of the *Confessions* (Penguin). For the French text I have used the Gallimard,
'Folio' edition (1973).

[17] 'J'ai fait le premier pas et le plus pénible dans le labyrinthe obscur et fangeux de
mes confessions. Ce n'est pas ce qui est criminel qui coûte le plus à dire, c'est ce qui
est ridicule et honteux. Dès à présent je suis sûr de moi; après ce que je viens d'oser
dire, rien ne peut plus m'arrêter' (p.48).

beaten I found the experience less dreadful in fact than in anticipation; and the very strange thing was that this punishment increased my affection for the inflicter. It required all the strength of my devotion and all my natural gentleness to prevent my deliberately earning another beating; I had discovered in the shame and pain of the punishment an admixture of sensuality which had left me rather eager than otherwise for a repetition by the same hand. No doubt, there being some degree of precocious sexuality in all this, the same punishment at the hands of her brother would not have seemed pleasant at all. But he was of too kindly a disposition to be likely to take over this duty; and so, if I refrained from earning a fresh punishment, it was only out of fear of annoying Mlle Lambercier; so much am I swayed by kindness, even by kindness that is based on sensuality, that it has always prevailed with me over sensuality itself.

The next occasion, which I postponed, although not through fear, occurred through no fault of mine – that is to say I did not act deliberately. But I may say that I took advantage of it with an easy conscience. This second occasion, however, was also the last. For Mlle Lambercier had no doubt detected signs that this punishment was not having the desired effect. She announced, therefore, that she would abandon it, since she found it too exhausting. Hitherto we had always slept in her room, and sometimes, in winter, in her bed. Two da''s afterwards we were made to sleep in another room, and henceforth J ..ad the honour, willingly though I would have dispensed with it, of being treated as a big boy. (pp. 25-6)

According to Rousseau, these whippings – scholars are agreed that the 'punition des enfants' in question was of the 'lower discipline' variety – influenced his sexuality for life:

Who could have supposed that this childish punishment, received at the age of eight at the hands of a woman of thirty,[18] would determine my tastes and desires, my passions, my very self for the rest of my life, and that in a sense diametrically opposed to the one in which they should normally have developed? At the moment when my senses were aroused my desires took a false turn and, confining themselves to this early experience, never set about seeking a different one. With sensuality burning in my blood almost from my birth, I kept myself pure and unsullied up to an age when even the coldest and most backward natures have developed. Tormented for a long while by I knew not what, I feasted feverish eyes on lovely women, recalling them ceaselessly to my

---

[18] In fact, Rousseau was eleven and Mlle Lambercier forty. See the Gallimard edition referred to in note 16, I, p.346.

imagination, but only to make use of them in my own fashion as so many Mlle Lamberciers. (p.26)[19]

Rousseau tells us that he was addicted to masturbation during his adolescence, and, reading between the lines, we can be sure that flagellant fantasies were vital to this activity. At the same time he was ignorant of the facts of sexual intercourse until unusually late, and indeed the vague intimations of the act that came his way as a child revolted him (he once saw dogs copulating and had the sudden thought that maybe human beings did the same disgusting thing). It was a long time before Rousseau realised that the feverish scenes of whipping he imagined to himself could have anything to do with sexual intercourse, as the passage just quoted shows. Later in the book he recounts how at the age of eighteen or so he used to exhibit his naked bottom to girls, from a distance, imagining that he was being beaten by them.[20]

Rousseau claims that as he grew older he was never free from flagellant fantasies, and that they and coitus became inseparably fused in his mind. Since, overwhelmed by shame and timidity, he was never able to *tell* any woman of his secret craving, never able to 'act it out' with a partner, we must assume that before and during intercourse he achieved and maintained erection by imagining flagellant scenes. As Krafft-Ebing's case histories would show a 100 years later, such tricks of the imagination are common in the sexual deviations. Who knows, indeed, what perverse fantasies may be enacted in the theatre of the mind during what may seem to be 'normal intercourse'?

The passage in which Jean-Jacques explains the consequences of his flagellant initiation at the hands of Mlle Lambercier is deeply moving, both for the personal tragedy it describes and for its fine psychological perception:

Not only, therefore, did I, though ardent, lascivious, and precocious by nature, pass the age of puberty without desiring or knowing any other sensual pleasures than those which Mlle Lambercier had, in all innocence, acquainted me with; but when finally, in the course of years, I became a man I was preserved by that very perversity which might have been my undoing. My old childish tastes did not vanish, but became so intimately associated with those of maturity that I could never, when sensually aroused, keep the two apart. This peculiarity, together with my

[19] This and the following quotations being too extensive to reproduce as footnotes, I have relegated them to Appendix A.
[20] *Confessions*, I, book 3.

natural timidity, has always made me very backward with women, since I have never had the courage to be frank or the power to get what I wanted, it being impossible for the kind of pleasure I desired – to which the other kind is no more than a consummation – to be taken by him who wants it, or to be guessed at by the woman who could grant it. So I have spent my days in silent longing in the presence of those I most loved. I never dared to reveal my strange taste, but at least I got some pleasure from situations which pandered to the thought of it. To fall on my knees before a masterful mistress, to obey her commands, to have to beg for her forgiveness, have been to me the most delicate of pleasures; and the more my vivid imagination heated my blood the more like a spellbound lover I looked. (pp. 27-8)

Rousseau had introduced his flagellant confession by exclaiming: 'How differently people would treat children if only they saw the eventual results of the indiscriminate, and often culpable, methods of punishment they employ! The magnitude of the lesson to be derived from so common and unfortunate a case as my own has resolved me to write it down' (p.25).[21] Rousseau knew what he was talking about, and corporal punishment would find no place in his *Emile, ou l'éducation* (1762).

After the publication of the *Confessions* the dangers of beating young children on their buttocks should have been obvious to all. It was possible to ignore Meibom, Cleland and the flagellant pornographers, who could all be lumped together as obscene. But Rousseau was another matter, a philosopher of international standing. As Freud wrote in 1905:

Ever since Jean-Jacques Rousseau's *Confessions*, it has been well known to all educationalists that the painful stimulation of the skin of the buttocks is one of the erotogenic roots of the *passive* instinct of cruelty (masochism). The conclusion has rightly been drawn by them that corporal punishment, which is usually applied to this part of the body, should not be inflicted upon any children whose libido is liable to be forced into collateral channels by the later demands of cultural education.[22]

Where Britain was concerned, Rousseau's warning was heeded by some doctors but not by the teachers or by Parliament. This despite

---

[21] 'Qu'on changerait de méthode avec la jeunesse, si l'on voyait mieux les effets éloignés de celle qu'on emploie toujours indistinctement, et souvent indiscrètement! La grande leçon qu'on peut tirer d'un exemple aussi commun que funeste me fait résoudre à le donner' (p.44).

[22] *Three Essays on Sexuality*, originally published as *Drei Abhandlungen zur Sexualtheorie* (1905). All my references to Freud in this book are taken from the *Standard Edition* of his works (see details in the bibliography). This quotation, VII, p.193.

the fact that the *Confessions* were well known in the country, the first translation having appeared as early as 1783. It was easier to pretend, as did a writer to *Notes and Queries*, that Rousseau was not as other men:

> Unfortunately the few who have investigated certain byways of literature and life know that the birch, like many useful things, has, in the hands of some quasi-maniacs, been terribly abused. But I cannot see why this should prevent the employment of this effective form of punishment by sane parents upon sane children. There can be little doubt that, putting aside certain very exceptional natures, such as Rousseau's, a sound whipping when deserved is extremely beneficial to an ordinarily healthy child. (16 December 1876, p.496)

By the time that Krafft-Ebing came to coin the word 'masochism' towards the end of the nineteenth century, Rousseau's flagellant confession, written with such honesty and insight, had become the object of widespread analysis and discussion among psychologists.[23] For the moment it is enough to say that, after the publication of the *Confessions*, the area of human experience opened to investigation by Meibom had, for the first time, been explored by a passive flagellant speaking in his own, and in this case very authoritative, voice. It would be only nine years before the Marquis de Sade, in *Justine*, would explore the active aspect of flagellation.

François-Amédée Doppet: 'Aphrodisiaque externe, ou Traité du fouet' (1788)

In the opinion of Henry Spencer Ashbee, the most important work on sexual flagellation after Meibom was Doppet's *Traité du fouet*. Ashbee gives no details of this treatise, however, nor of its bibliographical history.[24]

Doppet (1755- *c.* 1800) was a French doctor, writer and general. Although the author of numerous works, he is remembered, if at all, for his little treatise on flagellation, the first edition of which seems to have been that published anonymously at Geneva in 1788. Its full title was: *Aphrodisiaque externe, ou Traité du fouet et de ses effets sur le physique de l'amour. Ouvrage médico-philosophique suivi d'une dissertation sur tous les moyens capables d'exciter aux plaisirs de l'amour, par D****. There were several subsequent editions.

[23] See especially the essay by Alfred Binet, 'Le Fétichisme dans l'amour' in *Etudes de Psychologie expérimentale* (1888), pp. 1-85.
[24] Pisanus Fraxi, *Centuria Librorum Absconditorum*, p.445, n.

Doppet's treatise is a serious attempt to deal with a serious topic. It is written with clarity and underlying passion, and has as its main purpose that of persuading the French authorities to ban the beating of children on their naked buttocks. Doppet also disapproves strongly of ecclesiastical flagellation.

He begins by reviewing Meibom's account of the aphrodisiac effects of flagellation, referring to some of the German doctor's sources (including Pico della Mirandola and Coelius Rhodiginus). That flagellation of the buttocks acts as a sexual stimulant there can be absolutely no doubt, he insists. And if anyone thinks that Meibom was wrong he need only ask a modern prostitute.

Doppet has come to the conclusion that the childhood-habit theory of flagellation cannot of itself totally explain the phenomenon, and proceeds to elaborate a simple *physical* explanation which in practice differs little from that of Meibom. He points out that the latter's view that beating, by warming the lumbar region, caused the newly heated sperm to descend from the seminal vesicles to the testicles, is completely disproved. Meibom got his anatomy all wrong. What really happens is that the heat generated by flagellation applied to the lower back and buttocks is transmitted via the lumbar region to the neighbouring genitals, thereby stimulating erotic sensations – in both men and women.

Given the mechanical nature of the genital response to such whipping, it follows that children punished in this fashion may become sexually aroused. This is the worst aspect of the matter, for once children are excited by being whipped certain consequences become automatic: interest in the buttocks often leads to children whipping each other, to fondling and masturbation. The interest becomes an obsession and when, in later life, Nature demands that a man be able to copulate with his wife, what happens? He finds that he is impotent and unable to fulfil his marital obligations without having recourse to the rod. Man and wife are miserable, and the former can only find relief by visiting low women and being fustigated.

Doppet is outraged at the injustice done by teachers to children by prematurely enflaming their sensuality in this way, and encouraging it to run in unnatural channels. He has no doubt that some of the pedagogues, at any rate, positively enjoy whipping their pupils on the buttocks; and finds in the practice evidence of sodomitic inclinations. Moreover Doppet is certain that, if parents and teachers wished, they could easily find alternative methods of punishing their charges. Had not Rousseau in *Emile* made many valid suggestions for reforming education, and that without the need for corporal punishment? But of course the floggers will not listen. Doppet shows his appreciation of the central issues at stake in an incisive paragraph, to my mind the most important in the treatise:

> I suppose it is necessary, in certain cases, to inflict corporal punishment on children; but should we beat the miscreants on the lower back and loins? We are taught during our first five or six years to hide our buttocks and *parties honteuses* ['shameful parts']; then, after this period, along comes a teacher who forces us to unbutton our trousers, push them down, lift our shirt, show everything and receive the whip in the middle of the class. And don't these parts become even more 'shameful' when it's some uncouth pedant who's looking at them and touching them? (p.167)[25]

Doppet perceives clearly, that is, the shame component in flagellation, but no more than Rousseau is he able to integrate this insight into a general theory that might explain why it is that flagellation can act as a sexual stimulant. None the less, and despite his adherence to a 'physical' explanation of flagellation, Doppet comes close to sensing that, in the enforced revelation of what is forbidden, in the exposure of the *parties honteuses*, there might lie a clue to an understanding of the flagellant phenomenon.

About one thing Doppet is absolutely certain: children must not be whipped on the buttocks. French educationalists took the message, and it was not long before the beating of children was outlawed in French schools.

Sade: 'Justine ou les Malheurs de la vertu' (1791)

The Marquis de Sade's philosopher-libertines are compulsive talkers: having buggered, flogged, dissected or otherwise ravaged their victims they are only too happy to justify their behaviour – for pages on end if necessary. Many of these fluent apologists for cruelty appear in *Justine*, and it is not difficult to summarise their philosophy, which derives from one basic tenet of faith: namely, that our erotic desires are given to us by Nature, 'the celestial Mother' (p.221), with the intention that we should satisfy them, no matter how eccentric they may seem.[26] As one libertine insists, 'Nature ... never placed in us

[25] 'Je suppose qu'il soit nécessaire, dans certains cas, d'infliger aux enfants des peines corporelles; devrait-on frapper le coupable sur le dos et les reins? On nous apprend pendant les cinq ou six premières années que nous vivons à cacher notre derrière et les parties *honteuses*; au bout de ce temps vient un régent qui nous force à déboutonner nos culottes, à les abattre, à trousser la chemise, à tout montrer, pour recevoir les étrivières en pleine classe. Ces parties ne seraient-elles plus *honteuses*, quand c'est un cuistre qui les regarde et qui les touche?'

[26] I have used the Livre de Poche edition of *Justine* (1973), edited by Béatrice Didier.

any desire other than that of satisfying ourselves, at whatever price that might be' (p.300).[27]

It follows that virtue consists, not in accepting man-made moralities, which are relative and vary from society to society, but in attuning ourselves to the dictates of Nature. If we feel a powerful urge towards some form of cruelty, for example, we should follow it. Not to do so would be 'unnatural'. Nature in her wisdom has made some men strong, some weak; some sodomites, some straightforward heterosexual copulators. Everyone wants to be happy, everyone wants to enjoy orgasm, but the means of achieving this desirable end differ from person to person, and are implanted in us by the hand of Nature. Our tastes are there *ab initio*:

> The organs which render us unavoidably susceptible to this or that taste *(fantaisie)* are formed in our mother's womb, and the first objects we see and the first discourses we hear complete this determination of our natures: after that, our tastes are formed and nothing in the world can alter them. (p.217)[28]

Thus Clément, one of the libidinous monks who officiate in the subterranean torture chambers of the monastery (ostensibly Benedictine) of Sainte Marie des Bois. Clément is patiently trying to explain his philosophy to Thérèse, the much-belaboured 'heroine' of the book:

> Undoubtedly the most ridiculous thing in the world ... is the wish to argue about a man's tastes, to thwart them, condemn them, or punish them, if they happen not to conform either to the laws of the country in which one is living, or to social conventions. People will just never understand that there is no kind of taste, no matter how bizarre, no matter how criminal one may consider it, which does not depend on the type of personal organisation we have received from Nature. (p.213)[29]

---

[27] 'La Nature ... ne plaça jamais dans nous d'autre désir que celui de nous satisfaire, à quelque prix que ce pût être.'

[28] 'C'est dans le sein de la mère que se fabriquent les organes qui doivent nous rendre susceptibles de telle ou telle fantaisie, les premiers objets présentés, les premiers discours entendus achèvent de déterminer le ressort; les goûts se forment, et rien au monde ne peut plus les détruire.'

[29] 'La chose du monde la plus ridicule sans doute ... est de vouloir disputer sur les goûts de l'homme, les contrarier, les blâmer, ou les punir, s'ils ne sont pas conformes soit aux lois du pays qu'on habite, soit aux conventions sociales. Eh quoi! Les hommes ne comprendront jamais qu'il n'est aucune sorte de goûts, quelque bizarres, quelque criminels même qu'on puisse les supposer, qui ne dépende de la sorte d'organisation que nous avons reçu de la Nature!'

The characters in *Justine*, as elsewhere in Sade's work, realise that they are not 'normal' by other people's standards. Often they are unhappy and feel isolated by their perversion. Several of them make the point that, if they are cruel, it is not from choice but because they can only become sexually excited by inflicting pain. They feel that other people should make an effort to understand this.

One of the central episodes in *Justine* takes place at the house of the sadistic amateur surgeon Rodin who, as well as practising illegal operations, runs a boarding school (14 girls and 14 boys, all handpicked for their beauty and all between the ages of 12 and 16). Rodin is a flagellomaniac, and uses the 28 bottoms at his disposal mercilessly. As he explains to Thérèse, 'if an individual ... is unhappily so constituted that he can only become aroused by inflicting pain on the object of his attentions, you will admit that he ought to let himself go without feeling any remorse about it' (p.221).[30]

Rodin's 'strange taste' (*goût bizarre*, an expression Sade uses several times and which, as we have seen, Rousseau applied to *his* flagellant proclivities) consists not only in whipping but in being whipped. Like Cleland's Mr Barville, whom we met earlier, he is a 'sado-masochist'. And like Barville he uses flagellation not as an end in itself but as a stimulating prelude to intercourse, although in this case it is anal intercourse. It seems in fact that Sade, like Doppet, sensed a relationship between sodomy and gluteal flagellation. Most of the floggers in *Justine* are sodomites, and Thérèse soon realises that, whatever bit of her person may be penetrated, it will not be her vagina. These men are all like the Comte de Gernande, of whom Thérèse observes that he was 'a passionate votary of the backside (as are all libertines, alas!)' (p.257).[31]

It is of interest to note that none of the libertines in *Justine* has any notion of sexual tenderness (a characteristic which never fails to astonish Thérèse): these unfortunates are simply not turned on by loving caresses. Moreover, they are all – to a man – disgusted by the female genitals, impotent in their presence:

> Although the true temple of love is within his reach, Rodin, faithful to his cult, does not even look in that direction; he fears even its outlines and, if the position of her body reveals them, he covers them up; even the

[30] 'Si l'individu ... est malheureusement organisé de manière à n'être ému qu'en produisant, dans l'objet qui lui sert, de douloureuses sensations, vous avouerez qu'il doit s'y livrer sans remords.'
[31] 'Intime partisan du derrière (malheureusement, hélas! comme tous les libertins).'

slightest disarray would spoil his homage, and he wants to be disturbed by nothing.[32] (p.123)

In many ways Sade anticipated the investigations of the nineteenth-century sexologists, and his descriptions of sexual perversions, techniques and beliefs were without doubt based on his own experience and observations. Where flagellation was concerned, Sade saw clearly – as others had done before him – that it is solely concerned with the buttocks; and perceived that it also relates to impotence and dislike or fear of the female genitals.

It is little wonder that Sade's books have constantly been in trouble with the authorities, for not only in their exploration of sexuality but in their attack on conventional morality and Christianity they have been seen as a potent source of danger to governments and established religions.

Copies of Sade were extremely hard to come by in Victorian England, and were greatly prized by the collectors of erotica. Among the latter, Richard Monckton Milnes (created Lord Houghton in 1863) was the proud owner of the 1797 edition of *Justine*'s successor, *La Nouvelle Justine ou les Malheurs de la vertu*. This he lent to Algernon Swinburne in August of 1862 and, as we shall see later, the book made an extraordinary impact on the sensibility of that perverse young poet.

Virey (1816), Serrurier (1820) and Tartivel (1877)

Jules Virey, in his article 'Flagellation' published in the authoritative *Dictionnaire des sciences médicales* (vol. 16, 1816, pp. 7-14), adhered to the *ubi stimulus ibi affluxus* explanation of sexual flagellation: the 'vital force' (*esprit vital*) is drawn to the area beaten and 'there are too many sympathetic connections between the nerve branches at the base of the spine for flagellation of the buttocks and surrounding parts not to influence the genital organs' (p.13).[33] Virey mentions the source material we have seen in Meibom, and refers to the more recent case of Rousseau as an example of the way in which such flagellation may awaken prematurely the sexual impulse in children.

[32] 'Quoique le vrai temple de l'amour soit à sa portée, Rodin fidèle à son culte, n'y jette pas même de regards, il en craint jusqu'aux apparences, si l'attitude les expose, il les déguise; le plus léger écart troublerait son hommage, il ne veut pas que rien le distraie.'

[33] 'Il y a trop de communications sympathiques entre les rameaux nerveux de l'extrémité de la moelle épinière, pour que la flagellation sur les fesses et les parties environnantes ne porte pas ses effets aux organes génitaux.'

In the same dictionary Jean-Baptiste Serrurier referred to the dangers of beating children on their buttocks in his article 'Pollution' (vol. 44, 1820, pp. 92-140). We must be on the look out, warns the writer, for those who would seek to reintroduce a form of punishment which in France has been prohibited for many years. The effects of gluteal flagellation are perfectly well known to medicine, and there is a great danger that such beating applied to children may awaken premature sexual feelings, thus encouraging masturbation and the loss of that 'most vital fluid for the maintenance of life' (*la liqueur la plus importante pour l'entretien de la vie*) (p.126). Serrurier's horror of masturbation was typical of the medical profession of the day (we shall see its full flowering in Acton and Krafft-Ebing). He refers to a schoolfriend of his who experienced inexpressible pleasure (*un plaisir indicible*) while being whipped on his buttocks, and who sought every possible means of attracting this punishment from his teacher; and believes that the unfortunate man killed himself by his excessive attachment to masturbation, a habit originally caused by whipping and which eventually drained him of his 'life force':

> The first cause, therefore, came from this unnatural excitement which, at an age of continence, provoked in the young man an exaltation capable of awakening passions with which he should only have become acquainted at a time of life when a man can control his feelings and order them according to the wise laws of nature.[34] (p.126)

A. Tartivel, in his article 'Flagellation' published in the *Dictionnaire encyclopédique des sciences médicales* (vol. 2, 1877, 4th series, pp. 354-8) more or less repeated Virey's material and explanation, expressing at the same time his strong disapproval of those 'self-styled civilised nations' which still practised corporal punishment. There can be little doubt that Tartivel had Britain in mind when talking of these 'lamentable witnesses to human cruelty' (p.354).

Virey, Serrurier and Tartivel, then, see gluteal flagellation as a purely mechanical device for stimulating erection; and we may take it that this was the standard view of the French medical profession. By the 1880s, however, a new school of French psychologists would be looking, with their German and Austrian colleagues, for the *psychic* roots of sexual deviation. A new age was about to dawn.

---

[34] 'La cause première venait donc de cet excitement surnaturel qui, dans l'âge de la continence, avait déterminé chez ce jeune homme une exaltation susceptible de développer des passions qu'il n'aurait dû connaître qu'à cette époque de la vie où l'homme peut raisonner ses affections et les régler d'après les lois sages de la nature.'

Millingen (1837), Ryan (1839) and Acton (1857)

What of English doctors? It seems that they too held to the old Meibomian view of sexual flagellation. Among the many *Curiosities of Medical Experience* (1837) that had come the way of Dr John Gideon Millingen was the use of the rod in curing different ailments, particularly insanity. As regards flagellation as an aphrodisiac, Millingen is more coy than his French counterparts: 'As a remedy, it was supposed to re-animate the torpid circulation of the capillary or cutaneous vessels, to increase muscular energy, promote absorption, and favour the necessary secretions of our nature' (II, p.47). And again, 'Flagellation draws the circulation from the centre of our system to its periphery' (II, p.52). More than that Dr Millingen is not prepared to say.

Two years later we find a far more interesting reference to sexual flagellation in Michael Ryan's important book, *Prostitution in London, with a Comparative View of that of Paris and New York* (1839). In his chapter 'Causes of Venereal Excesses', Dr Ryan devotes three succinct paragraphs to the subject. He has studied the ideas of Meibom and accepts that 'friction and irritation of the skin, especially near the reproductive system, excites the genital organs' (p.381). Moreover, Ryan is aware that the method is still in use, especially in brothels: 'Impotent libertines resort to this process, and suffer its tortures until the blood flows freely' (p.381).

Ryan is also familiar with the famous passage in Rousseau's *Confessions*, although a careful comparison of his paragraphs with Virey's article on flagellation suggests that his source was the latter rather than Jean-Jacques himself. No matter, Ryan has strongly-held views on the beating of children:

> The effect is now so well known that scourging children is entirely abandoned in all well-regulated schools and families ... Flagellation and denudation are inseparable, and often excite erection in children ... It is now totally interdicted in all respectable schools and colleges, and ought also to cease in all families. Medical practitioners should explain the bad effects of this mischievous practice on modesty and on the senses. (pp. 381-2)

One might have thought that Ryan's words would be listened to attentively by the people responsible for the education of the young in Britain. But no. And it was, of course, astonishingly naive of the doctor to imagine that the practice of beating children on the buttocks had already been abandoned in 'all respectable schools and colleges'.

Nothing, as we shall see, could have been further from the truth.

It is possible to argue that Millingen and Ryan were not widely read outside the medical profession. No such idea can be entertained about William Acton's *The Functions and Disorders of the Re-Productive Organs in Youth, in Adult Age, and in Advanced Life. Considered in their Physiological, Social, and Psychological Relations*, which was first published in 1857 and which, by 1875, was in its 6th edition. Acton's celebrated book has been analysed in depth by Steven Marcus (*The Other Victorians*, 1964) and, less comprehensively, by Alex Comfort (*The Anxiety Makers*, 1967), and it will not be necessary to consider it at length here. Certainly no student of the Victorian period can afford to ignore Acton: in him coalesce all the sexual anxieties and assumptions of the age.

A genito-urinary surgeon of European reputation, Acton had worked for several years in Paris before returning to London. His book on prostitution, also published in 1857, showed a surprisingly sane, humane approach to a tabooed subject, and in it Acton made a valiant attempt to make society face up to the realities of prostitution and the necessity for its medical regulation. In England the notion of making prostitution legal was of course anathema to the puritan mind; and the fact that it was officially controlled *outre Manche* contributed not a little to the current view of Paris as the modern Sodom and Gomorrah rolled into one. The English preferred to ignore the problem, but Acton, who had studied the French system at first hand, was wiser.

In *The Functions and Disorders of the Re-Productive Organs*, Acton's sexual anxieties come closer to the surface than in the previous book. Indeed at times they break right through. Acton's approach to his subject is conditioned by fear largely unacknowledged and assumptions almost wholly unrecognised. It is a very male book, and we find hardly a reference to female sexuality. Why should we, since 'the well-brought up English maiden knows absolutely little or nothing on these matters' (p.84)?[35]

For men the dangers of sexuality are ubiquitous from the moment of entry into the world. Aphrodisiacs crowd in on all sides, often in the most innocent guise. No one is safe. The enemy is always ready to attack, to take us unawares. And once it is granted that genital

[35] Peter Fryer (1966) quotes from the 1862 edition of Acton's book: 'The best mothers, wives, and managers of households, know little or nothing of sexual indulgences ... As a general rule, a modest woman seldom desires any sexual gratification for herself. She submits to her husband, but only to please him; and, but for the desire of maternity, would far rather be relieved from his attentions' (Fryer, p.17).

sensations, erection and emission can be positively damaging to health except when well-regulated in marriage (where orgasm more than once every eight days is excessive), it follows that no effort must be spared to prevent boys from becoming prematurely aware sexually or from giving themselves over to libidinous indulgence.

In his section on 'Infantile Sexuality' in *Three Essays on Sexuality* (1905) Freud wrote: 'So far as I know, not a single author has clearly recognised the regular existence of a sexual instinct in childhood; and in the writings that have become so numerous on the development of children, the chapter on 'Sexual Development' is as a rule omitted' (VII, p.173). Had Freud known Acton's book (there is no reference to it in the index to the *Complete Works*), he would have found it typical of its age: for Acton, any manifestation of sexuality in children is abnormal, pathological. Among such manifestations, masturbation is of course the most disturbing. Acton speaks of it with absolute horror. It is classified by him as one of the 'Functional Disorders in Youth'. It is 'a cowardly, selfish, debasing habit, one which should preclude those who indulge in it from associating with boys of proper spirit, distinguished as they are by a love for manly amusements compatible with health' (p.61). Terrible consequences attend the boy who masturbates: 'His health fails, he is troubled with indigestion, his. intellectual powers are dimmed, he becomes pale, emaciated, and depressed in spirits; exercise he has no longer any taste for, and he seeks solitude' (p.56). It is easy to recognise the inveterate masturbator, and 'the haggard expression, the sunken eye, the long, cadaverous-looking countenance, the downcast look, which seems to arise from the dread of looking a fellow-creature in the face, may be carried to the grave' (p.58). A closer look at the wretched creature's anatomy affords further proof: 'Masturbators have often very small shrivelled-up organs' (p.30). The masturbator, unless he reforms and immediately begins to practise 'self-control', 'self-restraint', 'self-regulation and restraint', 'self-denial', 'self-command and restraint' – such terms occur on every page of the book – takes inevitably, along with all the other profligate sperm-expenders, 'the miserable road which ends at the lunatic asylum' (p.8). Too much orgasm leads to insanity, in other words. And this is a European authority speaking! Little wonder then that generations of masturbators suffered from excessive fear, shame and guilt, or that they presented a blushful, downcast exterior to the world. The anxiety makers had done their work well, and we can only guess how many lives were wrecked (and perhaps are still being wrecked) by the uncritical acceptance of so much mumbo-jumbo put out *ex cathedra* by medical practitioners and clergy alike. For Acton, all good men are called to participate in a perpetual struggle against sexual temptation, the inner daemon. And while Acton only refers to theological sin in passing, it is clear that his thinking has 'been deeply influenced by Calvinism. Duty, Control, Restraint, Responsibility – they stalk every page of Acton's book.

What has all this to do with sexual flagellation? A good deal. Masturbation, as Acton is forced to concede, is widespread and almost impossible to control. But we can at least avoid those practices and situations which are known to encourage it. One of these is undoubtedly flagellation of the buttocks. Acton confesses himself shocked that schoolmasters still have recourse to a practice that is known to be sexually stimulating:

> Before quitting the subject, I cannot help alluding to the ill consequences of whipping children on the nates. Of late years, this form of punishment has gone out of vogue; but, in some recent newspaper correspondence, it is urged that flogging cannot be dispensed with. The objections on medical grounds have not, probably, been stated; and, I think, its ill effects are not sufficiently known. That it has a great influence in exciting ejaculation, no one can doubt. Jean Jacques Rousseau, in his 'Confessions', admits that this was his first incitement to masturbation, as the floggings administered by his guardian first gave him sensual feelings. I am almost ashamed to say there are vile wretches who, to excite emission, have recourse to this means of stimulating their flagging powers: and I sincerely hope that, if flogging is still to be practised, it may be employed on the shoulders, and not on the nates, of youths. (pp. 59-60)

Despite the subtitle of his book, Acton understands little more about the psychology of sexual flagellation than did Meibom 200 years earlier; but it would hardly be possible to speak out more clearly about the *dangers* of corporal punishment applied to the buttocks. Again, why did the educational authorities of the country not listen? It is a question that we must constantly ask throughout this book.

Richard von Krafft-Ebing (1840-1903)

Krafft-Ebing's *Psychopathia Sexualis* (Stuttgart, 1886) was by far the most important study of deviant sexuality to be published before the coming of psychoanalysis, and it exerted a decisive influence on forensic medicine, psychology and, not least, Freud himself. The book, which on its appearance in 1886 was little more than a slim *plaquette*, became instantly famous, went quickly through numerous editions (Krafft-Ebing adding copious new material all the time) and was widely translated. It was a monumental work in every sense of the word.

Krafft-Ebing was a distinguished man – Professor of Psychiatry at the University of Strasbourg (1872-3), Graz (1873-89), where he was also director of the provincial mental hospital, and finally Vienna (1889-1902).[36] Given the standing of the author, the findings published in *Psychopathia Sexualis* could not easily be ignored by the educated world. And what an extraordinary panorama of bizarre behaviour the book unfolded, what an unprecedented range of odd sexual activities it classified, like so many rare entomological specimens! Nothing comparable had ever been seen before, and the fact that the juicier bits were given in Latin seems not to have affected sales:

> Occasionally he would obtain a prostitute, undress himself completely (while she was not to take off a thing), and have her tread upon him, whip him, and beat him. *Qua re summa libidine affectus pedem feminae lambit quod solum eum libidinosum facere potest: tum ejaculationem assequitur.* Then disgust at the morally-debasing situation occurred, and he retired as quickly as possible. (p.101)

That example is taken from the first English edition of Krafft-Ebing's work, published in 1892 (based on the 7th German edition); as the reader can judge for himself, it did not require much Latin to get hold of the general meaning of such passages.

One of the merits – and novelties – of *Psychopathia Sexualis* was that it drew extensively on Krafft-Ebing's personal case histories. During the 1880s there was a rapid acceleration of research into the sexual perversions, and in successive editions of his book Krafft-Ebing incorporated the case histories and findings of many fellow investigators, notably Albert Moll, Alfred Binet, Lombroso, Alfred Eulenburg, Jules Garnier, Magnan, Mantegazza, Leo Taxil, Tarnowsky, Hammond and Schrenck-Notzing. Krafft-Ebing was nothing if not thorough.

Before considering Krafft-Ebing's analysis of sexual flagellation, it should be pointed out that, among the many assumptions that underlie his thinking, two in particular stand out. The first has already been mentioned: it is that Krafft-Ebing, along with his contemporaries, considers childhood sexual activity *abnormal*. The second is that, for Krafft-Ebing, the sexual deviations are *congenital in origin* and only sprout in soil that is 'hereditarily tainted'. Again and again throughout *Psychopathia Sexualis* we find Krafft-Ebing talking of 'degenerative psychopathic constitution', 'hereditary sexual

[36] Details from the editorial note to Freud, *Standard Edition*, XIV, p.21, n.1.

hyperesthesia' (i.e. sexual hypersensitivity), 'degenerates infected with hereditary taint', 'heavily tainted by heredity' or 'born of a family with hereditary taint', 'congenital general psychopathic disposition' and so on. Where Freudians would soon be talking of *regression* to early childhood, Krafft-Ebing conceives of an atavistic resurgence of degenerate characteristics. And having adopted this explanation nothing can shake him from his position. If all of us come into the world trailing clouds of glory (and Krafft-Ebing pays lip-service to Christianity), many of us are also doomed to drag through life here below the inescapable shackles of inherited taint.

Believing that those who exhibit 'abnormal' sexual tendencies do so because of some inherited, congenital deficiency, cerebral or otherwise, Krafft-Ebing can almost always find an anatomical expression of such degeneracy in the cases that come to his attention. 'Without any emotional cause whatever,' he writes of a typical case, 'he often had thought of suicide.' Examination revealed, however, that there was a *physical* cause for the ailment, for this patient was found to have 'a large, rhombic, distorted skull' (p.94).[37]

Given Krafft-Ebing's basic assumptions, it follows that sexual deviation can never be simply the product of faulty childhood environment. For him, environmental factors cannot, in themselves, cause deviation, although they may and do assist its 'reawakening' and development. Thus, if Krafft-Ebing's patients experienced sexual sensations in early childhood or practised masturbation, this was on account of an inherited pathological disposition which had been brought to the surface by environmental influences. Like Acton, Krafft-Ebing holds infantile masturbation to be pathological and disgusting as well as injurious to the health. For Krafft-Ebing, however, the principal danger of masturbation is that it may awaken in children latent, inherited tendencies to homosexuality, sadism, masochism or some other 'deviation'. Moreover, Krafft-Ebing recognises that the solitary masturbator of today may easily become the mutual masturbator of tomorrow, in which case the likelihood of aberrant sexual development will be increased. At best, masturbation may lead to debilitation, 'weakening of the genitals', 'neurasthenia' and impotence, at worst to the mental asylum: 'It was certain that his brother was suspected of love for men, and that a nephew became insane as a result of excessive masturbation' (p.89).

Krafft-Ebing is aware that other psychologists and investigators of

[37] From this point on, all quotations from Krafft-Ebing are taken from the translation of *Psychopathia Sexualis* by Dr Harry E. Wedeck (New York, G.P. Putnam's Sons, 1965).

deviant sexuality, as of other areas of human experience, are tending towards 'environmental' explanations of behaviour, in particular Binet and Schrenck-Notzing. A certain Prussian tone can be heard in those emphatic passages in which Krafft-Ebing rejects the opinions of such fellow-researchers, suggesting that he was perhaps not totally blind to the possibility that his own assertions concerning the hereditary origins of the sexual deviations were closer to assumptions than to scientific fact. This comes through particularly clearly in Krafft-Ebing's discussion of sadism and masochism which, bearing in mind his basic assumptions, we may now review.

It was Krafft-Ebing who put the terms 'sadism' and 'masochism', commonplace today, on the psychological map. The first of these terms, however, was not of his invention, 'Sadismus' being current, if not widespread, in German by the 1880s. It derived from the French 'sadisme', the first appearance of which, according to the etymological dictionaries, was in 1836 or 1839 (there seems to be some disagreement). As regards the adjective 'sadique', the dictionaries I have consulted are also somewhat at variance, the most frequent dates proposed being 1862 and 1888.[38] Swinburne often uses 'sadique' in his flagellant correspondence (beginning in the 1860s), but not the noun 'sadism' or the adjective 'sadistic' (the *Oxford English Dictionary* ascribes the date 1888 to 'sadism').

'Masochismus' was a word of Krafft-Ebing's own coinage:

> I feel justified in calling this sexual anomaly 'masochism' because the author Sacher-Masoch frequently made this perversion, which up to his time was quite unknown to the scientific world as such, the substratum of his writings. I followed thereby the scientific formulation of the term 'Daltonism', from Dalton, the discoverer of colour-blindness. (p.160)

According to the OED, 'Masochism' is first recorded in English in 1893, yet in fact it appears in the first English edition of *Psychopathia Sexualis* published the previous year.

Let us try to detach from the 130 dense pages dedicated by Krafft-Ebing to the discussion of sadism and masochism his basic view of these phenomena. For Krafft-Ebing, as for many subsequent

---

[38] Paul Robert, *Dictionnaire alphabétique et analogique de la langue française* (VI, 1964, p.298) gives Boiste's 1839 definition of *sadisme*: 'Aberration épouvantable de la débauche; système monstrueux et anti-social qui révolte la nature', and 1862 for *sadique*. The *Dictionnaire de l'Académie Française* (1879) gives neither word. Nor does the Littré *Dictionnaire de la langue française* (1882). The *Dictionnaire étymologique de la langue française* (Presses universitaires de France, 6th edition, 1975) gives 1836 for *sadisme*, 1888 for *sadique*.

investigators, sadism and masochism are 'two different sides of the same psychical process' (p.241), active and passive expressions of the same drive ('the parallelism in perfect', p.239). True sadism and masochism, like the other deviations, only occur in pathologically predisposed persons, and both expressions are essentially heterosexual in direction: the male sadist aiming at the complete subjection of the female (Krafft-Ebing believes that female sadism is very rare, a finding confirmed by later investigators), the masochist craving to be dominated by his or her partner. For Krafft-Ebing it is this pattern of domination and subjection that is the vital aspect of the subject, the other details being of secondary importance:

> the primary and essential thing is the consciousness of active or passive subjection, in which the combination of cruelty and lustful pleasure has only a secondary psychological significance. Acts of cruelty serve to express this subjection: first, because they are the most extreme means for the expression of this relation; and, again, because they represent the most intense effect that one person, either with or without coitus, can exert on another. (p.241)

Krafft-Ebing examines sadism first. He finds it to be 'nothing else than a monstrous pathological intensification' of normal sexual aggression in the male, a perversion 'in which the need to subjugate the opposite sex forms a constituent element' (p.157). It is rarely encountered in women. As regards men, Krafft-Ebing finds that 'Sadism, especially in its rudimentary manifestations, seems to be of common occurrence in the domain of sexual perversion' (p.109) but that, in its developed forms, it is 'a relatively rare perversion' (p.156). When it does occur it is undoubtedly hereditary in origin. Among the various forms that sadism may take is flagellation. Krafft-Ebing gives four cases of this perversion (nos. 39, 40, 41 and 42). In three of these the patients claim to have been first aroused sexually by witnessing a real-life beating being inflicted on another child. This was an extremely important finding, showing that the many active flagellants who figure in the works of the Marquis de Sade were not simply the inventions of the author's unique imagination. Take case 39:

> P., aged twenty-two, of independent means, heavily tainted by heredity, by accident saw the governess chastising his sister (fourteen years of age) on the fundament. This made a deep impression on him and henceforth he had a constant desire to see and touch his sister's buttocks. By some clever stratagem he succeeded. When seven years old he became the playfellow of two small girls, one of whom was tiny and lean, the other rather plump. He played the role of the father chastising his children. The

lean girl he simply spanked over the clothes. The other, however, allowed him to smack her bare bottom (she was then ten years old). This gave him great sexual pleasure and caused erection. (p.147)

P. was by now a confirmed sadist. At the age of 9 he formed a flagellant relationship with a slightly older boy, and this continued into manhood. He took the active part, and always ejaculated during the beating. In action and fantasy, P.'s obsession centred on the naked buttocks, and it is clear that it made little difference whether they were male or female. The female body as such did not excite him sexually, but 'At last he found a woman with whom he could have coitus, as she permitted him to flagellate her during the act' (pp. 147-9).

Krafft-Ebing assumes that P.'s flagellant tendencies were congenital, although to us no such assumption appears to be justified. He also assumes that such flagellation is basically a substitute for sexual intercourse with females, even though the person being beaten may be a boy:

> The sadistic acts with females just now described are also practised on other living, sensitive objects – children and animals. There may be a full consciousness that the impulse is really directed towards women, and that only as a makeshift the nearest attainable objects (pupils) are abused. But the condition of the perpetrator may be such that the impulse to cruel acts enters consciousness accompanied only by lustful excitement, while its real object (which alone can explain the lustful colouring of such acts) remains latent. (pp. 149-50)

This last assumption, again, is not justified, as cases 41 and 42 show clearly. For here the first excitement occurred when the patients saw other *boys* being whipped, experiences that led immediately to masturbation and the elaboration of flagellant fantasies. In both of these cases the buttocks are again all-important; and, for both men, attempts at heterosexual intercourse later in life have proved unsatisfactory. Krafft-Ebing has not elaborated the concept of fixation, which would come soon afterwards with the psychoanalysts, but this is clearly what these patients are suffering from – the fixation of a childhood, pre-pubertal nexus of sexual excitement. All we can safely deduce from Krafft-Ebing's observations on sadistic flagellation is that, as in masochism, the practice originates in early childhood, is centred on the buttocks and becomes fixated before puberty to such a degree that sexual intercourse without the fantasy (whether 'acted out' or not) is difficult if not impossible. Krafft-Ebing's own evidence, moreover, suggests that not only are these flagellant fantasies not hereditary but that they derive from lived experience.

Krafft-Ebing's longer, more detailed and undoubtedly more important section on masochism throws the subject of sexual flagellation into sharper relief, and reveals clearly the German doctor's difficulties in dealing with the phenomenon. For Krafft-Ebing masochism, as has been said, is also congenital:

> Masochism is the opposite of sadism. While the latter is the desire to cause pain and use force, the former is the wish to suffer pain and be subjected to force.
>
> By masochism I understand a peculiar perversion of the psychical *vita sexualis* in which the individual affected, in sexual feeling and thought, is controlled by the idea of being completely and unconditionally subject to the will of a person of the opposite sex; of being treated by this person as by a master, humiliated and abused. This idea is coloured by lustful feeling; the masochist lives in fancies, in which he creates situations of this kind and often attempts to realize them. By this perversion his sexual instinct is often made more or less insensible to the normal charms of the opposite sex – incapable of a normal *vita sexualis* – psychically impotent. (pp. 159-60)

Krafft-Ebing has found that 'the number of masochists is larger than has yet been dreamed' (p.176), that it is 'a perversion of uncommonly frequent occurrence' (p.193). He never succeeds in explaining why this should be so, although undoubtedly it is a question that occupies his mind.

Among the forms of subjection sought by the masochist (foot fetishism, the desire to be ridden as if a horse, enforced cunnilingus, etc.), Krafft-Ebing has found that flagellation holds the most important position. The many flagellant case histories and fantasies supplied by his patients reveal a remarkable similarity, and show that almost always the first excitement in connection with beating occurred in early childhood while a whipping inflicted by an adult was being witnessed, undergone or read about. In this last connection, Krafft-Ebing, Freud and other investigators found that several of their flagellant patients were first sexually aroused by reading *Uncle Tom's Cabin*, where there are frequent references to the flogging of negro slaves.[39] Case 61 is typical of Krafft-Ebing's passive flagellants: '*Vita sexualis* suddenly aroused in him at the age of seven while being caned on the fundament; at ten, masturbation. During the act, he always thought of someone flagellating him' (p.184). Most of his patients were men, but Krafft-Ebing also supplies several of women who desire

---

[39] See, for example, Freud (1919), XVII, p.180; Sadger (1913), p.355.

to be beaten – a finding corroborated by psychoanalysis: 'Since her earliest youth she fancied herself being whipped. She simply revelled in these ideas, and had the most intense desire to be severely punished with a rattan cane' (case 84, p.224).

Krafft-Ebing, faced with such a mass of evidence, cannot but notice that, in flagellation, the excitement always centres on the buttocks. Moreover, he knows that this characteristic of the phenomenon has already been isolated by earlier investigators. Realising that the fact must be explained, he turns first to traditional theory.

To begin with, Krafft-Ebing assumes, following the standard medical view of the day, which derived from Meibom (and which we have seen repeated in Virey and Tartivel), that flagellation applied to the buttocks can act as *a purely physical stimulus to erection*. According to Krafft-Ebing, this 'mechanical irritation' of the 'spinal centre' (p.169) – Meibom's lumbar region – induces a 'reflex physical irritative effect' (p.170) on the recipient's genitals. In the case of the male, erection then takes place and coitus becomes possible. Elsewhere Krafft-Ebing speaks of 'reflex spinal influence' (p.236), 'reflex excitation of lust' (p.236), 'simple (reflex) flagellation' (p.169), the 'reflex effect of passive flagellation' (p.241) and so on. Although Krafft-Ebing does not make the point, it ought to follow from this formulation that *anyone* subjected to flagellation, male or female, will react sexually, given the essentially involuntary nature of a reflex action. If passive flagellation really were a question simply of 'reflex spinal influence', what a blessing it would be to the impotent of the world! An infallible aphrodisiac! It is, of course, nothing of the sort. For Krafft-Ebing this form of flagellation is akin to hanging: 'According to observations made on men who have been hanged, it is evident that the erection centre may also be aroused by excitation of the tract of the spinal cord' (p.56). Hanging, however, and flagellation applied to the buttocks are, to say the least, two very different forms of stimulation; and while modern medicine has no difficulty in explaining why the former may produce erection, it has no place for the 'reflex spinal influence' which flagellation of the buttocks has been alleged for centuries to exert on the 'erection centre'. The fact of the matter is that Krafft-Ebing, like his predecessors, is stuck with an antiquated theory whose inadequacy he fails to recognise. His uncritical acceptance of this theory (which he sees not as theory but as fact) leads him into insoluble difficulties.

For Krafft-Ebing, as we have seen, true masochism is a wider phenomenon than passive flagellation, and is congenital. It follows, therefore, that masochistic flagellation proper must be differentiated from the reflex action, Meibomian variety, which is a purely mechanical affair: we are dealing with two different phenomena, Krafft-Ebing insists, although to the unpractised – and even the practised – eye they may appear to be indistinguishable.

Krafft-Ebing has no doubt that passive flagellation of the 'reflex' type is much practised by profligates – 'this perversity – not perversion – is very common' and is 'used by weakened debauchees to help their diminished power' (p.169). Contemporary works on prostitution (such as those by Taxil and Coffignon) have shown Krafft-Ebing that prostitutes in modern brothels are frequently called upon to wield the rod, and he assumes that those seeking this service are not true masochists but jaded *roués* in need of the 'mechanical' stimulus which flagellation can provide. It is not made clear why these men could not be 'true masochists'.

Krafft-Ebing argues that, since many of his masochistic patients had their flagellant fantasies before, and indeed without, experiencing the administration of flagellation to their own persons, these fantasies must have been in the mind at birth: 'The desire is felt before there has been any experience of the reflex effect, often first in dreams ... there can, of course, be no thought of a reflex physical irritative effect' (pp. 169-70). It is clear from this and similar observations that Krafft-Ebing greatly underestimates the power of fantasy in children, despite the fact that so many of his patients give full details of these fantasies and their origins in early childhood. It is also clear that Krafft-Ebing, although he is the immediate precursor of psychoanalysis, has no notion of the concept of repression: it does not occur to him that the fact that a patient has no *conscious* memory of an event does not prove that no such event took place.

Case 85 illustrates very clearly the difficulties under which Krafft-Ebing was labouring. The patient is a woman of 35: 'At the age of six or eight I conceived a desire to be whipped. Since I had never been whipped, and had never been present when others were thus punished, I cannot understand how I came to have this strange desire. I can only think that it is congenital' (p.225). With our post-Freudian knowledge (and assumptions, too, let it be admitted) we might suggest to this lady that, since the whipping of young children was apparently endemic in Germany at the time of her youth, there is a strong likelihood that she would have heard about it from a playmate, or read about it. We might even suggest that perhaps she might have repressed the memory of some unpleasant incident or incidents involving beating. And we might add that the fact that, a year before coming to Krafft-Ebing, she had read Rousseau's *Confessions* could be held to be of some importance. Krafft-Ebing, however, has no doubt that here is a case of congenital, hereditary masochism:

On account of its original character and the reference to Rousseau, this case may with certainty be called a case of masochism. The fact that it is a female friend who is conceived in imagination as whipping her is explained by the circumstance that the masochistic desire was here present in the mind of a child before the psychical *vita sexualis* had developed and the instinct for the male had been awakened. (p.226)

Krafft-Ebing's explanation of male sadism, as we have seen, is coherent – the deviation constitutes for him an intensification, in predisposed persons, of what is basically a normal drive towards the 'conquest' of the female. Female sadism he finds so rare that it can virtually be ignored. Female masochism, too, Krafft-Ebing explains adequately enough, seeing it as a morbid extension of woman's social and sexual roles in a society that demands of them a passive, submissive position in relation to men.

That leaves male masochism as undoubtedly the most unusual category of the four. At the end of his long account of the perversion Krafft-Ebing tries to come to a conclusion. What are the hall-marks of 'true masochism'? He points out to start with that the 'psychical characteristics' of masochists are essentially feminine:

It cannot be doubted that the masochist considers himself in a passive, feminine role towards his mistress and that his sexual gratification is governed by the success his illusion experiences in the complete subjection to the will of his consort. The pleasurable feeling, call it lust, resulting from this act differs per se in no wise from the feeling which women derive from the sexual act. (p.237)

Krafft-Ebing adds a few pertinent observations on the masochist's ideal partner:

The masochistically inclined individual seeks and finds an equivalent for his purpose in the fact that he endows in his imagination the consort with certain masculine psychical sexual characteristics – i.e. in a perverse manner, insofar as the sadistic female constitutes his ideal. (p.237)

Given this general framework, masochistic flagellation is easily explained: 'that passive flagellation occurs so frequently in masochism is explained by the fact that it is the most extreme means of expressing the relation of subjection' (p.236).

These characteristics of masochism, allied to Krafft-Ebing's belief that like the other deviations it is a congenital perversion, lead him to the following conclusion:

From this emanates the deduction that masochism is, properly speaking, only a rudimentary form of antipathetic sexual instinct [i.e. homosexuality]. It is a partial *effemination* which has only apperceived the secondary characteristics of the psychical sexual life.

This assumption is supported by the fact that heterosexual masochists consider themselves merely as individuals endowed with feminine feelings. Observation shows that they really do possess feminine traits of character. This renders it intelligible that the masochistic element is so frequently found in homosexual men. (pp. 238-9)

What Krafft-Ebing's diagnosis boils down to is that male masochists have congenital feminine characteristics which prevent them from experiencing sexual excitement other than by placing themselves in a submissive role in relation to the female. It is to facilitate this process that the female is endowed (in imagination or in 'acting out') with a selection of 'masculine' attributes and props which vary from case to case to suit individual requirements (stern expression, riding boots, whips, etc.) and which alter her from the Victorian Angel in the House into a full-blooded, dominant sexual partner. Krafft-Ebing at no point accepts the possibility that such masochism could be the result, say, of submissive patterns of response imposed on male children in early childhood and subsequently fixated: this and other 'environmental' possibilities would soon be investigated by psychoanalysis.

Whatever we may think of Krafft-Ebing's assumptions concerning heredity, there can be no doubt that his picture of the broad characteristics of sadism and masochism constituted a tremendous advance on previous knowledge. Perhaps one of his most important contributions lay in the many instances he provided of the function of perverse fantasies in assisting erection before and during coition. Although Rousseau had been the first to throw some light on this little-known area of human experience, it was Krafft-Ebing who really illuminated it. His case histories also showed the vital link between such fantasies and impotence, even though his own analysis of the phenomena presented would prove to have been wide of the mark. Insights such as the following had never before been available to the reading public, and their widespread dissemination through the publication of *Psychopathia Sexualis* can be seen as a significant breakthrough in human understanding:

On his marriage night he remained cold until, from necessity, he brought to his aid the memory-picture of an ugly woman's head with a nightcap. Coitus was immediately successful. (Case 116, p.292)

From this time it was necessary for him to call upon ideas about boots, which had been latent, for help in order to be potent in sexual intercourse with her. In proportion as his power failed, these ideas arose spontaneously. (Case 137, pp. 382-3)

She accepted her conjugal duties merely as a matter of unavoidable necessity. Her only condition was that she should be in the upper position. In this position she obtained a sort of gratification, for she imagined his body to be that of a beloved woman in the lower position. (Case 160, p.435)

Female charms never attracted him. Coitus was only possible when aided by the thought of a beloved man. (Case 149, p.408)

In the hope of correcting his sexual life he married. He forced himself to coitus with the wife and produced potency by imagining her to be a young man. (Case 144, p.394)

Psychopathia Sexualis provides dozens of such examples, among them many flagellant ones, as we have seen. It was on the basis of such discoveries that psychoanalysis would be built.

Krafft-Ebing's warnings about beating children

Krafft-Ebing has no doubt that the practice of whipping children on their buttocks is extremely dangerous. Such a practice must be immediately discontinued for, as his examples show, real-life whippings in childhood, witnessed or experienced, have often led to the sudden awakening of sexual excitement:

The first sexual emotions he experienced when, a boy of eight, he witnessed other boys being caned on the fundament. Although he felt compassion for the boys, he yet had a feeling of lustful pleasure pervading his whole body. Some time afterwards he was late for school and on the way the anticipation of a caning on the fundament excited him so much that for a short time he could not move and had a violent erection. (Case 143, p.392)

Pondering on the many such cases that have come to his notice, Krafft-Ebing concludes:

It sometimes happens that in boys the first excitation of the sexual instinct is caused by a spanking, and they are thus incited to masturbation. This should be remembered by those who have the care of children.

On account of the dangers to which this form of punishment of children gives rise, it would be better if parents, teachers and nurses were to avoid it entirely. (pp. 62-3)

It was what William Acton had said forty years earlier. A child excited by beating may be tempted to share his discovery with his fellows. Moreover, if he is one of those unfortunates with a congenital homosexual taint, the premature awakening of sexuality occasioned by beating will bring those latent tendencies to the surface – with perhaps disastrous results. Teachers have therefore a definite responsibility to desist from beating their charges – and to be ever watchful:

> A boy with inverted sexuality should be rigidly excluded from all public educational institutions for boys and sent to a hospital for nervous disorders. Boys should not be permitted to sleep together at home. Swimming lessons and bathing *en masse* should be under careful and strict supervision of a competent person.
>
> Neither should a child with antipathic sexual instinct be placed under the isolated tuition of a tutor or private master, for frequently the first object of homosexual love is the instructor at home. Care should be taken that tainted children are not caressed and fondled by persons of the same sex. Flagellation on the fundament should never be permitted. (p. 467)

It is evident that beating on the buttocks was still widely practised in German homes and schools at the time Krafft-Ebing was writing; and he had no illusions about the sexual element involved, diagnosing many of the teachers without hesitation as sadists and referring twice to the findings of a certain Dr Albert, published in 1859, concerning 'cases in which lustful teachers whipped their pupils on the naked buttocks without cause' (p.150). Krafft-Ebing has come to believe that 'The cases in which lascivious tutors, governesses, etc., cane or spank their pupils without provocation are open to investigation as to the pathological condition of the malefactor' (p.570).[40]

[40] The *Cyclopedia of Education* (New York, 1913) states that, according to the Statute Book of the German Empire of 15 May 1871, teachers were legally empowered to inflict corporal punishment, subject to certain restrictions. Teachers in Prussia seem to have enjoyed even wider beating powers: 'In Prussia, by a decree of 1900, a record must be kept of all punishments inflicted by a teacher, and this must be inspected on all occasions when an inspector visits the school. Teachers have the right to inflict punishment on pupils of their class or school not only outside school hours but also beyond the limits of the school premises. In the higher schools corporal punishment is not recognized as a proper form of correction and is limited to the three lower forms' (V, p.87). It seems that the right of German teachers to inflict corporal punishment gave rise to criticism. Moll (1912) refers to 'the recent widely advertised public pronouncements' against the practice (p.318). According to Gervas D'Olbert (1967), Prof. Pfeiffer's *Allgemeine Einführung zur soziopsychologischen Geschichte des Begriffes des Körperstrafens* (Leipzig, 1899), which I have not seen, 'offers an exhaustive survey of corporal chastisement in German schools and homes through many centuries of history, with special emphasis on the nineteenth' (p.138).

It was clear to Krafft-Ebing, then, as it had been to Rousseau, Doppet, Ryan and Acton before him, that society must prohibit the beating of children on the buttocks. In France, by contrast with Britain and Germany, all corporal punishment of children in schools had been abolished long before the time at which Krafft-Ebing was writing. It cannot be a coincidence that the two countries which specialised in flogging children produced both the most flagellant pornography and the most books analysing flagellomania. In this last category the German bibliography is enormous.[41]

Conclusion

By the first decade of the twentieth century it could no longer be doubted by open-minded people that there was a connection between flagellation applied to the buttocks and sexual excitement; that the deviation could take a passive ('masochistic') or active ('sadistic') form or be a combination of both ('sado-masochistic'); and that children, especially boys, thus punished were liable to experience sexual problems and impotence later in life. Warnings had been given to parents and teachers about the dangers of beating children on the buttocks from Meibom onwards, but it was the rapid acceleration of sex research in the late nineteenth century, and especially Krafft-Ebing's *Psychopathia Sexualis*, which provided incontrovertible arguments in favour of abandoning the practice. Whatever the explanation of the sexual element in flagellation (and there was disagreement about this), it was generally agreed that children should no longer be beaten in this way. For Krafft-Ebing had proved beyond any doubt that beating fantasies (whether congenital or not) arise in early childhood in connection with witnessing, undergoing, hearing or

---

[41] Havelock Ellis (1942) has an interesting paragraph on this aspect of our subject: 'Whatever the precise origin of sexual flagellation in Europe, there can be no doubt that it soon became extremely common, and so it remains at the present day. Those who possess a special knowledge of such matters declare that sexual flagellation is the most frequent of all sexual perversions in England. This belief is, I know, shared by many people both inside and outside England. However this may be, the tendency is certainly common. I doubt if it is any or at all less common in Germany, judging by the large number of books on the subject of flagellation which have been published in Germany. In a catalogue of 'interesting books' on this and allied subjects issued by a German publisher and bookseller, I find that, of fifty-five volumes, as many as seventeen or eighteen, all in German, deal solely with the question of flagellation, while many of the other books appear to deal in part with the same subject' (p.131). In a footnote, Ellis adds that flagellation 'appears also to be common' in America, and refers to flagellant advertisements appearing in Chicago 'massage shops'. Krafft-Ebing (p.193, note) also refers to flagellant advertisements appearing in German newspapers.

reading about the whipping of the buttocks, with which part of the anatomy flagellomania is exclusively and obsessively concerned.

After the publication and widespread translation of Krafft-Ebing's great work, the advisability of discontinuing such punishments, one might have thought, would have become obvious, even in Britain. But in Britain the teachers were not prepared to listen.

One of Krafft-Ebing's most valuable contributions to knowledge had been to document the sadistic variety of sexual flagellation, and to suggest that many schoolmasters derived explicit pleasure from inflicting whippings on their pupils. Other researchers found similar cases, notably Albert Moll. In his *Das Sexualleben des Kindes* (1909) – published in English as *The Sexual Life of the Child* (London, 1912) – Moll wrote that he had received 'the direct confessions of schoolmasters and schoolmistresses, that they have struck their pupils for the purpose of thereby enjoying sexual stimulation' (p.317). Among these pedagogues were 'some extremely pious schoolmasters', and Moll warned that 'it is inadmissible to infer, because a schoolmaster is a religious man, that therefore he is the one to whom the right to inflict corporal punishment may safely be entrusted' (p.319).

The findings of continental psychologists and psychiatrists made slow headway in Britain – met fierce resistance, in fact. Several books by distinguished foreign doctors were banned, including, to the indignation of the French medical profession, an English translation of Charles Féré's important study *La pathologie des émotions* (1882), published by Carrington at Paris in 1899.[42] But little by little the views of the new school of French and German investigators filtered into the consciousness of the more enlightened members of the educated class. Thus Joseph Collinson of the Humanitarian League, who was indefatigable (as we shall see) in his fight against the beaters of Britain, could write in 1907 in his pamphlet *Facts about Flogging*:

> Those who have studied pathology, as expounded by Continental thinkers, know that the use of the rod, as at present inflicted, is evidence that flagellomania is a real and widespread disease ... birching has come to be regarded among medical men in France, Germany, and other parts of the Continent, as a sensuous gratification for people of morbid tastes. (pp. 6-7, 13)

---

[42] See *Le Progrès médical*, no. 52, 30 December 1899, p.503, 'Libéralisme anglais: Saisie d'ouvrages scientifiques'. Dr Bourneville, author of the article, observed: 'Nous attendons l'opinion de la presse médicale anglaise sur cette étrange mesure qu'on aurait pu croire impossible à notre époque.'

The pages that follow will show that until well into the twentieth century beating was endemic in Britain, especially in England, and that such beating was often extremely brutal and of the 'lower discipline' variety beloved of flagellants.

It is impossible that, in the face of the published evidence as well as that of their own senses, the schoolmasters of Britain can have been unaware of the dangers and delights associated with the beating of children. Many of them must have been familiar with Rousseau, Acton and the other critics of the beating system, as well as with the many references to the subject in English literature. Many of them, no doubt, were also familiar with the flagellant pornography that flooded the market in the nineteenth century – and is still with us.

How are we to explain the prevalence of flagellomania in Britain and the survival of beating in schools until our own time? One of my reasons for writing this book has been to attempt an answer to this question.

2

Home and School Beating in Nineteenth-century England and Later

Parental beating

Upper- and middle-class Victorians (and to a lesser extent Edwardians) never tired of reminding themselves that the beating of naughty children had been strictly enjoined upon them by God, through the mouth of Solomon. Again and again the same Old Testament maxims were pressed into service. We rarely hear of Christ's gentleness with children during the endless flogging debates that took place during the century. Indeed, apart from Christ's castigation of the Temple money-lenders, the New Testament proved to be of little use to the supporters of flogging, and was conveniently laid aside. It was felt that *Proverbs* had said all that was necessary on the matter – then, now and forever:

> For whom the Lord loveth he correcteth; even as a father the son in whom he delighteth.
>
> Proverbs, III, 12.

> He that spareth his rod hateth his son: but he that loveth him chasteneth him betimes.
>
> Proverbs, XIII, 24.

> Chasten thy son while there is hope, and let not thy soul spare for his crying.
>
> Proverbs, XIX, 18.

> Withold not correction from the child: for if thou beatest him with the rod, he shall not die.
> Thou shalt beat him with the rod, and shalt deliver his soul from hell.
>
> Proverbs, XXIII, 13-14.

These verses of Scripture, quoted *ad nauseam* during the nineteenth century, were of general application to cases of moral delinquency in the young (dishonesty, lack of obedience, 'self-will', rebelliousness, bad language and so on). Other similar verses could be used to justify the flogging of criminals; while two in particular lent themselves to cases of foolishness, and were suitable for application to children who, for example, were not working hard enough at their lessons:

Foolishness is bound in the heart of a child; but the rod of correction shall drive it far from him.
Proverbs, XXII, 15

A whip for the horse, a bridle for the ass, and a rod for the fool's back.
Proverbs, XXVI, 3.

There was one maxim that recurred more frequently than any other: 'Spare the rod and spoil the child'. This was universally attributed by the Victorians to Solomon, but in fact comes from Samuel Butler's satirical poem *Hudibras*, published in 1664 (Part II, Canto I, 1. 884). In this section of Butler's poem an amorous lady urges Sir Hudibras to undergo a whipping on her account – as a fitting and tradition-hallowed proof of knightly love and also, perhaps, as a parody on the practices of the religious flagellants. It is clear from her words that Butler has projected onto this lady a dubious interest in what the Victorians loved to call the *modus operandi* of fustigation. The relevant lines for our purpose read (it is the lady speaking):

But since our sex's modesty
Will not allow I should be by,
Bring me, on oath, a fair account,
And honour too, when you have done it;
And I'll admit you to the place
You claim as due in my good grace.
If matrimony and hanging go
By dest'ny, why not whipping too?
What medicine else can cure the fits
Of lovers, when they lose their wits?
Love is a boy, by poets styled,
Then spare the rod and spoil the child. (1885, pp. 113-14)

'The passage as a whole,' wrote Henry Salt, 'is hardly decorous enough for quotation.' Moreover, 'it is significant that a witty writer, who frankly treats the subject of whipping as what it is – an *indecent* subject – should have provided many generations with a supposed precept from the Bible!' (1916, p.28).

Occasionally some more thoughtful person would point out that the Biblical injunctions concerning the rod were perhaps intended to be understood in a figurative sense (as is obvious in the case of the 'rod of iron', for example). 'That passage in the Old Testament which speaks of sparing the rod and spoiling the child', wrote a lady to *The Queen* on 23 December 1865, confusing Solomon and Butler, 'ought not to be more literally taken than that in the New Testament of the "lilies of the field"' (p.435). A correspondent to another journal put it even more firmly, pointing out that Christ himself had never commended the use of the rod to His followers, and that He had distinguished Himself by His love and respect for children:

> Solomon has been quoted as an authority for the rod, but Jesus has said, 'A greater than Solomon is here;' and Solomon and his son Rehoboam are bad *examples* of life, whatever his *precepts* may have been to the Jews. Again, we cannot be Christians and Jews at the same time; and if we whip the children we must stone the adultress, etc. (*The Englishwoman's Domestic Magazine*, 1 March 1870, p.190)

To write thus was to incur the wrath of the floggers. The following outburst from 'One who was Flogged in his Youth, and Has Never Regretted It' is characteristic:

> Your correspondent would hardly require to be referred to our oldest and best authority; which, however, too many of our antibirchites, wise above what is written, are desirous of interpreting after a figurative manner. If, however, the following passages are figurative, I know not what is literal [a selection of quotations from *Proverbs* is then given]. Solomon had no hesitation either as to the instrument of castigation, or the part of the person to which it was to be applied. (*Notes and Queries*, 18 October 1862, p.312)

In 1904 Vice-Admiral Penrose Fitzgerald unwisely entered into debate with George Bernard Shaw in the columns of *The Times* on the subject of birching in the Royal Navy (of which more later):

> Mr Bernard Shaw tells us that more brains are wanted on the quarter-deck, and that 'the cane and the birch are essentially a fool's implements'; and yet Solomon is not usually counted a fool, and he said (Prov. 13, v.24), 'He that spareth the rod hateth his son; but he that loveth him chasteneth him betimes.'
> But a wiser than Solomon is here – Mr G. Bernard Shaw! (9 September 1904, p.6)

Shaw's rejoinder, in which the shortcomings of Solomon and his children were reviewed, infuriated the floggers:

I have gone carefully through the history of Solomon and his presumably well-birched son. I find that Solomon himself was the son of David, a successful warrior and ruler, who spoiled his children, as the case of Absalom shows. Solomon introduced the flogging system, which grew more severe in the family until scorpions were substituted for whips. And, as might have been expected, Solomon's children lost the kingdom his father had built up, and scattered the nation he had welded together ... As to Solomon himself, unrestrained authority, and the practice of flogging other people, had such an effect on him that, on reaching the age of an admiral, he turned to the worship of Ashtaroth, and never could be reclaimed. A more impressive warning against governing empires on Solomonic principles, and governing navies on the principles of Captain Kidd's boatswains,[1] is not to be found in the Scriptures. (14 September 1904, p.8)

In Protestant Britain, Christ's own scourging was overlooked, the point rarely being made that God, not content with providing flagellant advice for earthly fathers, had put His teaching into practice by permitting the flagellation of His only Son. It was left to Roman Catholic apologists for the rod, as we have seen, to remind the faithful of Christ's sufferings under the lash, and of the spiritual benefits to be obtained from their imitation.

The editorial views of the *Family Herald* (founded in 1842) afford us a clear insight into the religious assumptions with which the growing middle class approached the subject of corporal punishment in the family. Corporal punishment, explained the editor, derives its legitimacy from God, who 'is severe as fire if you transgress His immutable and inviolable laws; but gentle as warmth if you do not' (17 November 1849). As human parents created in His image it is our duty to emulate Him in the treatment of our children who 'are given in charge to us in order that we may teach them the nature of the Divine Law, and prepare them for manhood and womanhood' (17 November 1849). Nature, like God, is wise, and physical pain is part of her law: 'Look at Nature, our common mother. Is she not severe? There is no order in this world without severity. But the more kindness you combine with it the better' (4 September 1852). Children in the natural state are little beasts ('Me! me! me! is the soul of a child, and its selfishness is only beautiful and interesting because it is feeble and governable') (17 November 1849). It follows that children must be taught, and if necessary forced, to obey us. Obedience and duty: two imperatives which dominate all nineteenth-century discussions on the education of children. Two imperatives which forbade all insubordination to parental authority. The child is father to the man,

[1] Captain Kidd, the pirate, was hanged by the British in 1701.

and Victorian children, trained to fear their fathers and God, could hardly fail to continue the same system when they themselves became parents. The *Family Herald* and the middle-class mind it represents perceive 'self-will' and 'forwardness' (two terrible moral flaws) on all sides, not only in children but in the lower class. These dangerous traits must be eradicated:

> The world is a battlefield, an arena of fierce, or animated, or interested conflict. It is a world of authority and obedience, a world in which all must learn to obey before they can be authorised to govern. (24 November 1849)

A grim, Old Testament view of life it was. And one in which the male principle reigned supreme.

Upper- and middle-class Victorian fathers, then, could and did see themselves as created in the image of a punitive, flagellant God. But how did domestic discipline work out in practice? The evidence is that, in these social groups, there was endemic beating in the home in the nineteenth century. Lower down the social scale, on the other hand, it seems that ceremonial beating 'in the old-fashioned style' was much less common: children were knocked about, certainly, but not in the fashion favoured by the Biblical beaters.[2]

Memoirs, autobiographies, letters, novels – they all show that middle- and upper-class fathers had little hesitation in applying Solomon's maxims to their children. The rod was the rule. Jonathan Gathorne-Hardy's *The Rise and Fall of the British Nanny* provides further evidence that beatings were commonplace in upper-class and, increasingly as the century progressed, middle-class nurseries. He quotes Lady Anne Hill:

> My first Nanny was horrid. I am told that I was wrongly fed by her in infancy, and that in consequence I was ill for some years. Everybody who knew me then recalls how appallingly I used to scream. One of my brothers remembers her laying me over her knees when I was still in long clothes (I imagine aged eight months or younger), and beating me hard on the bottom with a hairbrush. This she continued to do frequently when I was bigger. (p.245)

Lord Curzon had a similarly monstrous nanny:

> She spanked us with the sole of her slipper on the bare back [read 'bottom'], beat us with her brushes, tied us for long hours to chairs in uncomfortable positions with our hands holding a pole or a blackboard behind our backs, shut us up in darkness. (p.17)

[2] Pearsall (1975), p.109.

Indeed, Curzon's nanny seems to have been a genuine sadist:

> She made me write a letter to the butler asking him to make a birch for me
> with which I was to be punished for lying, and requesting him to read it
> out in the servants' hall. When he came round one day with a letter and
> saw me standing in my red petticoat with my face to the wall on a chair
> outside the schoolroom and said, 'My you look like a Cardinal', I could
> have died of shame. (p.303)

As Gathorne-Hardy observes, this female, whose name was Miss
Paraman, sounds and looks as if she might have walked straight out of
a Victorian flagellant novel.

It seems, however, that when corporal punishment was required in
the nursery the *pater familias* was usually called in to do the job.
Gathorne-Hardy quotes Nurse McCallum:

> Nursery life was very strict. If they had jam for tea they didn't have cake.
> The parents were tough too. C.F. [the father in this instance] was a good
> example. The children were often given 'stick'. Right from the beginning,
> when they were very small, I've taken a child into the bathroom, father
> has come up, then slippered that boy till he couldn't sit for two days. A
> real good proper thrashing. You could hear him yell. And a very good
> thing. We never punished them. The father did. That gave them a lively
> respect for their father. As a result they were very good children. Very
> quiet. Very self-contained. (p.245)

Not all nannies were as unpleasant as these, certainly. Nor were all
fathers as harsh. But the fact remains that many decent people,
themselves victims of religious literalism and anxiety, doubtless
whipped their children out of a sense of duty. And when they did so
they whipped them on their bottoms 'in the old-fashioned style'. It is
no part of my purpose in this book to suggest that all those who beat
their children were – or are – conscious sadists. Edmund Gosse's
father, for example, was a kindly man. A well-known geologist with
several successful books to his credit, he was also a Plymouth Brother
who believed in the literal truth of the Bible (which he tried vainly to
reconcile with Darwin). On one occasion the young Gosse
misbehaved: 'My Father, after a solemn sermon, chastised me,
sacrificially, by giving me several cuts with a cane. This action was
justified, as everything he did was justified, by reference to Scripture –
"Spare the rod and spoil the child" ' (p.37). Either Gosse or his
father, it may be noted, makes the habitual mistake of confusing
Solomon with Samuel Butler. Victorian England was undoubtedly
full of men like Gosse senior.

Before leaving the subject of 'domestic discipline', let us have a look at the extraordinary activities of a woman whose services seem to have been rendered necessary by those parents who were too squeamish to put Solomon's advice into practice themselves, at least with their daughters.

Mrs Walter Smith, the girl-flogger of Clifton

When I first read about this lady in Ronald Pearsall's *The Worm in the Bud* (pp. 403-4), I confess that I felt sure the whole thing was a flagellant hoax of a type common during the nineteenth century. A hoax, I thought, which had even taken in Mr Pearsall. But no. Pearsall does not give the source of his information concerning Mrs Smith, which was in fact Henry Labouchère's journal *Truth*. The revelations published by *Truth* in 1889 proved beyond doubt that Mrs Smith really existed. *Truth*'s attention had been drawn to some dubious advertisements appearing in London newspapers:

> BAD TEMPER, Hysteria, Idleness, etc. CURED by strict discipline and careful training. Three GIRLS only received. – Address G., care of Mrs Clapp, St. John's-road, Clifton. (*Daily Telegraph*, 5 October 1889, p.6, col.2)

> UNTRACTABLE GIRLS TRAINED and EDUCATED. Excellent references. 'Hints on Management', 'Training of Children', and 'The Rod', 1s. each. Advice by letter, 5s. Address, Mrs Walter, Clifton. (*The Times*, 21 October 1889, p.2, col.5)

On 21 November 1889, *Truth* informed its readers that an acquaintance of the editor had persuaded a lady friend to answer these advertisements, explaining that she had an unruly daughter whom she wanted 'broken in' and asking for advice and for the pamphlets. 'Mrs Walter' rose to the bait. In her reply she said that her real name was Mrs Walter Smith (' "Walter" being my nom-de-plume') and offered to take the girl for £100 per annum, enclosing with her communication an impressive list of twenty references, headed by the Very Rev. Dean of Lincoln and including the names of clerics, an admiral, a general, aristocrats and so forth. She also sent a leaflet entitled 'Modus Operandi with Intractable Girls'. The latter, published in full by *Truth*, reads, in its obsessive concern with ritualistic detail, like a piece of flagellant pornography:

> First I warn of the consequences of repeated faults; then, when a direct act of disobedience, a lie, or very serious fault shows itself, I tell her that

presently I shall punish. *Never birch when angry.* During the interval she·
thinks over the fault. *I* make preparations. These consist in having ready
a strong narrow table, straps (waist-band with sliding straps, anklets,
and wristlets), cushions, and a good, long, pliable birch rod, telling her to
prepare by removing her dress, kinkers [sic], etc., and putting on the
dressing-gown (*hind part before*). Then I talk seriously to her, show the
nature of the fault, and the need of punishment as a cure. Next I put on
the waist-band, after having told her that if she submits quietly no one
need know; if she struggles I must call in help (girls generally prefer to be
quiet). Placing her at *the end* of the table (on which there are cushions to
protect the person), I turn her body over the table, and fasten the straps
underneath it. Then I fasten the knees together, wrists the same, unless I
anticipate a struggle – then I use anklets and wristlets, and fasten the
limbs to the legs of the table. This really takes less time to do than to write
about. Unfastening the dressing-gown, the orthodox surface is found at
the right angle for punishing. Taking the birch, I measure my distance,
and, standing at the side, proceed to strike slowly but firmly. By moving
gently forward each stroke is differently placed, and six strokes may be
enough if well given *with full force.* If the fault has been such as to need
severe correction, then I begin again on the other side and work back
again. For screams increased strokes must be given. If a girl tries very
hard indeed to bear it bravely, then, perhaps, I give ten instead of twelve.
(*Truth*, 21 November 1889, p.939)

Following upon these overtures, and having perused Mrs Smith's
account of her methods, the editor's friend has had three interviews
with her in London, and one at the school itself, 53 Oakfield Road,
Clifton:

He describes her as a tall, strong woman, arrayed in the dress of some sort of
Order, and wearing a medallion with the effigy of a 'Good Shepherd'
stamped upon it. As an inducement to him to confide his ward to her tender
mercies, she said that she had girls of twenty in the house, to whom a week
or two previously she had administered fifteen cuts with a birch-rod, and
she explained that she had a considerable number of clients in London
whose daughters she chastised.

This appears probable, for, when my friend called on her, it was difficult
to get more than a few minutes' conversation with her, there were so many
waiting for an audience. Each interview costs half-a-guinea. She had before
her a book, in which her flogging engagements were registered, and they
appeared to be numerous. (*ibid.*)

Successive issues of *Truth* published further revelations, including
some of Mrs Smith's replies to other spoof enquiries. It emerged that,
as well as her establishment at Clifton, she did indeed offer a 'have-
birch-will-travel' service to parents with unruly children. It also
emerged that these parents could be present to witness the infliction of

the birching. It looks very much as if Mrs Smith, wittingly or unwittingly, was catering to the needs of the true flagellants. Her fees were considerable:

> As I have been to town twice recently I shall not be there again until the end of the month unless I am called specially. In that case my fee is $2\frac{1}{2}$ guineas; when I am in town, 10s.6d. If desired I could go to Oxford. (28 November 1889, p.990)

Truth claimed that it had been 'overwhelmed' with letters about the Smith case; in particular it had received the aggrieved communications of some of the people whose names figured in the list of the girl-flogger's referees. It transpired that Mrs Smith was the widow of a clergyman who for many years had been headmaster of All Saints School, Clifton (perhaps she acquired her flogging propensities from her husband) and that, on his death, she had decided to set up a little girls' school; that, being a respectable lady, the people to whom she had applied for references were only too happy to acquiesce; and that, some years after these references had been supplied, her establishment underwent a sea-change, becoming an institute for the education of difficult girls. Of this change the referees, including the Dean of Lincoln, claimed they knew nothing. Hastening to express their disgust at her methods, they now publicly dissociated themselves from Smith. Not surprisingly a correspondence flourished for several weeks in the Bristol and Clifton newspapers, *Truth* noting that all the pro-flogging letters were anonymous. As we shall see, this was almost always the case when flogging discussions got under way.

I have suggested that, wittingly or not, Mrs Smith was catering to the flagellomaniacs. Perhaps she was one herself. It is of interest to note that, along with her own inflictions, she also did a line in the supply of birch rods and other pieces of flagellant paraphernalia, operating a mailing-service as well as a more orthodox retailing system. In her pamphlet 'The Rod' she wrote:

> To be effectual the rods should be of the right sort. They can be bought at Clifton of Mrs Clapp, St. John's-road, from 8d. upwards, trimmed if required. They can be sent post free for 3d. each. They should be made from 2 ft. to 3 ft. 6 in. long, very thin and pliable. I get mine from a family who have made them for generations. (21 November 1889, p.939)

When *Truth*'s revelations became known in Clifton, Mrs Clapp understandably got into a bit of a tizzy, and wrote to a local paper:

> Some time after, Mrs Smith again called on me, and wanted me to allow

Home and School Beating

my shop to be used as a depot for the sale of birch rods, and giving as a
reason that she was endeavouring to get them substituted for the schools. I
at once declined having anything to do in the matter, and have never had
any of the rods in my possession. (5 December 1889, p.1046)

Perhaps Mrs Clapp was indeed innocent, although it seems unlikely.
For, as *Truth* pointed out (keeping this bit of information back until
the end), the following announcement had appeared as long as six
months before in no less a journal than the *Church Times*:

BIRCH RODS. – These useful articles, for which there is a growing
demand, may be had from the depôt. Of different sizes. – Mrs CLAPP, St.
John's-road, Clifton. (12 December 1889, p.1093)

Were we really to believe, asked *Truth*, that such an announcement
could have been inserted by Mrs Smith without the knowledge of Mrs
Clapp?

I mentioned in the first chapter that both Krafft-Ebing and Freud
had patients who claimed that their libido had first been aroused at an
early age by reading about the whipping of Negro slaves in *Uncle Tom's
Cabin*. The passage that most affected them is likely to have been that
in which Mrs Beecher Stowe describes the arrangements made to
send the pretty quadroon Rosa to a whipping-house for the infliction
of 15 lashes:

Miss Ophelia well knew that it was the universal custom to send women
and young girls to whipping-houses, to the hands of the lowest of men –
men vile enough to make this their profession – there to be subjected to
brutal exposure and shameful correction. She had *known* it before; but
hitherto she had never realised it, till she saw the slender form of Rosa
almost convulsed with distress. All the honest blood of womanhood, the
strong New English blood of liberty, flushed to her cheeks, and throbbed
bitterly in her indignant heart. (1972, pp. 320-1)

The author does not describe the actual whipping meted out to
poor Rosa, but the hints given in the above passage leave little enough
to the reader's imagination. It seems clear that Rosa is to be subjected
to 'lower discipline' ('brutal exposure and shameful correction'), and
that the men will enjoy themselves. The whipping of female slaves on
the naked buttocks was apparently widespread in the South at the
time, as it had been some decades earlier in the West Indies when the
anti-slavers brought this fact to the notice of the British public.
Were it not for *Truth*'s exposure of Mrs Smith of Clifton, one would

have thought it impossible that a not dissimilar institution could have existed in England in 1889, forty years after the publication of *Uncle Tom's Cabin* and the American Civil War. A free-lance whipping service for parents reluctant to do the job for themselves? It seems incredible, yet as we have seen Mrs Smith really existed and advertised her activities openly, even in the columns of *The Times*.

When one sets Mrs Smith in context, however, and when one realises the extent of flagellomania in Britain during the nineteenth century, she becomes more credible. Indeed her activities seem almost benign when set beside some of the flagellant descriptions appearing in the correspondence columns of respectable newspapers and journals during the century. These we shall be examining in a later chapter. Only in a society so confused and anxious about corporal punishment while at the same time so sexually repressed could such a bizarre creature as Mrs Walter Smith flourish.

Flagellant advertisements

We have seen that Mrs Clapp was free to advertise her birch rods – 'these useful articles' – openly in the *Church Times* in 1889. Such insertions were not uncommon in respectable publications during the nineteenth century; and indeed it is often impossible to distinguish them from the advertisements for flagellant brothels that pullulated in the gutter press at the same time.

Swinburne and his friend Richard Monckton Milnes kept their eyes open for these advertisements. In one letter the poet writes to Milnes to thank him for sending a cutting from *Punch* which reproduced a juicy item from the Liverpool *Daily Post*:

> WANTED, a Young Lady, about 20, as Housekeeper to a Widower, and to take charge of three boys, the eldest ten years old. Must be of good appearance and address; accomplishments not essential. Salary £25. – Address, stating age, and if willing to give severe corporal punishment, A.Z., Post Office, Chester.

Mr Punch's comments on this ('A Literal Solomon', 31 January 1863, p.47; see Plate 7) showed that he, at any rate, believed it to be genuine. He disapproved. Swinburne, however, was delighted, and allowed his mind to run on the possibility of dressing up as a young lady and applying for the position himself.[3]

---

[3] *The Swinburne Letters*, edited by Cecil A. Lang (Yale and Oxford, 1960-1962, 6 vols.), I, pp. 76-7. I shall refer to this publication henceforth as *Lang*.

On 1 November 1876 a similar request was inserted in the religious weekly *The Guardian* in the midst of dozens of more conventional items (see Plate 8). The wording of this advertisement makes it pretty clear that it is a flagellant mystification:

> WANTED, by a Widow Lady, a PERSON who is experienced in the art of whipping, and well qualified to administer a severe flogging with a new birch rod to two young children of the ages of nine and ten. Wages 30*l.* per annum. The children are very wilful and troublesome. Address to S.N.N., Brooks' Club, Suffolk-street, London. (p.1431)

The editor of *Notes and Queries* quoted this advertisement and observed: 'It is a matter for astonishment that such an advertisement should have been admitted into a respectable paper. Even if it were a hoax, it is one of a shameful sort. It is to be feared, however, that the flagellants as a class are not extinct' (18 November 1876, p.419).[4]

The editor of *Notes and Queries* would have found the article inserted in *Home Chat* on 3 January 1903 even odder: ' "Spare the Rod and Spoil the Child." Birches are Coming Rapidly into Fashion Again!' (see Plate 10). Among the other pieces of information contained in this piece of flagellant fantasy was the following: 'Apart from the chastening of the young there is a small demand from the professional masseuse, who treats some patients with gentle applications of the rod to stimulate a sluggish circulation.'

Albert Moll showed (1912) that in that other haven for flagellants, Germany, whipping advertisements similar to those appearing in English newspapers were common. Moreover, many of the German insertions made their point by emphasising that 'English methods' were required:

---

[4] The French were intrigued by the impunity with which flagellant notices could be inserted into respectable English newspapers. *Le Paris* quoted one of Mrs Walter Smith's advertisements for her whipping pamphlet in the issue for 24 December 1889 (Henriques, 1969, p.236). Hector France (1885, p.308) quotes from several similar advertisements that appeared about this time in the *Standard*. Sometimes even odder things got into print. I cannot refrain from quoting the following publisher's advertisement (a compositor's joke, presumably) which appeared in *The Times*, no less, on 12 June 1882, listed among new books issued by Griffin and Farran's:

> A new and Cheaper Edition, fully Revised, price 6s EVERY-DAY LIFE in our PUBLIC SCHOOLS. Sketched by Head Scholars, with a Glossary of some Words used by Henry Irving in his disquisition upon fucking, which is in Common Use in those Schools. Edited by CHARLES EYRE PASCOE. With numerous Illustrations. Church Times. – 'A capital book for boys.' Record. – 'The book will make an acceptable present.'

Governess, from England, recommends her admirable boarding-establishment for pupils of fair age. Apply 'Hearneshouse'.

As Moll comments on this advertisement, 'No doubt is possible in this case, since "Hearneshouse" is the title of a sadistic novel' (p.243).

Energetic gentleman, severe disciplinarian, offers *English instruction* to boys and girls of fair age. (*ibid.*)

According to Moll, the fact that the key words are underlined makes the flagellant nature of these advertisements unmistakeable:

Gentleman offers strict instructions to older boys. Replies to 'English' ... (*ibid.*)

Parental beating in more recent times

We have seen that the parental beaters of Britain in the nineteenth century were able to convince themselves that they had divine backing in applying the Solomonic rod to their wayward children. Whether they *really* believed this deep down is another matter; and anyway I wish to leave such considerations until later in this study. Given that God had ordained the beating, not only of children but of various other categories of miscreant, it followed that the opponents of flogging were likely to come under fire from Bible-quoting birchites. We have already seen a typical specimen of vituperation from 1862, and another from 1904. Here is a final example, from 1905. Colonel P.F. Robertson (of Bray, Ireland) is attacking one particularly tenacious body of anti-beaters:

Think what the members of the Humanitarian League will have to answer for if they are able to induce any weak men and silly women to disobey God's command – to whip the naughty children under their control. (Henry Salt, 1916, p.29)

We shall be reviewing in a later chapter the discussions that have taken place during this century in Parliament concerning corporal punishment, judicial and scholastic. During a debate of 13 February 1953 in the Commons attention was drawn to the existence of a vocal and extremely dubious organisation in operation at the time. It was called the National Society for the Retention of Corporal Punishment, and had been founded by Eric A. Wildman. It transpired that Sir T. Moore had received a letter from the Society congratulating him on his work in favour of corporal punishment; and that he had been referred to in one of their pamphlets as 'a stalwart for our cause'. One of the Members, in no doubt as to the morbidity of Wildman's motives, read out a passage from the pamphlet in question, which was entitled *Juvenile Justice*:

> We are doing everything in our power, but so much depends upon the support we can command. With us is allied the Corpun Educational Organisation which exists to provide teachers, educational authorities, and parents with carefully selected and manufactured instruments of correction. Already there are 10,000 'satisfied customers'. Corpun also runs a unique literary service publishing the personal experiences of those entrusted with the care of the young of administering corporal correction and providing them with a media for the frank expression of opinion. Profits from these enterprises are ploughed back to further the work of the N.S.R.C.P. (Hansard, *Commons*, 13 February 1953, col.831)

Wildman's activities and advertising methods – among the latter, sandwich-men parading the streets of Kensington and public lectures at Caxton Hall, with the Society's founder arrayed in gown and mortarboard – led shortly afterwards to police intervention. His premises were raided, and a lorry-load of pamphlets, canes, birches, straps and other flagellant paraphernalia removed. Several of the documents were prefaced by clergymen. One of them was entitled *A Girl's Beating: Punishment Postures*, and was lavishly illustrated. Wildman – need it be stated? – was an advocate of 'old-fashioned discipline'. And being, as he claimed, a democrat, he felt it only right that girls should be punished in the same manner as their brothers.

Wildman was charged with obscene libel, and tried in May 1953. He was found guilty and sentenced to pay £500 within six months or go to prison for a year. Since then, to my knowledge, he has disappeared from public view.[5]

In *Exploring English Character* (1955), Geoffrey Gorer found that 21% of English fathers and 14% of mothers approved of 'some type of severe punishment for boys' (p.193). For girls, the figures were lower, 11% of fathers and 8% of mothers. Gorer's sample was 14,000, drawn from all levels of society, and his findings showed that 'spanking' (on the bottom implied) was at that time widely practised or approved of by English parents. It is unlikely that there has been a significant

[5] These details concerning Wildman's activities are drawn from Gervas d'Olbert (1967), pp. 183-91. According to Peter Fryer (1966), the British Library has in its Private Case 'five big parcels full of the duplicated material' issued by Wildman (pp. 120-1) as well as two of his booklets on flagellation, *Modern Miss Delinquent* (1950) and *Punishment Posture for Girls* (1951), which were withdrawn on legal advice before publication (p.147)

change in attitudes since then. Gorer found, moreover, that the English are peculiar about bottoms:

> It is generally assumed in English broadcast, television or music hall humour that the fact that human beings possess buttocks is inexhaustibly funny, an endless source of innocent merriment; and a great number of my respondents used somewhat facetious synonyms for the area spanked – 'the place nature meant for it', 'where it hurts to sit down', 'the b-t-m', 'the right place', 'the posterior' and so on. (p.192)

Though Gorer does not say so, this is just the sort of evasive language one would expect from members of a beating-obsessed society. Gorer came to the conclusion (and it is a related factor) that English parents were not unaware of the potentially sexual side to spanking:

> The quotations suggest that at least some English parents find pleasure without conscious guilt in inflicting severe pain on children as punishment. The majority disapprove of such behaviour, but the emphasis with which such disapproval is voiced suggests the possibility that there is an unconscious temptation against which such defences have to be erected. In many other societies, I very much doubt whether such heat and indignation would be engendered on the subject of severe punishment of children, or indeed whether the possibilities would be mentioned in answer to the vague and open question 'Are there any forms of punishment you don't approve of for boys or girls?' (pp. 195-6)

Gorer does not mention the Victorian background to the beating debate, but as we shall see, the 'heat and indignation' he found in the early 1950s were nothing new.

On 29 November 1968 the *New Statesman* published an article by Corinna Adam entitled 'Beating in Britain'. It contained some startling revelations. Miss Adam had located, in Bognor Regis, a certain shopkeeper called Eric Huntingdon who was doing a brisk trade in the sale of canes by post – more than 4,000 of them in the last two years. Huntingdon claimed that he had received enquiries:

> from the highest in the land to the lowest. Some of the names would surprise you. We even had an order for two dozen from a *very* respectable London club. But mostly it's just ordinary mums and dads, and education authorities of course. I don't think the people who write are kinky, I think we're supplying a need. If we didn't sell canes, these people would be hitting their children with something much worse. (p.740)

Five years (and presumably 10,000 canes) later, Huntingdon was still in business. On 28 March 1973 another journalist, Claire Marks, interviewed him for the *Guardian* ('A Beaten Path to his Door'). Huntingdon told her that 'the demand for canes for use in the school and home continues'. Were he to advertise widely, he said, he would be inundated with requests for the instrument. Again, top people were still using his unique service: 'Some of the most famous people in the land, cutting across all social classes, have used this service with the complete confidence that wild horses wouldn't drag their name out of me'. Eric Huntingdon was apparently aware of the sexual implications of 'old-fashioned discipline', for in his pamphlet 'Parents who Cane Care' he explained that 'we do not advocate the use of the cane on bare flesh, pants afford the modesty a child is entitled to'. How many of the requests for canes were from bona fide parents even Mr Huntingdon, presumably, could not know, but we can be sure that a sizeable proportion (including that one from the *very* respectable London club) came from the flagellants. Whoever they were, these clients knew exactly what they were ordering, for Mr Huntingdon had taken pains to provide a careful description of his wares:

SMALL: *Approximately 20in. long. Thin, pliable, curved handle. Made from junior school cane. Suitable for younger children.*

STANDARD: *Approximately 28in. long. Thin, pliable curved handle. Made from junior school cane. Although this has been purchased as a deterrent for children under the age of eight years, it is not recommended as such. For general exhibition in home or school among children of middle/late childhood.*

SENIOR: *Approximately 28in. long. Curved handle, made from stouter cane, but still lighter and shorter than the 'old fashioned' cane. This cane will truly sting, and is recommended to those with older children to control.*

Reading the excerpts from this document given by the *Guardian*, one might be forgiven for believing that Mrs Walter Smith of Clifton was again amongst us, at least in her capacity as supplier of instruments of correction. And doubtless Mr Huntingdon, assuming that he is still in business, would find himself even busier were he to include in his service the provision of birch rods.

If Victorian fathers were prepared to beat their own children, it followed that they would be prepared to have them whipped at school.

It also followed that they would be likely to approve of the judicial flogging of juvenile offenders. But the British (and especially the English) did not leave it at that: they flogged adults too. The English Vice began in the home, spread to the home's most obvious extension, the school (particularly the boarding-school), and thence to the courts, the prisons, the Army and Navy, the colonies – and the brothels. The British Empire, it might be argued, was founded on the lash.

Beating in schools

Beating has always been common in British schools, the schoolmaster's legal right to administer corporal punishment deriving from the fact that society has considered him to stand *in loco parentis* to the children under his care. Lord Collins put it succinctly: 'It is clear law that the father has the right to inflict reasonable personal chastisement on his son. It is equally the law, and it is in accordance with very ancient practice, that he may delegate this right to the schoolmaster' (Henry Salt, 1916, pp. 31-2).

One of the earliest protests against the prevalence of beating in British schools appeared in 1669 in *The Childrens Petition; Or, A Modest Remonstrance of that intolerable grievance our Youth lie under, in the accustomed Severities of the School-discipline of this Nation* (see Plate 5). In this document, 'Humbly presented to the Consideration of Parliament', the shameful nature of 'lower discipline' was made quite explicit by the author, who said that punishments 'were of that nature as to make our schools to be not merely houses of correction but of prostitution, in this vile way of castigating in use, wherein our secret parts, which are by nature shameful, and not to be uncovered, must be the Anvil exposed to the immodest eyes and filthy blows of the smiter' (quoted in Newell, 1972, p.13).

Two centuries later, this form of beating was still habitual in British schools.

Of the schoolmasters, the Anglican clerics who controlled the private boarding schools for the sons of the privileged and wealthy – still known today, to the bewilderment of foreigners, as the 'public schools' – were, as one would expect, the most ardent supporters of the Biblical rod: at once teachers and ministers of God, they felt themselves doubly authorised to apply corporal punishment to the boys who had been placed with them. Consider the case of the famous Dr Arnold of Rugby School. It is widely held that Arnold was a great educational innovator and a kindly, humane, Christian gentleman. Perhaps he was all these things. He was also a firm believer in the necessity of applying corporal punishment to the young, and had had experience of the system while a pupil at Winchester. In an article first published in 1835 ('On the Discipline of Public Schools'), Arnold argued that children *are* inferior to adults, that their disobedience originates in pride and is therefore sinful ('that proud notion of personal independence which is neither reasonable nor Christian') and that children must be taught, by corporal punishment if necessary, to acknowledge their true position:

> Impatience of inferiority felt by a child towards his parents, or by a pupil towards his instructors, is merely wrong, because it is at variance with the truth: there exists a real inferiority in the relation, and it is an error, a fault, a corruption of nature, not to acknowledge it. (1845, p.365)

It follows, continues Arnold, that corporal punishment cannot be degrading since the child is already 'without grade' (my words) in relation to adults. Arnold is obsessed by sin, by 'evil feelings', and is of the view that the rod is the best antidote – but only for boys up to 15. He does not say so outright, but hints that over that age (remember that for the Victorians sex only starts at puberty) there would be 'obvious objections'. As we shall see in examining the flagellant correspondence columns of the nineteenth century, these obvious objections are constantly adumbrated but rarely discussed openly.

At Rugby, as every reader of *Tom Brown's Schooldays* will deduce, Dr Arnold put his ideas on corporal punishment into practice. I have often wondered if he did so also with his son, the poet and critic Matthew Arnold; certainly the latter loathed beating, as can be seen from his comments on the prohibition of such a system in French schools. Flogging, he writes, 'will more and more come to appear half disgusting, half ridiculous, and a teacher will find it more and more difficult to inflict it without a loss of self-respect. The feeling on the continent is very strong on this point' (1866, p.502).

Very strong indeed. During the 1850s and 1860s Napoleon III commissioned reports on the educational methods of several European countries, including England. In 1866 two French commissioners, J. Demogeot and H. Montucci (both distinguished academics and men of letters), spent several months in the country studying secondary education. Their report was published in 1867. Demogeot and Montucci were deeply shocked to find that the birch was still in use at the public schools:

The English Vice

The whip ... is one of those ancient English traditions which continue because they have continued ... A foreigner finds it difficult to conceive of the perseverance with which English teachers cling to this old and degrading custom. We have read in Dr T. Arnold's works an eloquent dissertation in favour of flogging, which has not in the least convinced us ... Flogging is not fitting and not decent. One is astonished to see English teachers remove a garment which the prudery of their language hesitates even to name. Moreover this punishment is degrading, because it recalls that traditionally reserved for little children and which, therefore, is no longer logically applicable to the second age.[6] (pp. 40-1, 43)

During the nineteenth century successive French laws reiterated the ban on the beating of children at school.[7] They seem to have managed perfectly well in France, in fact, without that recourse to the rod which has always seemed so indispensable to the pedagogues of Britain. Notices placed in French schools today remind teachers and pupils alike that corporal punishment is a crime and that infringements of the law may have serious consequences. No school in France, it hardly needs saying, carries any instrument specifically designed for the infliction of corporal punishment. There can be no doubt about it: they order this matter better in France.

The British flogging system was given prestige by the public schools and imitated elsewhere; the assumption being that what was good enough for public school boys was good enough for everyone else. Any parent sending a son to a public school knew that he would be fortunate indeed to escape beating; and any man accepting the headmastership of a public school knew that he would be required to wield the rod frequently. It is impossible that among the schoolmasters of Britain there were not many who derived conscious sexual pleasure from the practice.

Among our main sources for facts concerning beating in boys'

[6] J. Demogeot and H. Montucci, *De l'Enseignement secondaire en Angleterre et en Ecosse* (1867). This passage reads in the original: 'Le *fouet* ... est une de ces anciennes traditions anglaises qui vivent parce qu'elles ont vécu ... Un étranger a peine à concevoir la persévérance avec laquelle les instituteurs anglais conservent ce vieil et dégradant usage. Nous avons lu, dans les oeuvres du docteur T. Arnold, une éloquente dissertation en faveur du *flogging*, laquelle ne nous a pas du tout convaincu ... Le *flogging* est peu convenable et peu décent. On s'étonne de voir les maîtres anglais écarter un vêtement que la pruderie de leur langue hésite même à nommer. En outre, ce châtiment est dégradant, parce qu'il rappelle la punition traditionnelle réservée aux petits enfants, et que par conséquent il n'est plus logiquement applicable au second âge.'

[7] For example, Article 20 of the decree instituting the 'école laïque publique et gratuite', dated 18 January 1887, reads: 'Il est absolument interdit d'infliger aucun châtiment corporel.'

schools in the nineteenth century are, for the nine oldest public schools (Eton, Winchester, Westminster, Charterhouse, St. Paul's, Merchant Taylors', Harrow, Rugby and Shrewsbury), the famous 'Clarendon Report' (1864);[8] for the other secondary schools, the *Report of the Schools Inquiry Commission* (1867-68); and the *Report on Industrial and Reformatory Schools* (1896).

But first let us take the 'preparatory schools', about which we shall find little information in the *'Clarendon Report'*. The preparatory schools (familiarly known as prep schools) were and are the boarding establishments that prepare boys (and some girls) for the public schools. With the rapid growth of the latter in the nineteenth century, there was more and more demand for prep schools. In 1892 about fifty headmasters formed the Association of Preparatory Schools, which was incorporated in 1923. There are today about 500 prep schools (compared to approximately 250 public schools), and they cater for some 73,000 pupils.[9]

These private schools (the great majority of them boarding) have traditionally been run like miniature public schools by men who have been through the system themselves; and they are obsessed by the public schools for which they prepare their pupils. At prep school a boy's life is overshadowed by the spectre of the Common Entrance Examination to public school, for which he is relentlessly crammed.

Until very recently (and perhaps still), boys were also 'prepared' at these establishments for the disciplinary methods they would encounter at public school, and beating, often severe beating, was common.

If ever there was a schoolteacher who felt himself to stand *in loco parentis* to his pupils it is the preparatory school headmaster (and his wife), the more so given the tender years of those committed to his care. To foreigners it is incomprehensible that English parents of the privileged classes could send their sons away at such an early age to be looked after by strangers. Jonathan Gathorne-Hardy has put it nicely:

It is an illustration ... of the enormous tenacity of ideas about education and bringing-up generally, that this ancient practice of sending children away at a cruelly early age persists to this day. In no other Continental country does the prep school play the part it does here. And an Italian seeing the droves of whey-faced, tearful, seven-year-old upper-class little

[8] *Report of Her Majesty's Commissioners appointed to Inquire into the Revenues and Management of Certain Colleges and Schools, and the Studies Pursued and Instruction Given Therein; with an Appendix and Evidence*, 4 vols., 1864.

[9] Details from *The Public and Preparatory Schools Year Book* (1976), published by Adam and Charles Black, p.796.

English boys, clutching the hands of their mothers – or even, still, their Nannies – at Waterloo or Paddington or Euston Stations at the start of another term, might well write home in exactly the same vein today as his countryman did five hundred years ago. (p.35)

Before Winston Churchill arrived at Harrow School in 1888 he had been a pupil at St George's preparatory school, Ascot. At the time, St George's was run by a young Anglican clergyman called Herbert William Sneyd-Kynnersley (1848-86),[10] whom Dr Anthony Storr has not hesitated to diagnose as a sadist.[11] It is likely that Churchill was removed from the school (at the instigation of his nanny) when it became apparent that he had received brutal beatings. 'How I hated this school', wrote Churchill in *My Early Life* (without identifying it or its headmaster by name), 'and what a life of anxiety I lived there for more than two years' (p.20). Of the disciplinary methods in force at the school he recalled:

Flogging with the birch in accordance with the Eton fashion was a great feature in its curriculum. But I am sure no Eton boy, and certainly no Harrow boy of my day, ever received such a cruel flogging as this Headmaster was accustomed to inflict upon the little boys who were in his care and power. They exceeded in severity anything that would be tolerated in any of the Reformatories under the Home Office. My reading in later life has supplied me with some possible explanations of his temperament. Two or three times a month the whole school was marshalled in the Library, and one or more delinquents were haled off to an adjoining apartment by the two head boys, and there flogged until they bled freely, while the rest sat quaking, listening to their screams. This form of correction was strongly reinforced by frequent religious services of a somewhat High Church character in the chapel. (pp. 19-20)

Churchill does not specify which 'reading in later life' had led him to a possible understanding of Sneyd-Kynnersley's predilection for the birch; and it is odd that he does not allow himself to use the word 'sadism', which is clearly what he means. Roger Fry, who was at St George's just before Churchill, was far more explicit in the account he gave to Virginia Woolf of his time at the school. This she published in *Roger Fry: A Biography* (1940):

When my parents told me there were to be no punishments it was quite true that the masters never set lines or kept boys in, but as Mr Sneyd-

[10] Dates given by Randolph Churchill in the index to his biography *Winston S. Churchill: Youth 1874-1900* (Heinemann, 1966), p.598.
[11] Storr (1973), p.231.

Kynnersley explained to us with solemn gusto the first morning that we were all gathered together before him he reserved to himself the right to a good sound flogging with the birch rod ... as I was from the first and all through either first or second in the school I was bound *ex officio* to assist at the executions and hold down the culprit. The ritual was very precise and solemn – every Monday morning the whole school assembled in Hall and every boy's report was read aloud.

After reading a bad report from a form master Mr Sneyd-Kynnersley would stop and after a moment's awful silence say 'Harrison minor you will come up to my study afterwards'. And so afterwards the culprits were led up by the two top boys. In the middle of the room was a large box draped in black cloth and in austere tones the culprit was told to take down his trousers and kneel before the block over which I and the other head boy held him down. The swishing was given with the master's full strength and it took only two or three strokes for drops of blood to form everywhere and it continued for 15 or 20 strokes when the wretched boy's bottom was a mass of blood. Generally of course the boys endured it with fortitude but sometimes there were scenes of screaming, howling and struggling which made me almost sick with disgust. Nor did the horrors even stop there. There was a wild red-haired Irish boy, himself rather a cruel brute, who whether deliberately or as a result of pain or whether he had diarrhoea, let fly. The irate clergyman instead of stopping at once went on with increased fury until the whole ceiling and walls of his study were spattered with filth. I suppose he was afterwards somewhat ashamed of this for he did not call in the servants to clean up but spent hours doing it himself with the assistance of a boy who was his special favourite. (pp. 32-3)

In Sneyd-Kynnersley (even his name sounds sadistic) we have the type of the English clerical flagellomaniac; and, as we shall see, the St George's birching ceremony was an almost exact copy of that used at Eton. Other pupils of Sneyd-Kynnersley who recalled his predilection for the birch were Sir Edmund Backhouse and Maurice Baring (see Trevor-Roper, 1976, and Baring, 1922).

Not only were the headmasters of these preparatory schools themselves great beaters but they often allowed boys in the sixth form to cane their juniors – in preparation, presumably, for the day when they would be prefects or otherwise privileged seniors at their public schools. Cyril Connolly, who was a contemporary of George Orwell (then Eric Blair) at St Cyprian's school at Eastbourne, recalled in *Enemies of Promise*: 'My last year at St Wulfric's [his name for the school] was rosy. I was in sixth form which had its own sitting-room ... We were about as civilised as little boys can grow to be. We were polite and we hardly ever caned anyone' (p.174).

Orwell's misery at the intensely snobbish St Cyprian's was almost unmitigated, and he described his time there in 'Such, Such were the Joys', a devastating essay published after his death in 1952. At St Cyprian's, rich and titled boys were never caned because they might complain. But Orwell was not from a well-off family, and moreover (unknown to himself) had been accepted on special terms. He was beaten with a riding crop by the headmaster-owner of the school, Mr Vaughan Wilkes ('Sambo') for the terrible crime of wetting his bed. Before the first beating, Mrs Vaughan Wilkes ('Flip') had gone out of her way to humiliate the boy before a female visitor, referring to his wicked incontinence and warning him that she would instruct the sixth form to cane him if he did not immediately learn to exercise control over his bladder. Many years later Orwell wrote in 'Such, Such Were the Joys': 'To this day I can feel myself almost swooning with shame as I stood, a very small, round-faced boy in short corduroy knickers, before the two women ... my dominant feeling was not fear or even resentment: it was simply shame because one more person, and that a woman, had been told of my disgusting offence' (pp. 380-1).[12]

By the time the average preparatory school boy went up to his public school (at the age of 12 or 13) he was thoroughly broken in to the beating system.

At the public schools the flogging of boys was an everyday practice which, along with other hallowed traditions, was felt to be essential to the development of the boys' characters. Over the centuries these schools had produced a steady stream of notorious flogging headmasters – Dr Keate of Eton (headmaster from 1809-34) being generally accorded top prize for efficiency with the rod, although he had many close rivals, including Westminster's Dr Busby, mentioned earlier. In most of the public schools, moreover, as at the prep schools, certain senior boys were empowered to inflict corporal punishment – characteristically of the 'lower discipline' sort – on their fellows. This was doubtless intended to train them in the exercise of Christian

---

[12] In the nineteenth century Eastbourne had produced a particularly nasty prep school headmaster. In 1860, at 'a private school of the highest class' in that town, a mentally deficient boy of good family, Reginald Cancellor, was beaten to death by a Mr Hopley. Hopley and his wife tried to hush the matter up, 'but mysterious stories of midnight shrieks and blood-stained instruments of punishment began to be whispered about. The servants had seen blood upon the linen in Mrs Hopley's room ...' When the body was uncovered, 'the appearance was that of a human creature who had been mangled by an infuriated and merciless assailant'. According to the *Annual Register, Or a View of the History and Politics of the Year 1860*, from which these quotations are extracted, 'The details of the evidence before the magistrates sent a thrill of horror through every family throughout the kingdom' (p.60). Hopley was sentenced to four years' penal servitude.

responsibility and restraint, but we can be sure that it also greatly increased the amount of flagellomania in these establishments.

During the nineteenth century many new public schools were founded. They tended to ape their illustrious predecessors in the matter of corporal punishment, so that as the century progressed the beating obsession became more and more prevalent throughout the upper reaches of British education.

Every so often during the century accounts would appear in the newspapers of flogging excesses committed in the schools – often by boy against boy. While the grammar schools had their share of such scandals (Bath Grammar School in May 1856, for example), the public schools were always the worst offenders. This was inevitable given their character as boarding establishments, where discipline was as a matter of course more difficult to maintain than in the day schools. In the public schools numbers were large, masters were few and classes unwieldy. It seemed to the authorities that only the traditional birch could keep order, and there was little original thinking about alternative methods. Although hardly a major public school escaped a flogging exposure at one time or another, one may assume that the majority of incidents were hushed up and went unreported. As private institutions run by a privileged sector of the community, the public schools did not take kindly to adverse criticism, and had means of protecting themselves.

In the next chapter we shall be investigating the everyday flagellant activities of Eton, *sanctus sanctorum* of the English worshippers of the rod. For the moment let us look briefly at some of the scandals that erupted at other public schools during the nineteenth century.

At Harrow in 1854 a monitor, Platt, inflicted 31 strokes of the cane on a lad named Stewart, 'from the effects of which,' wrote *The Times*, 'he suffered so severely as to require medical care' (13 April 1854). An exchange of letters in *The Times* followed, several of them discussing the rights and wrongs of the monitorial system which, on the model of Rugby, had been instituted at Harrow by Dr Charles Vaughan (headmaster from 1844 to 1859). Vaughan himself was a well-known flogger and not likely to sympathise with public criticism of one of his monitors. 'After forty years,' writes Ronald Pearsall, 'Sir Charles Bruce, Governor of Mauritius, trembled when he recalled Dr Vaughan's castigations' (1972, p.412). Vaughan was a homosexual, and behaving in 1858 rather too indiscreetly towards one of his favourite boys in the school, was denounced and forced to resign.[13]

The 1870s produced a spate of beating scandals at the public

[13] Pearsall (1972), pp. 552-3.

schools. The first, which concerned Winchester, arose in 1872, when it emerged that a boy had been brutally 'tunded' (the Winchester form of beating) by a prefect. The columns of *The Times* were again filled with angry letters – from the headmaster, Dr Ridding, and a wide range of supporters and opponents of the rod, including one from 'The Victim' and another from his father. The offending prefect was eventually constrained to apologise to his victim, and Dr Ridding distinguished himself by writing of him that 'I am most sorry that so good and so gentle a boy as he is should have allowed his zeal for discipline to have so far outrun his discretion'.[14] Like Vaughan at Harrow some twenty years earlier, Ridding was determined to stand by his prefects. Understandably, since he was a great flogger himself. 'It was not unusual of him after morning school,' wrote Bishop Wordsworth, 'to castigate not less than fifty boys at a time' (Pearsall, 1972, p.410). An editorial in *The Saturday Review* on the Winchester case revealed that brutality among the boys at Winchester existed on a scale unparalleled at other public schools ('Judicious Kicking', 23 November 1872).

Then there was the Shrewsbury case of 1874, which also received considerable coverage in *The Times*. On 21 July 1874 the newspaper published a letter from the headmaster, the Rev. H.W. Moss, who was disgruntled because of the adverse publicity he had been receiving in the local press. After all, what had he done? He had simply inflicted 88 strokes of the birch ('mere fleabites', one of his supporters called them) on a boy who, against the rules, had caused ale and porter to be conveyed to his study. The 88 strokes had been counted out ritually by a monitor. Ten days after the infliction of the 'mere fleabites' a surgeon found that the boy's body was still covered with weals. The Governing Body met and made pronouncement:

> The Chairman afterwards handed in a decision to the effect that they extremely regretted the misunderstanding between Mr Moss and Mr Loxdale [the boy's father]. They did not think the punishment excessive, but recommended that for the future punishments should be more in accordance with public feeling and the practice of other public schools. (*The Times*, 31 July 1874)

The last reference, to practice at other public schools, was not intended to be facetious, presumably. In an article on this case ('Flogging at Shrewsbury', 5 August 1874) *The World* expressed its suspicion that similar brutalities were in fact common at other public

[14] *The Times*, 20 November 1872, p.8.

schools, and offered an explanation that must have been as resented in some quarters as it was justified:

> We suspect that a careful investigation would bring to light many instances of ill-judged severity. Our grounds for this suspicion are, that clergymen are in all relations of life, as a body, less merciful, less ready to make allowances for human frailties, than laymen. The more conscientous they are, the better they are qua clergymen, the more intolerant they are of offences, all of which they place in the category of sins. To them there is no such thing as a little sin. Sin is sin simply, and as such, for the sake both of the sinner and society at large, to be sternly repressed. Again, they find it difficult to separate their position as teachers from their holy status as ministers of God, and resent offences against their rules as insubordination towards the Almighty. Finally, they have been so long free from contradictions and snubbings of their fellow men, that they are more impatient than other people, and, like captains of men-of-war, are apt to become despotic. These are no mere assertions. Look at their harsh social verdicts, at the heavy sentences they pass as magistrates on women and children guilty of infinitesimal acts of larceny. Consider the rigidity of their rule in their own families, the result of which is that it has become a proverb that clergymen's sons are the greatest scamps. (p.7)

The World finished by recommending that the governing bodies of schools should keep a much closer eye on the methods of these clerical disciplinarians.

Christ's Hospital, London, was a great flogging and bullying school in the eighteenth century, and the tradition continued well into the nineteenth. When in 1877 it became known that one of the pupils, William Gibbs, aged 12, had hung himself, questions were asked in Parliament. The Home Office appointed a special commission to investigate. Their report, published in *The Times* (11 August 1877), revealed that the disciplinary arrangements at the school were quite inadequate. Between 8 p.m. and 8 a.m. there were no masters in attendance, discipline in the 50-boy dormitories being entirely in the hands of the monitors (aged 13-16, not even the most senior boys in the school) and a few matrons and beadles. It must have been pandemonium. Each monitor had virtual carte blanche to deal as best he could with the boys in his dormitory; and the power was often abused. The commission found that Gibbs, having run away to avoid bullying by a particularly unpleasant monitor, had been severely birched on his return; that he had run away again; that, on being returned to the school a second time, he was locked up for the night in the infirmary; and that the following morning he had hung himself from a ventilator cord. It seemed clear that the thought of further bullying and flogging was too much for poor Gibbs. The commissioners went to some lengths to establish that the boy had bullying tendencies, was self-willed and obstinate; and upheld the verdict of the Coroner: 'Suicide while in a state of temporary insanity.' As always in such cases, the old boys of the school rallied round to defend the good name of their Alma Mater. Dozens of letters appeared in *The Times*. Several old Blue-Coats swore, however, that their own recent experience at the school had been of unmitigated unhappiness. As we shall see later, cases similar to that of the unfortunate Gibbs occurred in the Navy.

One final example (from just into our own century). In October 1906 the high master of Manchester Grammar School (a public school despite its name), Mr Paton, administered a severe birching on the naked buttocks to a boy who had been found guilty of telling a lie. There was an outcry. Paton, who in his previous capacity had been at the non-flogging University College School in London, declared in vindication of his action: 'I do not believe in a love that cannot be severe and stern against sin. If a boy comes to me and does some offence of mere animal spirits, or what I call *hanky-panky-tricks*, I tell him he has to take his punishment, and he usually takes it in a very philosophic way'.[15] Paton did not explain why the birch was found necessary in Manchester when in London it could be dispensed with.

Many more instances of beating excesses committed at the public schools during the nineteenth century (and later) could be given. More significant than the excesses, however, was the normal, everyday beating routine that prevailed in these schools. By looking closely at how that routine operated at Eton in the next chapter it is hoped to give the reader an insight into one of the oddest predilections of the English. For the moment, however, let us turn our attention to the secondary schools attended by the less well-off sectors of the community.

The Report of the Schools Inquiry Commission shows that, while beating was common in these schools, the use of the birch was almost unknown by the 1860s. The cane was the universal instrument of correction. In the majority of cases, it seems, canings were applied to the hand, although frequently we are told that they were given on the 'back', the stock euphemism for the buttocks, which not a single witness in this or the 'Clarendon Report' can bring himself to name. Two typical examples from the former Report:

[15] Bradley Hall, 'Flogging at Manchester Grammar School', *The Humane Review*, VIII (1907-1908), pp. 205-18.

3398. (*Lord Taunton.*) I suppose when you use the cane you only strike the hand? – Sometimes on the back, in a safe region; usually it is on the hand. (IV, p.349)

3728. (*Lord Taunton.*) Do you approve of the use of the cane? – As little as possible, I think.

3729. Do you prefer it to the rod? – I think so.

3730. Even upon the back? – I think so. (IV, p.375)

Another fact which the School Inquiry Commission's tables of evidence reveal is that these canings were more often inflicted in public than in private, presumably to enhance their alleged deterrent value. This practice is likely also to have had a stimulant effect on the spectators, given the strongly voyeuristic component in flagellomania.

Out of the welter of evidence (the minutes record no less than 18,125 questions and answers), certain exchanges in the Report have particular interest, especially those in which the relative merits of cane and birch come under discussion. Here is C.P. Mason, principal of Denmark Hill, Camberwell, a private school, on the subject:

3396. (*Lord Taunton.*) Do you think the cane a good instrument of punishment for a boy? – I do in some cases. Do I understand that you are drawing a distinction between the cane and the birch?

3397. Yes. – I think for older boys the birch involves an amount of exposure that is humiliating, so that in the case of the older boys if I ever have occasion to administer anything of the kind it is with the cane. With little fellows I think the birch is less likely to injure them by hurting their hands, so with little boys I use the birch. (IV, p.349)

Occasionally a headmaster, such as the Rev. J.S. Howson of Liverpool College, expresses disapproval of those who would beat boys on any part of their body other than the hand:

2692. (*Dr. Temple.*) Do you ever use the birch? – Never the birch, only the cane.

2693. (*Lord Lyttelton.*) Do you cane the boy on the hand? – Only on the hand. If a boy is caned anywhere else I am very much annoyed, because I think a cane is not an instrument to be used on other parts of the body. The muscles, for instance, might be injured by a blow of the cane across the arm or leg. (IV, p.276)

This same gentleman has been receiving some odd requests from parents:

2695. I have sometimes had very angry letters, saying this punishment is contrary to the spirit of the 19th century. On the other hand, I have had letters occasionally, in which parents have earnestly begged me, to use their own expression, 'to use the stick more', which I decline to do. (*ibid.*)

C.H. Pinches, headmaster of Clarendon House College and Commercial School in Kennington, has also had some strange letters from parents; and his reply concerning the use of the birch is a refreshing attempt at honesty, especially when one compares it with the marked reticence on the subject displayed by the majority of those questioned:

3925. (*Lord Taunton.*) How do you maintain the discipline of your school? – I will never undertake not to inflict corporal punishment, but it is very rarely inflicted, and when it is inflicted it is by the cane over the back; that does not occur perhaps more than three or four times in the year.

3926. Do you prefer the cane to the rod? – I object to the accompaniments of the rod, that is taking the trowsers down and so on, although it perhaps would surprise you to know that I refused two boarders the other day because I declined to use the birch in the way suggested by the lady who wished to place them with me. I think as far as the punishment itself is concerned the birch is preferable, but I do not like the adjuncts. (IV, p.391)

Had Pinches been the recipient of a spoof flagellant letter? Or was the lady genuine? We cannot know. Further quotations from the Report of the Schools Inquiry Commission are unnecessary, since the answers tend to be pretty stereotyped. What is striking is that, apart from Pinches's solitary objection to the unpleasant 'adjuncts' of the birch, there is not a single reference to the possible dangers of 'lower discipline'.

If beating was permitted in the schools for the upper and middle classes, one can imagine what the situation was like in those institutions existing for the benefit of the working class. And one can imagine even more easily what it was like in the Reformatory and Industrial Schools for boys. These institutions were semi-private in character, run by committees of 'philanthropists' (many of whom were no doubt genuinely well-meaning) and often presided over by disciplinarian clerics. The Rev. M.G. Vine, to take an example, was warden of the Farm School, Redhill, Surrey. In the 1896 Report we find him expressing the view to the Commissioners that, in the case of the 'very bad characters' who were sometimes sent to him, a 'severer punishment' than usual should be permitted:

6289. What is in your mind when you use the expression severer punishment? – The Government regulations – in their code of model rules – lay down a certain number of strokes which may be inflicted.

6290. Is that 18? – That is they lay down 18. We never at Redhill have felt ourselves bound by that – it is a very rare case that we should ever exceed it – but there are cases where I should not hesitate, and I have done it, to go beyond that number, where a great big fellow of 18 and 19 years of age is guilty of some offence that he requires to be thoroughly taken down. I think that such a case requires very severe punishment, and I do not think that 18 strokes of the birch rod is anything of a punishment for a great big, strong, healthy fellow.

6291. What would you propose? – I should give three dozen, and I have done it. (II, p.173)

The Rev. Vine would no doubt have denied that he derived any personal pleasure from inflicting such a punishment on the naked buttocks of a 'great big, strong, healthy fellow'. It was all for the lad's good. The Rev. E. St. John, warden of the Working Boys' Home in the Greyfriars Road, was another Biblical flogger, and had strong views on how to deal with a stubborn boy:

27,564. Supposing he did not do well, then what would you do? – I should make him; I should punish him.

27,565. He has to submit to punishment? – Yes, certainly.

27,566. You mean that you would flog him? – Yes.

27,567. But of course he may say, I will not take that? – I should not give him the option, but he could go afterwards if he liked.

27,568. Not go out first? – No, I should not give him the option; I should give him the flogging first.

27,569. And give him the option of going out afterwards? – Yes.

27,570. Can you legally do that? – I do not know whether I legally can, but certainly a parent would do this with his own son, and I think I am in the place of the parent. (II, p.811)

These clerics, let it be said, are in no way untypical of the men who were running such schools. But even they pale by comparison with Captain Beuttler, superintendent of Heswell Reformatory School, Liverpool. The activities of this man began to be bruited in 1910 and led eventually to a special Home Office Report which was debated in the House of Commons on 23 February 1911. The report revealed that the most appalling punishments had been meted out by Beuttler and his aides, and that several boys had died in suspicious circumstances. The medical officer of Wormwood Scrubs prison, who examined the bodies of some eighty-eight boys who had been caned during the previous twelve months, found that in twenty-seven cases 'the canings had left injuries of a permanent character'. The cane used was much heavier than the regulations allowed, and that 'which had been in use in the school for some time had been shown to him ... it had been split at the end, and was bound up by whipcord, which ... made it a great deal more unsuitable for the use to which it was applied' (Hansard, *Commons*, 23 February 1911, col. 2162). The birch, too, was a more vicious instrument than the regulations allowed, and even the Marquess of Tullibardine ('I do not in the least wish to pose as a humanitarian') conceded in the House that 'it is going a little bit too far when the birch rod used is of green willow twigs and hawthorn branches' (*ibid.*, col.2189). Winston Churchill, Home Secretary at the time, wound up the debate:

> There is no doubt whatever, to my mind, from investigation which I have been making into the subject that there is a great deal more flogging going on in these reformatory schools than is necessary or desirable. There must be corporal punishment, but the regulations under which it is administered appear to me to fall altogether short of the requirements and conditions which modern opinion imposes, and which the necessities of the case demand. (*ibid.*, col.2199)

Churchill, whose experience at the hands of the Rev. Sneyd-Kynnersley had made him sensitive to the subject of beating, announced his decision to appoint a strong Departmental Committee which, among other things, 'should be able to go into the whole question of the present methods of maintaining discipline in reformatory and industrial schools' (*ibid.*, col.2200).

The Committee set up by Churchill published its report in 1913. It felt unable to recommend that caning on the hand be discontinued because such caning 'is allowed in all public elementary schools and practised in almost all' (Salt, 1916, p.42). None the less the Committee made several humane recommendations which materially improved the lot of the unfortunate children committed to these establishments. Despite which the Old Guard were still in evidence. In the same year one of the benefactors of the Sheffield Blue-coat Charity School, Mr F.C.C. Fighiera, was reported as saying to the assembled boys:

> I don't know whether you have flogging in this school. I hope so. I can assure you from personal experience, and from the personal experience of

my sons, that there is nothing more pleasant in this world than to get a jolly good thrashing when you deserve it. (*The Humanitarian*, November 1913, p.184)

With the Industrial and Reformatory Schools may be included the various Poor Law Institutions (the Workhouses, Receiving Homes, Cottage Homes, etc.) in which children were often severely beaten. Most of these cases never came to the notice of the public. Some did. A flogging scandal broke at the Eye Workhouse in 1908 and led to questions being asked in the House of Commons. By now the Humanitarian League's campaign against flogging was having considerable success, and its secretary, Joseph Collinson, provided a carefully documented list of many other similar institutions where brutal floggings were inflicted day after day.[16] In October 1909 more questions were asked in the Commons following allegations about brutality at Ashton-under-Lyne Workhouse, where in the presence of two doctors a young boy had been badly cut and bruised by a birching.[17] Then in 1913 it was revealed that excessive floggings had been administered at Camberwell Workhouse:

Mr O'Grady asked the President of the Local Government Board whether his attention had been called to the flogging of boys who were convalescent in the Camberwell workhouse infirmary; if so, whether he was aware that the punishment was administered with a whip on the bare flesh for trivial offences, and that in four recent cases the ages of the boys were thirteen, eleven, nine, and seven years respectively; and whether, having regard to the indignation of the public locally respecting these practices, and the discussions at the meetings of the Camberwell guardians, he would cause a public inquiry to be made into the matter.
    Mr John Burns: My attention has been called to this matter. The punishment does not seem to have been excessive, and I see no necessity for a public inquiry. (*The Humanitarian*, July 1913, p.147)

The flogging of girls

The beating of schoolboys, then, was widespread throughout Britain in the nineteenth century. But what of schoolgirls? In view of the unflagging efforts of Victorian pornographers to convince themselves and others that fully-grown girls were as frequently subjected to the birch as their brothers, a few words must be said on the subject. The Report of the Schools Inquiry Commission states categorically that 'From our returns it would appear that in hardly a single case is

[16] *The Humanitarian*, August 1908, p.60.
[17] *ibid.*, December 1909, p.188.

corporal punishment known in Girls' Schools. In very many of them it is stated that they have no punishments at all' (vol. I, p.558). Presumably the Commissioners were satisfied that the headmistresses were not lying, and there can be little reason for doubting the accuracy of the returns in this matter. The truth is that the daughters of the affluent were not birched in British schools.

The situation was different, however, in schools for the less well-off, and poor, girls. Take the Royal Patriotic Asylum, for example. This was a girls' institution opened at Wandsworth in 1859 for the education of the children of victims of the Crimean War. When conditions at the school came to the notice of the House of Commons in 1863 it was found 'among other things, that a girl who was within two months of having completed her sixteenth year had been flogged with a birch rod by the lady superintendent under the express directions of the chaplain, the servants of the establishment refusing to inflict the punishment' (Hansard, *Commons*, 1 June 1863, col.193). The churchmen again. Other abuses came to light, but the names of the superintendent ('the daughter of a very distinguished naval officer') and the chaplain were carefully withheld from the public. The Wandsworth disclosures were a godsend to the flagellants, who repeatedly cited them as proof that the birching of girls was common in England.[18]

Then there were the girls' Reformatory and Industrial schools, details of which may be obtained from the 1896 Report. Here, as in the boys' schools in the same category, birch, cane and tawse were in frequent use. Most of the beatings seem to have been applied to the children's hands, but there are exceptions:

7744. Have you any corporal punishment? – Yes, we have.

7745. How often? – The average I should think is two or three girls in a month.

7746. Are they caned on the hand or on the back? – On the back – and not with the cane.

7747. With a birch? – With a leathern tawse.

7748. Of course it is done in private? – Yes.

---

[18] See, for example, *Notes and Queries*, 28 July 1866, p.72. A godsend, too, was the account published by the *Evening Standard* of 12 July 1866 according to which a seventeen-year-old girl had received an 'indecent whipping' from teachers, including a man, at her school at Cambridge, Massachusetts. See *Notes and Queries*, same day as above, which reproduced the *Standard*'s article.

7749. How many strokes do you give? – I have given as many as five for a very serious offense.

7750. Do you give that yourself? – I give that myself. I keep the weapons locked up. (II, p.208)

Thus Mrs Cameron, superintendent of the Maryhill School at Glasgow. Mrs L.J. Campbell, a member of the Committee of Managers of Toxtell Park Reformatory for Girls at Liverpool, preferred the birch to the tawse, and insisted on proper ceremonial when one of her charges was to come under the rod:

10,966. Do you have corporal punishment in your school? – Yes.

10,967. To what extent? – The birch rod is used on little girls, but it is only administered by the superintendent, four strokes across the shoulders, and done in the presence of the schoolmistress and the girls.

10,968. In the presence of the girls, do you say? – I do not say all the girls in the school.

10,970. Do you apply that to the old girls or young girls? – Only to the little girls.

10,971. Is it necessary that, for the punishment of a little girl, there should be a public ceremony? – The matron does it publicly as a protection from supposed abuse. (II, p.299)

Miss C. Hunter ('with a certain class of girl you must have a tawse, I consider') was superintendent of the East Chapelton Reformatory for Girls. She replied evasively when questioned about the part of the body on which she operated:

21,926. Will you tell me what a whipping consists of? – All strokes with the tawse.

21,927. And on what part of the body? – On the hand mostly.

21,928. Any otherwise? – Yes.

21,929. What, on the shoulders? – No, we put them to bed. (II, p.642)

The Chairman was not to be silenced by such a bizarre reply, and his further questioning of Miss Hunter revealed that, before a culprit was 'put to bed', she was 'stripped and whipped'.

One final example. On 14 February 1900 a report was read before a committee of the London School Board which stated that the managers of a certain girls' Industrial School had just passed a resolution that, in future, girls over thirteen *should only be birched across the shoulders*. Previously, that is, girls over that age had been subjected to the indignity of being birched on their bottoms. Honnor Morton added, in her discussion of this report, that out of the punishment records of sixteen such schools, two gave instances of birching, ten of caning, two of the infliction of the tawse and two of unspecified 'whipping'. She noted, however, that in recently founded Industrial Schools such corporal punishments were not allowed.[19] It seemed that some progress in humanity was, at last, under way.

Beating in boys' fiction

One important aspect of national flagellomania may be mentioned at this point: the descriptions of public-school-style canings which occur in the thousands of boys' yarns published in the Victorian period and later in books, twopenny weeklies (such as the *Gem* and *Magnet*) and annuals (the most famous being the *Boy's Own Annual* and *Chums*). In all these stories, caning of the (clothed) buttocks is taken absolutely for granted, and, in some, the account of the ceremony itself is explicit.[20] In many there are references to birching (I read in a recent reprint of *The Magnet*, 25 February 1926: 'Who is most kindly and humane,/And never, never wields the cane,/But wields the birch with mite and mane?/The Head!'). There can be little doubt, it seems to me, that this huge corpus of writing contributed to the dissemination of the flagellant message, for it was produced not only for the boys of the privileged classes, who were actually part of the beating system, but for those lower down the social scale who would not be so likely to experience 'lower discipline' in their daily lives.

> 'Thank you for telling me, sir.'
> He was wondering how many strokes it would be, whether it would draw blood, whether he would cry in front of all the form!
> Mr London picked up the ground-ash and pointed to a vacant desk in front.
> 'Bend over there,' he commanded.
> Chummy put himself in position and stuffed his handkerchief into his mouth.
> Mr London brought the stick down with all his force, four times, four deliberate, even strokes, and each stroke raised a purple weal under

[19] Honnor Morten, 'Inhumanity in Schools', *The Humane Review*, I (1900-1901), p.21.

[20] In this genre, an author called Desmond Coke, who flourished between 1909 and 1919, seems to have been outstanding. Representative titles of his books (which often included drawings of canings) were *The Bending of a Twig*, *The House Prefect*, *The Worst House at Sherborough* and *The Chaps of Harton*. See Gervas d'Olbert (1967), pp. 255-6.

Chummy's shorts ... and that is how Chummy came to worship Mr
London with all his heart and soul.

This choice piece of writing comes from the *Chums Annual* (vol. 50,
1927-8, p.94). It is typical of the genre and, one may think, not very
different from the endless descriptions given in Victorian flagellant
pornography, of which more later.

In his brilliant essay 'Boys' Weeklies' (1940), George Orwell
analysed the *Gem* and *Magnet*, weeklies that had been in existence for
many decades. Orwell found that life in 1939 at Greyfriars and St
Jim's, respectively the two public schools chronicled in these comics,
had not changed in 30 years: characters (including Billy Bunter) and
situations were ageless, outside time. Canings, described with relish,
were of course frequent at both establishments. Orwell would not, I
think, be surprised to learn that recently many issues of the *Magnet*
and *Gem* have been reprinted in facsimile (by the Howard Baker Press
Ltd., London) and that there has been a resurgence of interest in these
products of the fertile pen of Frank Richards.

Modern comics, too, often tend to project an image of the good old
beating days, particularly (it seems to me) the *Dandy* and the *Beano*,
both published, like the *Gem* and *Magnet*, by D.C. Thomson and Co.
Ltd. Whenever children get into trouble in either paper there is bound
to be a beating in store, both at school and at home. Schoolmasters
are invariably arrayed in mortar board and gown, and positively
bristle with canes. I have before me a copy of the *Dandy* dated 11
September 1976 in which there appears an item entitled 'Winker
Watson'. In this particular weekly appearance, it is Scragg, Winker's
friend at Greytowers School (shades of Greyfriars), who cops it, and
we see him issuing from the headmaster's study holding his bottom,
which is emitting what seem to be rays of lightning: 'Scragg confessed
to making additions to the artist's first portrait, and he, not Winker,
got a whopping. That day, he posed again for the art class – standing
up, of course!' One of his class-mates pipes up 'That's fine, thanks,
Scragg! We've drawn you standing up, so how about sitting down for
the next one?'

The Topper, also published by D.C. Thomson Ltd., does a line in
fathers who believe in the virtues of corporal punishment. 'Quiz Kid'
('He knows all the answers') gets his facts wrong in the issue dated 11
September 1976: 'Gulp! I hadn't forgotten about cul-de-sac. It's a dead
end, like I shall have when Dad has finished with me.' [21]

Why do those responsible for publishing these comics persist in

[21] In the issue of the *Beano* for the same date, Dennis the Menace's father himself
indulges in a bit of menacing: 'I reckon I can give you six of the best with one hand

presenting British fathers and schoolteachers, not only as beaters but as 'lower discipline' beaters? I hope that, as our investigation progresses, it may be possible to propose some answers to this and related questions.

Home and school beating since the 1940s

British children can still be beaten, legally, at home, at State primary and secondary schools, at preparatory and public schools, at approved schools and at those for the educationally sub-normal.

As regards beating in the home, it appears that methods vary widely. Geoffrey Gorer found it necessary to divide 'the more severe types of physical punishment' known to English parents (and approved of or disapproved of as the case might be) into several categories depending on the words used by his respondents.[22] Moreover, no single verb in English is as etymologically explicit as the French *fesser*, 'to beat on the buttocks' (from *fesses*, buttocks) or its noun *fessée*; and it seems that it may be the British embarrassment about bottoms, noted by Gorer, which has given rise to the large number of ambiguous beating words current in the language, words which, characteristically, are vague about the part of the body involved even when this is clearly the buttocks. Let us take a few examples (the reader will be able to find many more). 'Spanking' is almost certainly felt to apply specifically to the bottom, although there is no etmyological link; 'birching', while always administered to the buttocks, is no more related to them etymologically than are 'caning', 'belting' or 'whipping'; 'flogging' is also ambiguous, both as to the instrument and the part of the body involved; the onomatopoeiac 'smacking' and 'slapping' can be applied to different parts of the body, although a preference for the buttocks may be implied; 'tanning' ('I'll tan your hide/backside') certainly refers to the buttocks (treated, metaphorically, as leather-producing material – compare the verb to 'leather') while 'hiding', originally probably related to the tanning process, now seems to serve in a wider sense ('I'll give him a good hiding if he's not careful').

The lesson to be learned from this linguistic situation is that 'beating' can mean many different things to different people. Gorer's analysis also shows that parents who approve, for example, of caning

---

tied behind my back, Dennis'; while in 'The Bash Street Kids', teacher administers 'twelve of the best' with his cane to the bottoms of his pupils while a machine keeps count of the number of strokes. 'A hundred and eight whacks,' exclaims the sweating pedagogue, 'This machine is in perfect running order!'

[22] Gorer (1955), p.192.

may disapprove violently of 'belting': truly, one man's beat may be another man's poison. In this book I am principally concerned with the beating of the buttocks, the one form of corporal punishment with overt sexual implications. When teachers or others talk about bringing back the cane, it would be foolish to assume that they are necessarily flagellants. Where State schools are concerned, caning is usually applied to the hand and is therefore not so dangerous psychologically as the public school practice (although one may still strongly disapprove of it).

Bearing these distinctions in mind, let us review the beating situation as it has obtained in schools over the last few decades, taking first those run by the State.

To appreciate this situation, it needs to be understood that in England and Wales it has been, and still is, the rule that the Local Education Authorities (LEAs) should be allowed to arrive at their own decisions, without government interference, concerning the disciplinary methods to be used in the schools under their control. There are at present 104 LEAs in England and Wales. In practice this system has meant that many LEAs have been content to delegate to headmasters the responsibility for deciding whether corporal punishment should be used in their schools, and in what manner.

All attempts to abolish the cane in schools by Act of Parliament have so far been frustrated.

The 1944 Tory Education Act introduced no changes as regards beating in schools. When Labour came to power shortly afterwards, however, parliamentary support for abolition grew, and a new organisation, the Committee against Corporal Punishment in Schools, was formed, which at one time enjoyed the support of 50 MPs (Newell, 1972, pp. 23-4). In 1947 the Government commissioned the National Foundation for Educational Research to undertake an enquiry into the use of rewards and punishments in schools, and by the time their findings and recommendations were published, in 1952, the Conservatives were back in power. The writers of the report expressed themselves against total abolition (the cane, they felt, was necessary as the usual 'last resort'), and revealed that they had found teachers to be overwhelmingly in favour of retention:

In a sample of teachers chosen with considerable care to be as nearly as possible representative of all conditions and shades of opinion in the State service, 89.2 per cent agreed that corporal punishment as a last resort should be retained in schools; 77.8 per cent were strongly in favour of corporal punishment used with discretion; 8.8 per cent only agreed that more harm than good is caused by the retention of corporal punishment;

5.6 per cent only agreed that all corporal punishment should be abandoned in schools; 3.5 per cent only agreed that corporal punishment in schools should be made illegal. Analysis of the ground voting for abolition showed that it consisted mostly of women teachers.

Even more impressive is the evidence recorded by the head teachers of thirteen state schools in which corporal punishment had been voluntarily abandoned. Of these, two only registered absolute opposition to corporal punishment for all types of pupils. (Newell, 1972, p.26)

Naturally, the Tories were pleased. On · 13 March 1952, the Minister for Education, Florence Horsbrugh, was asked what action she proposed to take in the light of the report. 'Questions of school discipline are left to the discretion of local education and school authorities', she replied, 'and I see no grounds for action on my part' (*ibid.*).

During the 1950s and early 1960s the abolitionists seemed to be making little headway. Then, in 1967, there was a significant breakthrough with the publication of the Plowden Committee's report, *Children and their Primary Schools*. The Committee recommended that corporal punishment be abolished in primary schools. They had found that 'the overwhelming majority (between 80 per cent and 90 per cent) of the teaching profession are against the abolition of corporal punishment, though few support it except as a final sanction'.[23] The Committee pointed out that corporal punishment 'can be associated with psychological perversion affecting both beater and beaten' (p.271). Their recommendation has still not become law.

In 1968 Ms Gene Adams founded the Society of Teachers Opposed to Physical Punishment (STOPP), which since that date has campaigned vigorously against the use of corporal punishment in all English and Welsh schools. (Its headquarters are currently at 10, Lennox Gardens, Croydon, Surrey.)

In the same year, teachers in London were being issued with a confidential booklet when they started work:

Corporal punishment shall be given only with the open hand of the teacher used on the arm or the hand or with a cane of approved pattern. Two canes, a larger and a smaller, are approved. The smaller cane only may be used for boys below 11 years of age and for all girls, irrespective of age. The larger or the smaller cane may be used for boys above 11 years of age at the discretion of the headmaster or headmistress. Corporal punishment of girls shall not be administered by a headmaster or assistant master. (Quoted by Corinna Adam, p.740)

[23] *Children and their Primary Schools. A Report of the Central Advisory Council for Education (England)* ['The Plowden Report'], I, p.270.

In April 1970, however, the Labour-controlled Inner London Education Authority (ILEA) announced that it was going to abolish corporal punishment in the primary schools under its control, the ban to take effect from January 1973. There was the expected outcry from the London branch of the National Association of Schoolmasters and the Conservative press. The *Daily Express* pontificated on 27 November 1971: 'The time for firm training of youngsters is in the early years. By the time they reach secondary schools it will be much too late. "Spare the rod and spoil the child", runs the old maxim. And it is still true today.' The *Daily Telegraph* voiced similar sentiments (Newell, 1972, p.180).

Despite this opposition the ban on beating in London's primary schools went ahead in 1973 as planned. According to the Honorary Secretary of STOPP, Colin Bagnall (in a letter to the author, 27 May 1977), the ban has been 'fully accepted' by teachers; there has been no move yet, however, to extend it to the secondary schools of the capital.

In 1972 STOPP published in Penguin Books its report *A Last Resort? Corporal Punishment in Schools*. Unashamedly abolitionist in their views, the contributors had carried out their research with painstaking care, and expressed themselves with becoming dignity despite their obvious anger. The report showed that corporal punishment was far more common than was admitted by its supporters, and came to the conclusion that only an Act of Parliament could remedy the situation. Although the report avoided for the most part the sexual implications of beating, there could be little doubt that some of the cases of 'lower discipline' mentioned involved sadism (Newell, 1972, p.130).

Despite the activities of STOPP, beating continued. On 9 August 1975, the *Daily Express* reported that a working party on school discipline appointed by the Tory-controlled Oxfordshire county council had recommended that caning be restored in state schools. The working party had expressed in familiar terms their regret about having to make such a recommendation: 'We deplore the need for its use, but most members agree that such punishment has a part to play in maintenance of acceptable standards of behaviour in schools' (p.2). The editorial voice of the *Daily Express* commented the same day:

> So, at the very time when most authorities have banned corporal punishment, Oxford is to revert to the philosophy of 'spare the rod and spoil the child'. As Soccer's hooligans get their aggro ready for the start of the season, it's a nice question whether or not Oxford's example should be taken up outside school, too. It'll be surprising if the demand doesn't grow.

Very surprising indeed, if the *Daily Express* were to have its way, for whenever any M.P. (invariably Conservative) or J.P. recommends a return to corporal punishment you can be sure that this newspaper will give his words prominence.

A few days before the Oxfordshire recommendations became known, the National Foundation for Educational Research's report, *Frontiers of Classroom Research*, revealed that more than 50% of third and fourth-year primary school teachers in 871 schools in Lancashire and Cumbria admitted that they 'smacked' children.[24]

It seemed that the bring-back-the-cane virus was having one of its periodic outbreaks.

In the first week of January 1976 an entire mixed class of 24 ten-year-olds in a Glasgow primary school was strapped on the hand by a woman teacher of twenty years' experience. A Strathclyde education authority spokesman said, 'this is not the case of a raw young teacher cracking up' (*Daily Telegraph*, 14 January 1976).

A few days later there was a riot at Newcastle upon Tyne when the headmaster of Heaton Comprehensive School decided that the girl pupils were to become subject to the 'tawse' like the boys. At this news 200 girls rampaged through the school and the police had to be called.

Commenting on this affair, Ms Gene Adams, founder of STOPP in 1968, said: 'It bears out what we have been saying for eight years. Perhaps this incident will help people realise how prevalent corporal punishment is' (*Observer*, 11 January 1976).[25]

In view of these and other similar events, the head teachers decided that they must make their position on corporal punishment clear. The National Association of Headteachers is the largest single body in Britain of heads in all types of State schools. It has 18,000 members. On 17 January 1976, the Association's 30-strong Executive Committee recommended that in no circumstances should older girls be caned except on the hand (!) and stated that they saw 'nothing wrong' with such punishment. According to the *Observer*, the recommendations were 'to be incorporated in the Association's guidance documents to be published soon' (18 January 1976).

Despite the Association's misgivings about beating girls on their bottoms, an event occurred a few weeks later which one would have

---

[24] 'Humiliating Pupils as Alternative to Cane', *The Times*, 4 August 1975.

[25] In a letter to the *Observer*, Mr Edward T. Baker of the Portia Trust wrote (14 November 1976): 'The National Children's Bureau's recent report 'Britain's Sixteen-Year-Olds' found corporal punishment used in 80 per cent of schools attended by some 14,000 children born in a single week in March 1958' (p.10). According to the *Observer* (11 January 1976), STOPP 'estimates that corporal punishment exists, if only as a last resort, in two-thirds of British schools. In about one-third it is in common use'.

thought impossible, even in England. According to STOPP, at Camden Square School, Seaham, County Durham 'a fifteen-year-old girl was held down over a platform by the headmaster and a woman teacher and given six strokes of the cane across the buttocks by another woman teacher' (*Croydon Paper on Corporal Punishment*, prepared by STOPP for Croydon Teachers' Association, Appendix A, p.14). It sounds like an incident from the sort of flagellant pornography we shall be examining later in the book.

There are, as has been said, 104 LEAs today in England and Wales. In a recent article (May 1977), Michael de la Cour has explained that, of these, 68 impose some regulations concerning the use of corporal punishment in the schools under their control; 18 have banned beating for some children, mainly infants; 36 leave the question entirely to the discretion of individual headmasters; *and not a single one has abolished the cane completely*.

STOPP's research shows that children at British State schools are still frequently beaten on the 'part ordained by Nature', although it is not easy to obtain accurate figures. Girls, too, are more commonly liable to 'lower discipline' than might be imagined. We have seen the Camden Square School case. That of Hillingdon LEA might be termed recidivist. Michael de la Cour tells us that this Authority, which 'previously discouraged corporal punishment for girls – "only in exceptional cases" – and required that girls should only be caned on the hands, now discourages corporal punishment less strongly for all and both boys and girls can now be caned on the hands or buttocks' (1977, p.143).

The Approved Schools, descendents of the Reformatory and Industrial Schools, are boarding establishments for the education and training of children and young persons sent to them by the courts. In 1967 there were 123 approved schools in England and Wales, 90 for boys and 33 for girls. The schools, which are publicly financed, are run by local authorities or committees, religious bodies and so on. In the large majority of cases the children who end up in such establishments are from working-class backgrounds.

In 1967 revelations concerning excessive canings administered to boys at Court Lees Approved School at South Godstone, Surrey, and the official Home Office Report that followed them, focussed public attention on a little-known area in which the English Vice was still active. It will be recalled by many readers that Ivor Cook, the master who showed what was going on at Court Lees by writing (anonymously) to the *Guardian* and sending to the *Daily Mail* colour film of the badly bruised buttocks of the victims, was sacked and that he found it impossible to find subsequent employment.

The Home Office inquiry was carried out by Mr Edward Brian Gibbens, Q.C.[26] He found after some research that Cook's allegations were, in many cases, justifiable. The Approved School Rules, from which Gibbens quotes at the beginning of his report, show that caning was normal practice at these establishments, although officially discouraged except in extreme cases. As regards the *modus operandi*, the Rules state that 'Boys under 15 may be caned either on the hands or on the posterior. Boys over 15 may be caned only on the posterior' and that 'Caning on the posterior must be over a boy's ordinary cloth trousers. Boys under 15 may be given up to six strokes and those over 15 up to eight strokes. In exceptional cases, with the specific approval of a manager, a boy over 15 may be given 12 strokes' (p.9). It seems that no rules were laid down as to the severity with which the strokes might be applied.

Among other disturbing things, Gibbens discovered that at Court Lees the canes used were heavier, thicker and altogether more brutal than those supplied by the Home Office, and that they had been obtained illegally from the (highly disreputable) Eric A. Wildman Tutelage Supply Company, which has already been mentioned; that Mr Denis Haydon, the headmaster, had on occasion caned boys with 'excessive severity' (p.23); that, in contravention of the Home Office rules, boys had not only been caned in pyjamas but that, when beaten with their trousers on, Mr Haydon had been in the habit of first pulling out their shirts: 'Mr Haydon himself candidly admitted that he pulled out the shirt of boy No. 22 before caning him and that from time to time he does pull a boy's shirt out of his trousers *in order to make the caning more severe.* He thinks that this act also lends a certain drama to the occasion which impresses the boy' (p.17, Gibbens's italics). Gibbens also found that, during one of the beatings, the victim's head was held between the knees of another master: 'Mr Wright denied holding the boy's head as described between his knees, but I accept that this allegation is established and I think that it is an irregular method of controlling a boy during corporal punishment' (p.17). Wright was not the only person who lied to Gibbens.

Gibbens is extremely careful not to imply that there was anything sexually kinky about those in charge of discipline at Court Lees. The word 'sadism', for example, is never suggested, let alone used. Yet even the most blinkered reader of his report would surely put it down feeling that something was morbidly wrong at Court Lees. As regards the photographs, the experts agreed that they were authentic, and the

[26] Edward Brian Gibbens, Q.C., *Administration of Punishment at Court Lees Approved School. Report of Inquiry.* Home Office, Command 3367, 1967.

doctors that the injuries to the boys' buttocks were excessive: 'They were unanimous in saying that the photograph of boy No. 2 revealed injuries of quite unusual severity. Professor Simpson and Dr Teare declared that if such cases as boys Nos. 2 and 8 had been brought to them in their hospitals, they would have felt bound to call for an investigation by the police or other authority. Professor Simpson would add the case of boy No. 20' (p.19).

As a result of the Court Lees case it became apparent that at other approved schools there was also frequent caning. Following the rumpus, however, approved school beatings halved, from 1,449 in January-June 1967 to 705 in January-June 1968. Commenting on these figures in the *New Statesman*, Corinna Adam observed: 'Had it not been for Ivor Cook, there would presumably have been about 1,500 beatings in 1968 which would have been claimed to be quite justified, but now have somehow been found unnecessary' (29 November 1968). The approved school headmasters and managers, it would seem, had been scared by the publicity afforded to the Court Lees affair.

None the less, in 1968 there occurred another instance of brutality which caught the attention of the public. William Byrd, headmaster of Cholderton College, a private boarding school for difficult boys, was sentenced to five years' imprisonment for his cruelty towards some of his charges. According to STOPP's report, *A Last Resort?* (Newell, 1972, p.54), Byrd 'had caused a sixteen-year-old boy to be twice thrown naked into the school swimming pool and made him run in bare feet round rough ground of a garden nearby, because he called another boy a 'Nazi'. He had also punished boys for stealing and being in possession of cigarettes, by making them strip and caning them excessively. The judge at Assizes had considered that he had used the boys to gratify his own sadistic urges'.

Byrd appealed, and 'the appeal judges merely considered that in moments of impatience he had gone further than he should. They reduced his total sentence to two years' (*ibid.*).

A similar case was reported in the press in February 1976 when the housefather of Besford House, Shrewsbury – a council home for 29 children – was sentenced to four years imprisonment for brutally beating some of the boys with, among other things, a horse-whip. He pleaded guilty to 23 charges, 19 of causing actual bodily harm and four of common assault. The boys had been beaten frequently on the naked buttocks. The judge said 'There is undoubtedly an element where you got sadistic pleasure out of what went on' (*Daily Telegraph*, 28 February 1976, p.3).

As regards the preparatory and boarding schools, the principal

The English Vice

breeding-grounds of English flagellomania, the evidence suggests overwhelmingly that traditional attitudes to beating were still widespread ten years ago. Graham Kalton, in his book *The Public Schools: A Factual Survey of Headmasters' Conference Schools in England and Wales* (1966) has shown that at that time caning was very frequent at these establishments. To start with, Kalton found that 'In all the schools except four independent boarding or mainly boarding schools the headmaster can administer corporal punishment; in three of these four schools, two of which are Quaker schools, no one can do so, while in the fourth the headmaster does not allow himself to administer corporal punishment but delegates the task to other members of his staff' (pp. 124-5). As regards beatings inflicted by housemasters and the boys themselves at all the other schools surveyed, Kalton made some interesting discoveries. This passage deserves to be quoted in full:

> In 124 of the 134 schools with boarders the housemasters can use corporal punishment, and in addition in 44 of these schools other masters are so empowered. The power to administer corporal punishment is given to some boys in three-fifths of the schools and, moreover, it is seldom confined to the head boy, being so restricted in only 16 of the 95 schools for which the information is available. All the 11 day schools for which information is available restrict the number empowered to administer corporal punishment to less than twenty boys, and five of them restrict the right to the head boy. In 40 of the 84 schools with boarders the right is given to between six and ten boys. Of the remainder, 11 give the right to one boy only, and 12 to between two and five boys, leaving 21 schools where more than ten boys are entitled to administer corporal punishment. In fact in six of these schools more than fifty boys can do so. In nearly every case corporal punishment cannot be administered without the approval of the headmaster or a housemaster; in other cases, where this approval is not required, the boy always has the right of appeal to the headmaster. In three schools it is stipulated that only a slipper or gym shoe may be used, and in four more schools only a few boys can use a cane, the majority being allowed to use only a slipper. (pp. 125-6)

In view of the mass of evidence regarding the sexual implications of 'lower discipline', these figures strike one as most disturbing. It is as if the public school Establishment had learned nothing for the last hundred years about psychology.

Two years later, in *The Hothouse Society: An Exploration of Boarding-School Life through the Boys' and Girls' Own Writings* (1968), Dr Royston Lambert and his team of researchers confirmed Kalton's findings: 'In public and similar schools, the senior boys can usually cane the serious offenders. In most state boarding schools the prefects are not allowed to do so, while in progressive schools the senior pupils have few sanctions over the others and caning is unknown' (1974 ed., pp 202-3).

Lambert's research was used by the Public Schools Commission, whose report ('the Newsom Report'), published in the same year, came out strongly against the retention of corporal punishment in the public schools, arguing that, in the event of integration with other schools, such a practice would be unacceptable to the rest of the population. The Report also deprecated fagging and, in particular, the beating of boy by boy. After the morbid refusal over the years of the public school Establishment to change its disciplinary methods, and its constant repetition of the same old arguments in favour of the cane, this document comes as a relief.

Punishments

235. Many people picture the public schools as places where corporal punishment is frequently used, often for trivial offences. It certainly was so in the past. But there is good evidence that a marked change has taken place in the last decade, and beating is on the decline. This is in line with the view of the then Secretary of State (in answer to a Parliamentary Question on 19th December 1967) that 'the practice of corporal punishment should be dropped from our schools' and his hope that 'the local authorities, the governing bodies of schools and the teachers themselves will all use their power and influence to achieve this end'. We think all boarding schools, and in particular any public schools which are going to accept assisted pupils, should review most carefully the ways in which they sanction corporal punishment. In day schools such punishment can be checked by parental and public opinion. In boarding schools this is more difficult and it is not easy for boys to complain, for that would be to flout the conventions of the school. Nor, in independent schools, do their parents have recourse to the local education authority, as have parents of children at maintained schools.

236. While we hope that this form of punishment will decline and disappear, there is one feature of it which should now cease – as indeed it has already ceased at a number of public schools. This is the beating of boys by boys. For years the public schools have been criticised for permitting this practice to continue, and we are unconvinced by any of the defences which have been made to us. If, as it is claimed, the practice is dying out, why not abolish it? We agree with the statement made by the headmaster of a famous public school: 'It is worse for those who inflict this punishment, and for those who watch it being inflicted, than for the boy who suffers it'. We would not be prepared to accept for integration any school where the practice continued.

237. There are other physical punishments which should be reconsidered at the same time. We have been told of punishments such as restriction of diet or of sleep. These are not wise. Nor are they typical. Before assisted

pupils are sent to public or other independent boarding schools, the
Boarding Schools Corporation ought to satisfy themselves that the scale
and type of punishment within a school is sensible. (pp. 115-16)

Quite apart from the factual evidence concerning the survival of
beating today in the prep and public schools (ask any teacher), there
are many symptoms of the continuing interest shown by the British
public in the subject. Allusions to beatings appear in many
autobiographies published recently, for example; and they may crop
up in the most unlikely places elsewhere whenever the Old Boys start
to reminisce. To take but one example. In the *Sunday Times*'s long-
running column 'One Man's Week', in which Successful People were
engaged to titillate us, or make us envious, with an account of their
richly varied hebdomadal doings, an item germane to our subject
caught my eye one day. It was contributed by Hugh Johnson
('journalist and author of books on wine and trees'). Johnson had
been yachting in the Channel: 'We're going too fast, motoring. We're
meant to take five days. We put in to Brest to kill time. *Histoire d'O* is
playing to an empty house ... The Bretons aren't fools; it is a silly
film. We had better beatings at Rugby' (12 October 1975). That sort
of remark is apparently irresistible to the public school man.
    Another symptom of the interest people take in beating may be
found in the television series 'Whacko!', in which Jimmy Edwards
was perfectly cast as the beefy, caning headmaster. This sort of
programme is obviously considered quite normal by the British public
– quite normal, that is, as a picture of what goes on in the public
schools where the privileged are educated. As Corinna Adam
remarked in the article already quoted, 'Britain is run by people who
were beaten at their public schools and don't-think-it-did-them-any-
harm'. She went on to observe that Ivor Cook, who exposed the Court
Lees excesses, 'has often been told – and I've heard the same – that,
after all, "it's no worse than what goes on in a public school" '. As we
shall see throughout this book, this has been the traditional view of the
ruling class.
    The public school system has naturally thrown up, along with the
'hardened' type to whom 'it never did any harm' and out-and-out
flagellants such as Swinburne, a large category of sensitive creatures
such as George Orwell who felt themselves to have been marked
indelibly by their school experience. At public school many men who
have achieved eminence later in life first sensed the connection that
exists between sexuality and cruelty. One of these men, it seems, was
Laurence Olivier. On 21 November 1965, the *Observer* published a
letter from Olivier, then Director of the National Theatre, headed

'Violence and the Censor'. It was an intelligent, searching piece of writing in defence of Edward Bond's *Saved*, currently playing at the Royal Court. Olivier recalled his school experience, or one aspect of it, in a pungent paragraph:

> The first time a schoolmaster ordered me to take my trousers down I knew it was not from any doubt that he could punish me efficiently enough with them up. The theatre is concerned, whether in the deepest tragedy or the lightest comedy, with the teaching of the human heart the knowledge of itself, and sometimes, when it is necessary – and we are obviously going through such a time – with the study, understanding and recognition of that most dreaded and dangerous eccentricity in the human design, the tripartite conspiracy between the sexual, the excretory and the cruel.

Sir Laurence, at any rate, seemed to be in no doubt about the element of active sadism involved in this form of punishment.

On 1 December 1975 the *Times* diarist published a photograph of what he called a 'viciously self-contradictory sign' spotted by a reader outside a school in Herefordshire. It read: 'Much Birch. Voluntary Controlled School.' Only in England, one feels confident, could such an insertion be guaranteed to provide merriment. It was a joke right into the 'Whacko!' class.

David Niven, predictably, is very old-boyish about his experience, including his beating experience, at Stowe, one of England's newest public schools, founded in 1923. From the film star's best-selling autobiography *The Moon's a Balloon* (1971) one gathers that the Stowe authorities had made little effort to devise modern methods of discipline. Niven's housemaster was one of the flogging brigade:

> 'Go next door into the Gothic Library. Lift your coat, bend over and hold on to the bookcase by the door. It will hurt you very much indeed' ... The first three or four strokes hurt so much that the shock somehow cushioned the next three or four, but the last strokes of my punishment were unforgettable ... In the bathroom mirror, I inspected the damage. It was heavy to say the least. Suddenly, Major Howarth's cheery voice made me turn, 'Pretty good shooting I'd call that'. (pp. 50-1)

One could quote from any number of similar accounts. But the most original book containing beating reminiscences to have appeared recently is undoubtedly *The Autobiography of an Englishman* by 'Y', which caused something of a stir in London literary circles on its appearance in 1975. The publisher claimed that 'Y' was a well-known author and critic in his sixties, and that 'he enjoys considerable public standing'. Reviewers wondered in vain who 'Y' might be.

But more interesting than the author's identity was the story, the pathetic story, he had to tell, of his progress from a late-Victorian home to preparatory and public school, and thence, burdened with sexual problems, out into the world. Particularly unusual is the frankness with which 'Y' discusses his obsession with flagellation. While it is a pity that 'Y' could not bring himself to reveal his true name, the critics agreed that the book is authentic history and not a fictional concoction. Its value as a social document is therefore considerable.

The author's father, to begin with, was a Victorian pater familias of the old school: 'When my father caught me at the age of sixteen or so smoking secretly, he was grieved rather than angry. He used to smack us with his hand on our naked buttocks by way of punishment ... I bitterly resented the smacking, which was sharp and painful and had no lasting physical effect. My father smacked on principle and with a certain proportion of the wrath of God' (p.11). One is reminded of Edmund Gosse's father, whom we met earlier.

And so to prep school – 'in the home counties' ('Y' calls the establishment Newton Lodge). Beating at this school followed the usual pattern: 'Life at Newton Lodge implanted in me my lifelong obsession with flagellation' (p.20). To start with, the beautiful school captain was something of an expert in the art of beating (already, at the age of 14!): 'It was his practice, for a time, to order the younger boys out of bed and beat them on the bottom, asking them first to bend over their beds ... He allowed us to choose between a beating with the back of a hairbrush and one with a dressing-gown cord' (p.19). Another flagellant variation in vogue at Newton Lodge seems to have been borrowed from Eton:

> In the big schoolroom there were high sash windows, raised or lowered by means of thin, hard blind cord. It was an amusement of the prefects to make smaller boys bend over the window sill and lay their heads beneath the open window in the manner of one on the execution block. Then the window was gently lowered, and the boy was whipped on the bottom with the blind cord. (p.21)

The Head, too, was a beater, caning 'with some frequency, never getting nearer to our flesh than the seat of a pair of pyjamas' (p.20). 'Y' makes it clear, however, that the Head's hesitation to cane on the naked buttocks made little difference, since it only needed a bit of imagination to conjure up the real thing. And after a beating there was always a rush to the nearest mirror to study the effects of the strokes: 'The excitement caused in the school by this mass punishment was intense. As we rose next morning, the whole of another dormitory came into ours to see us strip and show off our weals. The showing of weals on the bottom is one of the keenest pleasures known to schoolboys' (pp. 20-1). In this respect one of 'Y''s reminiscences is of particular interest for the light it throws on the voyeuristic element in flagellomania:

> One boy whom I loved, called Clifford, was caned by the Head with some force on one occasion, and I was privileged to be shown his naked bottom privately in the lavatory. I was shocked to see a huge livid purple bruise where all the strokes must have fallen on the same spot. I felt a wave of fascinated horror and compassion sweep over me. I longed to soothe the place in some way, but could only utter some exclamation of sympathy ... I feel certain that an obsession with flagellation, practical or theoretical, never leaves anyone once he has acquired it at school. (pp. 21-2)

There can be no doubt that 'Y' is right. Since caning on the buttocks, naked or not, has always been the pride and privilege of the preparatory and public schools; since that is probably still the case today, State school canings being usually applied to the hand; and since, as is well known everywhere except apparently in those establishments that practise it, flagellomania is always exclusively centred on the buttocks, we can be absolutely sure who is to blame for the English Vice.

We need not delay over 'Y' 's subsequent experience at his public school (tantalisingly disguised as 'Praed'): it was in all respects typical, from the headmaster's canings to the other traditions of the school; nor need we linger over his encounters with caners at other schools when he himself became, temporarily, a schoolmaster, or his love affairs, homo- and heterosexual. After reading his book, one cannot but agree with Jill Tweedie, who wrote in the *Guardian*: 'For those who still believe that sex education, permissiveness and sparing the rod is spoiling the child, I suggest they contemplate the pathetic loneliness of this tableau. And read the book' (27 February 1975).

Finally, it must be said that there are still some people in both the House of Commons and the Lords who are fighting to see school beating abolished in Britain by Act of Parliament. Among them one should mention Dennis Canavan, who, as Labour Member for West Stirlingshire, moved on 20 January 1976 a Ten-Minute Private Member's Bill to abolish completely all such punishments in British schools. Canavan, himself for many years a teacher, asserted that corporal punishment has a brutalising effect on the pupil-teacher relationship and that, moreover, 'In extreme cases the excessive use of corporal punishment could lead to sadism on the part of the teacher

and to masochism on the part of the pupil' (Hansard, *Commons*, 20
January 1976, col. 1154). It was a dignified, controlled speech. 'Surely,'
Canavan asked, 'it is not beyond our wit or the wit of the teaching
profession to think of some alternative, non-violent form of punishment'
(col. 1155). When he had finished, Patrick Cormack, Conservative
Member for Staffordshire, South-West, rose to put the traditional
public school view, beginning his contribution by saying 'I do not think
that this House has ever heard so much rubbish in so short a period'
(col. 1156). Cormack went on to say that 'I feel that the proposals which
the hon. Gentleman has put before us ought to be thrown out as the
ludicrous set of specious, do-gooding nonsense that they are' and that
'People who have the future of our children truly at heart will agree that
there is something to be said for the old adage that if one spares the rod
one spoils the child' (col. 1157).[27]

There were only 300 or so Members present when the House
divided. The motion was defeated by 181 votes to 120.

---

[27] The conservative *Daily Telegraph*, it is interesting to note, printed its account of
these proceedings under the heading 'Demand to Abolish the Cane is Rejected as Do-
Gooding Nonsense' (21 January 1976).

3

Eton, the Birch and Swinburne

That birching was a habitual form of punishment at Eton before, during and after Swinburne's time there (1849-53) is well attested. Indeed there has never been any secret about it. In 1864 the Royal Commissioners, having been informed that flogging was still inflicted as often as five or six times a week, commented that, if that was so, 'it is much more frequent at Eton, in proportion to its numbers, than at other great schools to which our inquiry has extended' (*Clarendon*, I, p.96). Dr Goodford, the Provost, claimed that flogging had diminished during his time as headmaster (1853-62), but the Commissioners found that the evidence from various sources did not 'entirely tally' with such a claim:

> 8519. (*Lord Clarendon.*) Has flogging diminished since the time when you first went to Eton? – No.
>
> 8520. (*Mr Vaughan.*) Is it any great dishonour to a boy to be flogged, or is it regarded as a natural incident of the day? – It is regarded quite as a natural incident of the day.[1] (*ibid.*)

The numerous memoirs published by Old Etonians during the nineteenth century and later often refer to these 'natural incidents of the day', and they do so with an odd mixture of coyness, euphemism and fascination. In his letters we find Swinburne harping back to them with compulsive interest, particularly when writing to his friend Richard Monckton Milnes, Lord Houghton, who shared a taste in flagellant matters with the poet, 28 years his junior. We shall have occasion to return to Milnes later.

[1] There seems to have been some public confusion as to whether birching had or had not diminished at Eton at this time. On 23 November 1861, the *Family Herald* advised ANXIOUS PARENT: 'We believe "birching" to be abolished at many of our great schools; and if, as you state, you are rich enough to send your son to Eton, you may do so safely' (p.476).

At Eton the official school birchings were only administered by the Head Master and the Lower Master, each dealing with his respective part of the school. The Lower School was made up of all divisions below the Fourth Form.

The Lower School was numerically much smaller than the Upper. In 1850 it comprised about thirty boys, while the Upper School had about 600. By 1862 it had 140. The average age at which boys entered the Upper School was twelve, and most of these never attended the Lower School, having been coached for Eton either by a private tutor (as was the case with Swinburne) or at a preparatory school. According to the evidence submitted to the Royal Commissioners, ten out of every 50 boys sitting the entrance test to Eton might fail and have to enter the Lower School or apply elsewhere. Occasionally it might happen that a boy older than twelve would have to enter the Lower School, or that a boy already there would 'stick' in the Lower School beyond the age of twelve. It must have been an unenviable position.[2]

The Head Master and Lower Master of Eton needed a strong arm. Any man accepting either post knew perfectly well that he would be required frequently to administer a particularly nasty form of corporal punishment. But such men were habitually clerics, and no doubt felt themselves Biblically justified in applying the Solomonic rod to their pupils.

In the normal course of events a boy 'complained of' by a master or tutor (for any one of a staggering number of possible offences, most of them trivial, and also for idleness at lessons) would be 'put in the bill' – the flogging list. Then, at the appointed hour, he would be birched by either the Head or the Lower Master, depending on his position in the school.

Each part of the school had its own flogging block. The 'block', as it was familiarly known, was a portable wooden step on which the victim knelt with his trousers down to receive his punishment on the naked buttocks. In that position he was attended by two 'holders down' whose duty it was to lift up his shirt tails and keep him there until the full quota of strokes had been administered. The ceremony was referred to, accurately enough, as the 'execution', although on the Eton block nates, not necks, were cut.

The Eton birches were grotesque instruments (see Plate 12) consisting of three feet of handle and two of a thick bunch of birch

---

[2] The information contained in this paragraph is derived from *The Eton Register Part I 1841-1850* (1903) and *Clarendon*, III, pp. 206-16. The latter source, which gives the evidence of the Rev. W.A. Carter, Lower Master from 1857, provides a detailed account of the working of the Lower School at the time.

twigs. The preparation and supply of birches was one of the duties of the Head Master's servant, in the days of Dr Hawtrey (1834-52) one Finmore. Ralph Nevill (at Eton 1846-51)[3] tells us in *Floreat Etona* (1911):

> A dozen new rods were supposed to be at hand in the cupboard every morning, for there was no calculating the number of floggings that might be inflicted in a day. Finmore used to make the rods at his own house, with the help of his wife, and brought them to the library[4] quietly after Lock-Up, or in the morning before early school. Sometimes, however, when the supply of rods ran short Finmore had to bring in fresh birches in the middle of the day, which, for several reasons, was a somewhat hasardous task. (p.91)

In the Lower School the 'executions' were always fully public, and the boys would gather to watch the fun. Upper School boys were permitted to attend. It must have been humiliating for sensitive victims. Lower School birchings were inflicted in the 'Schoolroom', where there was plenty of seating for spectators. Questioned about these floggings, Dr Goodford agreed that they took place in the Schoolroom:

> 2929. (*Lord Devon.*) Then in the lower school it is done in the presence of the boys? – I do not know whether they are present or not. (*Clarendon*, III, p.94)

That was a lie, or at best a deliberate evasion. Goodford had been a boy at Eton (1826-30), an Assistant Master from 1835-52 and Head Master from 1853 to 1862; he was now Provost.[5] He knew perfectly well that in the Lower School birching was indeed 'done in the presence of the boys'. It is of interest to note that Lord Devon, who must also have realised this, did not press the Provost on the point: both the Commissioners and the men under examination tended to become shy when the 'indelicate' possibilities of birching were adumbrated.

In his *Seven Years at Eton* (1883), James Brinsley Richards gives us an account of the first Lower School birching he witnessed. Richards (whose original name was Reginald T.S.C. Grenville-Murray) attended Eton between 1857 and 1864 and was, therefore, almost a contemporary of Swinburne. The officiating Lower Master in his

---

[3] *The Eton Register* (1903), p.87.
[4] The 'Library' was, in fact, the headmaster's study.
[5] *Dictionary of National Biography* (1908), VIII, p.126.

description is the Rev. Adolphus Carter, who ascended to this position in 1857 and was notorious for his severity in handling the birch:

> I had never been chastised since I was in the nursery after the manner in use at Eton, and I thought that manner infinitely degrading. When I first came to the school, and was told how culprits were dealt with, when I was shown the block, and the cupboard under one of the forms, I fancied I was being hoaxed. I never quite believed the stories I heard until I actually saw a boy flogged, and I can never forget the impression which the sight produced upon me. It was on a cold rainy morning, when that corner of the Lower School where the block stood looked funereally dark, and the victim doomed to execution was a very white-skinned, curly-headed boy called Neville. He was a boy very fond of fun, and had a squint which enhanced the comical expression of his countenance. As we were all flocking out of school at the end of early lesson, I beheld him standing ruefully alone among some empty forms. A cry arose behind me: 'Hullo! there's going to be a swishing!' and a general rush was made towards the upper end of the schoolroom.
>
> In the Lower School floggings were public. Several dozens of fellows clambered upon forms and desks to see Neville corrected, and I got a front place, my heart thumping, and seeming to make great leaps within me, as if it were a bird trying to fly away through my throat. Two fellows deputed to act as 'holders down' stood behind the block, and one of them held a birch of quite alarming size, which he handed to the Lower Master as the latter stepped down from his desk.
>
> I had pictured a rod as nothing more than a handful of twigs, but this thing was nearly five feet long, having three feet of handle and nearly two· of bush. As Mr Carter grasped it and poised it in the air, addressing a few words of rebuke to Neville, it appeared a horrible instrument for whipping so small a boy with. Neville was unbracing his nether garments – next moment, when he knelt on the step of the block, and when the Lower Master inflicted upon his person six cuts that sounded like the splashings of so many buckets of water, I turned almost faint. I felt as I have never felt but once since, and that was when seeing a man hanged. (pp. 70-2)

The writing here is perceptive; while still rather shy, Richards has managed to convey just what an Eton birching was like, and the degree of humiliation it involved to the novice. From his account we can surmise that the ceremony as often generated sexual excitement as disgust in the onlookers. The 'thumping heart', the 'splashings' of birch on bare skin, the recollection of a real execution – can we fail to recognise the signs, even if Richards is not himself fully aware of what is going on?

Books on Swinburne have tended to assume that, in his day, birchings in the Upper School were private. It is a fact, however, that this was not necessarily the case. John Delaware Lewis was at Eton between 1841 and 1844, five years before Swinburne's arrival.[6] Lewis left the school when he was in the upper division of the Fifth Form. According to an article published by Lewis in 1875, floggings were public, and it is clear that he is referring to the Upper School:

> It was, in my time, so far from being a punishment administered on special occasions only, or with any degree of solemnity, that some half-dozen to a dozen boys were flogged every day. It was entirely public; any one who chose might drop in. I have sometimes been one of three spectators, and sometimes one of a hundred. These latter large assemblages were collected, of course, only on occasions of very great interest, either as to quantity or quality – a member of the eight, or the eleven, to be 'swished' as they used to term it, or a number of culprits to catch it for doing something or other particularly heinous – smoking or drinking, or going to Ascot on the sly. (pp. 46-7)

These Upper School birchings were inflicted in the Head Master's room, otherwise known as the Library; and Lewis describes the crush of excited boys on the stairs outside waiting to be admitted to the show:

> That a young man of eighteen, nineteen, or even it might be of twenty years, should be made to kneel down after the fashion of a little boy, *nudis natibus*, and on that portion of the frame which I have taken the liberty of clothing (it must be thought of as having no other clothing) in a dead language, should receive successive strokes from a huge birch rod, before a large concourse of spectators – all this constitutes a picture which would have presented itself to any one but the Eton authorities as a caricature, and what is worse, an indecent caricature. (p.47)

The Rev. A.G. L'Estrange's *Vert de Vert's Eton Days and Other Sketches and Memories* (1887), an account which covers the years 1845-50, describes a similar incident, with Dr Hawtrey again officiating:

> Eleven o'clock school was over in half an hour, and at twelve all the lower boys in our house assembled with undisguised delight to see Spratt 'swished'. Everyone but himself seemed to think it capital fun. We accompanied him upstairs to the headmaster's room – a small chamber adjoining the upper school. Here were the full terrors of the law. The block, with all its appalling associations, had been drawn forth, and beside it stood two collegers in their long black gowns, as if about to assist at a real execution. The centre of the scene was formed by the doctor

[6] *The Eton Register* (1903), p.27.

himself; but how changed from the obsequious courtier of yesterday! There he stood, stern and statuesque, with his nose sublimely elevated, and the birch rod in his hand – eternal thunder 'settled on his head'.

'Spratt minor!' he demanded with marked and awful brevity.

'Here, sir,' replied the culprit, emerging from the crowd with an elongated countenance, and wearing a pair of thick leather gauntlets.

'Go down!' commanded the doctor airily.

'Please, sir, it's my first fault,' urged Spratt, in a tone of injured innocence.

'Why, you were here last week!' replied the doctor indignantly.

'No; please, sir, that was my major' (elder brother).

'I know your face perfectly,' insisted the doctor.

'And more than his face,' suggested a boy behind me.

'At all events,' concluded the doctor, 'I only allow first fault for lessons. Go down!' (pp. 17-18)

Poor Spratt minor realises that all is lost, and resigns himself. L'Estrange continues:

There was no contradicting this, and his only plea having failed, Spratt was soon kneeling on the block. The object of the gauntlets, which I could not at first understand, now became manifest, for every time the birch descended he thrust his hand in the way to break its force. The collegers did all in their power to prevent this evasion of justice, but he nevertheless sometimes succeeded, and accordingly the doctor, who was conscientious, gave him a sly cut just as he was rising, to square accounts and make up for all deficiencies. (p.19)[7]

The usual number of strokes inflicted seems to have been six, although for particularly heinous crimes it could be higher. In *Recollections of Eton* (1870), 'An Etonian' writes:

The victim did as he was told; his trousers were turned down, and the two collegers held up his shirt, each by one corner, really making a very effective tableau. The birch then descended, and after six successive cuts, the performance as far as regarded Robinson was at an end. Edwards was the next, and as his complaint was for impertinence, he received two extra cuts, making eight. (pp. 136-7)

[7] Further confirmation that Upper School birchings could be public comes from Ralph Nevill (1911): 'In the case of big boys there is some humiliation in being flogged. A certain captain of the boats, who had indulged too freely in champagne, a very tall and powerful young man, about to be flogged by Dr Hawtrey, begged hard that he should receive his punishment in private, and thus escape the degradation of being observed on the block by a large crowd of boys looking through the open door. The Headmaster, however, would not hear of this for a moment, declaring that publicity was the chief part of the punishment' (pp. 84-5).

Depending on the severity of the beater and the relative hardness or delicacy of the victim's posteriors, the effects would be more or less severe. In every case there would be the immediate and considerable reddening of the buttocks that must automatically result from a birching:

> 'How do you feel?' said Jackson, as I made my appearance at the bottom of the stairs.
> 'Very warm and comfortable,' I answered, laughing. 'It did sting a little, though.'
> 'Yes; you'll be like a plum-pudding behind, I dare say, for the next fortnight. However, as it's not the time of year for bathing, nobody will be able to chaff you about it.' (p.137)

Sometimes blood would be drawn on these occasions. It was hardly an edifying sight for clerical, let alone young, eyes. Henry S. Salt, who was at Eton under Hornby (Headmaster from 1868 to 1884) and who later became a champion of the anti-floggers and editor of *The Humanitarian*, said that 'One cannot speak in detail on this unpleasant subject' (1910, p.103). In a later book, however, he allowed himself to be more explicit:

> In my early days at Eton I had to be present at floggings on many occasions, first as one of the two Lower-boy Collegers who then acted as 'holders down', and afterwards as Sixth Form praeposter; and I certainly think that (in *Punch's* words) anybody who can be disgusted by anything would have been disgusted by *that* spectacle. (1928, p.70)

Even humanitarians such as Salt had difficulty in talking about bottoms. The buttocks could only be alluded to, not named, forming as they did a prominent item on the list of English 'unmentionables'. Despite the fact that during the nineteenth century boys were being constantly beaten on their bottoms, especially at Eton, few people were able to talk openly about the subject – few people, that is, apart from the flagellant pornographers. A jingle published in the anonymous *Guide to Eton* is typical of this coy attitude (it should be noted again that Dr Keate, Head Master of Eton from 1809 to 1834, was one of the school's greatest floggers of all time):[8]

[8] For information on Keate, see the Rev. C. Allix Wilkinson, *Reminiscences of Eton (Keate's Time)* (1888).

THE OLD ETONIAN AND DR KEATE

An old Etonian once met Keate abroad
And seized his hand; but he was rather floored
To see the Doctor seemed to know him *not*.
'Doctor,' quoth he, 'you've flogged me oft, I wot,
And yet it seems that me you've quite forgot.'
    'E'en now,' says Keate, 'I cannot guess your name;
Boys b-s are so very much the same.' (Anon, 1860, p.11)

The word 'bottom', that is, could not easily be printed. It was not decent, and its referent was a subject for sniggering, blushing – and, very often, flagellant fantasy.

Many of those who went through the flogging system as practised at Eton were likely to end up either completely hardened to the shame involved in birching or else as flagellants. Brinsley Richards comments perceptively on what modern psychologists would call his 'desensitisation' to such scenes:

I gradually came to witness the execution in the Lower School not only with indifference, but with amusement. I took no pleasure, however, in the thought that I might some day be scourged myself; for, in the first place, the physical sensations produced by birching did not seem to be pleasant; and in the next, I never could divest myself of the idea that it was shameful to be whipped in the way I have just described. (p.72)

But the awful day came and Richards found himself on the block:

Mr Carter whipped me with little less severity than if I had committed an offence which was morally heinous;[9] and I rose from my knees completely hardened as to any sense of shame either in the punishment I had undergone, or in others of the same kind I might have to suffer thereafter. (pp. 76-7)

Fifty years before the publication of Brinsley Richards's book, the *Edinburgh Review* had discussed the 'hardening' effect of the Eton flogging system. Criticising the 'unseemly punishment' in vogue at Eton, the anonymous writer stated:

We are ... convinced that nothing but habit, which deadens the minds of honourable men to the impropriety and indecorum of such an exhibition,

[9] Of Carter, Lord Redesdale wrote: 'clever, but perhaps a little too eager to exact a heavy payment for the pleasure of idleness' (1915, I, p.64).

could have concealed from them the inexpediency of the mode of punishment itself. (Anon, 1830, p.78)

In terms analogous to those employed by Brinsley Richards, the article referred to the brutalising effect on boys of witnessing such scenes, and pointed out that human nature being what it is, 'eyes and nerves soon get accustomed to cruel sights'. Bernard Shaw would say the same thing in his preface to *Misalliance* (1914) (and Shaw had had ample opportunity to study the mentality of modern birchites):

> We are tainted with flagellomania from our childhood. When will we realise that the fact that we can become accustomed to anything, however disgusting at first, makes it necessary for us to examine carefully everything we have become accustomed to? (1972, p.78)

In other words, we are all capable of becoming sadists. The floggers of Britain would have strongly resisted any such suggestion. They had been through the beating system and had become 'hardened'. At Eton the fear of being thought unmanly, of showing weakness under the rod, must have added to the efficacy of the hardening process, to the formation of tough hide and stiff upper lip. Any boy who flinched or cried when being birched was mercilessly 'chaffed' afterwards, and there was strong pressure on the victims to take their punishment 'like men'. During the debates on flogging that filled the nineteenth century, the pro-birchers would always remember *their* experience at school: 'We took our 'licking' stoutly, like the lad in Mr Kingsley's Westward Ho!', wrote 'Civilian' to *The Times* (16 November 1872). Having being hardened themselves, they naturally expected others to share their fortitude.

Not all parents took this attitude, however, and the case of Mr Morgan Thomas deserves more than a rapid glance.

The Morgan Thomas case

On 17 October 1856 the *Coventry Herald and Observer* printed part of a correspondence that had been exchanged the previous summer between a Mr Morgan Thomas of Sussex and the Provost and Headmaster of Eton; two letters written by Mr Thomas to his son's tutor, Mr Day, were also published in the same newspaper.

Mr Thomas claimed that the sole object of the correspondence was to achieve 'the abolition of that most glaring and disgraceful system of flogging practised at Eton', that 'ignoble and degrading punishment', that 'filthy and degrading practice'.

Here is what had happened. Morgan Thomas's eighteen-year-old son, Dalrymple, having been instructed by his father that from the age of 14 he must not submit 'to the, at his age, degrading and inappropriate infliction of the Rod', has taken his father at his word. Suspected of smoking – a cardinal sin at Eton – he has been 'complained of' by his tutor, sentenced to execution – and expelled for not submitting. It transpires further that Dr Goodford, the Headmaster, has offered 'no opportunities for mediation or argument', despite the fact that he is aware that the boy acted on his father's instructions. Nor has Goodford been in touch personally with the boy's father.

Morgan Thomas insists in his letter to Dr Hawtrey, the Provost, that but for the paternal injunction his son would willingly have submitted to the punishment, 'for strange to say! Eton boys have been so accustomed to these beastly exposures, that they have lost the disgust which otherwise nature and decency thus outraged would impart'. Referring to the 1847 Act under which a Justice had not the right to order a boy over 14 to be whipped, Thomas comments: 'If the Legislature spares the adult posteriors of juvenile offenders (even privately), surely the authorities of Eton might evince an equal indulgence (publicly) to those young gentlemen who have reached maturity?'

Morgan Thomas has no doubt about the dangers of Eton birchings, about the influence they may have on young boys:

> But surely it is not in vain to appeal to your own knowledge of what is decorous; it should be unnecessary to suggest that different ages as well as different offences merit and permit different punishments whether in quality or degree. Even nature proscribes this obscene practice, nor is much advancement in Physiology required to ensure adhesion to her mandate. *Why* do the boys crowd round to see a 'big fellow' – an adult – flogged?

In 1856 you could hardly get more explicit than that (note that at this time Upper School floggings, as we have seen, were still public). What did Dr Hawtrey make of the letter, the celebrated Dr Hawtrey who, as Headmaster from 1834 to 1852, had acquired for himself a considerable reputation as a flogger? Now Provost of Eton, Dr Hawtrey received Morgan Thomas's communication at his vicarage beside the Thames at Mapledurham (of *Wind in the Willows* fame). His reply was a masterpiece of evasion:

> SIR, – The subject to which your letters draw my attention seems to lie within a very narrow compass.

When you brought your son for admission to Eton you were fully aware of the system of discipline to which you were committing him.

You ordered your son to resist that discipline, when, by any offence usually so punished, he should incur the penalty.

Had you given this information in the proper quarter, the Head Master would have immediately told you that he could admit no boy on such conditions.

Such an occasion, as you had apparently contemplated, occurs; your son acts on your authority, and resists. The Head Master then for the first time hearing what had been your private instructions to your son, declines to retain him as his scholar.

Of course he will decline to retain your second son on similar conditions, and he will do rightly.

Hawtrey's letter provoked Morgan Thomas's scorn: 'I take leave to remark that it is no answer to that which I wrote to you ... I have a right to infer either that you feel ashamed of the practice of adult flogging, or are unable or afraid to justify it.'

Hawtrey played no further part in the debate.

Morgan Thomas's two letters to Mr Day, his son's tutor, are similarly frank. Flogging in the Eton style is seen, again, as an outrage to decency and self-respect, particularly when applied for some trivial offence. The survival of birching is a blot on the honour of a very great school and its practice unnecessary to the maintenance of discipline:

I hope that I am not the only gentleman who has made the same stipulation respecting submission to the degradation of the filthy punishment treated with such levity at Eton. There are reasons both physical and moral against this dirty practice after a certain time in life ... Up to a certain age, the boy may be thus punished with greater or less effect ... but after that age, the man should be made to feel that such an indecent exposure of his person is an impossibility, and such an assault insupportable.

That 'certain time in life' is, of course, puberty, and we remember again that these are pre-Freudian days. For the Victorians, sexuality was held to begin only on the appearance of the first pubic hair; and, for boys at any rate, fourteen was the critical age.

Morgan Thomas, in short, claims that he has the good of Eton at heart and feels that, if the school is to be improved, there must be 'a proper respect for young men's posteriors' as well as for the rest of their persons:

If discipline is to be maintained among gentlemen, it cannot be done by brute force but by a sensible appeal to their honour. And this must be instilled into their hearts, and not by the road of their naked bottoms!

It comes as a shock to see that last word published in a respectable newspaper in the 1850s. And as a relief, in the midst of so much cant and hypocrisy.

Morgan Thomas was by now up against the public school Establishment. He had mentioned in passing during the correspondence published by the *Coventry Herald* that, although he was no lover of *The Times*, this would not prevent him from airing his views there should the need arise. It seems that he sent a copy of the relevant copy of the *Coventry Herald* to *The Times*, for on 14 November 1856 that august newspaper commented on the case. It was a muddled and, one is tempted to say, hypocritical, leading article. *The Times* made no bones about its dislike of Morgan Thomas, and refrained from publishing the correspondence. In particular the leader insisted that Thomas had acted foolishly in not informing Dr Goodford of his instructions to his son. A fair point. But in a peculiar sentence *The Times* then went some of the way with the offended father:

> In the next place, with regard to the discipline of the rod, as practised at our public schools, no one will affirm it to be a suitable punishment for lads of 18, or to be such as they ought, under any other circumstances and in any other position, voluntarily to submit to. So far we agree with Mr THOMAS.

In other words, public school boys are different from the rest of humanity. The leader continues:

> But lads of 18 ought not to commit things worthy of punishment; and the question is, how are they to be dealt with when they do so? ... some short and simple mode of punishment must be devised, and rigidly enforced, if anything like discipline is to be maintained. The punishment of flogging answers this description; and we suppose it is retained for want of a better. No 'big boy' need submit to it unless he chooses; he has always the alternative of leaving the school.

Nor will *The Times* swallow all that nonsense about indecency and outrage to self-respect:

> As to the alleged indecency and degradation of such exhibitions as those referred to, we are greatly mistaken if 99 out of 100 Etonians would not pronounce it to be downright nonsense, and yet we have never heard it alleged that gentlemen who had been educated at that school were more deficient in self-respect and less governed by a sense of honour than others who had not smarted under the same rough discipline.

The lack of thought in the leader did not escape Morgan Thomas, and it was to the credit of the newspaper's editor that he was allowed to fire his Parthian shots a few days later (on 21 November 1856). *The Times*, he claimed, had evaded the issue, had attacked the man and not the argument. That issue was quite simple: is it right or wrong to flagellate, publicly or privately, the naked buttocks of schoolboys in their nineteenth year? If wrong, should it not be immediately abolished? These 'boys', after all, were fully-grown men. *The Times*, he pointed out, had itself admitted that to anyone but a public school boy such discipline would be unacceptable. Why are these lads to be treated differently from other mortals? Eton alone, apparently (but propped up by the attitudes represented by *The Times*) is incapable of even beginning to look for an alternative to flogging.

There is no overt indication that Morgan Thomas had read his Meibom, or that he believed that a schoolmaster might actually *enjoy* flogging a boy: 'I cannot for an instant harbour the thought that the Masters of Eton can take any pleasure in these unnatural exposures.' Yet one cannot resist the suspicion that such a thought had crossed his mind. Of course such an allegation made in a serious newspaper in the 1850s would have been received with fire and brimstone: it was better simply to hint at the sinister possibility by denying it.

On 19 November 1856, a few days after the publication of the leader in *The Times*, an anonymous letter appeared in *The Morning Post*, a newspaper which took a consistent pro-flogging line until well into the twentieth century. I quote it here because it shows how tenuous was the line between the genuine and the fake, the sincere and the pornographic, whenever corporal punishment was under discussion:

Flogging at Eton

To the Editor of the Morning Post

'Chasten thy son while there is hope, and let not thy soul spare for his crying.' Proverbs, XIX. 18.

SIR, – Your contemporary, *The Times*, has lately made a leading article out of the 'flogging at Eton'. He has *complained of*, and tickled up finely that father who would everlastingly be appealing to the honour of the boys. Let us hope the father will never repent the course which he has adopted. I knew a fond mother who, relative to this subject, exclaimed, 'It is quite shocking. Why does not the doctor *talk* to the boys?' – *talk* to 600 boys!

Now, I can vouch that, from the earliest days to the days of the immortal Keate, and thence to those of the present head-master, they have, one and all, appealed to the *very seat of honour*. 'Experientia docet.' And, mark me; flogging, used with sound judgement, is the only *fundamental* principle upon which our large schools can be properly conducted.

I am all the better for it and am, therefore,

ONE WHO HAS BEEN WELL *SWISHED*

This could be, and perhaps is, Swinburne (who particularly enjoyed using the joke about *fundamental* education) or one of his flagellant friends; I see no justification for accepting Ronald Pearsall's assumption that the writer is necessarily an 'elderly flagellant' (1972, p.409). But that it is the invention of some Etonian wit, elderly or otherwise, can hardly be doubted; nor can the fact that it is typical of hundreds of similar letters that appeared during the century and which we shall be looking at in a later chapter.

And there the Morgan Thomas case rested. It would be fifty-five years before the birch was abolished, and then only temporarily, in the Upper School. As for Dalrymple Thomas, it may be of interest to record that he seems to have survived the incident. He became a Colonel in the Royal West Kent Regiment; married Agnes, Countess Waldstein; and, in 1903, was living at San Remo.[10] One wonders if he continued to smoke in later life.

Tutors, fagging and bullying

Every boy going to Eton had first to be committed by his parents or guardians to the care of a *tutor*, whose private *pupil* he then became. The financial arrangements were made directly between parents and tutor. The tutors, all of whom had been *Collegers* at Eton themselves (that is, boys on the foundation), were also, of course, masters in the school. They were officially termed Assistant Masters ('Classical' being understood). Most of them had taken the usual course from Eton to the sister foundation of King's College, Cambridge, before returning to teach at their old school. It was a pretty incestuous, and a very traditional, system.

The 600 or 700 *Oppidans*, as opposed to the 70 Collegers maintained on the foundation who actually lived in the school, lodged either with their tutor or with a *dame* – the name for anyone, male or female, excepting tutors, who kept a boarding house. The tutor's house contained a *pupil room* where he instructed his boys and helped them with their preparation for school. And it was felt to be an advantage to board with one's own tutor.

[10] *The Eton Register* (1903), p.105.

The 'Clarendon Report' of 1864 provides detailed information on the running of the tutorial system at Eton.

Each tutor had approximately 40 private pupils, about 25 or 30 of whom might board in his house. In his *division* at school there would be a further forty or so boys, some of whom would inevitably be his own pupils. A tutor's life was busy – but lucrative.

Oscar Browning, who became an Assistant Master in 1860, has described the dual system of teaching that prevailed at Eton in his *Memories of Sixty Years* (1910):

> An Eton boy's education was given to him by two sets of teachers in two different places, by the division master in school, and by the tutor in his pupil-room; one the law, the other the equity of instruction. The school work, as it was called, was absolutely rigid, confined to certain Latin and Greek books, read again and again, until they were learnt by heart. (p.66)

It was part of a tutor's duty to help his pupils in the preparation of this school work and to hear their lessons before they went into school. This activity was known as 'school business'. But the tutor also engaged his pupils in extra-curricular 'private business'. Browning continues:

> Side by side with this school teaching was the work of the tutor, a thing difficult to explain to, or to be understood by, any one who has not personally experienced it ... The tutor was in the place of a parent, and did more for his charge than many parents do or can do. He had complete control of the boy, body, mind, and spirit, for six years. His duty was to know him thoroughly, to understand his character, the quality of his disposition, and how he might be trained and moulded to the greatest advantage. (p.66)

It follows that a pupil might suffer considerably at the hands of an incompetent or otherwise unsatisfactory tutor. And there is no doubt that the tutor was held to represent the child's parents:

> 3271. (*Lord Clarendon.*) I will ask Mr Balston's opinion regarding the tutorial system, which in most of the reports we have received is considered the keystone of the Eton system. Do you consider that the tutor does really stand *in loco parentis* to the boy? – Yes.

> 3272. That he attends not only to his educational progress during school, but to his individual character and to his moral and religious training? – Yes.

> 3273. Then, as far as can be, he represents the boy's parents? – Yes. (*Clarendon*, III, p.106)

It follows that, if the tutor stood *in loco parentis* to his pupil, he would be entitled to inflict corporal punishment upon him. This aspect of Eton discipline is never directly raised by the Clarendon Commissioners, although the Report does make it clear that offences committed in the boarding houses were dealt with there. W. Evans, for example, a well-known *dame*, stated that he 'never had occasion to appeal to the school to maintain discipline' (*Clarendon*, III, p.260). If this was so in the case of a man who was not even a Master at the school, then we can be certain that in matters of house discipline the tutors would have felt themselves quite competent to deal with their pupils themselves. The answers show, moreover, that each house had its own 'captain' chosen from among the pupils, and that this privileged boy might have the right delegated to him to 'lick' (beat) offenders. There is no doubt that some if not all tutors did inflict corporal punishment *in loco parentis* for misconduct or for other offences, which might include laziness at 'private business'. In *Eton in the Forties* (1898), Arthur Duke Coleridge recalled that one tutor, the Rev. William Cookesley, used to apply the cane with gusto to his charges:

> I was sent for by C–y, and found him raging at one of the boys in the pupil room. He addressed me thus: 'You are captain of the school. I want you to take and lick that boy within an inch of his life' – pointing to the delinquent. 'He has told me a lie, and he was to have been confirmed by the Bishop next week.' My plea was obvious. I was no longer a schoolboy, and whatever was to be done in the way of executioner's duty must be done by my successor. It was a merciful escape for me. I think I should have appealed to Hawtrey, and besought him to take the case out of my hands. I have since heard from a pupil of C–y's, that he had no objection whatever to administer personal chastisement to his own pupils, and that he could be very free with the 'doctor', as he called the cane which he kept for enforcing, or rather trying to enforce, discipline in his house. (pp. 357-8)

The relevance of these considerations will become apparent in a moment when we examine the relations between Swinburne and his tutor. But first, a word or two about fagging and bullying at Eton.

As has been mentioned, the staff-pupil ratio in the public schools was very low in the nineteenth century (about 17 masters to 600 or 700 boys at Eton during the 1840s). This encouraged the establishment of monitorial systems whereby power was delegated to particular senior boys to maintain discipline among their fellows. The advocates of the monitorial system felt that such an arrangement was character-building for all concerned: for those who were subject to the authority of their elders and for those wielding that authority. It was also maintained, by Dr Arnold among others, that such an institution helped to check bullying. During the 1872 Winchester controversy, to which reference was made earlier, Bonamy Price, Acting Headmaster of Rugby, spoke up in defence of the system and of the right of senior boys to administer corporal punishment to their wayward juniors:

> I hold now, as I did then, that the right of the Sixth Form or of its individual members to punish, subject to the considerations I have mentioned ... is an excellent element of our public school system; but no one felt more intensely than Dr Arnold that it imposed a most real responsibility, that never ceased for a moment, on both the Head Master and the Praeposters. It was his incessant effort not only to train the Praeposters and the school to self-government, but also to awaken and keep alive in them the sense that such powers could be justified only by a fitting development of character in the rulers. To rear the sixth first to govern themselves and thus to govern others was the very soul of the institution of a ruling Sixth Form at Rugby. (*The Times*, 19 November 1872)

The opponents of the system (and they were not thick on the ground) argued that what was needed was a fourfold increase in the number of masters; and that it was wrong that boys should be placed in a position of such power over their fellows, especially in the matter of corporal punishment.

Eton did not have monitors or prefects as such. It did, however, have a Sixth Form comprising the ten most senior boys in the school; and these enjoyed what were virtually monitorial powers, particularly over the 70 Collegers:

> 8761. (*Lord Clarendon.*) What punishment have they the power of inflicting? – They may thrash a boy, in rare cases, for very serious offences, but they generally content themselves with setting what are called epigrams. (*Clarendon*, III, p.281)

The evidence laid before the Commissioners showed that the Sixth Form's licence to inflict corporal punishment (with the cane) was frequently used and not infrequently abused; and that other brutalities were tolerated. The memoirs of Old Etonians corroborate this finding. Particularly instructive is Arthur Duke Coleridge's *Eton in the Forties* (1898), which has already been cited. The first chapter of this book gives a lurid account of the cruelty rampant in the College at the time. Coleridge became Captain of the School, and knows what he is talking about:

I would not unnecessarily hurt the feelings of any old colleger, but one of them hurt mine very considerably, and if he lives and reads my anathema, he will see I have not forgotten him for scoring me heavily with a birch on that part 'which cherubs lack',[11] and indulging at my cost in other pleasantries of a revolting description. The offence supposed to warrant amateur scourging was that I had escaped the headmaster's *triste lignum*, often probably as I had deserved it. The captains of Long Chamber, Upper Carter's and Lower Carter's Chamber, were good and merciful, but they winked at the ruffianism of my tormentor, who, as a sixth-form boy, could do as he pleased. It pleased him to steal a birch from the headmaster's cupboard; it pleased him still more to wield the instrument of justice, and rehearse all the formalities of a public execution upon an unoffending victim. (pp. 4-5)

Coleridge recalls another instance of bullying which deserves to be quoted for its lucidity:

Old Wykehamists are still to be found who defend 'tunding' as a wholesome form of chastisement; they will never bring me round to their opinion. Eton borrowed many of the good customs, and some of the bad, from the older foundation of Winchester. Amongst the bad, I reckon a traditional connivance at tyranny, in which upper boys, armed with a little brief authority, could, with impunity, indulge. I do not admire even a partial and limited power of corporal punishment vested in the sixth-form of certain schools, and I think that any sixth-form is in a bad way if it cannot enforce discipline amongst the lower boys without a cane, and a traditional license to use it. This conviction was forced upon me in my first year as an Eton colleger. My tormentor operated on other subjects besides myself, and one evening took to battering a friend of mine about the face and head so savagely, that the poor lad was kept in bed for days, until his bruises were healed. I was a witness of that performance, and shall not forget it to my dying day. I marvelled at the sixth-form boys at their supper-table, conscious of all the brutality going on, and never lifting a finger to interfere with their comrade's all-licensed cruelty. The chief executioner was safe – safe from the vengeance of his fellows, who dared not interfere with the exercise of his power; safe from the higher authorities, who must have screened such iniquity, from the fear of a public exposure of the system. (pp. 37-8)

Linked to the monitorial system was the institution of 'fagging',

---

[11] The phrase is from Samuel Coleridge via Charles Lamb. Lamb and Coleridge were contemporaries at Christ's Hospital. Their headmaster, James Bowyer, was a notorious flogger. According to Lamb, Coleridge exclaimed on hearing of Bowyer's death: 'Poor J.B.! – may all his faults be forgiven; and may he be wafted to bliss by little cherub boys, all head and wings, with no *bottoms* to reproach his sublunary infirmities' (Lamb, 1962, p.24).

which in one form or another existed at almost all the public schools. The anonymous *Guide to Eton* explains:

> Fag, a Lower Boy who performs some trifling offices for an Upper Boy, such as laying his breakfast or tea; sometimes (but uncommonly, as it is against the Rules), lighting his fire. Upper Boys are sometimes mean enough to send Lower Boys to the tobacconist, which is a certain flogging if the boy is caught. The *gentlemen* of the fifth Form would not do this ... Fagging is the remains of the old feudal idea. The Fag performing any small offices of which he is capable for his master, who on his side is bound to protect and assist his Fag, saving him from being bullied, reproving and advising him, should reproof or advice be needful ... A Fag's 'master' may have great influence for good or bad on his Fag, and is most culpably responsible if he does not use it for good. They should be most careful that attendance on themselves should not interfere with their Fag's meals or lessons. (Anon, 1860, pp. 20-1)

'Lower Boys' were all boys below the Fifth Form and should not be confused with those in the Lower School. In practice the fags were drawn from the Fourth Form, and this meant that a boy entering Eton at the age of twelve could expect to spend two or three years as a fag, since the Fourth Form was divided into several 'divisions'. In a perfect world the fagging system might have had its merits; but all too often it degenerated into a licence for sadism. This was all the more likely to happen since the right to have a fag was conferred at puberty.

Bullying was widespread at Eton, and there is no doubt that the fag's lot was often not a happy one. The fifth- and sixth-formers, having been bullied themselves as Lower Boys, frequently abused their power. The anonymous 1830 *Edinburgh Review* article already quoted put the anti-fagging case vehemently. 'A boy begins as a slave, and ends as a despot,' it said. 'Corrupting at once and corrupted, the little tyrant riots in the exercise of boundless and unaccountable power; and while he looks back on his former servitude, is resolved that the sufferings which he inflicts shall not be less than those which he endured' (p.76). The system of fagging is 'the only regular institution of slave-labour, enforced by brute violence, which now exists in these islands' (p.75), and the fag-masters 'are restrained by nothing but their own forbearance and sense of honour' (pp. 75-6). If the fag fails in any way to perform his duties satisfactorily, 'he is liable to be beaten, at the will of his master, by his master, and at the moment of passion, either with the fists, or any other instrument' (p.76). The author of the article has no illusions, either, concerning the pleasure to be derived from the exercise of such power: 'We only wish,' he exclaims, 'that these inflictions never proceeded from wanton cruelty – from that extraordinary pleasure of inflicting physical pain, which seems to reign in the breasts of many boys and children' (p.76).

There were frequent discussions in the newspapers during the nineteenth century about the fagging systems in operation at the public schools. A correspondence headed 'Bullying at Eton' ran in *The Standard* between the 6 and 19 November 1862. One of the letters deserves to be quoted:

> SIR, – I observe in your impression of yesterday various letters, professing to be from men who have been, or are just now being, educated at Eton, advocating the system of fagging at present carried on there. According to their statements one would naturally suppose that fagging is one of the most beneficial customs in existence. The accounts given of it, and the arguments adduced in its defence, smack rather strongly of the sixth form; and appear to me, who have lately been subjected to its baneful influence, to be rather more rosy-coloured than the bare facts of the case would warrant.
>
> Sir, I, and no doubt other men, could lay before you instances of persistent cruelty, perpetrated on juniors at that school, for no better reason than that their blood was a little darker than that of their persecutors or that they refused to pander to the odious vices of their worthless tyrants. Is it possible for an Etonian of a few years standing, to forget the ill-usage, in consequence of which R– drags out an existence burdensome to himself, and remains a monument of those excesses into which, through fagging, he was forced? To many of your readers what I here say may appear exaggerated and utterly unworthy of credence; but had they suffered as I have done they would feel that the language which I have employed is only too tame, and that the pages of any other than a medical journal are not the place for enlarging on this painful subject..I think it is high time that the press should advocate the appointment of a commission of inquiry in reference to this matter, and I leave to them the duty of making public the innumerable abuses of which the system of fagging is the immediate cause ... (18 November 1862, p.2)

This letter, signed 'An Old Etonian', caught the eye of Richard Monckton Milnes, who commented in his commonplace book: 'a dreadful example of the excesses brought on by the fagging system.'[12]

Gilbert Coleridge's *Eton in the Seventies* (1912) shows that, at that time, the fag masters enjoyed their privilege to beat as much as they had done during the days of his father (whose *Eton in the Forties* has

---

[12] Milnes's commonplace books, eighteen of them, dating from 1840 to 1865, are among the Houghton Papers in Trinity College Library, Cambridge. The writing is at times extremely difficult to decipher. This quotation is from Houghton 213 (1860-61-62-63-64), p.111 recto (by my calculation – the pages are not numbered).

already been mentioned): 'A slipper, or if the fag-master was possessed of that badge of ineffable superiority, a cane, applied smartly to the tight trouser of a bent figure was a sufficient incentive to efficient carrying and cooking' (p.9).

From what has been said, it can be seen that beating and the threat of beating pervaded the Eton system at every level, not to mention the other forms of bullying common among the boys. To study the effect that such a system could have on sensitive children, let us now turn our attention to Algernon Charles Swinburne, who must surely rank as England's and Eton's most distinguished flagellant.

Swinburne and the birch

Swinburne's life-long obsession with birching is now – after many years of obfuscation and hesitation by the scholars – a well-known fact, although the notorious flagellant MSS in the British Library have still not been published. It has not been easy for the English Establishment to come to terms with the realities of Swinburne's 'secret life', his visits to flagellant brothels and his involvement in the world of flagellant pornography. Perhaps this reluctance derives from the fact that the poet's flagellant writings can be considered a product of public school practices that still obtain, albeit in a modified form, in our own time. Nonetheless, we have come a long way from Gosse's biography (1917), in which not a single reference to this aspect of Swinburne's personality and work is to be found; and recent studies of the poet, notably those by Jean Fuller (1968) and Philip Henderson (1974), have placed due emphasis on flagellation. It must be said, however, that neither of these writers is particularly perceptive on the subject.

Swinburne entered Eton in the spring term of 1849 at the age of twelve, having been coached for six months by the Rev. Collingwood Forster Fenwick, Rector of Brook in the Isle of Wight. He had passed the entrance examination to the Upper School successfully, and was placed in the upper division of the Fourth Form.[13] Swinburne, that is, was never in the Lower School.

There is no doubt, from the endless and detailed descriptions of Eton-style birchings that fill the unpublished flagellation pieces, that the future poet exercised his right on numerous occasions to be present at public birchings. The lurid evocations that pack the 165 MS sheets of Swinburne's mock-epic poem *The Flogging-Block* (154 of

---

[13] Lafourcade (1928), I, p.86.

them written on both sides)[14] have a ring of authenticity, although, to
be sure, they are much exaggerated:

> Daily rations of birch have been Algernon's fare
> For a fortnight at least, on the whipping-block, where
> He is kneeling once more, and exposing a bare
> Broad tawny big bottom – Algy's red head
> Is no redder, perhaps, than another boy's, bred
> Of a stock whose red hair is proverbial, it's said:
> But where shall we find a boy's bottom as red?[15]
>
> ('Charlie's Flogging')

> His recent sores had just begun to heal,
>   But every eye that looked his bottom o'er
> Saw many and many and many a bloody weal
>   And many and many and many a red ridge raised before
> By many and many a stripe that left it sore
>   From many and many a birch worn out in vain
> On Redgie's bare posteriors, bared once more
>   To feel once more the red rod plied amain
> And writhe and smart and burn and tingle with the pain.
>
> ('Reginald's Flogging')

The concentration on the buttocks we know to be a *sine qua non* of
the flagellant phenomenon, and Swinburne is no exception to the rule.
Indeed he is bottoms-mad, and there is no reference in any of the
flogging pieces to the genitals: the eyes feed greedily on the buttocks,
but only on the buttocks. Swinburne's flagellant compositions are
notable for their rampant voyeurism, for their insistence on the
pleasure with which the boys view the sufferings inflicted on the
posteriors of their fellows. When their own turn comes they never
enjoy the experience. The master, also, is portrayed as deriving overt
pleasure from the performances at which he is only too happy to
officiate:

> There's one thing all present agree in hating
> To be kept overlong in prolonged expectation
> Of the sight and the sense of a boy's flagellation.
>
> ('Charlie's Flogging')

---

[14] For the full title page of this work, see the Bibliography (Swinburne).
[15] Swinburne's red hair was by all accounts magnificent.

How those great big red ridges must smart as they swell!
How the Master does like to flog Algernon well!
How each cut makes the blood come in thin little streaks
From that broad blushing round pair of naked red cheeks.

('Algernon's Flogging')

Hard as the hard old wooden Flogging-Block
The Faces are, that meet my Face and mock:
My Cousin chuckles, and my Brother grins,
To see their Junior suffering for his sins:
At each fresh Birchen Stroke they smile afresh
To see 'the young one' suffer in the Flesh.
Each time the Twigs bend round across my Bum
Pain bids 'Cry out', but Honour bids 'Be dumb'.

(Prologue to *The Flogging-Block*)

Swish! Fiercer the master's dark eyeballs grow now than the eye of a dragon
is!
Each schoolboy is thrilled by the sight of his bare-bottomed schoolfellow's
agonies.

('Rupert's Flogging')

The two poems contributed by Swinburne to the anonymous *The Whippingham Papers* (1888)[16] also stress the master's pleasure:

'What makes you late, sir?' with a smile and a frown
Of outward wrath and cruel inward joy,
Replied the master ...

('Arthur's Flogging')

So Arthur's bottom seems, between the cuts,
To vibrate under his tormentor's hands
Who, gloating on it, as he flogs it, gluts
His eyes with the full prospect, while these great
Cheeks contract at each cut, and dilate ...

('Reginald's Flogging')

Swinburne, we can be sure, witnessed many floggings at Eton. But was he himself ever whipped by Dr Hawtrey, or by his successor, Dr Goodford? We know that he was 'sent up for good' to Hawtrey on two occasions (that is, to receive the headmaster's compliments for his work), and there is indirect evidence that he was also sent up to be

---

[16] For details of this curious work and Swinburne's contributions to it, see in the Bibliography under (1) anon. (1888) and (2) Swinburne. It is worth pointing out that Whippingham is a town on the Isle of Wight near Cowes. Swinburne spent the greater part of his childhood on the island, at Bonchurch. The name of Whippingham must have greatly amused him.

beaten by him. Certainly Dr Birkenshaw, the flogging headmaster of *The Flogging-Block*'s Much Birchingham School, Rodbury, Northumberland, seems to owe something to Hawtrey who, as we know, was a proficient flogger and given to sarcastic or witty observations between strokes. In 'Another Epilogue' to 'Reginald's Flogging' we find the following exchange between Redgie and a voyeuristic Old Etonian who has been privileged to witness the latter's birching (the cancelled passages in the MS are italicised):

> *Reginald*. Please, were you often swished, sir?
> *Old Etonian*.   Twice a week,
>   *can?* Hawtrey
>   At least. *You wonder how he deigns to speak*
>   *To me* But *you* just beat us all for cheek.

The fact that Hawtrey came into Swinburne's mind as he was working on this passage is of some interest, and may indicate that the headmaster's dexterity with the rod had made an impression on the boy's body as well as on his imagination. And a revealing letter to his Old Etonian friend, George Powell (at Eton from 1855 to 1860)[17] dated 13 August 1867 does suggest that Swinburne had on occasion found himself 'in the bill': 'I don't think I ever more dreaded the entrance of the swishing room than I now desire a sight of it. To assist unseen at the holy ceremony some after twelve I would give *any* of my poems.'[18]

But despite the likelihood that Swinburne had tasted Hawtrey's rod, it is to his tutor that we must turn if we wish to know the real villain of the piece.

Swinburne's tutor, with whom he lodged, was the Rev. James Leigh Joynes (1824-1908). Like all the tutors at Eton, Joynes had himself been a Colleger (1836-44) and King's, Cambridge, man before returning to Eton as an Assistant Master. This he did in the spring term of 1849, that is to say at precisely the same time that Swinburne entered the school.[19] Joynes was then 23, Swinburne 12. Joynes had taken his degree at Cambridge in 1848 and been ordained deacon in the same year.[20] In 1854, a year after Swinburne left Eton, he was

---

[17] *The Eton Register, Part II, 1853-1859* (1905), p.60.

[18] Lang, I, pp. 259-60 (details of this edition of the Swinburne letters have already been given in Chapter Two, note 3, p.58).

[19] *The Eton Register* (1903), p.2.

[20] From the obituary published in *The Times*, 30 June 1908, p.1.

ordained priest.[21] Years later, in 1878, 'Jimmy', as he was known to the boys, was elevated to the position of Lower Master, and on his retirement in 1887 a celebrated caricature in *Vanity Fair* (16 July 1887) showed him brandishing a large birch rod and pointing grimly to the block (see Plate 14). This portrayal, according to A.C. Benson, 'was like the original in a sense, but only in one, and that a rare mood' (p.90). The writer of the *Vanity Fair* commentary accompanying the caricature, however, asserted that Joynes

> is old-fashioned in his notions, has a pious horror of modern innovations, has handled the birch with an unsparing hand and has usually accompanied his stripes either with a grim word of warning, or a biting jest addressed to the victim at the block; so that he has left a lasting impression on many generations of little boys. Personally he is the most genial of men.

The *Vanity Fair* description, of course, is of a later Joynes whom Swinburne never knew, but there is little reason to believe that he had been a milder man in his early days at Eton – the years when, to take Oscar Browning's words quoted earlier, he would have had 'complete control' of Swinburne's 'body, mind and spirit'.

In his published letters Swinburne only refers twice to Joynes by name, and neither mention has much interest for our purposes (Lang, IV, p.171; VI, p.254). On another occasion he recalls how infinitely kind Mrs Joynes had been to him 'at an age when I most needed kindness' (Lang, IV, p.321). But there is one letter, one extraordinary letter, which seems to refer to Joynes and which has caused many an eyebrow to rise since its publication by Professor Lang. At this time the poet was obsessed with the Marquis de Sade's *Justine*, which Richard Monckton Milnes had lent him in the summer of 1862,[22] and in the letter in question (to Milnes) he criss-crosses his outpourings with references to the fustigations administered in that book by the sinister Rodin to the unfortunate inmates of his sadic school. 'Redgie' is, of course, Swinburne himself. Lang dates the letter *ca.* 10 February 1863:

> If I might add one criticism [of a flagellant effusion by Milnes] I should say no one birching was sufficiently circumstantial. Redgie and I used to suffer more than that in the simple orthodox way at the hands of the tutor

[21] *ibid.*

[22] According to Lang, I, p.54, note 3, Swinburne read, not the 1791 *Justine* but the 'preposterously ruttish and scatological' *La Nouvelle Justine ou Les Malheurs de la vertu* of 1797.

I have told you of. His great idea (I believe *really* he had some idea of the sort) was *to inflict no pain elsewhere while the swishing proceeded.* I should have been thankful (barring the *insult* which we should have resented) for the *diversion* of a box on the ear, such as Rodin's superincumbent John 'bestowed'.[23] I have known him (I am really speaking now in my own person) perfume the flogging-room (*not* with *corduroy* or *onion* but) with burnt scents; or choose a *sweet* place out of doors with smell of firwood. *This* I call real delicate torment. Please tell me what you think. Once, before giving me a swishing that I had the marks of for more than a month (so fellows declared that I went to swim with), he let me saturate my face with eau-de-Cologne. I conjecture now, on looking back to that 'rosy hour' with eyes 'purged by the euphrasy and rue'[24] of the Marquis de Sade and his philosophy, that, counting on the pungency of the perfume and its power over the nerves, he meant to stimulate and excite the senses by that preliminary pleasure so as to inflict the acuter pain afterwards on their awakened and intensified susceptibility. If he did, I am still gratified to reflect that I beat him; the poor dear old beggar overreached himself, for the pleasure of smell is so excessive and intense with me that even if the smart of birching had been unmixed pain, I could have borne it all the better for that previous indulgence. Perhaps he had no such idea, and I, grown over-wise through perusal of Justine and Juliette, now do him more than justice; but he was a stunning tutor; his one other pet subject was *metre*, and I firmly believe that my ear for verses made me rather a favourite. I can boast that of all the swishings I ever had up to seventeen and over, I never had one for a false quantity in my life. (Can you say the same? I should imagine you *metrical* as a boy). One comfort is, I made it up in arithmetic, so my tutor never wanted reasons for making rhymes between his birch and my body.

You must excuse my scribbling at this rate when I once begin, for the sake of that autobiographical fact about perfume and pain, which you can now vouch for as the experience of a real live boy. I always wanted to know if other fellows shared the feeling. Conceive trying it in a grove of budding birch-trees scented all over with the green spring. Ah-h-h! (Lang, I, pp. 77-8)[25]

[23] This is almost certainly a reference to the flagellant poem *The Rodiad*, in my view composed by Milnes. This matter is discussed more fully in Chapter Six. In the next line, Lang has transcribed 'perfume' incorrectly as 'prepare'. The MS of the letter is among the Houghton Papers in Trinity College Library, Cambridge.

[24] Lang (I, p.78) identifies the source of this allusion: Milton, *Paradise Lost*, Book XI, 1. 414.

[25] Milnes's (almost illegible) reply to this letter is in the British Library, Ashley B. 1984. It is dated August 22 [1862]: 'I think you underrate the intelligence of the book ... Rodin, to my mind, is the hero of the book: after I read it I saw him in every doctor and naturalist[?] that came in my way.' There are references in Milnes's letter to 'Frank Fane' and 'Reggie', much birched schoolboys who appear in many of Swinburne's flagellant pieces. Another letter from Milnes to Swinburne, dated 'Thurs. 1st November' [1866] (Ashley B. 4362, VI, p.64) is also concerned with flagellant matters.

Swinburne, while himself allowing the influence of *Justine* (and *Juliette*) on these musings, nonetheless insists that the birchings really took place as described, and that they were inflicted by 'the tutor I have told you of'. That Swinburne had indeed talked to his friend before about these beatings is confirmed by a passage in one of Milnes's commonplace books. The entry, published here for the first time, was made in November 1862. It reads:

> Algernon Swinburne with a tutor who flogged him over the fallen trunk of a tree, till the grass was stained with his blood and another time when wet out of the water after bathing: the last much the more painful! His dreadful disappointment at seeing the big boys at Eton getting off with a few unimpressive switches. Tutor telling him he had no pleasure in flogging boys who were not gentlemen: the better the family the more he enjoyed it. The tutor once flogging him in 3 different positions till he was quite flayed. A.S. very fair, the tutor often flogging a very dark boy by way of contrast, making them hold [?] each other. Using different rods – sometimes made of the lower [?] twigs of fir with the buds on. Calling A.S. Pepper-bottom.[26]

If Swinburne was telling the truth, it would seem from this account that Bertie Seyton's birching when wet from bathing in *Lesbia Brandon* derived from the author's own experience.[27] Perhaps on the occasion he was birched by his tutor, Swinburne had broken bounds to swim at Cuckoo Weir on the Thames, for in his densely autobiographical (and appallingly bad) tragedy *The Sisters* (1892) we find the following exchange:

Frank.	Let's be cool.
	I have not seen you quite so hot and red
	Since you were flogged for bathing at the Weir.
Reginald.	Which time? the twentieth?
Frank.	That at least.
Mabel.	Poor fellow! (Act III, sc.i, pp. 57-8))

The smell of firwood seems to have been specially connected in Swinburne's mind with birchings, for echoing his words to Milnes he

---

[26] Houghton 213 (1860-61-62-63-64), p.21. Cf. 'Reginald's Flogging' in *The Flogging-Block* where the master says to Reginald:
'You are nicknamed, I hear, in the lower division,
Pepperbottom – a term of appropriate derision.'

[27] *Lesbia Brandon* was not Swinburne's title for this work, which was edited and published for the first time by Randolph Hughes in 1952. For the episode in question, see p.19.

wrote to Charles Augustus Howell in 1865: 'I send you a fresh sample of Dolores. If you are amiable and write me something stimulating as the smell of firwoods, you shall have the rest' (Lang, I, p.123). The 'something stimulating', as the remaining paragraphs of the letter make clear, is to be a flagellant dialogue between a schoolmaster and boy.

A group of three letters written by Swinburne in the autumn of 1864 to his cousin Mary Gordon, who shared his interest in the birch, also refer to a flogging he received from his tutor, this time for daring to indulge in some unorthodox metrical experiments with galliambics: 'I *tried* ... to do my week's verses in it once, and my tutor said it was no metre at all and he wouldn't take them, because it was an impertinence to show such a set up, so it counted as if I had done nothing, and the consequences were tragic' (Lang, I, p.110). The second letter records Swinburne's triumph when another master, to whom he showed the condemned exercise, expressed the opinion that the galliambics were very competent. 'But that,' recalls the poet, 'did not heal the cuts or close the scars' (Lang, I, p.110). Swinburne liked his phrase concerning the 'tragic consequences'. In a letter to W.M. Rossetti some years later (1869) he noted of a critic that 'he *could* mis-spell in a way the consequences of which at Eton ... would have been tragical – not to say Sadical' (Lang, II, p.10); and, in describing to Milnes (1864) a colourful flogging scene, he observed that 'the consequences in that case were tragic' (Lang, IV, p.136).

Two further references to Swinburne's birching tutor occur in the letters to Milnes. In the first of these, written in 1863, the poet alludes to their rival undertaking to produce flagellant material: 'If I can't match them [Milnes's 'revelations' concerning *his* victim, Frank] it must be my tutor's fault. I could put in delicious and pungent details from memories not much more than seven years old yet. (Less by a year or two now I think of it. Signed – Reginald) Voyons!' (Lang, I, p.72).

Then in 1876, during the Wilberforce scandal (see pp. 150-1), Swinburne reminded Milnes of what he told him some years earlier (recorded, as we have seen, in the latter's commonplace book):

> My tutor, I know, used always to say – indeed I've sometimes heard him myself – there was no perfect satisfaction but in flogging a boy of good family ... *I* have always maintained that he used to whip his pupils according to the number of their quarterings – increasing the quantity and severity of the cuts inflicted in a direct ratio. And I know I've got sixteen at least (quarterings, not cuts). (Lang, III, p.192)

The evidence, then, that Swinburne was birched by Joynes is very strong. And it looks as if the tutor was something of a dilettante flagellant. I have spent some time setting out the evidence because there has been a tendency to assume that Swinburne's flagellant writings of Etonian inspiration were the product of perversity rather than experience: to see Swinburne as one of Krafft-Ebing's congenital degenerates and not as the unfortunate victim of English flagellomania. With this tendency has often gone sheer ignorance of the ways in which Etonian discipline functioned. Thus A.E. Housman, to take but one example, wrote to Edmund Gosse in 1919 after reading the latter's confidential paper on Swinburne's 'moral irregularities': 'The Eton anecdote on p.19 is perplexing, because Etonians tell me that the only person privileged to flog is the headmaster' (1971, p.159).

As regards Swinburne's brief experience as a fag (he entered the non-fagging Fifth Form in 1850) we have virtually no information, except that he himself recalled that he was frequently neglectful (Lang, III, p.229). We can assume that he was subjected to the usual rigours, and one wonders if he may have been thinking back to his own days in the Fourth Form when he made Reginald Harewood say in the densely autobiographical *A Year's Letters*:

> They want to diplomatize me; I am to have some secretaryship or other under Lord Fotherington. If anything comes of it I shall leave England next month. I shall have Arthur Lunsford for a colleague and one or two other fellows I know about me. A.L. was a fearful swell in our schooldays and used to ride over the heads of us lower boys with spurs on. I wonder if Frank remembers what a tremendous licking he got once for doing Lunsford's verses for him *without* a false quantity, so that when they were shown up he was caught out and came to awful grief? I don't know if I ever believed in anything as I did once in the get-up of that fellow. To have him over one again will be very comic; he never *could* get on without fags. Do you think the service admits of his licking them? I suspect he might thrash me still if he tried: you know what a splendid big fellow he is. (Sylpher ed., p.111)

The hero worship of the smaller boy for the bigger that this passage reveals is typical of Swinburne, as we shall see later, and a vital element in his flagellant MSS. It should be recalled in this connection that Joynes, when Swinburne was placed in his care, was only twelve years his senior – little more than a Sixth Former. Given that most young boys are likely to find an idol among their older schoolfellows, there can be no doubt that the power of the latter to inflict corporal punishment must greatly enhance the development of homosexual and sado-masochistic tendencies and attachments.

Before leaving the subject of fags, we can take it that Swinburne himself took advantage of the system when he entered the Fifth Form in 1850. The only Swinburne scholar to mention this aspect of the poet's time at Eton, to my knowledge, is Lafourcade. I have not been able to identify the source of his information (which I translate from the French):

> In 1850 Swinburne obtained third place in the 'Fagging Division Trials', examinations which gave successful candidates the right to have a fag.[28] By one place he beat the future Dr Warre, a famous scholar who would later become headmaster of Eton. His first thought was to choose among his comrades available as fags the biggest and strongest boy he could find: 'Davis, carry these books to my room', the huge boy doing as he was told with a sense of humiliation. Intelligence had triumphed over brute force.[29] (1928, I, p.83)

If Lafourcade's information is correct, the only possible candidate as Swinburne's fag seems to be a certain Francis Byam Davies (sic) (at Eton, 1848-52) who was still 'stuck' in the Fourth Form in 1850, by which time the clever Swinburne had progressed to the Fifth, and who may therefore have been physically large (*énorme?*) while at the same time not very good at his lessons. Davies was killed at Sebastopol in 1854, and one would like to think that he nurtured no grievance against the future poet.[30]

Swinburne left Eton suddenly at the end of the summer term in 1853. He was sixteen, and had not yet reached the top of the school. He had proved himself an excellent classical scholar, had won the Prince Consort's prize for French and Italian in 1853 (having taken second prize in French in 1852). He seemed destined to be one of the most outstanding boys in the school. What had happened? Gosse states that serious friction had developed between Joynes and his pupil during 1853, and his source may well have been the poet himself: 'He became less amenable to discipline and idler at his work' and had 'increasing trouble with Joynes of a rebellious kind' (1917, p.26). Fuller (1968) suggests that Swinburne's 'peculiar attitude to

[28] It seems clear that the 'Fagging Division' was another way of referring to the Fifth Form.

[29] 'En 1850, aux "Fagging Division Trials" (examens qui permettent aux candidats reçus de prendre un *fag*), Swinburne obtient le troisième rang (avant le futur Dr Warre, érudit fameux qui sera principal d'Eton) et son premier soin est de choisir parmi ses camarades disponibles comme *fags*, le plus gros et le plus fort qu'il puisse trouver: "Davis, portez ces livres dans ma chambre", et l'énorme garçon de s'exécuter avec humiliation. L'intelligence triomphe de la force brutale.'

[30] *The Eton Register* (1903), p.100.

punishment' may have been a contributory factor in the decision of the Eton authorities to request or suggest his removal (p.27). Certainly one's impression of Joynes is that Swinburne, as he matured, would have found him intolerably stuffy;[31] and one is not surprised to discover that the tutor's own son was also a rebel – and a Socialist one at that.[32] There are numerous touches in Swinburne's 'autobiographical' works which suggest that a battle of the wills may indeed have developed between the two, and it seems likely that it was Joynes who suggested that it would be preferable if Swinburne were to be removed from the school. Swinburne's *alter egos* in the 'autobiographical' writings and the flogging poems are always in trouble with the authorities, especially for their rebelliousness. In this respect Reginald Harewood in *A Year's Letters* is particularly Swinburnian.

Swinburne never forgot his experience of the birch or the scenes he witnessed when other boys came under the rod. After his invocation to the Muse of Whipping at the beginning of *The Flogging-Block*, inspiration descends in a passage of Etonian reminiscence:

She hears! She hears! Already on my Eyes
Scenes once but too familiar seem to rise:
Again I see, and shudder at my Doom,
The dark high Precinct of the Flogging-Room;
The Block so long familiar to my Knee,
The Birch to none more cruel than to me;
With Arm raised high I see my Master stand
And grasp the brandished Rod with sinewy Hand;
The supple Twigs, the swelling Buds I view
That once too well my burning Buttocks knew ...

[31] According to A.C. Benson (1924), 'in spite of this almost roguish cheerfulness of demeanour, I do not think that Joynes had any deep sense of humour. Indeed he was generally rather shocked by it' (p.97). A.C. Ainger wrote (1917): 'He was a good scholar and a good disciplinarian, but his intellectual and literary range was limited, and, though he was kind and sympathetic with the boys, he did not make much attempt to adapt himself to their various natures and dispositions. Swinburne was his pupil, and boarded in his house – an awkward duckling for such a hen' (pp. 236-7). Henry Salt, who married Joynes's daughter, probably gives the most balanced view of the man (1928). For Salt, 'of the sense of humour he was by no means devoid' (p.127). When Salt met Swinburne at Putney, 'the poet made many most friendly inquiries about his "dear old tutor" ' (*ibid.*).

[32] Wrote Benson (1924): 'His eldest son was for a time a master at Eton, but he adopted somewhat extreme socialistic and vegetarian views, and was actually arrested as a political agitator in Ireland in the late seventies, where he had gone as a propagandist on a self-sought mission. He was a writer of considerable force and charm, but died prematurely' (p.96).

In the poet's letters to Richard Monckton Milnes, which span the years from 1861 to 1882, the theme of Etonian birchings recurs constantly. Milnes himself had not attended any public school, let alone Eton, and was incurably inquisitive about all matters concerning inflictions of the pedagogical rod.

George Powell, unlike Milnes, had been to Eton – shortly after Swinburne. To him, at least, the poet did not have to explain what birching was all about. On 3 August 1867 he wrote to Powell:

> I should like to see two things there again the river – and the block. Can you tell me any news of the latter institution or any of its present habitués among our successors? the topic is always most tenderly interesting – with an interest, I may say, based upon a common bottom of sympathy. (Lang, I, p.256)

Powell, as always, was only too happy to oblige his beloved poet. Having two cousins at Eton at the time, he began informing himself about current executions at the block. In this he was brilliantly successful, and not long afterwards Swinburne wrote delightedly to a friend that Powell had not only culled for him 'some newly-budded "blossoms of the block" ' (*ibid.*, p.258) but had actually managed to procure – gift of gifts! – a real birch, fresh from the bloody fray. On 13 August he wrote to Powell 'I long to thank you in person and to enjoy the sight and touch of the birch that has been used' (*ibid.*, p.259).

Powell also used his good offices to obtain for Swinburne a photograph of the block. The poet was somewhat disappointed both with its size and unavoidable lack of animation:

> What a pity the scene is imperfect, a stage without actors, a hearth without fire, a harp without cords [sic], a church without worshippers, a song without music, a day without sunlight, a garden without flowers, a tree without fruit! I would give anything for a good photograph taken at the right minute – say the tenth cut or so – and doing justice to *all sides* of the question. As it is the block is just at the right angle for such a representation. If I were but a painter – ! I would do dozens of different fellows diversely suffering. (*ibid.*, p.265)

Simeon Solomon *was* a painter, and a flagellant. In a letter to Swinburne of 1863[33] he promised 'on my return I will make you many drawings' (*ibid.*, II, p.35). The same letter contains a sketch of the

---

[33] Lang (II, p.32) proposes the date 1869 for this letter but admits that this is the 'merest guess'. Fuller (1968) has shown that 1863 is almost certainly the correct date (p.177).

Queen 'presenting rods to the Schoolmasters of the United Kingdom', all kneeling to receive the priceless gift.

We have seen that another close friend of Swinburne, the Anglo-Portuguese Charles Augustus Howell, was involved in the composition of flagellant scenes for the poet. A competent draughtsman, Howell also turned out flagellant drawings that Swinburne seems to have much appreciated. 'There's a note for you which deserves a *lovely* sketch of switching by return of post,' the poet wrote to him in 1866. 'Send one, and make a day to call soon' (*ibid.*, I, p.179). In 1873 he made a similar request of Howell: 'Dis donc, Charlie, tu serais bien bon enfant de m'envoyer un croquis tel quel pour me désennuyer – never mind how rough it is, it would always amuse and give me pleasure to look at.' In return for this drawing Swinburne promised Howell 'a sonnet or a stanza. Voilà' (*ibid.*, II, p.229). Clearly the poet felt that such an exchange would be advantageous to both parties.

Randolph Hughes believed that Howell was also prepared to make a more robust contribution to Swinburne's need for flagellant stimulation: 'It is pretty evident,' wrote Hughes to Helen Rossetti Angeli, 'that when Swinburne was in town Howell was at least occasionally one of those who played the part of a flagellant schoolmaster to him, and thus gratified a *penchant* acquired by the poet during his troublous Eton days'.[34]

It seems that, while mainstream pornographic photographs were widely available by the 1860s, flagellant pictures were more difficult to come by. Flagellant etchings accompanying the types of publication which will be mentioned in a later chapter tended to be of poor quality. As a result, any good illustrations were bound to be prized by the connoisseurs. Little wonder, then, that Swinburne became impatient with his publisher John Camden Hotten (who did a special line in flagellant books), to whom he had unwisely lent his photograph of the Eton block: 'Will you get back and send me *at once* the photograph I lent long ago of the 'Eton block' etc.? *today if possible* I want it' (Lang, I, p.306).

Photographs of the flogging block appear to have become openly available at Eton later in the century, for in 1874 Powell received the following complaint from the poet: '*how* could you be at Eton and not remember to invest for me in at least two of the large photographs of the flogging-block, when you knew how I wanted them and was shy of writing to order them? Oh monsieur!' (*ibid.*, II, p.290).

[34] Helen Angeli Rossetti, *Pre-Raphaelite Twilight. The Story of Charles Augustus Howell*, 1954, p.178.

In 1890 Eton celebrated its 450th anniversary. Swinburne was invited to contribute a poem to mark the occasion, and came up with 'Eton: An Ode', which began:

> Four hundred summers and fifty have shone on the
>   meadows of Thames and died
> Since Eton arose in an age that was darkness, and shone
>   by his radiant side
> As a star that the spell of a wise man's word bade live and
>   ascend and abide.
>
> And ever as time's flow brightened, a river more dark than
>   the storm-clothed sea,
> And age upon age rose fairer and larger in promise of hope
>   set free,
> With England Eton her child kept pace as a fostress of
>   men to be.[35]

The ode continues in this vein for a further seven stanzas. It was not one of Swinburne's finer efforts. The school, however, seems to have been pleased with it, and when the poet died in 1909 a wreath was sent 'with grateful homage' from Eton with a card quoting some lines from the poem.

The joke is that Swinburne composed at the same time an alternative piece, 'Eton: Another Ode', in which he sang the one aspect of the school that really interested him. The manuscript of this effusion (British Library, Ashley 5271) is dedicated to 'M', whom the Swinburne scholars agree is none other than Mary Gordon, the poet's cousin, of whom more in a moment. The composition is attributed to 'A(lfred) C(ecil) S(herburne) 185-'. I give the opening stanza and stanza four (the poem contains eight stanzas in all):

> Dawn smiles sweet on the fields of Eton, wakes from
>   slumber her youthful flock,
> Lad by lad, whether good or bad: alas for those who at
>   nine o'clock
> Seek the room of disgraceful doom, to smart like fun on
>   the flogging-block!
>
> Swish! Swish! Swish! Swish! O, I wish, I wish, I'd not
>   been late for lock-up last night!
> Swish! that mill that I'm bruised from still (I *couldn't* help
>   it – I *had* to fight)
> Makes the beast, – (I suppose, at least) – who flogs me,
>   flog with all his might.

[35] Published in *Astrophel and Other Poems*, 1894. *The Poems of Algernon Charles Swinburne*, Chatto and Windus, VI, pp. 191-93.

It has been my principal purpose in this chapter to document the Etonian background to Swinburne's flagellant writings, to show the context in which his flagellomania developed. We may be certain, however, that before he went to the school he was already interested in the subject, already aware of the fascination it held for him.

It is not possible to do more than touch on this aspect of his development here. To start with, the poet's father, Admiral Swinburne, seems to have had the naval notions of discipline that one would expect from an old salt of his day and age.[36] That he believed in the paternal rod there can be little doubt. Swinburne scholars are agreed that the birching Captain Harewood of *A Year's Letters* is modelled on the poet's father, although the latter himself denied it on one occasion.[37]

Then there is Swinburne's tutor who prepared him for Eton, the Rev. Collingwood Forster Fenwick. I was surprised to find that modern Swinburnians seem to have done no research on this cleric, adding nothing to the scant details provided by Mrs Mary Leith (1917) and Edmund Gosse (1917). Yet it is fair to assume that Fenwick exerted a considerable influence on the future poet.

Fenwick (1790-1858) was, like the Swinburnes, a Northumbrian, and was born a few miles from their country seat, Capheaton, at Lemington Hall. His published sermons show that he was an Anglican fundamentalist of the old school; and suggest strongly that he held Solomonic notions on the disciplining of the young.[38] During the period that Swinburne lodged at Fenwick's rectory at Brook in the Isle of Wight, it may well be that the birch was applied *in loco parentis*. It suddenly occurred to me one day as I was reading *Lesbia Brandon* that perhaps Bertie Seyton's flogging private tutor, Mr Denham, was based on Fenwick. For not only does 'Den' rhyme with 'Fen', but

---

[36] Leith (1917), p.245.

[37] Letter to W.M. Rossetti, 21 August 1905 (Lang, VI, p.195).

[38] Rev. Collingwood F. Fenwick, LL.B., *Sermons*, etc., Bath, 1831 (see full title in Bibliography). The *Sermons* contain many references to the punishing God of the Old Testament. Fenwick's God is the God discussed in Chapter Two – the stress is on Duty, Obedience, Responsibility, Submission. Fenwick talks a great deal about 'the rebellious wickedness of man's nature constantly striving against the goodness of God' (p.27), 'wilful disobedience to God' (p.29) and so on. He does not approve of 'the wilful indulgence of a sensual propensity' (pp. 106-7). God, when provoked, is capable of administering the schoolmaster's rod ('The servant that knoweth his master's will and doeth it not shall be beaten with many stripes', p.244). Why do we not recognise that God loves us?: 'In every affliction, in every sickness, in every loss, in every untoward event in life, he might have seen, had he not shut his eyes and heart, this very God, who he says has never visited him, chastising him with a parent's rod, and striving to bring him to himself by judgement' (p.18). Fenwick died at Ryde, Isle of Wight, in 1858.

'ham' and 'wick' both mean 'little village'. Surely this cannot have been a coincidence? Moreover, although Fenwick does not seem to have attended Eton, as has Denham, his brother, Robert Orde Fenwick, was educated there.[39] So there was a family connection with that establishment, and doubtless Fenwick could have provided the young Swinburne with information about matters Etonian, including disciplinary matters.

A novel by Swinburne's cousin, Mary Gordon (later Mary Leith), who shared his interest in the birch, lends confirmation to the suspicion that Fenwick was a flogging parson;[40] while Swinburne's references to his and Mary's shared childhood lead one to believe that on occasions the future poet underwent the ordeal of the paternal rod in expiation of faults in which Mary had had a part.

Finally, there was another cousin, Algernon Bertram Freeman-Mitford (1837-1916), later Lord Redesdale. Mitford had gone up to Eton three years before Swinburne, in 1846,[41] and looked after him on his arrival there in 1849. A passage in *A Year's Letters*, together with

[39] According to the 1864 edition of the *Eton Lists*, p.39b, Robert Orde Fenwick was in the Upper Fifth form in 1802.

[40] I have not space enough to go into this aspect of the matter in detail. The novel is *Trusty in Fight; Or, the Vicar's Boys: A Story* (1893). The vicar in question, the Rev. Thorburn, is similar in many respects to Fenwick. He has numerous sons, as had Fenwick, and there can be no doubt that, in portraying Fred Thorburn, Mary had Swinburne very much in mind. She stated, moreover, that Swinburne had 'more or less revised' the story during his stay at her home, Northcourt, in the Isle of Wight, in 1863-4 (Leith, 1917, p.20). Fenwick had died in 1858. The Rev. Thorburn believes in the exercise of the Solomonic rod, as does the headmaster of Fred's school – and Fred receives many beatings, especially at school. In revising her story for publication, Mary seems to have toned down its flagellant character. Writing to Swinburne on 2 February 1893 after hearing a rumour that the birch was to be abolished at Eton, she said, employing the childish cipher that she and the poet used on such occasions, 'I fear ... that we may expect a capid deradence of England's screatest ghool. Beside which I fear the (even revised version of) *Fusty in Tright* will be too *antiquated* for publication! though do remark that the very Worthie the Vicar had *old fashioned ideas* of discipline' (British Library, Ashley 5752, ff. 42-5). It is significant, I believe, that in this same letter Mary recalls her visit to Swinburne when he was living with Fenwick at Brook Rectory. For further information on these cipher letters, see Fuller (1968), pp. 270-8; and the following letters to the *Times Literary Supplement* arising from the publication of Fuller's book: F.A.C. Wilson, 16 January 1969; T.A.J. Burnett, 23 January 1969; F.A.C. Wilson, 30 January 1969.

[41] *The Eton Register* (1903), p.90. Lord Redesdale described his contact with Swinburne at Eton in *Memories* (1915). The Mitfords had a family seat in Northumberland at Newton Park, $8\frac{1}{2}$ miles from Capheaton, the Swinburne seat; and a house at Exbury, on the shores of the Solent looking across to the Isle of Wight (the latter property is now owned by the Rothschilds). It seems to me that Swinburnians have failed to take into account the probable influence of Mitford on his younger cousin. There is an interesting reference to Mitford in one of Milnes's commonplace

what Mitford himself has told us about Swinburne at Eton, suggests that he may have informed the future poet all about the block before the latter arrived at the school. In this passage, Reginald explains to his cousin Frank, who will shortly be following him to school, how disciplinary matters are arranged there:

> No description can express the full fleshy sound of certain words in his mouth; he talked of *cuts* with quite a lickerish accent, and gave the technical word *swish* with a twang in which the hissing sound of a falling birch, or the clear hard ringing noise of a tough stroke on the bare flesh, became sharply audible. His eyes glittered and his lips caressed the tingling syllables. The boy was immeasurably proud of his floggings, and relished the subject of flagellation as few men relish rare wine. (Sylpher ed., p.24)

But whatever the antecedents of Swinburne's flagellant obsession, we can be certain that it was at Eton that it became fixed and confirmed. We may be certain, too, that many of his fellow Etonians before and after his time developed similar tendencies as an inevitable reaction to the birching system. What makes Swinburne different from that system's other victims is that he wrote about the obsession and tried to understand it. Leaving aside his strictly pornographic exploitation of flagellation, *A Year's Letters* and *Lesbia Brandon* tell us a great deal about the inner workings of the flagellant mind. I shall refer to *Lesbia Brandon* in a later chapter of this book, where an attempt is made to understand the dynamics of the flagellant fixation.

A last word on Eton

In the early 1860s, as we have seen, the Clarendon Committee found that flogging was more frequent at Eton than at the other public schools it had examined, despite the assurances of the authorities that such punishments had much diminished in recent years. It seems that the situation disimproved further under the long headmastership of James Hornby (1868-84) for, according to Henry Salt, who was a pupil at that time, 'rarely did a day pass without a number of boys being "swished"' (1910, p.103). Hornby's successor, the Rev.

---

books (Houghton 214, p.22): 'Nothing can exceed the 'spooning' of the handsome little boys by the bigger ones at Eton ... [Warburton?] says he had never got on because he would not let himself be 'spooned' – Swinburne soon after he got there being asked "if he was Bertie Mitford's [woman?]"'. Mostly handling and toying and rarely anything more.'

Edmond Warre (1884-1905) appears to have been less fond of the rod, for he 'contrived to render birching so odious that it has become rare and discreditable, instead of being frequent and honourable' (*Vanity Fair*, 20 June 1885).

Birching, as the everyday form of punishment for serious offences at Eton, seemed therefore to be on the way out by the turn of the century. None the less, it was widely recognised in the world outside Eton that any man accepting the headmastership of the school would still be required to wield the birch. Thus, in 1908, the *Humane Review* told its readers that the President of Harvard was reported to have said recently, in relation to the Etonian birch, that 'no self-respecting educationist in America would accept the post of head master of Eton if it involved the performance of such a ceremony' (Vol. VIII, p.210).

In 1905 the Rev. Edward Lyttelton succeeded Warre as headmaster of Eton. Five years earlier, in 1900, Lyttelton had published the third impression of a little treatise entitled *Training of the Young in Laws of Sex*. For its time, and given the profession of its author, this was an enlightened work, arguing that parents should be prepared to talk more openly to their children about the facts of reproduction. Lyttelton was clearly very anxious about masturbation, however (there is much talk of 'the unclean thing', of 'trials and temptations' and of the 'heroism' needed to overcome sin), and there can be no doubt that he had read William Acton's famous and much-reprinted work, discussed earlier. Acton, it may be recalled, had warned in 1857 of the great dangers attending flogging: 'I cannot help alluding to the ill consequences of whipping children on the nates ... that it has a great influence in exciting ejaculation, no one can doubt ... I sincerely hope that, if flogging is still to be practised, it may be employed on the shoulders, and not on the nates, of youths' (pp. 59-60). Acton's book must have been known to all headmasters of public schools, although little attention seems to have been paid to his strictures about flogging. Lyttelton, however, may have taken note, for in 1911 he announced that the use of the birch had been discontinued in the Upper School, and its place taken by the cane. Acton, followed by Krafft-Ebing and others, had made it perfectly clear, however, that boys well before the age of puberty could be sexually aroused by being whipped on the nates or seeing others thus punished. Lyttelton seems not to have grasped this point, and his treatise shows no awareness that children may have sexual feelings before puberty. As a result he did not abolish the birch in Eton's Lower School.

Lyttelton's decision, as may be imagined, created an uproar, and there was much comment in the newspapers: such was the importance of Eton in the consciousness of the nation, a thing not easily to be understood by foreigners, then or now. On 5 April 1911, the *Daily Telegraph* published a selection of views emitted the previous day by Old Etonians on hearing the extraordinary news. Most of these men regretted the passing of a centuries-old tradition. Earl Winterton was reported as saying:

> I regard the proposal as part of a tendency which is one of the least desirable symptoms of the age. It is a ridiculous presumption that there is something wrong or unnatural in administering corporal punishment to children. To give them instead such punishment as writing out lines, which injure their eyes, is far more harmful to the health than suitable corporal correction. As to the originators of the change, the Humanitarian League I believe, I think their efforts might be better directed against such brutal practices − of everyday occurrence in the summer-time − of catching flies on fly paper, or − a cruel custom found among infants − of trying to lure birds by putting salt on their tails.

Witty, too, was Ian Malcolm, M.P.:

> It is a great pity that a good, old-fashioned, and healthy form of castigation should have to make way for a form of punishment which has for many nothing like the same historical and classic, not also to say personal, memories. It makes it obvious that the art of birching has died out. It was no easy thing, I imagine, to administer a birch with a nice appreciation of anatomy and a clever calculation of effect, whereas any tyro can use a cane. Besides, the new system precludes the romantic excitement of stealing the birch or the swishing block. Nobody would want to thieve a halfpenny cane!

The letter from Henry Salt, secretary of the Humanitarian League, published in the *Daily Telegraph* the following day, deserves to be quoted:

> As Earl Winterton has referred to the Humanitarian League as the originators of the discontinuance of the birch in the Upper School at Eton, permit me to say that this is an honour which we can hardly claim. We have long condemned birching as a form of punishment which is often cruel and always indecent, but we have not addressed any special appeal to the Eton authorities on the subject, because we felt that sympathy is due less to the sons of wealthy parents, who are lightly handled, than to the children of the poor, who, whether in reformatories or in the precincts of police-courts, are liable to be very severely beaten.

In 1917 Cyril Connolly and George Orwell went up from their prep school, St Cyprian's, to Eton. They found that the birch was very much in use in the Upper School. Lyttelton had retired from the headmastership of Eton in 1916, and it is clear that one of the first things done by his successor, Dr Alington, was to reinstate the traditional instrument of Etonian discipline.[42] Connolly – who described his time at Eton in *Enemies of Promise* – discovered that 'the masters could not cane. They punished by lines, detentions, and 'tickets' or chits of misbehaviour which had to be carried to the housemaster for signature. Serious offences or too many tickets, meant being complained of to the headmaster and might end in a birching' (pp. 178-9).

Connolly gives an example of what was considered a 'serious offence' during his time at Eton, and of the consequences following indictment:

> Consider Jacky; playing fives with me one afternoon he said 'Damn and blast' when he missed a ball. The Headmaster, who was passing, heard him and told Sixth Form. That night he was beaten. In the excitement of the game he had forgotten to prepare his construe. Others had prepared theirs but after the silence before boys are put on to construe, when all divisions have been tried in vain, it was he who was called upon. He was ploughed and given a 'ticket' 'Failed in Construe' to get signed by his tutor. He had not the courage to show it him, forged his tutor's initials on the bottom and handed it back. By chance the two masters met, the ticket was mentioned and the fraud discovered. Within three days of the game of fives the Praeposter came with the terrible summons. 'Is O'Dwyer K.S. in this division? He is to go to the Headmaster at a quarter to twelve.' The wide doors are open which means a birching will take place. The block is put out. Two boys in Sixth Form are there to see the Headmaster does not raise his arm above the shoulder, and an old College servant to lower his trousers and hold him down. (pp. 255-6)

So the disgusting old ritual was still being carried out, with other boys forced to watch. Connolly found, moreover, that the caning of boy by boy was rife at the time, and not only by the Sixth Form: 'The whole school, ruled in theory by Sixth Form and the Captain of the School, was governed by Pop or the Eton Society, an oligarchy of two dozen boys who, except for two or three *ex officio* members, were self-elected and could wear coloured waistcoats, stick-up collars, etc., and cane boys from any house' (p.178).

[42] Commenting on this retrograde step, Henry Salt observed (1928): 'I have not made inquiry, but I have heard it rumoured that Dr Alington, sacrificing to medieval superstition what must surely be his own personal feeling, has restored the rank old practice which his predecessor discontinued. If this be so, St Hudibras ought to be adopted as the school's Patron Saint' (p.76).

Boys could cane, that is, where masters could not. And the canings were administered on the buttocks (clothed, admittedly, a small advance on the nineteenth century), the victim being forced habitually to adopt a position that most emphasised the roundness of his posteriors (a vital element in flagellomania). Both Connolly and Orwell received their share of such beatings, and from the description given by the former it is not possible to deny the presence of explicit sadism on the part of the beaters:

> The chair was only put in the middle of the room when beatings were to take place and sometimes the fag was sent beforehand to get the canes with which he would himself be beaten.
>
> The worst part was the suspense for we might make a mistake the day before and not be beaten for it till the following evening. Or we could get a day's grace by pleading a headache and getting 'early bed leave' or by going out to the shooting range, the musical society or to a mysterious evening service, held once a week to expedite the war ...
>
> Often mass executions took place; it was not uncommon for all the fags to be beaten at once. After a storm of accusation to which it was wiser not to reply since no one, once the chair was out, had been known to 'get off', the flogging began. We knelt on the chair bottom outwards and gripped the bottom bar with our hands, stretching towards it over the back. Looking round under the chair we could see a monster rushing towards us with a cane in his hand, his face upside down and distorted – the frowning mask of the Captain of the School or the hideous little Wrangham. The pain was acute. When it was over some other member of Sixth Form would say 'Good night' – it was wiser to answer. (pp. 181-2)

To judge from *Enemies of Promise*, the fag's lot was every bit as unhappy in Connolly's day as it had been in the nineteenth century. Nothing much had changed.

In 1962 David Benedictus, who had recently been a pupil at Eton, published his novel *The Fourth of June*. While the author explains that 'all the characters in the book ... are entirely imaginary', there is no doubt that it offers an accurate picture of, among other things, beating at Eton in the 1950s.

A central episode in the novel concerns the brutal caning of Scarfe by the house captain. Scarfe has the misfortune to be from a rather 'common' family, a fact which does not endear him to his superiors. Benedictus has no doubt about the sadism involved in Etonian boy-to-boy beatings:

> 'When Defries was beating him, I felt just as I do when I'm seeing a lobster boiled.'
> 'Hungry?'

'No, you stupid bastard, objective.'

'Oh, objective; yes, of course, Objective.'

'Why, didn't *you* feel objective?'

'No,' said Morgan after a pause, 'I felt more like the lobster actually. Defries would make quite a chef.'

'Yeah. Morgan, em, do you approve of – well, of the *way* he cooks?'

'Oh yes, it's very much to my taste.' Morgan was in a strange mood. Physically he was very relaxed, but his mind was unusually alert, his imagination active. He was almost alive. He took down the cane from the picture-hook on the wall and bent it between his hands.

'A fable of our time,' he said suddenly, 'by Adrian Stuart Anstey Morgan. Once upon a time I was a great, big oak-tree growing in the forest.'

'But it's a bamboo,' complained Pemberton. (pp. 129-30)

Although *The Fourth of June* is by no means a great novel, it does contain some memorable scenes, phrases and vignettes, among the latter the portrayal of Manningham, the ineffectual housemaster.[43] As regards Etonian beating, the following sarcastic passage sums up the author's attitude:

When out of a school population of under twelve hundred perhaps sixty boys wield the cane and when the Headmaster and Lower Master swing the birch to great effect, most housemasters let them get on with it, and add nothing to the general swishing tumult all around them.

And in passing, who can argue that, from these sixty boys and thirty masters who find themselves flogging the hell out of a recalcitrant child, there will be many who abuse that privilege? No, in any given year there will be but a handful of abuses. And who would maintain that even such abuses as do arise from time to time are of any importance when set against a system that produces so high a proportion of, say, our incorruptible parliamentary leaders. And if they in their turn sometimes seem thick-skinned, then their childhood discipline which hardened their bottoms for sitting on government benches, may in part seem to blame; but how often does a thick skin hide a sensitive spirit? – and we must not criticise this or that minister because he subordinates his aesthetic sensibilities to the cares of state.[44] (p.89)

[43] Manningham observes at one point: 'I have never met the boy who would not enjoy in some measure seeing someone beaten' (p.146).

[44] In late 1976, as I was working on this book, I happened to find myself sitting at lunch next to an Old Etonian of 1950s vintage. The revelation that I was including a chapter on Eton in my book was greeted with disbelief. 'Surely you could do something more useful for the country?', he exclaimed. Benedictus was written off as a crank. 'He was already disturbed before he went to Eton. Parents divorced ... He should have been taken away from the school ... Out of twelve hundred boys there are always a few eccentrics ... We were contemporaries ... I was a house captain and had

Eton Microcosm (1964), edited by Anthony Cheetham and Derek Parfit, is quite unashamed about beating at Eton. The inside covers of the book are embellished with the reproduction of a remarkable mediaeval woodcut which shows a bare-bottomed scholar being birched over the knee of a pedagogue 'in the old-fashioned style' (as the Victorians called it), with his genitals visible (see Plate 15). In their section 'Discipline' (pp. 46-50) the editors show that at the moment of writing fagging and caning continued as at Connolly's time forty years earlier. Moreover

> The ultimate punishment is again a flogging – this time with the Birch, beloved legacy of Dr Keate. If any opponent of corporal punishment has managed to hold out this far, here are two comforting notes to cheer his anguished soul. First, nobody is ever birched twice at Eton, because a second offence is punished with expulsion. Second, a member of Sixth is always present at the execution to ensure that the Headmaster does not raise his arm above the shoulder before striking.
>
> But as always the School wins the last trick of all by charging the offender 10s.6d. for the Birch, which invariably disintegrates during the proceedings. (p.50)

As late as the 1960s, therefore, the Headmaster of Eton was still exercising the traditional rod on the naked buttocks of those pupils who had been careless enough to commit a 'serious offence'. It seems unbelievable, does it not? One would have thought that by that date, even at Eton, the possible consequences of such a practice might have become known.

Fagging, too, was still in operation a few years ago, and presumably is today. On 31 May 1975 the *Guardian* published a little piece entitled 'Demo at Eton on Fagging':

> The Eton branch of the National Union of School Students has chosen today – the day of one of the college's big cricket matches of the year – for an anti-fagging, anti-tails demonstration. As parents and Old Etonians stroll round the grounds, they will be handed leaflets informing them that 'Etonian minds are polluted by their surroundings'.

On the subject of fagging, the leaflet informed these people, according to the *Guardian* report, that 'almost no other school students would

---

to cane boys sometimes. Did them good. Hurt like hell, mind you. You need discipline in such a large school. Of course there's nothing sexual in it ... In my time both the Head and Lower masters birched, but not often ... Yes. Pop canings were really brutal, I admit ...'

accept this kind of degradation and humiliation. Slavery was abolished hundreds of years ago. They seem to have forgotten about fagging.'

Referring to the prevalence of flogging at the public schools during the nineteenth century, Ronald Pearsall has written 'It is very doubtful ... whether even the most unworldly headmaster failed to realize the power he had to form an addiction, an addiction sanctioned by English literature' (1972, p.412). Are we to believe that Dr Hawtrey, to take an example, had no awareness of the sexual implications of Etonian birching? No knowledge of what many medical men had said on the subject of flogging and impotence? No inkling of the flagellant pornography flooding the market? I find it impossible to believe. Hawtrey was no clerical recluse. Wrote Lord Redesdale:

> He was a traveller, a man of the world, and a linguist, proficient in French, German and Italian, able to hold his own, and always welcome, in the political and learned society of many continental cities and universities. His personality was as well-known in Paris, Rome, and the great German towns as in London or at Windsor. (p.53)

According to the *Dictionary of National Biography*, Hawtrey 'is said to have spent £40,000 on his library, which included alike Aldines and rare editions of the classics, besides recent issues from continental presses' (vol. IX, p.248). He may not have read Meibom, of course, but it seems unlikely, to say the least, that such a scholar could have been unacquainted with Rousseau's *Confessions* or the allusions of other serious writers to the subject of sexual flagellation. The question therefore arises – and we must try to answer it later in this book – as to why Hawtrey and his peers at other public schools, past, future and present, have not been more anxious to suppress a mode of punishment widely held to be dangerous to health: widely held, that is, outside the public schools.

How many people were emotionally stunted or rendered sexually impotent by their experience at Eton we shall never know; for, as Pearsall says, 'very few of those men who passed through the public schools were keen to broadcast the fact that they had acquired a taste for the whip' (1972, p.412). But every so often we are given unexpected glimpses into the secret lives of some of these victims. Swinburne is a case in point. So too, perhaps, is Gladstone. The recent revelations concerning the latter's self-flagellant activities after paying 'charitable' visits to prostitutes make one wonder about the effect on him of Etonian discipline,[45] a discipline which, as George Bernard Shaw reminded readers of his preface to *Misalliance*, it was well known he had undergone: 'Can anything be more disgusting,' Shaw asked, 'than the spectacle of a nation reading the biography of Gladstone and gloating over the account of how he was flogged at Eton, two of his schoolfellows being compelled to hold him down whilst he was flogged?' (1974, p.77).

But if Drs Keate and Hawtrey were ignorant of the dangers attending these ceremonies – and I think it would be naïve to assume that they were – no such indulgence can be afforded to their successors in the twentieth century. Until a few years ago these men continued to wield the birch, and allowed senior boys the right to cane their juniors. Recently, however, things seem to have improved somewhat. Desiring to inform myself about the present beating situation at Eton, I wrote to the Head Master, Mr Michael McCrum, in April 1977. In his reply (28 April 1977), Mr McCrum told me that no boys have been birched at Eton since he arrived there in 1970 and that he should be surprised if this 'anachronistic form of punishment' were ever to be reinstated. In a second letter (18 May 1977), Mr McCrum added that senior boys are no longer allowed to inflict corporal punishment at Eton 'and have not done so for many years'. The Head Master, Lower Master and House Masters still use the cane, however, and this is administered to boys 'in their normal clothes on their backside'. 'Lower discipline', that is, has still not disappeared from England's most famous school, and our authority for this statement is the Head Master himself.

[45] Gladstone was at Eton under Dr Keate, that most notorious flogger. When, in March 1975, the third and fourth volumes of *The Gladstone Diaries*, edited by M.R.D. Foot and H.C.G. Matthew (Oxford University Press) were published, reviewers revealed that, after indulging with prostitutes in 'strange and humbling pursuits' (Gladstone's words), the great man used to flagellate himself (lower or upper discipline?) when he got home, introducing a special sign into his diary to record the infliction of these fustigations. It also transpired that he had succumbed to the temptation of reading pornography. In view of the fact that Gladstone left a paper at the end of his life in which he affirmed that he had never 'been guilty of the act which is known as that of infidelity to the marriage bed', but limited himself to this negation one wonders if flagellation without sexual intercourse played a part in his relationships with prostitutes. See Philip Howard, 'Secret Life of Mr Gladstone' (*The Times*, 10 March 1975); Nicholas de Jongh, 'Gladstone Whipped Himself out of a Frenzy' (*Guardian*, 12 March 1975); Asa Briggs, 'Conflicts still Secret' (*Guardian*, 13 March 1975); Stephen Koss, 'The Meshes of Impurity' (*Times Literary Supplement*, 14 March 1975); John Raymond, 'Portrait of a Giant' (*Sunday Times*, 16 March 1975); Derek Parker, 'The High Price of Virtue' (*The Times*, 20 March 1975); and Bryan McAllister's cartoon in the *Guardian* (13 March 1975) which shows a bowler-hatted English gentleman in an antiques shop. 'This is the genuine Gladstone bag,' explains the attendant, 'complete with riding crop, rubber boots, and handcuffs.'

4

Judicial, Prison, Army and Naval Flogging in Britain

The most convenient source of information on the history of judicial flogging in Britain up to 1938 is the Home Office *Report of the Departmental Committee on Corporal Punishment*, published in that year (Cmnd. 5684). This is known as the 'Cadogan Report', from the name of the Committee's Chairman, the Hon. Edward Cadogan, C.B., J.P. The recommendations of the Cadogan Committee became law in 1948, when judicial flogging was finally abolished in Britain except for some prison offences. The Cadogan Report was followed, in 1960, by *Corporal Punishment. Report of the Advisory Council on the Treatment of Offenders* (Home Office, Cmnd. 1213). This Report ratified the findings of its predecessor, and recommended that there be no return to judicial flogging. It is a remarkable fact that judicial inflictions of the lash and birch continued in Britain long after they had been abolished in other civilised parts of the world; and there are indications that many people would like to see them reintroduced. Let us look at the history of this predilection.

The judicial flogging of juveniles

Juvenile offenders, as one would expect, were widely subject to judicial whipping in Queen Victoria's Britain.

In 1847 an Act empowered Justices 'to deal summarily with offences of simple larceny committed by persons under fourteen years of age, and provided that boys so dealt with might be ordered to be once privately whipped, either instead of or in addition to imprisonment' (*Cadogan*, p.3). Under this Act children could be brutally beaten for the most trifling offences. On 18 March 1861, *The Times*, under the heading 'Strong Meat for Babes', published a letter from one 'J.O.' on the subject of the judicial flogging of children. He had come across a recent Parliamentary Return giving details of whippings inflicted on juveniles throughout the country a few years earlier, and had decided to raise his voice in protest:

> Here is what we administered in 1857-8-9 to the children of the poor. Sixty-seven criminals of 12 years of age, 41 of 11, 34 of 10, 12 of nine, three of eight, and one of *seven*, appear in the lists before me as having been thus punished, – some with the birch, and others – I shudder while I write it – with the 'cat'. In Chester gaol a child of *eight* is stated to have received 24 lashes for 'repeated misconduct'; a child of nine, to have received the same for 'house-breaking'; and at Bodmin a boy of twelve got two separate floggings of 36 lashes each for 'horse-stealing'. At Hertford a boy of 10 received 36 lashes for stealing a piece of beef, while a man of 29 only received the same punishment for stealing 29 fowls. Two children, of nine years old, received 15 lashes each at Faversham – one for stealing a cocoanut, value 3d.; the other for stealing a half-pound weight, value 7d.; while a man of 36, at Maidstone, received but 18 for running away and deserting his wife and family!
>
> At Salford, in Lancashire, a boy of 12 received 48 lashes for 'most artfully and wantonly destroying the books in his cell'; a boy of 11 got 36 lashes for shouting in his cell; and a boy of ten 48 lashes for putting the cotton given to him to pick into his cell pot. In the same prison another boy of 11 got 48 lashes, also for shouting in his cell; and a boy of ten was similarly maltreated. A boy of 14 got 60 lashes for idleness at crank labour.

And so on. J.O.'s summary of the Parliamentary Return makes sickening reading. He concludes his letter:

> The well-fed children of the rich, when they come to be stripped for punishment, are at eight, nine, or ten years of age but frail, delicate-skinned, little creatures, very ill-fitted to bear even a dozen cuts of the cane or the birch; the under fed children of the poor are frailer and punier still, and I appeal to every member of the House of Commons who has young children of his own to put a stop to these wanton and unnecessary cruelties. (p.5)

These were kindly sentiments, but few members of the House of Commons were interested in reforming the whipping system. Indeed, as the century progressed, the flogging powers of judges and magistrates increased. Paralleling brutalities in the schools, many cases of appalling judicial beatings administered to children came to the notice of the public.

Under the Larceny Act, 1861, the Malicious Damage Act, 1861, and the Offences against the Person Act, 1861, the Superior Courts were empowered to sentence boys under 16 years of age who had been convicted on indictment of a wide range of possible offences to receive a whipping. The whipping clauses of these three Acts were retained with little modification until judicial flogging was finally abolished in 1948.[1]

The Juvenile Male Offenders Act of 1862 made an attempt to regularise the rather haphazard whippings that were being meted out by magistrates, especially in country districts. It was provided that the instrument used should be a birch rod; that this should be applied to the naked buttocks; that Justices ordering whipping should specify the number of strokes in their sentence; and that the maximum number of strokes should not exceed twelve.[2]

Justices were still not empowered to sentence a boy over 14 to be whipped.

The powers of the 1862 Act were extended by the Summary Jurisdiction Act of 1879, which increased the number of offences for which whipping could be ordered: 'children' up to twelve years of age could receive a maximum of six strokes with the birch, 'young persons' up to fourteen years, twelve strokes.[3]

In 1885 the Criminal Law Amendment Act empowered judges to order a boy under 16 convicted on indictment of unlawful carnal knowledge of a girl under 13 to be whipped in lieu of imprisonment.[4]

This Act encouraged those people who wished to see further whipping amendments made to the law and, in particular, wider powers for the flogging of boys up to the age of sixteen.

In 1889 a second Summary Jurisdiction Act further increased the number of petty offences for which whipping could be ordered by magistrates to children under 14.[5]

Then, in 1900, Lord James of Hereford produced his Youthful Offenders Bill which, in his own words, was intended 'to substitute a punishment other than that of imprisonment upon young persons under sixteen years of age' (Hansard, *Lords*, 5 March 1900, col.5). That punishment, of course, was the birch. In practice the Bill would have empowered justices to have children birched up to the age of sixteen for a wide variety of offences. The Bill laid down that children under twelve could receive up to a maximum of twelve strokes of the birch; those under sixteen up to eighteen strokes. Some of the Lords quipped about their own experience under the birch at public school. Earl Carrington was more serious: 'Eighteen strokes is the maximum number which can be inflicted on a boy of any age, but I regard that

---

[1] *Cadogan*, p.61.
[2] *ibid.*, p.10.
[3] *ibid.*, pp. 10-11.
[4] *ibid.*, p.4.
[5] *ibid.*, p.10.

number as rather too high. Noble Lords who were at Eton will remember that no one had more than twelve. I remember that twelve well' (*ibid.*, col.8).

When Lord James's Bill reached the Commons there was a heated debate, as always on such occasions. It became obvious that the drafter of the Bill had been unable to envisage any alternative to prison for the 14-16 age group other than whipping, despite provisions which already existed in law; and it was clear that the Bill would penalise the poor yet again, since parents were to be allowed to pay a fine in lieu of a birching sentence.

The remarks of several public school men during the Commons debate demonstrated that it had not yet dawned on them that birchings inflicted at Eton or Harrow on the sons of the affluent were different in kind to those administered by a strong policeman to poor children. It is pitiful to see these privileged men emitting the old platitudes, men such as Arthur Jeffreys, who exclaimed:

> Surely it would be better to give them a good birching. At the present time the sons of the upper classes – even Dukes' sons – are birched, and why should not other people and the children of other classes be birched? (Hansard, *Commons*, 21 May 1900, col.834)

Or Vicary Gibbs:

> Members talk of this Bill as a question of class legislation. That is perfectly ridiculous. It is admitted on all hands that the sons of the richer classes are subjected to corporal punishment in their schools, and why should it be any degradation to the sons of the poorer classes to be subjected to the same treatment? (*ibid.*, col.839)

To the credit of the House, and the brilliant oratory of Messrs. Carvell Williams, Serjeant Hemphill, T.P. O'Connor, Broadhurst, Sir Walter Foster and others, the whipping clauses of Lord James's Bill were thrown out.[6]

Under changes introduced by the Children's Act, 1908, six strokes of the birch became the maximum whipping penalty that could be imposed by Justices on boys under fourteen.[7] The law was gradually becoming more humane.

We have seen the letter from 'J.O.' giving details of the whippings

---

[6] It is worth noting that the National Society for the Prevention of Cruelty to Children expressed itself in favour of the birching clauses in Lord James's Bill (*Humanity*, August 1900, pp. 58-9).

[7] *Cadogan*, p.11.

imposed on children in the 1850s. One or two other instances may be mentioned from the nineteenth century. The 1887 Ilkeston case, for example, in which a child of seven was brought before the magistrates and charged with stealing a watch. He was found guilty and sentenced to receive four strokes of the birch. The *British Medical Journal* reproduced an extract from the surgeon's certificate:

> James Buckbury, aged seven, was brought to me on July 7, suffering from lacerated wounds over the side and belly, which had that day been inflicted by the policeman's lash. The wounds which I counted were over fifty in number, and had penetrated deep into the cellular and muscular tissue, those on the belly being especially deep. The child was very feverish and sickly. Its little heart was in a most excitable condition, and it complained of acute pain. I prescribed some soothing medecine, and some ointment, etc., to dress the wounds. I have been attending the child since. He is progressing favourably, and the wounds are healing nicely. For a few days he complained of occasional twitches of internal pain, pointing to slight pleurisy. It seemed to me a monstrous thing that a child of such tender years should be beaten in such a brutal manner. (Quoted by the *Pall Mall Gazette*, 22 July 1887)

Thirteen years later, in the debate on the Youthful Offenders Bill in the Commons, Sir Walter Foster recalled that in his capacity as Member for Ilkeston he had brought the Buckbury case before the attention of Parliament:

> That was a comparatively mild sentence. I saw the boy two or three days after the infliction of this punishment, and his little back was covered with wounds which extended right through the skin to the muscles, and not only was his back a mass of rawness, but the wounds had come round to the front of the abdomen, and they had cut down to the muscles on the front of his frame. (Hansard, *Commons*, 21 May 1900, col.836)

In October 1901 Mr Alfred Binns wrote to *The Humanitarian* to describe the effects of a similar police birching:

> I was near the West Ham Police Court, and noticed four women leading four small boys, with a group of people following. They entered a public house with the boys, whose ages would be from nine to eleven years. I followed, and in a few minutes the children were partially stripped by the women. A cry of horror from all present at once arose at the hideous and revolting sight of the bodies of the boys. A mass of bloody-looking sores and half-broken wounds were shown on the right hip and flank, extending round to the front of the thigh and abdomen. The feeling of the spectators was so strong that I thought for the moment that they might

1. Action in an early eighteenth-century flagellant brothel; frontispiece of the 1718 London edition of Meibom's treatise. Note the voyeurs at the window. Courtesy of the British Library Board.

2. The frontispiece of Paullini's *Flagellum Salutis* (1698), a lengthy treatise (in German) describing the medical benefits of flagellation. Courtesy of the British Library Board.

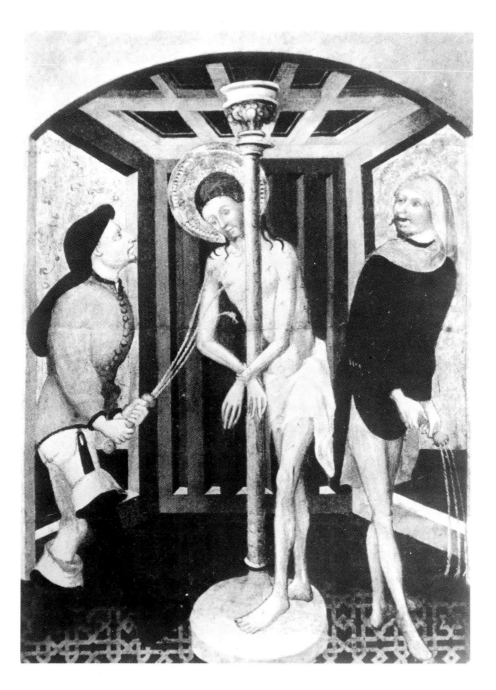

3. Surely one of the most remarkable Flagellations of Christ ever painted. Early fifteenth century, attributed to the Catalan artist Luis Borrassá. The whip handles are equated by the artist with the floggers' penises, the thongs with seminal emissions. Note the crude expressions on the executioners' faces. Courtesy of the Musée Goya, Castres, France.

4. Fanny Hill applies the Meibomian rod to Mr Barville; from the 1766 edition of Cleland's *Memoirs of a Woman of Pleasure*.

THE
Childrens Petition:

OR,

A Modest Remonstrance
of that intolerable grievance
our Youth lie under, in the
accustomed Severities of the
School-discipline of this Nation.

---

*Humbly presented to the Consi-
deration of the Parliament.*

Licensed, *Novemb.* 10. 1669.
Roger L'Estrange.

London, Printed for *Richard Chiswel*
at the two Angels and Crown
in *Little-Brittain,* 1669.

5.   Title page of the *Children's Petition* (1669).

AUNT MOLLY'S LETTER.

My dear Chicks,—

I am so very busy that I have only time for a very short letter this week. I expect you are all feeling awfully excited at the thought of the glorious 25th of December, which is coming along so quickly. Mind you keep a VERY big corner for the plum-pudding and turkey. **Your loving**

AUNT MOLLY.

Little Alta, who was four years old, had been into some mischief for which her father considered she deserved punishment. To make the punishment more impressive he gave fifteen minutes for her to decide the kind of chastisement most appropriate. To his utter astonishment, she said : " Scold me."

Poor little Georgie had heard his father say that dog-days would begin early in May. Accordingly, the next morning he seated himself on the front doorstep. His mother asked what was the matter.

"Nothing," was Georgie's reply. " I'm just waiting for the dogs to come along. I want to get a Newfoundland."

"Isn't it funny, papa?" said Willie, as he played with the typewriter. " When I use a pen my writing is very different from yours, but with the machine you can't tell one from the other."

3. – Till he cried !

Gertie (returning from school) : " Mamma, we have been reading of such a dreadful time. I should not have liked to have lived then, and I am sure you would not, for people were tied to a leg of mutton, and, after gunpowder had been put round, they were all blown up !"

Mamma : " Are you sure it was not a stake they were tied to ?"

Gertie : "Oh, yes, mamma, it was a steak ! I knew it was meat of some kind."

Cecil was greatly pleased at being told that his granny was coming to see him, as it was his birthday.

After having given the child a present, she said to him : "Do you know, Cecil, that it is also my birthday to-day ?"

" Oh, granny !" exclaimed Cecil, " then we are twins !" And he could not be persuaded to the contrary.

6. Illustration to the children's page in the family magazine *Home Chat* in 1903. Courtesy of the University of London Library.

A LITERAL SOLOMON.

Has the reader the rare advantage of knowing any young lady who is cross and spiteful, and especially hates children? If so, let him buy an extra number of this periodical, not to damage his set, and send her the annexed copy of an advertisement, cut out of the *Liverpool Daily Post* :—

WANTED, a Young Lady, about 20, as Housekeeper to a Widower, and to take charge of three boys, the eldest ten years old. Must be of good appearance and address ; accomplishments not essential. Salary £25.—Address, stating age, and if willing to give severe corporal punishment, A. Z., Post Office, Chester.

Housekeepers are generally supposed to know all about pickling, but that knowledge is not taken to include the pickle to keep a rod in, as it appears to be in the foregoing advertisement for a young lady who will have to take charge of children, and is "willing to give severe corporal punishment." The author of this notification belongs to a past age. He should have lived formerly. Above a century ago his advertisement might have been satisfactorily answered by a most eligible party, under the maiden name which she bore whilst she was "servant to a merchant in Goodman's Fields," and before she "became the wife of JAMES BROWNRIGG, a plumber." The lady, now famous under the name of BROWNRIGG, might then have conferred immortality on that disguised by the letters A. Z. The desired condition of willingness to inflict severe corporal punishment, coupled with the necessitudes of good appearance and address, amount to an inquiry for a stepmother. The lady who accepts A. Z.'s situation may reckon on becoming MRS. A. Z.; and it is by no means unlikely that MRS. A. Z. may become a second MRS. BROWNRIGG. When ELIZABETH BROWNRIGG was hanged for whipping her apprentices to death, her husband got off with six months' imprisonment. Perhaps MR. A. Z. will be less fortunate than MR. BROWNRIGG, and may accompany his lady to the halter.

CAN any Lady recommend a good GOVERNESS, English or foreign, for two little boys of ten and seven? She must be Protestant and able to teach thorough English, French, German, Latin, music, and drawing. Apply, stating age, salary, and full particulars, to M. M., care W. H. Smith and Son, 79 and 80, Middle Abbey-street, Dublin.

WANTED, in a gentleman's family in the country, a Young Lady, about twenty-five years of age, as GOVERNESS to four children, ages ten, nine, seven, and six. Must understand how to teach good English and music, and must have been out before. Apply to E. M., Rose Place, Claines, Worcester.

WANTED, by a Widow Lady, a PERSON who is experienced in the art of whipping, and well qualified to administer a severe flogging with a new birch rod to two young children of the ages of nine and ten. Wages 30l. per annum. The children are very wilful and troublesome. Address to S. N. N., Brooks' Club, Suffolk-street, London.

A CLERGYMAN'S WIFE recommends her GOVERNESS. Continental French, German, good music.—Rector, 1, Duchess-road, Birmingham.

7. Mr Punch (31 January 1863) seems not to have suspected that the advertisement in question might be a flagellant hoax.

8. A flagellant advertisement finds its way into more staid company in the columns of the religious weekly *The Guardian* (1 November 1876). Courtesy of the British Library Board.

— En Angleterre, les petites filles sont très jolies... mais trop souvent fouettées.

9. A nineteenth-century French comment on the English Vice. Presumably the little girl's bottom is about to receive a post-birching sponging from Nanny. Courtesy of Faber and Faber.

The collar is of the tucked chiffon and lace, adorned velvet.

A short length of brocade, say, some three-quarters of a yard, should be induced to suffice for this pretty little vest.

And the same may be said of the two following examples, the first (No. 3936) whereof would demand a daintily-coloured Orient satin, simply gathered into the neck and waistband ; while for ornamentation comes a jabot of lace, flanked either side by bands of Oriental embroidery.

The last vest depicted (No. 3937) is of black satin, with front empiècement of coloured satin veiled in Alençon punched lace, with collar of the coloured satin.

Two New Skirts.

No. 3938 presents itself as a skirt of most enticing genre, and would look extremely well carried out in a rough zibeine or hopsack, allied to a fur bolero or pretty habillée blouse.

A silk, linenette, or satin foundation is indispensable, on to which is first laid the lower volant, this, together with the second one, being adjusted with a raw edge at the top, which demands the neatening influence of Prussian binding or ribbon. The uppermost volant comes over all, while the entrance is arranged for at centre-back as invisibly as possible.

In cutting out, the centre of each volant must be placed to a fold of the material, any join that may occur coming at either side.

No. 3939 is quite one of the best-approved skirts of the hour, with its shaped yoke band terminating in a long front empiècement.

As is clearly shown in the picture, a seam comes in front and entrance at centre-back, the fulness occurring there being gauged into the shaped yoke. A prettier or more thoroughly up-to-date skirt it would be impossible to find.

"SPARE THE ROD AND SPOIL THE CHILD."
Birches are Coming Rapidly Into Fashion Again!

The children of Royalty, the nobility, and the gentry are severely corrected, at first with laying on of hands or a slipper, but when their sins and their skins are more hardy, with that ancient and venerated instrument the rod. The cane is used at high-class schools with a frequency and heartiness which would horrify the Board-school child and shock his parents into violent protest. The Board-school spares the rod and produces hooligans.

When a child of the nobility or gentry is badly in need of correction the unhappy parent tries to buy a birch-rod, but usually finds that the shop is "out of stock." So he looks up the trade section of the London Post Office Directory and finds "Birch-rod makers, Dukas and Co., 20, Red Lion Square, W.C."

Then he sends a special messenger to Messrs. Dukas to buy a birch-rod, and bring it back carefully wrapped up to look like something else.

With this he rebukes the child, in such a manner that the said child will be reminded of his sins every time he happens to sit down.

The prescription, for external application only, is to be taken when required. It stimulates and refreshes the most torpid skin, produces vivid blushes and excruciating howls, and is strongly recommended for the young.

Messrs. Dukas, who are wholesale dealers in brooms and brushes, inform us that the birch-rod —once almost a forgotten implement—is coming rapidly into fashion.

They flatly declined to state whether the Royal Families of Europe are among their customers, or disclose the names of prominent applicants for rods.

People apply for rods through the post, send

special messengers or servants, or call in their carriages. One client sent an anonymous letter, enclosing money, ordering rods, and requesting Messrs. Dukas to announce the completion of the contract in the agony column of the "Daily Mail."

A client wrote not long ago: "If I send my boy, will you birch him?" This request was declined.

A lady wrote minute particulars as to her two little girls, asking the firm to prescribe a strong rod for the elder, and a tiny birch to threaten the younger, who was very delicate.

One of last week's customers Messrs. Dukas know to be a member of the Peerage with a fractious son.

Apart from the chastening of the young there is a small demand from the professional masseuse, who treats some patients with gentle applications of the rod to stimulate a sluggish circulation.

The birch twigs come from Kent

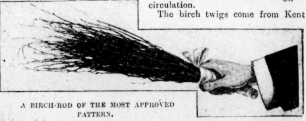

A BIRCH-ROD OF THE MOST APPROVED PATTERN.

and Sussex, and are cut from the undergrowth. They are brought in wainloads to two dealers in South-East London, from whence Messrs. Dukas are supplied. A number of twigs are bound together to make one rod, which is then supplied with a gay handle of coloured ribbon. One lady orders handles of chamois leather to save her fingers from being stung.

The rods vary in length from 18 to 20 inches, and in price from 1s. to 3s.

---

10. *Home Chat* again (in 1903). The joke about 'sluggish circulation' was an old one (and it recurs in James Joyce's *Ulysses*). Courtesy of the University of London Library.

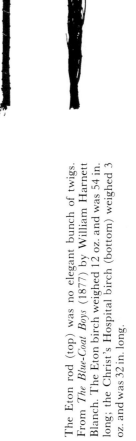

11. A bit of modern English fun from the weekly comic *Smash*. Courtesy of Syndication International Ltd. and the editors of *Smash*.

12. The Eton rod (top) was no elegant bunch of twigs. From *The Blue-Coat Boys* (1877) by William Harnett Blanch. The Eton birch weighed 12 oz. and was 54 in. long; the Christ's Hospital birch (bottom) weighed 3 oz. and was 32 in. long.

13. The 'Library' at Eton, from Ralph Nevill's *Floreat Etona* (1911). Courtesy of Macmillan of London and Basingstoke.

14. Swinburne's tutor, the Rev. James Leigh Joynes, Lower Master of Eton 1878-1887. The cartoon was published in *Vanity Fair* on his retirement. Courtesy of the British Library Board.

15. Birching at Eton in the good old days. Note the exposed genitals of the victim. Courtesy of Anthony Cheetham.

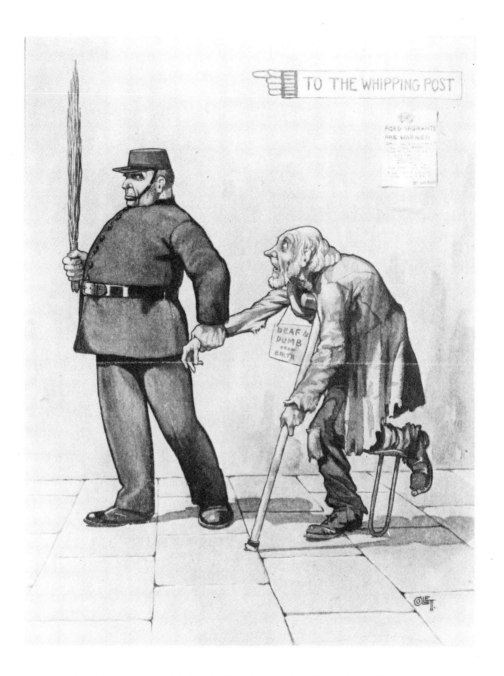

16. Anti-birching cartoon published in *The Humanitarian*, November 1909.

NEIGHBOURS IN COUNCIL.

France. "WHAT *AM* I TO DO WITH MY 'IRRECONCILABLES?'"
Britannia. "I KNOW PERFECTLY WELL, MY DEAR, WHAT I'M GOING TO DO WITH MINE!"

17. The birch for Irish rebels. O'Donovan Rossa was elected MP for Tipperary in 1869 while serving a prison sentence in England for his Fenian activities. The remedy of the rod had clearly not suggested itself to France as a means of putting down such troublesome political dissidents as Henry Rochefort. Courtesy of *Punch*.

THE BLOCK FOR TRAITORS.

MASTER O'SULLIVAN CORK. "PLEASE, SIR, I DIDN'T MEAN WHAT I SAID, SIR; AND I DIDN'T SAY WHAT I MEANT, SIR. BOO—HOO—BOO—HOO—OO!"

HEAD MASTER. "O, YOU DIDN'T, DIDN'T YOU? WELL, I WON'T FLOG THIS TIME, BUT IF YOU 'RE UP TO ANY MORE TRICKS, YOU 'LL CATCH IT. YOU MAY GO."

18. The mayor of Cork on the Etonian block, with Gladstone in the guise of headmaster. The mayor had disgraced himself by making a pro-Fenian speech. Courtesy of *Punch*.

19. A mother birching her son on a mediaeval French misericord. Courtesy of Dorothy and Henry Kraus (*The Hidden World of Misericords* (1976), published by Michael Joseph).

20. 'Lower discipline', Spanish style, from a mediaeval misericord in Zamora Cathedral. Courtesy of Ruedo Ibérico, Paris (Xavier Domingo, *Erótica hispánica*, 1972).

21. Hogarth's harlot was evidently required to exercise the rod. Plate 3 of *A Harlot's Progress*.

'School beatings? Never
did me any harm!'

22. The scopophobic Englishman, from
Hector France's *La pudique Albion*
(1885). Courtesy of the British
Library Board.

23. Arthur Horner's view of the English
Vice. Courtesy of the cartoonist and the
New Statesman.

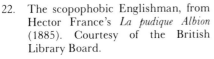

24. Flagellant advertisements published in *Society*, March 31, 1900. Courtesy of the British
Library Board.

25. Flagellant advertisements published in *Society*, November 18, 1899. Courtesy of the British Library Board.

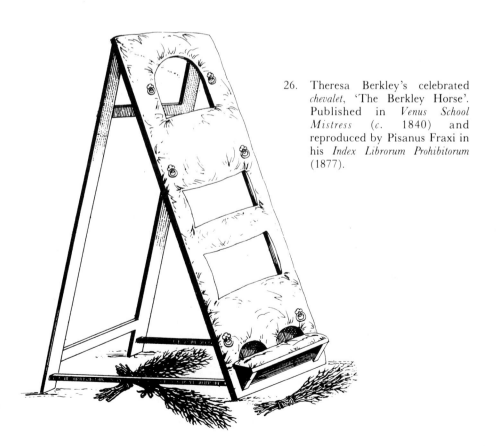

26. Theresa Berkley's celebrated *chevalet*, 'The Berkley Horse'. Published in *Venus School Mistress* (*c.* 1840) and reproduced by Pisanus Fraxi in his *Index Librorum Prohibitorum* (1877).

LADY TERMAGANT FLAYBUM going to give her STEP SON a taste of her DESERT after Dinner
Scene performed every day near Grosvenor Square to the annoyance of the neighbourhood

27. The full-breasted Lady Termagant Flaybum prepares to excoriate her stepson. From Pisanus Fraxi's *Centuria Librorum Absconditorum* (1879).

28. Another birching scene, from Pisanus Fraxi, *Centuria Librorum Absconditorum* (1879). Attributed by Ashbee to H.F. Gravelot. Note again the large breasts of the flagellatrix.

attempt to mob those who had ordered the infliction of such a barbarous and indecent punishment. (Henry Salt, 1916, pp. 46-7)

The Victorians were obsessed by the *modus operandi* of flagellation, as we shall see, so it is not surprising that there was considerable curiosity as to how judicial birchings were actually carried out. William Stead (of 'The Maiden Tribute of Modern Babylon' fame) was editor of the *Pall Mall Gazette* and an ardent campaigner against brutality. A few weeks after the Ilkeston revelations, the *Pall Mall Budget* published an allegedly eye-witness account of a police birching administered to two youthful offenders of about twelve and thirteen. The author of the piece is likely to have been Stead himself. While the writing is somewhat sensational, there is no reason to doubt the accuracy of the description:

> Immediately the birch had touched the poor little fellow's skin the weals or marks of the lashes were plainly visible, and after two or three strokes had been laid on the culprit's right buttock resembled nothing so much as a piece of raw beef, and when the whole complement of six strokes had been inflicted, I say it to the disgrace of the nation, blood was drawn, and, as his comrades viewed the matter, the official who held the birch had proved himself a clever fellow; for it is the acme of ambition on the part of the officers who are told off to administer the punishment to draw blood. The detective with the birch then moved his precious body to the other side of the form and inflicted the remaining six strokes in a similar manner on the tiny culprit's left buttock, the other little boy being put through the ordeal with exactly similar results. (4 August 1887, p.8)

Writing of such honesty was rare at the time, and it gave rise to a heated response. Letters poured in. Some were revolting, some silly, some decent and some indistinguishable from the kind of flagellant communication we shall be examining in the next chapter. Among the latter category came one purporting to give the 'Personal Experiences of a Parson', an obvious hoax. This cleric claimed that he had persuaded a friend to give him a sound birching in order that he might be in a better position to assess the sufferings of young miscreants at the hands of the police:

> I wanted to have a distinct impression of the pain the lad felt, and though not perhaps equal in quantity it probably exceeded it in quality. I was tightly buckled down to a saddle-horse, for, 'he never feels the proper smart who there unharnessed kneels',[8] and I let my operator have what he truthfully called 'a good fair cut at me'. But, after all, though a little skin

[8] The quotation is from *The Rodiad* (1871) which, as I have said (Chapter Three, note 23), was almost certainly composed by Richard Monckton Milnes.

was broken and a little soreness left, there was not much harm done, and the fresh recollection, combined with worse impressions of the dim and distant past, made me rather despise the people who fetched down a London barrister over a tiresome whelp who had had a few strokes with a light cut-whip. Many of the good people who cry over the poor little thieves who roar behind the police-court would be rather amazed if they saw the punishments sometimes given at our large boys' schools; yet the. lads laugh when it is over. It is not uncommon for under-masters to cane where the head master alone has the right to give what is technically called a flogging. This latter, of course, involves stripping, though the first does not, and it makes a distinction with a difference. (*Pall Mall Gazette*, 5 August 1887, p.3)

Those who approved of birching, it becomes increasingly clear, were the men who had been through the public school system. Those who imposed birching sentences were out of the same stable. Among the latter the magistrates stood out for their whipping proclivities. The Justices, as we have seen, had perfect liberty to order boys up to fourteen to be birched for a wide variety of offences. They did so as a matter of course. As Sir Walter Foster remarked in the House of Commons in 1900, the sympathies of the magistrates, especially in country districts, 'are rather with the game than with the children' (Hansard, *Commons*, 21 May 1900, col.836). Naturally when one of these country squires had a juvenile before him charged with poaching or stealing partridges' eggs, the temptation to give him a good birching was overwhelming. But no Justice could legally order a child of fourteen or over to be whipped. This could be exasperating and magistrates not infrequently tried to get round the law. Such a man was the Sussex Justice, R.G. Wilberforce (a relative of the anti-slaver). Two youths of fourteen and seventeen had been caught on Wilberforce's grounds digging out a rabbit's burrow in a hedgerow. Wilberforce interviewed the father, said the case was too frivolous to be taken to court, and offered as an alternative to birch the boys himself. This he did, brutally, in the approved fashion: 'scarcely any of the skin on the lower part of each boy's back remained unbroken, and ... the marks of the punishment were visible fully two months after the floggings were inflicted' (Hansard, *Commons*, 2 May 1876, col.2010). When the Agricultural Labourers Union took Wilberforce to Court, he was found guilty and fined £15. He was also roundly condemned by the Lord Chancellor, but not, apparently, removed from the Bench, despite demands in the Commons.

Swinburne was delighted with this case, and in a letter to Milnes he gave an extract from the republican speech which *he* would have made on the occasion to the House of Commons:

For centuries the birch had been the hereditary apanage of the young aristocrat – the heirloom of patrician adolescence – the feudal emblem of class divisions, the bloody badge of social exclusiveness, distinguishing by a crimson sign, even when his back was turned on them in scorn, the noble or gentle boy from his humbler fellows; and now that a patriot reformer had made a first attempt to break down those barriers and extend this jealously guarded privilege to the hardy sons of honest toil, was it for a republican to revile him? Was it only blue blood that had a natural right to blush on the birch-twigs? (Lang, III, pp. 191-2)

Swinburne was joking in the way that only he could (especially when writing to Milnes); but in putting his finger on the aristocratic associations of the birch he was showing that he, at any rate, knew where English flagellomania was nurtured.

Wilberforce was not alone in his dissatisfaction at not being able legally to order boys of fourteen and fifteen to be birched. His feelings were shared by many magistrates. *The Humanitarian* published several accounts of extra-judicial birchings imposed in the early years of the 20th century by magistrates on boys in that age group: it emerged that these men, unable to have the job done legally, were in the habit of allowing parents the 'voluntary' option of choosing a birching for their children instead of a fine. It appeared also that every so often the police took matters into their own hands and carried out an illegal birching.[9]

Little by little these malpractices decreased, but not so the magistrates' cry for more whipping. The Humanitarian League had warned that, in the event of the whipping clauses of the White Slave Bill of 1912 becoming law, there would be an inevitable demand for yet more flogging. We shall be examining the 1912 Bill in the next section, but one may say here that the League was right. In particular, the magistrates seemed determined that the flogging age for boys should be raised to 16. On 8 May 1913, for example, the *South Wales Daily News* informed its readers:

At the quarterly meeting of the Cardiff magistrates yesterday, Alderman W.J. Trounce presiding, the resolution passed by the Halifax justices, 'that it is desirable that the courts of summary jurisdiction be empowered to order whipping to male children under 16 years with or without any other punishment, in all cases of summary conviction, and in all indictable offences which may be dealt with summarily', was approved. (*The Humanitarian*, July 1913, p.147)

[9] See, for example, *The Humanitarian*, August 1902, pp. 42-3; July 1903, pp. 133-4; November 1904, pp. 86-7; December 1904, pp. 92-3; July 1908, pp. 53-4; August 1908, p.60; September 1908, p.67.

Many other magistrates up and down the country expressed similar views, although of course not all justices succumbed to the flagellomania of the moment. One who did was Mr E.J. Turner, a Visiting Justice of Winchester Prison (where perhaps he had awarded his share of flogging sentences for breaches of prison discipline). On 7 October 1913 Turner wrote to the pro-flogging *Morning Post* to protest about the 'class distinction' which prevented justices from ordering boys over thirteen to be birched:

> It is a matter for congratulation that in this sentimental age flogging is not yet forbidden in our Public Schools, but the punishment which is considered salutary for the gentleman's son is not available for the son of the poor man, and the only thing the Magistrate can do to a boy who has been guilty of an offence for which he would be flogged at a Public School is either to let him off with a caution, to put him on probation, or to fine his father. The Magistrate is not allowed to sentence him to the punishment which would appeal to the boy himself, which would probably deter him from repeating the offence, and which would certainly deter others from following his example.

It was the same old story. A few months earlier, a request was made by the Nottingham magistrates 'with the blessing of the Duke of Portland, for power to flog pit-boys who ill-treat ponies' (*The Humanitarian*, March 13 1913, p.117). Of course, there was no such request for power to flog fox-hunters or those who promoted the sweated labour of women and children.

Some of the sentences passed on young children at the time make one think one is back in the early nineteenth century: in 1913, for example, a boy of 10 was sentenced at Blackpool to be birched for the crime of stealing half-a-crown—from his own mother![10]

The official statistics show that, for the period 1900-1911, magistrates in England and Wales ordered 28,781 birchings to be applied to the naked buttocks of young offenders; their Scottish counterparts ordered 5,727.[11]

The judicial flogging of adults

The public flogging of women was abolished in 1817. This was followed in 1820 by the abolition of the private flogging of women.[12]

Male offenders, however, were still widely subject to the lash, and

[10] *The Humanitarian*, July 1913, p.147.
[11] *Cadogan*, pp. 19-20.
[12] *ibid.*, p.1.

there were in force at the time many Acts with flogging clauses.[13]

Under the Vagrancy Act, 1824, 'incorrigible rogues' and some other offenders could be flogged, mainly for second or subsequent offences.[14]

The Treason Act, 1842, provided that a person could be flogged for discharging or aiming a firearm at the Sovereign.[15]

In 1843 the Commissioners on the Criminal Law declared themselves against flogging except in the case of offences under the 1842 Treason Act. Their Report is notable for its humanity: 'It is a punishment which is uncertain in point of severity, which inflicts an ignominious and indelible disgrace on the offender, and tends, we believe, to render him callous, and greatly to obstruct his return to any honest course of life' (*Cadogan*, p.2).

As a result of changes in the law introduced in 1861, the whipping of adult males was abolished except under the provisions of the 1824 Vagrancy Act, the 1842 Treason Act, and two earlier Acts which allowed for the penalty of flogging for instituting certain actions against an Ambassador or his servants (the Diplomatic Privileges Act, 1708) and for indulging in the irregular slaughter of horses and cattle (the Knackers Act, 1786).[16]

In 1862 the Whipping Act provided that no offender should be flogged more than once for the same offence. In the same year the judicial flogging of adult males was abolished in Scotland – and was never reintroduced.[17]

Also in 1862, Parliament's panic over 'garrotting' (an attempt to choke or strangle a victim to facilitate the commission of an indictable offence) led to the hasty enactment, against the advice of the Home Secretary of the day, of a Private Member's Bill, the Security from Violence Act, 1863; this Bill reintroduced flogging for robbery with violence.[18] Several flogging sentences were carried out under the provisions of the Act, and were fully reported in the press. When, in December 1871, for example, two felons were to be whipped in Newgate, *The Lancet* – one of the leading medical journals in the country – sent along a representative to witness the infliction. He reported:

No. 1 convict received forty lashes well laid on in twenties by the two executioners. The marks became apparent across the shoulders after the

[13] *ibid.*, pp. 1-2.
[14] *ibid.*, p.1.
[15] *ibid.*, p.2.
[16] *ibid.*, pp. 2-3.
[17] *ibid.*, p.4.
[18] *ibid.*

second stroke, but blood did not flow till the eighth. After this the part became more or less livid and bruised, but the actual amount of haemorrhage was trifling, and the blood did not trickle below the seat of punishment. The effect upon the culprit as regards pain was undoubted, for after the third cut he began to moan and sob, and continued to do so to the end ... The punishment appeared to me to be about as severe as in the navy, where the number of stripes is limited to four dozen on the back; and not so severe as the same punishment inflicted with the 'cat' on the nates, as was formerly the case with boys in the navy. I do not think the health of either culprit will in any way suffer from the infliction of the punishment, and only regret that other prisoners were not paraded, as a ship's company would be, to witness the carrying out of the sentence of the law. (23 December 1871, pp. 899-900)

The Lancet's representative was clearly a product of the old (naval) school.

Under the 1863 Act the total number of lashes of the 'cat' that could be inflicted was restricted to 50, but provision was made for a second and a third instalment if that was felt desirable by judges. The provision of the Whipping Act of the previous year, that no offender should be flogged twice for the same offence, was thus rescinded. It gradually emerged that, before the 1863 Act became law, garrotting had already diminished and that, anyway, the 'epidemic' had been grossly exaggerated and was largely the work of one gang.[19] Despite this the pro-flogging faction would go on claiming until well into the twentieth century that the 1863 Act had put down robbery with violence. This assumption was used again and again to justify the reintroduction of flogging for the repression of crimes of violence.

A word might be said here about British methods of discipline in the colonies. India seems to have been the country that suffered most under the lash, particularly from 1864 when, following the Mutiny, flogging was reintroduced as a judicial penalty. Flagellomania quickly assumed monstrous proportions as the authorities gave free rein to their desire for revenge, to such an extent that in 1878 alone 75,223 floggings were inflicted.[20] These floggings were habitually administered with a rattan or cane to the naked buttocks in public. As one Indian writer commented mildly: 'It is now generally admitted that Indians feel a peculiar degradation in being subjected to whipping. It is a curious fact that those who were responsible for the Whipping Act [of 1864] knew nothing of this sentiment of the people for whom they were legislating' (Chakravarti, p.181). It could be argued that

[19] *Humanity*, April 1900, p.27.
[20] Sir Henry Cotton (1906), p.219.

those responsible were only too aware of the sentiment in question. The rage continued. There were 64,087 judicial floggings in 1897, 45,054 in 1900 and 23,186 in 1902;[21] 19,034 in 1908;[22] 12,559 in 1909, 9,876 in 1910, 9,519 in 1911 and, in 1912, a figure approaching 9,500.[23]

In 1875 Sir Richard Cross introduced a measure in the Commons which proposed to extend the punishment of flogging for crimes of violence. Fourteen years later Sir H. Selwin-Ibbetson recalled that 'we obtained for the Bill the sanction of every Judge in the Kingdom but two, and practically of every Quarter Sessions in the country, in favour of an alteration of the law in this particular way' (Hansard, *Commons*, 8 May 1889, col.1478). There was an important debate in the House, opposition to the Bill being led, brilliantly, by Peter Taylor, Member for Leicester. The House decided that the case against the Bill was conclusive and the Government was forced to drop it.

Following the outcry over W.T. Stead's revelations concerning child prostitution in 'The Maiden Tribute of Modern Babylon', the speedily-enacted Criminal Law Amendment Bill of 1885 raised the age of consent to 16; made procuration of women and children a criminal offence punishable, on conviction of indictment, by imprisonment for any term not exceeding two years; and, as we have seen, introduced flogging as a penalty for youths under 16 convicted of assaulting a girl under 13. The subject of flogging was hotly debated. in Parliament, but the weight of opinion came down in the end against the application of this penalty to adult males.[24]

Demands for increased flogging continued to be made, however. On 8 May 1889 a new Corporal Punishment Bill (not intended to apply to Scotland) passed its second reading, but was withdrawn a few months later before it became law. This Bill, had it been successful, would have empowered magistrates, first, to order boys up to the age of 16 to be birched instead of being sent to prison. It was an extension after which the magistrates had long hankered. As always the argument ran that it was preferable to birch youths rather than subject them to the degrading experience of prison. It seemed that no possible alternative could be envisaged. Mr Swetenham put the pro-flogging view in a nutshell, and at the same time showed himself most insensitive to the feelings of schoolboys:

[21] *ibid.*
[22] Sir Henry Cotton (1910), p.76.
[23] Sir Henry Cotton (1914), p.30.
[24] Details from the debate on the Criminal Law Amendment Bill (1912), Hansard, *Commons*, 1, 5, 6, 12 November 1912.

There are no persons who have acted as Chairmen of Quarter Session, and no persons who have acted as Judges of Assize, who have not from time to time felt most painfully the duty of being obliged to commit young boys under the age of 16 to prison, having no opportunity of administering instead the salutary punishment of a good flogging similar to that administered in schools, and we know that a boy is never degraded or brutalized by a flogging at school. (Hansard, *Commons*, 8 May 1889, col.1467)

As regards adult offenders, this Bill's opponents were even more alarmed, for it provided that magistrates should be empowered to order burglars, rapers of children, sodomites and those found guilty of bestiality to be flogged. Such a provision was absolutely novel. The floggers insisted that in cases such as these the lash would undoubtedly have a deterrent value (there were the habitual references to the 'success', long disproved, of the 'Garrotters Act' of 1863); they also insisted that, while they disliked the lash as much as everyone else, there was no alternative. They jeered at the suggestion made by the Bill's opponents that, in the matter of punishing criminals, Britain lagged behind the rest of the civilised world (Mr Shaw Lefevre had exclaimed 'Even Russia has now abandoned the knout. We are the only country that has made any retrograde step in the matter', *ibid.*, col.1465). Moreover, they claimed, it was ludicrous to talk of degrading a man who had already shown that he was a beast. As T. Milvain, the mover of the Bill, put it:

As to the argument about the punishment being brutalizing, in my opinion you cannot brutalize a person who has already brutalized himself by the commission of any of these offences. I cannot help thinking that the class who commit the kind of offences which I incorporate in this Bill are entirely lost to all moral sense, and I maintain that the only way to get at them is by appealing to their animal feelings. (*ibid.*, col.1442)

The Bill's opponents, on the other hand, expressed the view that, with flogging, everyone is brutalised and that the main victim of the system is not the criminal but society itself. Mr Pickersgill, who had put down the notice for the rejection of the Bill, explained this point of view with exemplary patience to the House:

I heard the hon. and learned Gentleman say that we sympathized with criminals. I wholly repudiate that statement. I think, indeed, it needs no repudiation; it answers itself. It is not the criminals we regard, but it is those who are not criminal. We have regard to the effect of a brutal punishment of this kind on the Judge who passes the sentence; upon the people in Court who hear it pronounced; upon the people outside who discuss the sentence; and the officials of the prisons, who are most unfortunate of all in having to inflict the punishment. In fact, it is not the criminals for whom we care, but the community. (*ibid.*, col.1475-6)[25]

One supporter of the Bill, to his credit, made a point all too rarely discussed in the flogging debates (or, indeed, the capital punishment debates) that occupied Parliament in the nineteenth century – and later. 'It does not follow,' said Mr Matthews, 'that because a punishment is deterrent, it is therefore justifiable' (*ibid.*, col.1458). When, a few years later, the Humanitarian League took up the fight against judicial flogging, it was precisely this argument that would come to the fore.

In 1898, in the belief that the White Slave traffic was getting worse, the Government introduced a Bill to extend the 1824 Vagrancy Act 'by providing that any male person living on the earnings of prostitution or soliciting for immoral purposes should be deemed a rogue and vagabond within the meaning of that Act' (*Cadogan*, p.4). This meant in effect that any person convicted under this provision would be liable to a whipping on a second or consequent conviction of the offence. The Government seems not to have realised fully the flogging implications of the Bill, and accepted an amendment repealing the whipping sections of the 1824 Act. The Lords rejected this amendment, however, and eventually the Bill was passed in its original form. The new Act did not apply to Scotland (where, as has been noted, the flogging of adults was abolished in 1862).[26]

On 24 March 1898 Bernard Shaw gave a lecture at Essex Hall entitled 'Flagellomania'. Shaw had no illusions about the motives behind the cry for the lash, and was one of the very few people in the country who had the courage and honesty to draw attention to the sexual implications of flogging. *Humanity* published a summary of the lecture:

[25] A similar view was expressed by the humane Recorder of Liverpool, Mr Hopwood, Q.C.: 'Flogging sentences brutalise and corrupt all society where it is practised. Its baneful example engenders deterioration in the judge who avails himself of it, as shown by his increasing use of the lash; the warder who administers it, who is paid extra for his disgusting service; the gaoler, who is bound to witness the torture and urge the warder if he prove too tender; the surgeon, who must stand by to ascertain the moment when the extreme of suffering a poor wretch can bear has been reached; while the spectators in court are taught the lesson that bodily suffering is approved by the law' (quoted by Joseph Collinson in *The Saturday Review*, 8 October 1898, p.473).

[26] *Cadogan*, pp. 4-5.

> With reference to the title of his lecture, Mr Shaw quoted from *Reynold's Newspaper* a notice of a recent book on 'Flagellation',[27] and pointed out that flogging is a form of debauchery which is perfectly well known, a mania which is based on a *sensual* instinct, though in some cases it takes the retaliatory form ... In our own century gentlemen have made up parties to see women flogged. (April, 1898, p.26)

In a later chapter we shall see that, concurrently with their reports of the periodic flogging debates in Parliament, the newspapers published regular accounts of raids on flagellant brothels, giving details of the birches, canes and other paraphernalia which the police could always be sure of finding in such establishments. Despite the fact that, as Shaw had pointed out, these practices were 'perfectly well known', those responsible for legislation could never bring themselves to mention them – with the rarest exceptions, and then enveloped in euphemism.

In 1900 Mr Lloyd Wharton, who had many years' experience as a magistrate, introduced his Private Member's Corporal Punishment Bill to the Commons. As he pointed out, this Bill was in fact 'precisely the same' as the abortive 1889 Bill (Hansard, *Commons*, 28 March 1900, col.547). Many fighting speeches were made in opposition to the Bill, notably by Serjeant Hemphill, Mr Asquith, Dr Farquharson and the Irish member Mr Dillon. The Bill's opponents were united in their conviction that further whipping powers must be withheld from the magistrates, on whose lack of legal training and frequent lack of judgement many caustic observations were passed. Farquharson was particularly outspoken:

> I want a man trained in his profession. In Scotland we have a better course of procedure. We have no amateur gentlemen aping the airs and graces of lawyers; we have no clergymen on the bench, the most pitiless of all people to deal with questions having any practical bearing on Christian charity ... You have country gentlemen steeped in all the prejudices of their class, sitting on the bench and aping knowledge of a profession in which they have not been trained. (*ibid.*, cols. 574-5)

Hemphill spoke up in support:

> We are now asked to return to the time when corporal punishment was inflicted at the discretion of justices; we are asked to go back almost to the days of the pillory and the stocks, when the character of the English

[27] I looked in vain for this notice. *Reynold's Newspaper* regularly published at this time a titillating list of 'Curious and Rare Books', however, so it is not unlikely that such an advertisement appeared in its columns.

people was more or less disgraced by the way in which country justices administered justice. (*ibid.*, col.576)

It is of great interest to note that the Tory Secretary of State for the Home Department, Sir Matthew White Ridley, spoke against Lloyd Wharton's Bill. In 1889 he had supported the Bill. He had changed his mind because, as he said, 'I have seen something of the administration of the criminal law from another point of view since I entered the office which I now hold; and I do not hesitate to say that in my belief it is not a desirable change to make in the law' (*ibid.*, col.583). Faced with such opposition the Bill could not hope to succeed, and was heavily defeated.

Between 1898 and 1912 many men were sentenced by magistrates to be flogged under the provisions of the original Vagrancy Act of 1824 and the new one of 1898. In the twelve months ending on 31 October 1912, for example, 23 flogging sentences were imposed.[28] Such floggings did not have to be confirmed by the Home Secretary, although if he heard about a sentence he might intervene. Thus in Dorset five old tramps were convicted of sleeping out and begging, and birched before the Home Secretary knew of the sentence.[29]

In 1907 Lord Hatherton, Chairman of the Staffordshire Quarter Sessions, sentenced a man in his sixty-sixth year to be birched (on the naked buttocks, remember) for vagrancy. There was a heated response in the press; the Humanitarian League protested; and the Home Secretary remitted the sentence. Lord Hatherton was the same age as his intended victim, and a retired Colonel of the Grenadier Guards.[30]

More advanced legal minds were strongly opposed to the antiquated provisions of the 1824 Vagrancy Act. The *Law Times* commented on 25 January 1908:

> To any reform party in the House of Commons, we take leave to commend that anomalous Vagrant Act under which magistrates may order the 'incorrigible rogue' to be flogged. The 'incorrigible rogue' is often an old, worn-out tramp who has been convicted of begging and sleeping in the open air, and we fear that he is sometimes a genuine labourer who has failed in the effort to provide himself with work. (*The Humanitarian*, April 1908, p.27)

But there were still magistrates who would not listen. In June 1909

---

[28] Hansard, *Commons*, 12 November 1912, col. 1856.
[29] *The Humanitarian*, February 1908, p.13.
[30] *ibid.*, December 1907, pp. 188-9.

Mr Montagu Sharpe passed a birching sentence on another old man at the Middlesex Sessions. This 'incorrigible rogue', sixty-five years of age, had been found guilty of begging. The sentence was remitted by the Home Office. Mr Montagu Sharpe, it emerged, was Chairman of the Royal Society for the Protection of Birds.[31]

As regards flogging sentences imposed for robbery with violence under the 1863 Security from Violence Act, there had been a decrease from 65 in 1894 to only 5 in 1906.[32] Then, in 1908, there was a rash of such sentences at Cardiff under Mr Justice A.T. Lawrence. Lawrence began his flogging campaign by imposing a sentence of 12 months' imprisonment and 12 strokes of the 'cat' on a 17-year-old soldier who had been involved in a brawl. Other sentences followed and, as a result of the excitement these generated, there was a lurid correspondence on flogging in the local papers.[33]

In the same year Mr J. Lloyd Morgan, K.C., introduced his one-clause Corporal Punishment Restriction Bill in the Commons. The aim of the Bill was to abolish the 'cat' and birch entirely for male offenders over the age of sixteen. The Bill was not successful.[34]

In 1912 alarm about the White Slave traffic revived, encouraged by exaggerated reports appearing in the newspapers, and the Liberal Government introduced the Criminal Law Amendment Bill, better known as the White Slave Bill. It was claimed that white slaving was getting worse, and that existing penalties, including the whipping provisions of the 1898 Vagrancy Act, were ineffectual. Once again the flogging debate got under way. The supporters of the Bill affirmed that the trade was largely in the hands of foreigners:

> A very large proportion of them, I am glad to say, are not Englishmen. I regret that some are, but if hon. Members could see not merely foreigners, not merely debased Englishmen, but dozens of negroes in the West End of London running white English girls on the streets, they would see at whom we wish to get. (Hansard, *Commons*, 12 November 1912, col.1901)

Thus Arthur Lee, one of the Bill's promoters. The pro-floggers assumed that, in the case of such men, whipping would act as a deterrent, as it was taken for granted that anyone engaged in such a trade would automatically be a coward. Reginald McKenna, the Home Secretary, put the flogging case mildly: 'We are dealing with a particular class of persons that have recently come into this country,

---

[31] *ibid.*, June 1909, pp. 141-2; July 1909, p.149.
[32] *ibid.*, May 1908, p.36.
[33] *ibid.*, May 1908, p.37.
[34] *ibid.*, July 1908, p.53.

and who can be driven out of it, as the police advise me, because in fact they will be intimidated by the fear of flogging' (*ibid.*, 1 November 1912, col.769).

The military men in the House were more virulent in their sentiments. Colonel Lockwood was cheered when he affirmed that 'A man who is found guilty of a crime of the description mentioned in this Bill is not a man; he is an animal' (*ibid.*, col.770). Colonel Burn agreed: 'When you do deport such a man I should like him to have the hall-mark of some British muscle on his back' (*ibid.*, col.786). Burn was echoed by Gershom Stewart: 'If we are to let him out in a week, we ought at least to let him out with the hall-mark of British muscle on his back, so that he will carry away some appreciation of the sentiment of Great Britain towards procuration' (*ibid.*, col.791). The most honest statement of the flogging position, however, came from the Marquess of Tullabardine. In answer to the charge of the humanitarians in the House that flogging with the 'cat' was torture – a charge habitually denied by the floggers – he exclaimed:

> I dislike flogging as much as hon. Members opposite, and probably I have seen a good deal more of it than many Members of this House. I quite agree that it is a brutal punishment, that it is a torture, and that it draws blood, and it is for that very reason I want to see it applied. I do not say that with any vindictiveness, and while I agree that the idea of flogging is repulsive, I cannot honestly see in what other way you can possibly deal with this crime. (12 November 1912, col.1917)

As regards the flogging clauses in the Bill, it was provided (1) that male persons convicted of a second or subsequent offence of procuring under the 1885 Act should be liable to be once privately whipped and (2) that male persons charged with living on the earnings of prostitution or soliciting for immoral purposes might be proceeded against on indictment and might, on a second or subsequent conviction, be ordered to be privately whipped. George Greenwood, in an eloquent plea for humanity, first moved that (1) be deleted from the Bill.[35]

He was ably supported by a handful of fellow anti-floggers. When it came to the division on (1), the Government insisted on putting on the official Whips. The House voted overwhelmingly in favour of the clause, by 297 votes to 44.[36]

During the debate that followed the acceptance of (1), the pro-floggers attempted to have the clause altered to provide for whipping

[35] Hansard, *Commons*, 1 November 1912, cols. 756-64.
[36] *ibid.*, 1 November 1912, cols. 789-90.

for a *first* offence. The Government allowed the amendment to go to a free vote. It was a close thing, the Government winning by 136 votes to 132, a majority of only four in favour of the Bill as it stood.[37]

Flagellomania had gripped the House and, had the amendment been carried, flogging would undoubtedly have become much more frequent.

When it came to (2), George Greenwood rose again to move that the flogging provisions be deleted from the Bill.[38] As before he was ably supported. But to no avail. The House divided 288 to 74 in favour of the Bill.[39]

The pro-floggers then pressed, as they had done with (1), to have the clause altered to provide for whipping for a *first* offence, but when it went to the division the Government won again, this time by the slightly larger majority of 188 votes to 164.

How did it come about, it may be asked, that a Liberal Government promoted a Bill which was remarkably illiberal in spirit? The Humanitarian League, at least, was of the view that the Government's real motive for introducing the Bill at this time was to placate the suffragettes and shift public attention from their claims:

> They will not give women the vote, which would be in accordance with Liberal principles, but they try to console them by whipping White Slave traffickers, which is in violation with those principles. As the Parliamentary correspondent of the *Daily News* shrewdly remarked: 'Any one who has watched the treatment of this sort of Bill can hardly avoid the conclusion that the defeat of weakening amendments is the direct result of the franchise movement.' (*The Humanitarian*, December 1912, pp. 90-1)

One of the most remarkable features of the 1912 debate was that not a single reference was made in either House to the by now well-known sexual associations of flogging, especially in connection with prostitution. The humanitarians did allude, however, to the 'brutalising' effect of the practice on the man inflicting the punishment and on those forced to witness the ceremony. Lord Eversley broke new ground when he stated in the House of Lords:

> I have consulted at different times persons who have seen the infliction of flogging as it is carried out at present in our gaols. It is carried out by warders, who receive additional pay for it, and the prison officials have to be present to see that it is properly carried out. I am told that the effect

[37] *ibid.*, 1 November 1912, cols. 801-04.
[38] *ibid.*, 12 November 1912, cols. 1892-6.
[39] *ibid.*, 12 November 1912, cols. 1933-8.

upon these men is decidedly bad. The warders who have to inflict it begin by a feeling of disgust at it, but that passes away soon, and there seems to be a strange fascination connected with the system which has a bad effect in stimulating the passion of the men who are engaged upon it, and not only them, but also the officials who are bound to be present. For my part I think that the State has no right to put these men in a position where they are compelled to be parties to scenes of that kind. (Hansard, *Lords*, 9 December 1912, col.111)

Lord Eversley's views were corroborated in the House of Commons by Mr Llewellyn Williams who, in his capacity as a justice, had himself witnessed judicial flogging:

I saw a warder administering twelve lashes with the 'cat'. At first he shrank from administering it, but, after four or five lashes had been laid on the naked back, and blood was squirting from it, that warder, instead of shrinking from his task, seemed to be taken with a blood lust, and could hardly stop himself from inflicting the punishment. A more brutalising thing never happened in my experience. This House has no right to brutalise men who have committed no crime against the law. It has no right to brutalise warders or policemen. (Hansard, *Commons*, 12 November 1912, col.1900)

Such statements, while not, perhaps, outstandingly frank, were certainly a step in the right direction; and although one scans the debate in vain for the word 'sadism', by then quite common, it is clear that there is a growing awareness, a vague uneasiness, about the perversity involved in judicial flagellation.

It took Bernard Shaw to see through the cant, ignorance and sheer viciousness involved in the passing of the White Slave Act. On 16 November 1912 he published an article in which he expanded his 1898 lecture on 'Flagellomania'. The vital part of this document reads:

As to the flogging from which all our fools expect so much, it will certainly give a lively stimulus to the White Slave traffic. That traffic makes a good deal of money out of flogging, which is a well-established form of vice. White Slaves make money for themselves and their employers by allowing men to flog them. Whenever a flogging is described in the papers they have a rush of custom. The literature of their trade is full of flogging. Men actually pay women to flog them. In the last epidemic of prostitution in London, when brothels boldly advertized themselves in all directions as massage establishments, the 'treatments' always included 'Russian flagellation', which was impudently announced on posters. The new Act will produce another epidemic; and it will also drive the whole business of direct procuration into the hands of women, who are not to be flogged under the Act; though any unemployed laborer whose wife, in desperation

at the children's hunger, solicits a man in the street, can be flogged under
it. The action of the House of Commons was not sane legislation; it was an
explosion of blackguardism, excusable in a bargee whose daughter has
been abducted by a White Slaver, but appalling in the rulers of a civilized
empire. The subject they were dealing with infected them; and they fell
below the level of the men they were legislating to flog.

If any man doubts that this is the real secret and nature of flogging
legislation, let him ask himself this question. Why, out of all the many
methods by which pain can be inflicted on a criminal, is this particular
method chosen? You can hurt a man with an electric brush worse than
with any instrument of flagellation. There are intolerable methods of
torture actually in use in some American prisons rather than face which I
myself would take any flogging that public opinion would stand. Flogging
is not more deterrent: on the contrary, the same men get flogged for the
same offence again and again. Why, then, is flogging chosen? Why do
people frantically keep protesting that it is the only punishment that these
people fear – that it put down garrotting – that its opponents are
sentimentalists – any absurd and ten-times-disproved falsehood put
forward recklessly in the agonies of a ridiculous longing for this relic of the
Cities of the Plain? The answer is obvious. The Act is a final triumph of
the vice it pretends to repress. (Shaw, 1912, p.7)[40]

As was mentioned in the previous section, the Humanitarian
League had warned that the White Slave Bill would lead to an
increase in the demand for flogging. They were right, and the
magistrates raised their voices yet again at this time in favour of wider
powers for whipping boys. The flogging of drunkards was advocated
by Dr H.C. Miller, and the birch for militant suffragettes was the
novel recommendation put forward by Ernest Vizetelly in the *Daily
Telegraph*. A long correspondence on the whipping of girls appeared in
the *Leeds Mercury* in early 1913, and the Rev. G.E. Thorne expressed
his desire 'to see the birch used on Mormon Elders' because, in his
opinion, Mormonism was another form of the White Slave traffic.[41]
Observing the symptoms of flagellomania on all sides, one
correspondent wrote to the *Star*:

Sir, – Ought not everybody to be flogged? The question is really becoming
urgent, in view of the clamour that is being raised, day by day, for the
whipping of somebody or other. Thus, to give a few recent instances only,
it has been proposed to flog the following:

[40] Shaw returned to this theme in the preface to *Misalliance* (1914).
[41] All four cases from *The Humanitarian*, May 1913, p.130.

Criminals who carry revolvers.
Persons who throw missiles at motor cars.
Motorists who drive recklessly.
Men guilty of violence to women.
Suffragettes who break windows.
Men who assault young girls and children.
Foreigners who insult English girls.
Parents who neglect their children.
Children who disobey their parents.
Midshipmen who cannot manage a boat.
Boys who steal fruit.
Persons who ill-treat animals.

It is not time that some Member of Parliament should introduce the Universal Whipping Bill?

                                                    J. BIRCHALL.

(*The Humanitarian*, December 1912, p.92)

In February 1914 it was reported that the local Parliament of the Channel Islands had passed a Bill making 'any person', without distinction of sex, liable to corporal punishment for offences against the Criminal Law Amendment Act of 1885. An amendment excepting women from the lash (presumably the birch applied to their naked bottoms) was defeated by 27 votes to 11. The London Government suppressed the Bill.[42]

As regards whippings inflicted under the White Slave Act itself, in 1913 there were 17 flogging sentences for 'procuration' and 5 for 'attempts to commit unnatural offences'. The number of such sentences sank to 7 and 2 respectively in 1914. In commenting on these figures, *The Humanitarian* noted that there had been little recent talk of the Act: 'What has really happened is, of course, that the greater excitement of the war has, for the time, drawn away attention from the minor excitement of flogging white slavers. That there will be a recrudescence of the flogging craze later on, we have no doubt whatever' (April 1916, p.143). In 1917 the Humanitarian League found ample evidence that just such a recrudescence was under way.[43]

Prison floggings

One would expect a flagellant Establishment to approve of the lash for breaches of prison discipline. Such was the case in England (and Wales). By contrast, prison flogging was not found necessary in

[42] *The Humanitarian*, August 1914, p.63.
[43] *ibid.*, April 1917, pp. 23-4.

Scotland, Ireland – or on the Continent. 'England,' wrote Henry Salt, 'shares with Russia, Turkey and Morocco the disgrace of being unable to preserve prison discipline without recourse to the lash' (1916, p.63). Under the Prison Offences Act, 1898, the offences for which corporal punishment could be awarded in both local and convict prisons were limited by statute to three – mutiny, incitement to mutiny and 'gross personal violence' to an officer or servant of the establishment. The same Act provided that all prison floggings must first be confirmed by the Home Office.[44] In a brief section tucked away at the end of the annual Reports of the Prison Commissioners, details of the number of prison floggings inflicted each year were provided. The 'ground for the sentence' was almost always given as 'gross personal violence to an officer of the prison' and it was sometimes stated that 'the offence was entirely unprovoked':

> That the assaults are always 'entirely unprovoked' [commented Henry Salt] only a very rigid faith in officialism is likely to believe; for, human nature being what it is, and the relations of warder and prisoner being what they are, the certainty seems to be absolute that *some* warders will occasionally so act as to provoke *some* prisoners against whom they happen to have a grudge. (1916, p.61)

It was even suggested by some critics of the system that warders might deliberately provoke prisoners in order that, when sentence was passed, they might have the pleasure of themselves inflicting a flogging while at the same time receiving the special fee.[45] The trials for breaches of prison rules, it should be understood, were held entirely in secret before Visiting Justices – often old Army officers, landed squires and so on, people who might be expected to side with the prison authorities against the miscreant. Since their deliberations were secret, the public could have no means of knowing what was said. News of prison floggings rarely appeared in the press. The prisoner, moreover, was undefended and seems to have had no right of appeal. In 1909 the *Law Times* expressed its dissatisfaction with this state of affairs:

> One objection to the authority of this tribunal is that it holds its trials in secret. By what process of reasoning the Visiting Justices reach their decisions, who among us shall say? We turn, for example, to the latest report of the Prison Commissioners, and read that at Birmingham Prison a certain 'W.W.' received sentence of twelve strokes with the birch. The

[44] *Cadogan*, p.6.
[45] *The Humanitarian*, April 1908, p.27.

entry immediately below this had reference to one 'M.B.' at Knutsford Prison, whose sentence was thirty-six strokes with the same instrument. Yet the 'grounds for the sentence' in the two cases are identical, and nothing is said which might warrant the inference that one prisoner had a worse record than the other. (*The Humanitarian*, November 1909, p.180)

The Visiting Justices could order that the flogging be inflicted with either the 'cat' or the birch, as they wished. As we have seen, the sentence had to be confirmed, under the 1898 Act, by the Home Office. In the vast majority of cases confirmation was given. In the two years ending 31 March 1907, for example, Herbert Gladstone and his predecessor confirmed between them 67 prison floggings and only remitted 3.[46] Between 1910 and 1936, 302 flogging sentences were imposed by Visiting Justices; of these, 241, that is 79.8%, were confirmed by the Home Office. 47.3% of these floggings were inflicted with the 'cat', 52.7% with the birch.[47] It would seem, therefore, that the preferences of the Visiting Justices were split more or less equally between the two instruments. The 'cat', of course, was applied to the bare shoulders, the birch to the naked buttocks.

The Report of the Prison Commissioners for the year ending 31 March 1910 showed that, in all, there had been 31 prison floggings in that year. Of these, 12 had been administered with the birch and the rest with the 'cat'. Winston Churchill was then Home Secretary, and the Humanitarian League, which had consistently maintained that birching was indecent as well as cruel, suggested to him that 'he might well refuse to confirm sentences of this kind, on the ground of their sheer indecency' (*The Humanitarian*, November 1910, p.85). Had the League known of Churchill's experience at the hands of his preparatory school headmaster, whom we met earlier, they might have made their plea more personal. Churchill did remit some birching sentences but he confirmed others, as he did many floggings with the 'cat' (including one of 30 lashes inflicted on a prisoner at Portland Prison in 1911).[48]

It came as a shock to me to discover that prison floggings were only finally abolished in England and Wales in 1967, under Section 65 of the Criminal Justice Act of that year. Between 1911 and the year of

[46] *ibid.*

[47] *Cadogan*, pp. 101, 141.

[48] *The Humanitarian*, commenting on the figures for 1911, remarked that out of the 23 prison floggings imposed in that year, in three cases only had the number of strokes been reduced by the Home Secretary. 'We regret to note,' the writer added, 'that the disgusting practice of birching grown men is on the increase, there being eleven sentences in which the birch was specified in place of the "cat"' (November 1911, p.179).

abolition, as the annual Reports of the Prison Commissioners reveal, some 350 prisoners were flogged, the tables showing again that the magistrates' preferences regarding the instrument of infliction were more or less equally split between the 'cat' and the birch. The last flogging sentences were awarded in 1962, when four prisoners were birched.

Floggings in the Army and Navy

Until well into the nineteenth century flogging was common in both the Army and Navy whereas in France, by contrast, the practice had long been abolished. Often the floggings, normally inflicted with the 'cat', were of sickening brutality, the Duke of York being considered humane when, in 1812, he recommended that the number of lashes be reduced to a maximum of 300.[49] Not infrequently men died as a result of illness brought on by an excessive flogging. Men such as John Frederick White, for example, who received 150 lashes at Hounslow in 1846,[50] or Robert Sim, who died after the infliction of 50 lashes at Limerick in 1867.[51] The 'cat' had, literally, nine 'tails' or thongs, which were separated by the flogger between each stroke, so that the number of lashes actually inflicted was greatly in excess of the apparent total.

In 1867 an Act was passed abolishing flogging in the Army in peace time.[52] This was followed in 1881 by an Act that totally abolished flogging in the Army except as a prison punishment.[53]

It was little wonder that British officers and soldiers, trained in the flogging system, ran amuck on occasions, and indulged in a flagellant orgy. Probably the most notorious instance occurred during the repression of the Morant Bay rioters in Jamaica in 1865. The reprisals were carried out with ferocity by Governor Eyre, whose troops embarked on a three-week binge of hangings, torture, rape and floggings. 600 men, women and children were indiscriminately killed, 1,000 houses burned down and many hundreds of other innocents executed.[54] It was the floggings inflicted on the negro women,

---

[49] Cooper (1870), pp. 353-4.

[50] For this incident, see the articles by the surgeon, Erasmus Wilson, listed in the bibliography.

[51] See 'Flogged to Death', *The Lancet*, 16 February 1867, p.219. *The Lancet* commented (forgetting Meibom, Acton, etc.): 'Flogging should be inflicted on the buttocks and not on the back over important vital organs.'

[52] Cooper (1870), pp. 354.

[53] Henry Salt (1916), p.17.

[54] Sandwith (1871), p.39.

however, which received most publicity in Britain, particularly when it emerged that they had been beaten on their naked buttocks, sometimes with piano wire (which cut their flesh to shreds). In the midst of the controversy during which a high-powered committee was set up in defence of Governor Eyre, H. Pringle, a former Jamaican Stipendiary Magistrate, wrote a frank letter to the *Daily News*:

> Men are flogged on their bare backs and shoulders. It is otherwise with women – they are flogged, according to Jamaican fashion, on their naked posteriors. However shocking this may be to mention, it is not the less necessary that the fact should be known. The person of a woman flogged is publicly and indecently exposed in shameful nakedness. The revelation of the facts relating to such floggings of women by the West Indian slave-owners was the circumstance that most powerfully roused the indignation of the people of this country against negro slavery, and most prominently conduced to its abolition. I am altogether at a loss to conceive that, under any possible circumstances of insurrection or warfare, it could be necessary to resort to this abominable and ferocious punishment of women. The subject is quite unfit for a woman to think of, but it is absolutely necessary for the ends of justice, and a due regard for outraged humanity, that these things should be made known to the women of England. (6 January 1866)

These revelations excited the flagellants, but Swinburne, for once, dropped his banter and confessed his disgust with Governor Eyre, who had been one of his childhood heroes.[55]

Floggings in the Navy were even more brutal than in the Army, and depended solely on the whim of individual captains. At sea, far from home, far from the newspapers, many abuses were undoubtedly committed. One has the impression that ships were run like floating boarding schools for adults, on public school lines. An article entitled 'Britannia's Shame' published in *The Leader and Saturday Analyst* on 11 February 1860 analysed a startling Return, dated 14 July 1859, made to the House of Commons. This document, 'Flogging in the Navy', gave full details of all floggings inflicted in 1858. It showed that, out of 47,646 sailors liable to be flogged, 997 were in fact so punished, receiving between them 32,420 lashes of the 'cat': 'and if we suppose,' the writer observes, 'that only six of the tails struck each time, they felt the anguish of 194,520 stripes. On every back, on the average, thirty-two lashes and something more were struck.' The writer went on to muse about the feelings of the aristocratic mothers of England whose

---

[55] Lang, III, pp. 230-3.

dear sons were forced to witness these revolting ceremonies (to which
they were not themselves liable, of course); but absent is any reference
to the mothers of the victims:

> It must be a horrible reflection for the aristocratic mothers of England,
> that the gentle boys who go from their arms or the care of kind preceptors
> to be Britannia's sea captains, are compelled to attend such cruel scenes,
> and are thus corrupted and hardened in the very beginning of life, to
> delight afterwards, perhaps, in cruelty originally abhorrent to their
> natures. Thus, however, by continually hardening youngsters,
> instruments are created for perpetuating the barbarous system from
> generation to generation, and amongst the youth whom it corrupts and
> debases we find, judging from the return, the worst examples of its
> abominations. (p.135)

There was good sense in the *Leader*'s article, but the writer might have
pointed out that most of these young sons of aristocratic mothers had
doubtless already been pretty well hardened to being flogged and
seeing others being flogged while at their public schools, or earlier –
long before they went to sea.

William Stables was a naval medical officer at about this time, and
in his book *Medical Life in the Navy* (1868) he described several of the
floggings at which he was forced to be present. His account of the
punishment meted out to the 16-year-old Tommie gives us a good idea
of the appalling conditions that prevailed aboard these ships.
Tommie, who ought to have been keeping his watch, had been found
by a brutal corporal gazing at a picture of his sister.

> 'That is my sister,' cried Tommie, with tears in his eyes.
> 'Your sister!' sneered the corporal; 'she is a –' and he added a word that
> cannot be named. There was the spirit of young England, however, in
> Tommie's breast; and the word had scarcely crossed the corporal's lips,
> when those lips, and his nose too, were dyed in the blood the boy's fist had
> drawn. For that blow poor Tommie was condemned to receive four dozen
> lashes. And the execution of the sentence was carried out with all the
> pomp and show usual on such occasions. Arrayed in cocked-hats,
> epaulets, and swords, we all assembled to witness that helpless child in his
> agony. One would have thought that even the rough bo'swain's mate
> would have hesitated to disfigure skin so white and tender, or that the
> frightened and imploring glance Tommie cast upward on the first
> descending lash would have unnerved his arm. Did it? No, reader; pity
> there doubtless was among us, but mercy – none. Oh! we were a brave
> band. And the poor boy writhed in his agony; his screams and cries were
> heartrending; and, God forgive us! we knew not till then he was an
> orphan, till we heard him beseech his mother in heaven to look down on

her son, to pity and support him. Ah! well, perhaps she did, for scarcely had the third dozen commenced when Tommie's cries were hushed, his head drooped on his shoulder like a little dead bird's, and for a while his sufferings were at an end. I gladly took the opportunity to report further proceedings as dangerous, and he was carried away to his hammock.

I will not shock the nerves and feelings of the reader by any further relation of the horrors of flogging, merely adding, that I consider corporal punishment, as applied to men, *cowardly*, *cruel*, and debasing to *human nature*; and as applied to boys, *brutal*, and sometimes even *fiendish*. There is only one question I wish to ask of every true-hearted English lady who may read these lines – Be you sister, wife, or mother, could you in your heart have respected the commander who, with folded arms and grim smile, replied to poor Tommie's frantic appeals for mercy, 'Continue the punishment'? (pp.98-9).

Naval floggings gradually became less severe as the century progressed. In 1881, when flogging was completely abolished in the Army (except for prison offences), the use of the 'cat' was suspended in the Navy, though not technically abolished. This meant, in fact, that the Admiralty might at any time reinstate the lash; it also meant that every ship still carried a supply of the brutal instruments, just in case.[56]

As regards the flogging of 'cadets' (boys up to 18) in the Navy, traditional ideas prevailed. New regulations had been issued in 1858 abolishing the 'cat' and substituting the birch – a more humiliating punishment taking the place of a physically more brutal one (if only marginally so).[57] As in the Lower School at Eton, the birch was always administered in public, to the naked buttocks. The revelant section of the King's Regulations reads:

Section 759. – 'Birching is to be confined solely to boys rated as such, and is to be inflicted with the birch as supplied from the dockyard; the birching is to be given over the bare breech, and is never to exceed 24 cuts; it is to be inflicted by the ship's police in the presence of the executive officer, a medical officer, two or more petty officers, and all the boys.'[58]

[56] On 1 November 1909, the First Lord of the Admiralty, Mr McKenna, was questioned in the Commons about the suspension of the 'cat':
Mr McKenna: The use of the cat has been suspended by Admiralty order since 1881.
Mr Byles: Can it be renewed by Admiralty order?
Mr McKenna: Yes, it can be renewed by Admiralty order, but I imagine my hon. friend would take the earliest opportunity to draw attention to it.
(*The Humanitarian*, December 1909, p.188)
[57] Cooper (1870), pp. 371-2.
[58] Quoted in a letter to *The Times*, 13 June 1904, p.5.

According to a Parliamentary Paper of 6 May 1903, the weight of the naval birch was 9 ounces, that is 4½ ounces heavier than the official birch supplied by the Home Office to the Police Courts.[59] The naval birch, moreover, was apparently steamed over the coppers to make it as tough as possible.[60]

The cane was also in use in the Navy for the punishment of cadets, and was also applied in public. Up to twelve cuts could be administered 'on the breech with clothes on'.[61] Used brutally, the cane was an even more vicious weapon than the birch.

A return for 1900 showed that 315 public birchings had been inflicted summarily on naval cadets in that year, all of them, of course, being witnessed by the other 'boys'.[62] Given the strong voyeuristic element always associated with sexual flagellation, there can be no doubt that these exhibitions must have been found most titillating by many of those present, as Bernard Shaw began to point out as early as 1897:

> Imprisonment and dismissal from the service are severe punishments; but they can afford no gratification whatever to officers who have no personal grudge against the sufferer. They are purely troublesome; and the fewer of them we are forced to inflict the better for everybody concerned. But corporal punishment is a completely different matter. It is capable of being used as a sport, a debauch, masquerading as a deterrent or as 'justice'. There is a flagellation neurosis, well known to psychiatrists and some less reputable persons. A public flogging will always draw a crowd; and there will be in that crowd plenty of manifestations of a horrible passional ecstasy in the spectacle of laceration and suffering from which even the most self-restrained and secretive person who can prevail on himself to be present will not be wholly free.[63]

The great strength of Shaw's argument against flogging was that he recognised that everyone, including himself, was likely to be brutalised by the system. Naturally such an argument was unacceptable to the public school mind.[64]

[59] *The Humanitarian*, June 1904, p.43.

[60] *ibid.*, July 1905, p.146.

[61] As for note 58.

[62] *Humanity*, December 1901, p.191. The corresponding figure for 1903 was 238 (*The Humanitarian*, July 1904, p.51).

[63] Letter to *The Saturday Review*, 28 August 1897, p.224. This was the first of five brilliantly argued letters on flogging in the Navy published by Shaw in this journal between August and November 1897. Several irate naval men entered the lists, and the correspondence continued until December of that year.

[64] Thus Charles Crauford wrote to *The Saturday Review* in favour of the birch for naval cadets: 'A whipping, that is to say, not so very much more severe than those

Several newspapers opened their colums to the Naval and other pro-floggers.[65]

The birch was used on Naval cadets until 1906 when, after years of indefatigable exertion by Shaw, Joseph Collinson and Henry Salt (both of the Humanitarian League) and a handful of M.P.s led by Swift MacNeill, the Admiralty was forced to capitulate: in that year summary inflictions of corporal punishment were abolished in the Navy and the cane was substituted for the birch. Public beatings were no longer allowed.[66]

The Admiralty had made a pitiful showing both in the House of Commons and in the various journals in which its spokesmen expressed themselves. The outbursts of Vice-Admiral C.C. Penrose Fitzgerald in *The Times* when goaded by Bernard Shaw made particularly sickly reading:

Mr Bernard Shaw then treats your readers to some blood-curdling details about a 'flagellant epidemic,' an 'official executioner,' 'physical torture,' 'the flaying of the unfortunate wretch's bare breech,' and a heap more nauseous cant of a similar description. As if British youths had not been birched and caned from time immemorial, not only at our public schools, but elsewhere; and yet the race has not turned out badly on the whole.

It is singularly opportune that a Commission has been appointed to inquire into the treatment of the feeble-minded and epileptic just at this epoch of our national development; for truly there never was greater need for such an inquiry, and if the members of the Commission are men of robust common sense they will give their first attention to the pseudo-philanthropists and effeminate doctrinaires who compose all the ranting brotherhoods and shrieking sisterhoods which are responsible for

inflicted at our Public Schools for inattention to studies' (4 September 1897, p.262). H.W. Wilson shared Crauford's view (on the same date): 'At any public school a lower-form boy who struck a monitor or prefect would be badly beaten. In a military force, such as our navy is, such crimes – and they are recurring with unpleasant frequency – deserve nothing but the severest punishment' (p.263). In fact, naval birchings were very much more severe than those at the public schools – up to 24 strokes could be administered and frequently were. As Shaw pointed out, these naval men's 'notion that the boatswain's mate, under orders to make an example of a mutineer, handles a birch as an Eton master does, is entirely worthy of their credulity' (*The Saturday Review*, 18 September 1897, p.318).

[65] Among them the *Morning Post* and the *Globe*, which Shaw termed as 'harbours of refuge for military gentlemen afflicted with this disease' (*Humanity*, April 1898, p.26).

[66] *The Humanitarian* published full details each month of events leading up to abolition. See especially the issue for April 1906, pp. 25-8. The Humanitarian League had greatly embarrassed the Admiralty by repeatedly asking for facilities to publish photographs of naval birchings 'in order to inform the public' of the brutality and humiliating nature of these ceremonies – see *The Humanitarian*, June 1904, pp. 42-3.

humanitarian leagues, anti-vivisectionist leagues, anti-vaccination leagues, and numerous other anti-commonsense leagues, supported by feeble-minded cranks who would be otherwise quite unable to attract any public attention.[67] (*The Times*, 9 September 1904, p.6)

It must be stressed that up to 1906, the year of abolition, the birch was frequently applied publicly to the naked buttocks of cadets *in their eighteenth year*, a practice which by that date would have been considered unacceptable at most of the public schools. Once again the feelings of working-class Britons were not considered by the Establishment to be as sensitive as those of boys from more privileged families.

Such was the shame involved in these birchings that several lads committed, or attempted to commit, suicide rather than undergo them.[68] It is hardly surprising. There are many first-hand descriptions of these morbid ceremonies. Two may suffice. The first comes from the *Naval and Military Record*, a journal opposed to flogging:

Another (I forget his offence) would utter no sound. Towards the completion of the number of strokes the corporal began to be anxious for his reputation, so he resorted to the unfair and terrible upward stroke, but his aim was not true. The poor fellow gave a yell which I shall never forget, and fainted at once. Your readers must conjecture what had happened. Until he had been surgically examined there was some anxiety, but when it was known that no permanent injury had been inflicted the matter became one for jest among those sufficiently lost to all sense of decency and humanity. (*The Humanitarian*, January 1905, p.103)

The second was published by *The Humanitarian* in an article entitled 'Flogging in the Navy (By One who has Experienced It)':

The most degrading and truly demoralising chastisement is, however, the

[67] In October 1904 the views of the pro-flogging brigade were ridiculed in a spoof publication calling itself *The Brutalitarian: A Journal for the Sane and the Strong*, a parody of *The Humanitarian* presumably prepared by members of the Humanitarian League. This single issue contained a leading article in favour of flogging ('It is through flogging that the Englishman has developed that toughness of fibre and splendid moral stamina which is the wonder of an envious world', etc.), an article on 'School Discipline', a letter in defence of 'The Jewish Method of Slaughter' and an anthology of quotations from real-life advocates of the rod. According to Henry Salt many people were taken in by the hoax, including the religious journal *The Rock* which stated: 'It is a healthy sign of the times that at last there seems to be a stand against the mawkish humanitarianism that would spare the criminal classes at the expense of their innocent victims' (Salt, 1916, p.140).

[68] For example, see *Humanity*, March 1901, pp. 115-16, and *The Humanitarian*, November 1905, pp. 181-2.

birch. The offender is strapped hand and foot, in this case, over the bitts or the breech of a small gun, his trousers are allowed to fall below the knees, a broad canvas band is passed round the middle of his body, and his clothing is strapped up by this means, leaving thighs and buttocks perfectly nude. The same preliminaries are gone through as in caning, and the strokes are deliberately delivered on the bare flesh, not in rapid succession, but with a slight pause between each stroke, making the torture and agony of as lengthy duration as possible. With each stroke the flesh is seen to turn red, blue, and black, with bruising; after six or eight strokes the skin usually breaks, and copious streams of blood trickle down the unhappy victim's legs; at the twelfth stroke a halt is called, and a fresh corporal with a fresh birch supersedes the first, and the boy is allowed to drink water, which is always provided. The officer orders, 'Carry on the punishment', and the second instalment is laid on; splinters of broken birch wet with blood whizz and fly in all directions, and not infrequently the exuding excrement of the sufferer goes to make up one of the most revolting and inhuman spectacles that can be imagined – it can hardly be described. Often he swoons, and has to be supplied with restoratives before he can be half led, half carried, to the sick berth below. (March 1905, p.115)

The reader will note that this account is strikingly similar to that given by Roger Fry of events in the Rev. Sneyd-Kynnersley's study.

When the birch was abolished in the Navy in 1906 the opponents of corporal punishment were, naturally, elated. It had been a long battle. It soon became clear, however, that an excessive number of *canings* were now being meted out to cadets. The Admiralty was extremely defensive when questioned on the subject in the Commons, and refused on a number of occasions to issue figures showing how many canings had been administered in given years. Eventually an approximate figure leaked out:

Mr T.F. RICHARDS asked the First Lord of the Admiralty if he was aware that 4,566 cases of flogging with the cane were reported to have taken place in the Navy during 1907.

Mr McKENNA replied that he was unable to trace the meaning of the figure suggested in the question unless it were the average number of boys borne on board ship. The actual number of canings in 1907 was under a thousand. The hon. member was mistaken in using the word 'flogging'. Flogging and birching had been suspended by Admiralty orders. The King's Regulations authorised caning with clothes on in the case of boys and buglers under eighteen, and by an Admiralty order, dated March, 1906, that punishment was only to be inflicted under the actual orders of the captain, and was not to be carried out in public. (*The Humanitarian*, November 1909, p.183)

In 1911 the First Lord of the Admiralty stated that the approximate number of canings administered in the Navy in 1909 was 1,500. That is, a little under 30% of all the boys in the Fleet were caned in that year. McKenna was questioned by Sir William Byles:

> Mr McKENNA: I am informed that the number of canings in 1907 was abnormally low, and that there is no ground for supposing the number for 1909 is above the average. In view of my hon. friend's desire for publication of an annual return I will inquire further as to the practicability of such a return.
>
> Mr BYLES: Do we get a particularly bad type of boy in the Navy, seeing that one in every three has to be annually whipped? (Laughter.) (*The Humanitarian*, April 1911, p.126)

In May 1912 the Humanitarian League wrote to Winston Churchill, the new First Lord of the Admiralty, to express its disquiet over the large number of canings being administered in the Navy. Churchill replied that the matter was being examined by a Committee which had been set up to inquire into the system of summary punishments in the Navy.[69] In 1913 this Committee recommended that the cane should only be applied for offences of a grave kind 'such as theft, drunkenness, insubordination, and deliberate or continued disobedience of orders'. The Humanitarian League expressed its gratitude to Churchill, but continued to press for an annual Parliamentary return giving details of the number of canings inflicted.[70]

By 1913 the anti-floggers had a right to feel considerable satisfaction about their efforts on behalf of boys entering the British Navy. The attitude of the Admiralty had been so consistently rigid that, without the dedication of the humanitarians, the birching and caning of cadets would undoubtedly have continued far longer than it did.

It may be recalled that flogging had been abolished in the Army in 1881. It was retained, however, as a punishment for prison offences – but not for officers. In 1897 a pamphlet by E. Livingston Prescott showed that both birch and 'cat' were in frequent use in the military prisons – largely unknown to the public and, apparently, even to a majority of Army men. The birchings were felt to be particularly ignominious:

[69] *The Humanitarian*, June 1912, p.43.
[70] *ibid.*, March 1913, p.115.

The prisoner is strapped down in a half-kneeling, half-lying position, with his head over the end of a wooden frame following the curves of the body, called in humorous prison parlance the 'Pony', whipped as a schoolboy is whipped, but with a strong rod pickled in brine, and with so much severity, experts inform us, that the flesh is more or less raw – 'like raw beef' – and the marks are indelible. (1897, p.6)

Quoting from the official 'Rules for Military Prisons', Prescott demonstrated the wide range of offences, often of the most trifling nature, for which a prisoner could be subjected to corporal punishment – and this at the whim of the prison authorities.

To the credit of the Army, corporal punishment in military prisons was abolished in 1906.[71]

Sometimes, however, the flogging fervour reasserted itself clandestinely. There was a scandal in March 1903 when it became known to the public that an illegal caning of considerable brutality had been inflicted on a young officer of the 1st Battalion Grenadier Guards who had broken out of barracks on an August evening in 1902. The Sergeant-Drummer who had administered this and other similarly illegal chastisements was reduced to the rank of corporal but reinstated six days later.[72] Commenting in the *Morning Post* on this incident, Sir John Gorst referred to 'our passionate attachment to corporal punishment which appears from recent disclosures to permeate even the mess-rooms of our fashionable regiments' (23 April 1903).

Finally, a last word about flogging in the Navy. The 'cat', as has been said, was suspended in 1881 but could, in theory, have been reintroduced at any time by the Admiralty. It never was. The possibility of such an eventuality was removed definitively by an Order-in-Council of 29 March 1949.[73] Boy ratings, however, were still liable to receive a maximum of 12 strokes with a cane.[74]

As regards naval prisons, flogging was retained after 1881, and indeed long after it was abolished by the Army in 1906. According to the statutory rules and orders as to discipline in such prisons, the authorities were empowered to inflict a maximum of thirty-six lashes or strokes with either 'cat' or birch on prisoners over eighteen years of

[71] Salt (1916), p.59.
[72] *Reynold's Newspaper*, 29 March 1903; Joseph Collinson, 'Brethren of the Birch', *The Humanitarian*, April 1903, pp. 110-11.
[73] The Criminal Justice Act, 1948 (Adaptation of Naval Discipline Act) Order, 1949, No. 597.
[74] A. Covey-Crump, *Naval Information*, 1955 (a type-written pamphlet which can be consulted at the Naval Historical Library, Earl's Court).

age.[75] Prison flogging was finally done away with by Section 122 of the Army Act, 1955, which applied to the Navy. The Naval Discipline Act, 1957, contained no flogging provisions.

Judicial flogging up to our own time

The law relating to judicial corporal punishment remained unchanged from 1912 to 1948.

Between 1912 and 1936, magistrates in England and Wales imposed 32,219 birching sentences on young offenders (up to the age of fourteen); in Scotland, 8,731 birching sentences were passed on offenders in the same age group.[76]

As regards adult offenders, approximately 100 flogging sentences were passed during the same period under the provisions of the various Acts containing flogging clauses.[77] It is of interest to note that 47 of these sentences (by far the largest category) were imposed in cases of a second conviction of indecent exposure under the Vagrancy Act, 1824.[78]

The whole question of judicial flogging was exhaustively studied by the Departmental Committee on Corporal Punishment appointed by the Home Office in May 1937 and chaired by the hon. Edward Cadogan, a former Conservative M.P. The Committee's Report (the 'Cadogan Report'), to which I have referred throughout this chapter, was published in February 1938 (Command 5684, reprinted in 1952). The Committee had come to the conclusion that corporal punishment was not an effective deterrent, and recommended its abolition except for certain prison offences. It pointed out that judicial corporal punishment had been abandoned without ill effects in every civilised country in the world except those in which the criminal code was influenced by English criminal law; and insisted that it was 'a specially unsuitable penalty for sexual offences' (p.66) – as George Bernard Shaw had said years earlier and, clearly, as the magistrates refused to believe.

The Report gave detailed, cool descriptions of how the 'cat' and birch were applied both to juvenile and adult offenders. As regards the former:

The punishment is usually administered in a cell or private room either within the precincts of the court or at a neighbouring police station. The

[75] *The Humanitarian*, December 1909, p.188.
[76] *Cadogan*, pp. 19-20.
[77] *ibid*., pp. 66-79.
[78] *ibid*., p.69.

birch is applied across the buttocks, on the bare flesh. The method most commonly adopted is to bend the boy over a low bench or table. His hands, and sometimes his feet also, are held by police officers. This is done in order to ensure that he shall not move, for if he moved a stroke of the birch might fall on some more sensitive part of the body. This method, though probably the most common, is not universal. In some Police Forces one constable takes the boy on his back, drawing the boy's hands down over his shoulders; and another constable holds the boy's feet, drawing his legs round the sides of the first constable; the first constable then leans forward, and the birch is applied by a third. We have also heard that in one Police Force the custom is for one constable to bend the boy over and hold his head between his knees, while a second officer administers the birch. And in one district the boy is strapped to an apparatus similar to the triangle used for corporal punishment in prisons. (p.18)

The *modus operandi* with adult offenders could be seen to be even more grotesque:

A prisoner who is to undergo corporal punishment is strapped to an apparatus, known as a triangle, which is best described as a heavier and more solid form of the easel used to carry a blackboard in a school-room. His feet are strapped to the base of the front legs of the triangle. If the cat is to be administered, his hands are raised above his head and strapped to the upper part of the triangle. If he is to be birched, he is bent over a pad placed between the front legs of the triangle and his hands are secured by straps attached to the back legs of the triangle. In both cases he is screened, by canvas sheeting, so that he cannot see the officer who is administering the punishment. The birch is administered across the buttocks, on the bare flesh. The cat is administered across the back, also on the bare flesh, so that the ends of the tails fall on to the right shoulder-blade. When the cat is to be administered, a leather belt is placed round the prisoner's loins and a leather collar round his neck, so as to protect these parts from any injury which might arise from a mis-directed stroke. (pp. 52-3)

The Cadogan committee had 'heard evidence from medical-psychologists, psychoanalysts, and doctors who have had practical experience in examining boys ordered to be birched and in supervising the administration of the punishment' (p.31). For the first time in an official government publication the question of the possible sexual associations of whipping was raised, although the Committee was guarded in its response to the views put forward by the psychoanalysts on this aspect of the subject. This passage demands full quotation:

The psycho-analysts' view of this question is based very largely on a theoretical analysis of the impulses underlying the desire to inflict corporal punishment. It is very difficult to do justice to this view in the small space which we can allot to it. Briefly stated, it is that the impulse to punish – as opposed to the treatment, reform, or even preventive detention of an offender – derives from an element of sadism which, in a conscious or (more often) unconscious form, exercises an influence over the thoughts and actions of a majority of the community. Punishment, in so far as it is imposed merely for punishment's sake, is an expression of the hatred felt by the community towards the person who has offended against the laws of the community. This element of sadism, which is present in all punishment *qua* punishment, is accentuated when the punishment takes the form of inflicting physical pain: for corporal punishment is not only an expression of hate impulse, but is also a direct or indirect expression of sexual impulse. Conscious sadism is recognised as a form of sexual perversion, and a system of judicial corporal punishment may pander to unconscious impulses which in essence are sadistic and sexual. The practical implication of this view is that corporal punishment has a bad psychological effect on all concerned – in satisfying sadistic impulses in those who order it or inflict it, and possibly in appealing to masochistic tendencies in those who suffer it. This view applies equally, of course, to the corporal punishment of adults. We do not feel qualified either to assent to, or to dissent from, this theoretical analysis of the impulse towards corporal punishment. We feel compelled, however, to point out that the full implications of this view would affect many forms of punishment other than corporal punishment and would extend far beyond our terms of reference. Psycho-analysis is a comparatively new method and we do not think that its development has yet reached the stage at which its hypotheses can safely be made the basis for a drastic and far-reaching reconstruction of the whole of our penal code. We do not feel that we can go further than to record the view that corporal punishment, whether of juveniles or of adults, may be liable to bring out in certain individuals unwholesome tendencies connected with sadism and perverted sexual impulses. We are unable to base any practical recommendations on the views expressed to us on behalf of psycho-analysts; and we feel obliged to add that none of the witnesses who has had actual experience of supervising the administration of corporal punishment has ever observed any overt signs indicating that either the victim or the person administering the punishment was deriving from it any masochistic or sadistic satisfaction. (pp. 32-3)

What, one wonders, did the Committee expect – erections all round? For it is unlikely, to say the least, that any such 'overt sign' of sexual response would have manifested itself in a public situation, even if beater or victim were of flagellant disposition. Still, the airing of such views in an official publication signified a remarkable advance in thinking on the subject of corporal punishment in a country where crass ignorance and hypocrisy have been the rule. It ought henceforth to have been impossible to discuss the matter without reference to the sexual implications of beating.

The Government immediately accepted the validity of the Cadogan Committee's recommendations on flogging and other penal matters and incorporated them quickly into a very liberal Criminal Justice Bill. The ensuing debate in the House of Commons was remarkable in that the Bill was praised, with few reservations, from all parts of the House. While some Members did indeed speak in favour of retaining flogging, and while not a single one mentioned the sexual implications of the practice, the tone of the debate was much higher than in previous discussions. As one Member commented 'I must say that I have been extremely surprised at the very moderate and one might almost say apologetic attitude of those who oppose the abolition of flogging. When one compares the extraordinary bitterness with which in the past flogging has been defended, it is astonishing to see how immense an effect the report of the Departmental Committee [that is, the 'Cadogan Report'] has had' (Hansard, *Commons*, 29 November 1938, col.351).

Several Members, however, were dismayed by the Bill's retention of flogging as a punishment for some prison offences. As Sir Stafford Cripps argued,

> If corporal punishment will not deter, and has not in experience deterred, in cases of robbery with violence, what conceivable evidence or argument can there be that it will have a deterrent effect in the case of prison offences? ... once it is established that flogging does not alter people outside prison, I can see no argument whatsoever for its maintenance inside prison. It's a brutal method, and brutal methods will never drive out insanity. (*ibid.*, 1 December 1938, cols. 716-17)

In the flogging debate of 1952-53, to which we shall come in a moment, the supporters of the lash would argue that, if flogging was considered a deterrent *inside* prisons, it must surely be effective *outside* them.

Although the 1938 Bill passed its Second Reading and proceeded to a Standing Committee (where a great deal of work was done on it), its enactment was held up by the war. It was ten years before the Cadogan recommendations were implemented, by a Labour Government, in Section 2 of the Criminal Justice Act, 1948.

During those ten years the number of birchings awarded by the Magistrates' Courts (including the Juvenile Courts) to boys under 16 was 3,002.[79] In Assizes and Quarter Sessions, 310 flogging sentences were passed on adults in the same period.[80] In the words of Labour M.P. George Benson, at this period 'the judges were flogging more frequently than they had ever flogged in any previous period of this century' (Hansard, *Commons*, 13 February 1953, (cols. 801-2). Benson showed, moreover, that 84% of these floggings were applied with the birch – 'lower discipline' was clearly on the increase.[81]

The floggers were not deterred by the passing of the 1948 Act. In 1952, with a Conservative Government under Winston Churchill in power, it seemed from newspaper accounts that there was taking place a sharp rise in the number of violent assaults being committed, especially in London. Lurid coverage was given to the activities of cosh-wielding gangs of 'thugs'; and soon the bring-back-the-birchites were once again in full voice. It was reminiscent of the panic over 'garrotting' in 1862, and, as in 1862, the amount of violence had undoubtedly been exaggerated.

On 22 October 1952 the Lords debated the subject of violence and corporal punishment, the pro-flogging faction being championed by no less a personage than the Chief Justice of England, Lord Goddard. His principal opponent was the eloquent Lord Templewood, a life-long abolitionist. Goddard explained that he was for the reintroduction of the birch, not the 'cat': the 'cat' made a man look a hero but the birch made him look a fool. Moreover, Goddard wanted wider whipping powers for judges than had been available since the early nineteenth century: 'What I venture to submit to your Lordships is that, with this increase of violent crime, the superior courts should be given power, in their discretion, to inflict corporal punishment for all forms of felonious violence' (Hansard, *Lords*, 22 October 1952, col.855). Every judge who spoke in the debate was in favour of reintroduction. No supporter of judicial flogging seemed aware of the possible sexual implications of birching; and Goddard, whose reading of the Cadogan Report must have been cursory at best, was even of the opinion that birching would be a useful deterrent against sexual crimes.[82]

[79] *Corporal Punishment. Report of the Advisory Council on the Treatment of Offenders* ['The Barry Report'], Command 1213, 1960, Appendix B, p.31.

[80] *ibid.*, Appendix D, p.33.

[81] Hansard, *Commons*, 13 February 1953, col. 803.

[82] As Fenton Bresler points out in his biography of Lord Goddard (1977), the Lord Chief Justice 'did not even deign to mention the [Cadogan] Committee's unanimous finding' (pp. 182-3). It came as no great surprise to the present writer to learn from Mr Bresler's biography that Goddard scorned psychiatrists and homosexuals, and believed that even murderers proved insane should be hung. Nor was one surprised to learn that Goddard applied 'lower discipline' to his own children, all girls. Bresler

Several public school men repeated the old argument that 'it never did us any harm'. Lord Asquith of Bishopstone produced a variation on the theme:

> It cannot really be said that the birch brutalises its victims. If it did, we should have to say that practically the whole of the governing classes of this country in the first half of the nineteenth century had been brutalised because they had all been birched by Dr Keates. (*ibid.*, col.876)

Some opponents of flogging did refer briefly to sadism, it is true; but one finds in the debate none of that clear thinking on the subject that one might have expected 14 years after the publication of the 'Cadogan Report'.

It became clear in the course of the Lords debate, however, that, despite the fact that a Conservative Government was in power, Government support could not be expected for a flogging Bill.

There can be little doubt that the Lords debate increased the hysteria which seemed to be taking hold of the country once again. The magazine *Picture Post*, always on the alert for a sensational story, inaugurated a public discussion on the subject 'Should we Flog the Thugs?'. The opening feature appeared on 22 November 1952, and was headed by extracts from the speeches of Goddard and Templewood in the House of Lords. Readers were invited to write to the magazine, and the correspondence ran for months. Some of the views expressed by the pro-floggers were little short of barbaric. Others gave the public school party line:

> The public schoolboy who snatches a puff at a cigarette in some dark recess is given eight strokes with a cane. The boy who wantonly coshes a helpless old lady is sent to a home more comfortable than most public schools.

---

quotes Goddard's daughter Pamela as saying: 'Many a time did I have to bend over and receive six of the best from his hands on that portion of the anatomy which, so I was advised by him and implicitly believed, was specially designed for the purpose' (p.22). On a later page the same witness recalls that 'he never said a word, but removed his slipper, dealt each of us a resounding whack on that part of our anatomy best fitted to receive it, and stalked out again' (p.49). We have met these standard euphemisms before. In 1958 Goddard, by then in his eighties, said of the Approved Schools that 'they don't seem to be able to give them a pat on the place ... the place it was meant for' (p.292). Mr Bresler tells us nothing of Goddard's experience of beating at his prep school (near Reading, but not identified) which he hated, nor at Marlborough, which he apparently loved. One imagines that beating at both these establishments followed the normal public school pattern.

Treat the Borstal boy in the same way as the average public schoolboy
and there will be a rapid decrease in juvenile delinquency.

    G.S. Partridge,
      Giggleswick School,
      Yorks. (29 November 1952, p.9)

Let the incredulous reader be assured at once: this implausibly-
named establishment really existed – and still does. One wonders if
boys caught smoking in the dark recesses of Giggleswick School
nowadays receive eight strokes of the cane.

Only one letter out of dozens mentioned the word 'sadism', despite
the views expressed in the 'Cadogan Report'. R.S.W. Pollard's letter
therefore deserves to be quoted:

> The desire to flog is a desire to have cruelty inflicted on another person. It
> can too easily provide satisfaction for the sadistic impulses latent in all of
> us. It would be a disgrace to English law if flogging were restored here. (20
> December 1952, p.6)

Justices of the Peace up and down the country were becoming daily
more uneasy about the flogging question. *The Times* published details
of ballots and resolutions. On 8 November 1952 it reported that the
Derby Magistrates had just resolved that 'her Majesty's Judges of
Assize should have the right restored to them to order whipping in
cases of robbery with violence' (p.3). Other magistrates followed suit
and, on 11 November, *The Times* reported that the Manchester City
justices also wanted whipping restored. Then, on 15 November,
readers of *The Times* learnt that Wing Commander Eric Bullus,
Conservative Member for Wembley North, with considerable support
in the House, was to introduce a Bill to reimpose corporal punishment
for crimes of violence. The debate was put down for 13 February 1953.

That left plenty of time for the controversy to rage before
Parliament debated the Bill.

The Anglican voice was soon raised in support of flogging, as one
would expect. Dr Garbett, Archbishop of York, was reported as
saying:

> I am not against birching in principle. Indeed, I think some children might
> well be birched by their parents. The strong demand for the restoration of
> corporal punishment is not a demand for flogging, but it is very natural that
> we should wish to express by physical punishment our indignation at some
> brutal outrage or violence. (*The Times*, 10 January 1953, p.3)

Not all Christians would have agreed with such a view, of course.

The inhabitants of Wimbledon had also got the wind up. It appeared that women were afraid to go out of doors after dark. What was to be done? Someone had the idea that the people of the borough should sign a petition asking the Government to bring back the lash. On 13 January 1953 *The Times* reported that the petition already had 7,000 signatures.

Wing Commander Bullus's Private Member's Criminal Justice (Amendment) Bill was debated in the Commons on 13 February 1953. On the same day the Magistrates' Association announced the result of a ballot that had been held among its members. Of the 6,298 votes cast (there were 3,000 abstentions), 4,412 were in favour of reintroducing corporal punishment, 1,886 against (Bresler, 1977, p.234). Like Lord Goddard, Bullus wanted corporal punishment introduced for a wide range of crimes of violence. And like Goddard he was in favour of reintroducing the birch, not the 'cat'. Good old public-school-style birching was what the thugs needed. During the debate all the pro-flogging clichés, without exception, were to be heard once again. To the credit of the House, however, it soon became clear that opposition to the Bill was strong in all quarters, not least from the Conservative Government itself. In fact it was the brilliant, humane speech of the Home Secretary, Sir David Maxwell Fyfe, that killed the Bill – 'killed it as dead as mutton', as one Member put it.

It is evident that the Bill's opponents had become extremely aware of the adverse criticism that its proposals had aroused on the continent of Europe. Geoffrey de Freitas tried to explain this to the Bill's supporters, and was interrupted by laughter:

> I beg hon. Members to consider this from the point of view of men who grew up on the Continent in which corporal punishment, whether in schools or as a sentence, is quite unknown. We are accustomed to corporal punishment. We do not realise that everyone else in Europe thinks of it as a mediaeval conception and a symbol of the past ... We can laugh, but we do not seem to appreciate the point that to Continentals degradation is inevitably associated with corporal punishment. I beg hon. Members to try and see this from the point of view of countries which are looking towards us for leadership out of their past period of violence by servants of the State. (Hansard, *Commons*, 13 February 1953, col.817)

As regards the sexual implications of birching, which its advocates have always refused to admit, two opponents of the Bill had been pondering on this aspect of the 'Cadogan Report'. Their remarks were more guarded than might have been expected – had this not been England. None the less the Rt. Hon. J.C. Ede came closer to the heart of the matter than any other Member of Parliament in any of the flogging debates of the twentieth century when he said:

> I am not convinced that in this House we have yet discovered the proper
> way to deal with sexual crimes, but I am certain of this – that flogging is
> no remedy for them, neither is it a deterrent. In fact, in certain
> circumstances it is an incentive.
>
> If we faced that honestly, taking medical as well as legal opinion into
> account, I think that we should be very ill-advised to pass any words that
> made it possible to apply corporal punishment to sexual offenders. (*ibid.*,
> col.793)

A few moments later, Ede was interrupted by a question from the Bill's
begetter which demonstrated the quality of his understanding:

> Wing Commander Bullus: Would not the right hon. Gentleman admit
> that there is a real difference between the cat and the birch?

Ede replied:

> Curiously enough, all expert evidence, including that of the people who
> have suffered both, states that there is no great difference but that, if
> anything, birching is more painful and indecent than the cat. (*ibid.*, col.794)

This was the only occasion in the entire debate that anyone had
suggested that birching was 'indecent'. As we shall see in the next
chapter, in which I examine the lurid flagellation discussions that filled
the columns of many nineteenth-century newspapers and journals, it
is a word with a history. In this respect, one final quotation from the
debate deserves to be made – from the speech of Captain C.
Waterhouse, Conservative Member for Leicester South-East.
Waterhouse made two novel suggestions:

> We should allow magistrates if necessary to order the cane or to send the
> culprits back to school to be caned. If a policeman should be too strong,
> put a stout policewoman on the job. (*ibid.*, col.796)

I have seen an English flagellant magazine in which it is precisely such
a 'stout policewoman' who is in charge of disciplinary operations.[83] It
is astonishing that such suggestions could be put forward by a Member
of Parliament.

By 159 votes to 63 the House voted against the immediate Second

---

[83] *Janus*, vol. 5, no.2 (1975), pp. 40-1.

Reading of the Bill, which was put off for six months. It was, of course, the end of the Bill.[84]

But not the end of the debate – these were the heady days of Eric A. Wildman and his National Society for the Retention of Corporal Punishment, which was mentioned in the second chapter. The newspapers continued to publish letters and articles on the subject, and, to the surprise of many people, the editorial policy of *The Times* seemed to swing in favour of the reintroduction of judicial flogging for certain crimes of violence. This despite the fact that the newspaper had supported the 1948 Act.

Flagellomania, as we know, can attack even the most apparently robust minds.

In 1960 the Advisory Council on the Treatment of Offenders was asked by the Home Office 'to consider whether there were grounds for reintroducing any form of corporal punishment as a judicial penalty in respect of any categories of offences and of offenders'. The Council's report was published in November 1960 (Command 1213).[85] The Council supported the recommendations of the Cadogan Committee. It had found during its investigations that the subject of corporal punishment was of widespread interest and that 'There can be little doubt that a large number of people in the country would at present support the reintroduction of corporal punishment as a judicial penalty' (p.7). According to the Report, a public opinion poll published in March 1960 showed that 74 per cent of the population of Britain 'considered that corporal punishment should be the penalty for some offences' (p.7). Although this estimate called for some caution, the Council found that it was supported 'by the opinions expressed by our own correspondents ... and in letters received by the Home Office during our inquiry which were brought to our attention' (p.7). It had become clear to the Council, moreover, that very many judges desired a return to the whipping system and that 'it seems that among magistrates generally there is a majority who favour corporal punishment as a judicial penalty' (p.8). Of the 3,500 letters the Council received, 77% were in favour of the reintroduction of judicial corporal punishment with only 17% against. Moreover:

> The general consensus of opinion, among both correspondents and witnesses, was that if judicial corporal punishment were to be reintroduced it should be available for a wider range of offences (particularly offences of violence) than before its abolition in 1948; and that it should be available for juveniles convicted of any offence, so that

[84] Hansard, *Commons*, 13 February 1953, cols. 840-41.
[85] For details of the Report, see note 79 above. This quotation, p.1.

the courts could, at their discretion, use it to check a young offender before he was too far gone in delinquency. (p.8)

Several of the Council's correspondents even 'suggested that females should be liable to judicial corporal punishment as well as males' (p.9). None of the letters received by the Council are published in the report, but it is hard to resist the suspicion that those in the last category at least may have been pornographic.

In stark contrast to the 'general consensus of opinion', the opinions given to the Council by medical men and probationers were unanimously against the reintroduction of corporal punishment. These professions, the report makes clear, were much in advance of both the judiciary and the people of Britain at large. Particularly relevant were the views of the probationers, who, after all, knew better than anyone else the psychology of juvenile offenders.

The report pointed out that, under the provisions of the 1948 Act, many new forms of treatment for young culprits had been introduced and that, in theory, 'the courts now have at their disposal a wide range of methods from which they can select the one that appears to offer the greatest chance of success with the individual offender, but for various reasons these new methods have not yet been fully developed' (p.17). The Council hoped that they soon would be and, while it did not state so explicitly, there was implied a severe criticism of those who believed that the return to the birch was the correct way to deal with juvenile or adult offenders.

In view of the recommendations of the Advisory Council the law remained unchanged. This meant, in practice, that prison whippings (which the Council did not examine) were the only survival in Britain of judicial corporal punishment, with the exception, as we shall see in a moment, of the Isle of Man.

Every so often since 1960 the pro-flogging voice has been raised, especially by Tory M.P.s, clergymen and the judiciary. It is impossible to read English newspapers regularly, in fact, without coming across the utterances of these people. Any sign of an increase in violence on the part of the less fortunate classes may be guaranteed to call forth the old response.

Some examples, taken at random. On 5 February 1975, the *Daily Mail* reported that the previous day Judge King-Hamilton, Q.C., had said at the Central Criminal Court that 'a great number of people would not be in the dock if they had corporal punishment when they were younger'. The judge, addressing the 18-year-old who had stolen a car and knocked down a schoolgirl, said: 'If corporal punishment had been administered when you were younger I am quite positive you would not be where you are now. You are a classic case of the saying, "spare the rod and spoil the child" ' (p.12). Some of us might well feel that the judge was also a 'classic case', but of another order.

On 9 June 1975 the *Guardian* reported that the Rev. Frederick Flood, rector of the much-vandalised parish of South Normanton, Nottinghamshire, had said: 'If vandals don't understand the graciousness shown them by magistrates, they must be punished in a way they do understand. I can't advocate birching as a punishment without being willing to carry it out myself. I believe in chastisement and I would do it willingly as a citizen' (p.7).

On 29 August 1975 the *New Statesman* published the following item in its 'This England' column (taken from the *Daily Telegraph*): 'Referring to Gary Paul he said: "In my view I did my best to strike him on the buttocks where it would hurt but not cause any physical damage. I did not consider I gave him an excessive caning." Judge Bertrand Richards commented: "Buttocks were ordained by nature for the purpose" ' (p.248). No teacher has ever admitted that he caned a boy excessively, of course; and it is interesting to see that in 1975 judges were still able to mouth the old rubbish about nature's purposes for the buttocks.

Then, of course, we have recently been hearing the inevitable cry to bring back the birch for football rowdies. Referring on 9 August 1975 to the decision of the Oxfordshire county council (Tory-controlled) to restore the cane to the schools under its control, the *Daily Express* commented: 'As Soccer's hooligans get their aggro ready for the start of the season, it's a nice question whether or not Oxford's example should be taken up outside school, too. It'll be surprising if the demand doesn't grow.'

Given the British public, and the *Daily Express*, it would indeed have been extremely surprising had the demand not grown. It did so steadily. On 26 September 1976 Mr Freddie Burden, Conservative M.P. for Gillingham, was reported in the *Sunday Express* to have said: 'This is the only way to deal with these thugs. Fines are a waste of time' (p.15). Note the words: *the only way*. We have heard them before, and doubtless shall again. On another page of the same issue (p.18), Anne Edwards put forward the evergreen, eye-for-an-eye view familiar to any student of English attitudes to corporal punishment:

It frightens me that so few people seem to equate the disappearance of Six of the Best with the increase in school thuggery, with teachers being physically attacked, with the more and more frequent reports of bullying in schools resulting in misery or broken bones or even suicide among the sad little victims ... Abolishing the cane protects the bullies – and leaves the weak defenceless.

A few weeks afterwards, it was reported in the *Daily Express* (14 October 1976) that, the previous day, a gang of teenage rapists had left the Old Bailey 'laughing over their sentences'. The newspaper published on its front page a picture of Tory M.P. Nicholas Winterton, who had declared: 'The cane would have done all these people the world of good'.

On 20 April 1977, in the midst of the football birching controversy, *The Times* (which in the past has vacillated in its attitudes to corporal punishment), nailed its colours to the wall in a leading article on 'cult violence':

> Inevitably, the call has arisen (with the manager of Manchester United being in the vanguard) for the reintroduction of corporal punishment for football hooligans. Understandable though such a reaction may be, it should be resisted. Birching has never been proved to have had any positive effect in the past, it carries with it for the offender a certain element of heroism, it is unlikely to prove a deterrent, and it is in any case contrary to the European Convention on Human Rights, as the recent finding by the European Commission on the practice in the Isle of Man indicates.

The Rev. Arundel C. Barker was upset by this leader, and on 22 April 1977 (p.19) expressed himself thus in a letter to the editor:

> It is my belief, shared by my children, that corporal punishment for juveniles *is* a human right, being the most biblical, simplest, least expensive, quickest and most effective way in which genuine love can be expressed, discipline and authority can be established and society can be safeguarded in the face of most forms of anti-social behaviour by children and young people.

The tone of this not very clear piece of writing is familiar, and abolitionists may be prompted to rejoice at the decline in the influence of the Anglican Church, which has traditionally upheld *biblical* notions on beating.

In view of the demands for the introduction of judicial birching for soccer hooligans (and many more could be quoted), it was obvious that some Conservative M.P. would soon take up the cry in the Commons. This time it was the turn of Graham Page, M.P. for Crosby, who moved the Second Reading of his Corporal Punishment Bill on 29 April 1977. Page said that he was not an advocate of a national referendum on birching, but that in his opinion 'if there were one on this subject, nine tenths of the votes would be in favour of physical punishment for physical violence' (*The Times*, 30 April 1977, p.4). The M.P. had come to the conclusion that 'corporal punishment would be most effective upon the under-18s'; and observed that 'he did not think the European Convention for the Protection of Human Rights and Fundamental Freedoms was meant to ban the modest form of physical pain inflicted by the birch or that birching was any more inhuman or degrading treatment than imprisonment' (*ibid.*). There was no indication that Page had read the 'Cadogan Report' or any other publication in which the dangers and drawbacks of corporal punishment are discussed.

Following Page, Michael Alison, Conservative M.P. for Barkston Ash, distinguished himself by repeating the threadbare argument that birching is not flogging ('He was glad the Bill did not have the old idea of flogging'). Brynmor John, Minister of State at the Home Office, expressed the Government's view that Page 'presented the spectacle of marching backwards to the nineteenth century', and pointed out that, among other considerations, there was no evidence that corporal punishment is a deterrent to violent crime. A closure motion was rejected by 17 votes to 6, and there for the moment the matter rests. If the Conservatives come to power at the next general election, however, it would not surprise the present writer if the call for the reintroduction of the judicial birch were to receive considerable support in Parliament.

Finally, a source of perennial interest to the newspapers is the survival of birching as a judicial penalty for juvenile offenders in the Isle of Man, which is governed by its own Parliament, the Tynwald.

In August 1975, a seventeen-year-old boy was given six strokes of the birch at Douglas. Commenting on the sentence in a letter to the *Guardian* (25 August 1975), Ms Millicent Faragher wrote:

> The severity of last week's sentence of six strokes can be imagined as this is the official specification of the Manx birch: four branches must be stripped of twigs and be 40 inches long: 15 inches are made into a handle by binding with twine; the circumference of the handle must be $3\frac{1}{4}$ to $3\frac{1}{2}$ inches with the circumference of the spray not more than six inches. The weight must be nine ounces.
>
> It will be noted that six strokes of the birch would be something like 24 lashes with a knotted instrument ... In 1969 another six-stroke sentence was passed on a 15-year-old who had been caught stealing liquor from an off-licence yard, and before that the same six-stroke punishment was inflicted on another 15-year-old who had spent the night in a flat sleeping with a willing girl of his own age, consequently being charged with indecent assault.

The chairman of the magistrates, in passing this latter sentence, is quoted by the same correspondent as saying 'We feel the boy has lacked a father's hand, and have taken that into consideration in assessing sentence'.

On 20 October 1976, *The Times* announced that the previous day the Tynwald had decided, by 29 votes to 2, to retain birching as a penalty for offences of violent crime. It comes as a shock to discover that, so far as the Manx legislators are concerned, a 'juvenile' may be a young man of 20 years of age. The sentiments of Manx supporters of the rod quoted in *The Times* article read like something straight out of the nineteenth century. All these people seem to assume that the island's freedom from violent crime is the direct result of the crude 'deterrent' prescribed by the law. Mr Howard Simcox, a Douglas solicitor and a member of the Legislative Council, was quoted by *The Times* as having said: 'There are always some people who can visualise the spectacle of a youth being birched but who are somehow incapable of lifting their eyes to see the thousands of people, some of them elderly, who may have been saved from violent attack by that birching and its deterrent effect.' Note the 'may have been saved': perhaps Mr Simcox is not *quite* sure. No one quoted by *The Times* makes any reference to the fact that, by the existence of such birching, many people 'may' also have been sexually excited, although it is known that those who have been birched in the Isle of Man have received flagellant letters from sexual deviants. As Ms Faragher wrote in her letter to the *Guardian* which has already been quoted: 'As this recently birched boy is to be returned to his special school he will presumably avoid receiving the usual crop of obscene anonymous letters which sometimes arrive for the recipients of a birching. (I have seen some of them.)'.

Imagine trying to explain the Manx system to one's children – the lowering of the trousers, the baring of the buttocks, the whole degrading ceremony. Yet presumably this is what Manx parents are often required to do. The European Commission of Human Rights at Strasbourg, to which some of the Isle of Man's birched offenders have appealed, naturally takes a very dim view of the whole thing, but the Tynwald is determined to resist outside interference in the running of what it considers to be its own affairs. As I correct the proofs of this book, a report in *The Times* (6 July 1977) states that, in the autumn, the Manx government intends to maintain at Strasbourg 'its right to birch young people guilty of crimes of violence' (p.3). It seems, moreover, that some of the birching diehards in the Tynwald have said that the island should break away from the United Kingdom if the British Government were to attempt to enforce a ban on judicial corporal punishment. Perhaps this would be a good idea. In order to boost its revenues, the island could then advertise itself as the world's first holiday centre for unruly young masochists.

It has been my purpose in the last three chapters to document the *facts* about legally-sanctioned beating in Britain up to the present time. It can hardly be denied such beating has been endemic, nor that the opponents of corporal punishment have habitually met with fierce resistance from the upholders of the system. From now on we shall be more concerned with the effects of the English Vice on the emotional and sexual life of the nation.

5

The Flagellant Correspondence Column in Nineteenth-century England

One of the more extraordinary features of the English flagellant phenomenon is the extent to which the corporal punishment of children was discussed in the respectable press of the nineteenth century, and the degree to which (while much of the discussion was clearly pornographic) almost all overt reference to the possible sexual implications of the practice was excluded from debate. At the same time the semi-pornographic scandal papers churned out masses of flagellant material which differed only in a slightly greater explicitness from that appearing in 'polite' publications. In perhaps no other area of Victorian life were the boundaries between truth and falsity so blurred; perhaps in none was there so much hypocrisy, such a refusal to confront things as they really were, such scope for pretence, for sexuality masquerading as responsibility towards the young or simply as moral outrage.

In the eighteenth century there seems to have been, along with a healthier attitude towards sex in general than was to become current in Victorian times, less hesitation in admitting that flogging could be a pleasurable activity under certain circumstances. Reference has been made in the first chapter to the exchange on the subject published in *The Gentleman's Magazine* of 1780 which shows that Meibom's findings had not yet, at that date, been repressed from the consciousness of thinking men. An earlier writer to that journal had no illusions at all concerning the aphrodisiac virtues of beating. In a witty article entitled 'A Dissertation upon Flogging' he explained that '*Flogging* is an Art which teaches us to draw Blood from a Person's Posteriors in such a Manner as may twinge him most severely without Danger of a Mortification ... I have seen a Professor foam with Extacy at the Sight of a Jolly Pair of Buttocks' (January 1735, pp. 17-18). *That* you would not be able to say in Victorian England! Yet, as we have seen, the 'Professors' of the nineteenth century more than emulated the flogging achievements of their predecessors.

Later in the eighteenth century two scabrous monthlies, *The Rambler's* (1783-90) and the *Bon Ton Magazine* (1791-6) gave ample space to the subject of flagellation, and inaugurated what was to become the flagellant correspondence column of the nineteenth century.[1]

Among the *Rambler's*'s flagellant contributions we find such items as 'The Laws of Flagellation. Extracted from the Common Law and Statutes of this Realm', 'The Boarding-School Insurrection; or, Mrs Flogger literally making a Rod for her own - '; an 'Essay on Flagellation'; and a series of spoof letters on the same topic. One of these letters, signed 'Viator', is of particular interest. The writer tells us of a female friend whose lover has a flagellant 'propensity' or 'penchant'. This young man, however, can fulfil his duties quite effectively without fustigation, and simply enjoys whipping as an extra stimulus. 'Viator' is perplexed: 'I should be glad to hear from any of your learned correspondents whether this story does not contradict the doctrine of Meibomius, etc. [for whom] such a taste has its foundations in the coldness of the constitution' (May 1783, p.177). A genuine enquiry? Hardly, yet the question is relevant. Perhaps the more enlightened flagellants were beginning to suspect that Meibom's 'doctrine' was untenable.

The letter from 'Fanny Quintickler' places no strain on one's credulity. It deserves almost full quotation because (1) it sets the broad pattern for subsequent communications in the nineteenth century and (2) being inserted in a semi-pornographic magazine it can refer, albeit flippantly in this case, to the genitals:

Nothing is more common now, particularly in our day schools, than to see a lady, sometimes very young, take a boy (very often 10 or 12 years old) to task, and, for a trivial offence, unbutton his breeches, and flog his posteriors with a birch rod, as she would a girl of that age. – I hate indeed to see a rod in the hands of a man; there is something in it so effeminate, so unmanly, that I would rather have a woman perform the birchin correction: and some grown up gentlemen will allow, that many ladies are no bad hands at handling a rod. – But why should the boys be flogged in the school, when the girls are very properly whippt in a private closet? Not long ago, in a day school not far from C.G. a boy about ten years old, having beaten and scratched a girl about his age, the governess, or rather her niece, (a girl not much above 17, for the governess is an old infirm lady) wishing very justly to punish the boy severely, pulled his breeches to

---

[1] *The Rambler's Magazine; Or, the Annals of Gallantry, Glee, Pleasure, and the Bon Ton, Calculated for the Entertainment of the Polite World; and to Furnish the Man of Pleasure with a Most Delicious Banquet of Amorous, Bacchanalian, Whimsical, Humorous, Theatrical and Polite Entertainment*, 1783-90, 8 vols. *The Bon Ton Magazine; Or, Microscope of Fashion and Folly*, 1791-6, 5 vols.

his heels, and, with a large bundle of new birch, flogged him till his bum and thighs were as red as scarlet: but, though she held him fast between her thighs, and even had one of her legs over his, and her left arm round his waist, the smart of the new birch caused the young culprit (a remarkable fine boy) to plunge and twist his body in such a manner, as to show a *little curious thing*, to the no small diversion of the schoolgirls. – The young school mistress having, however, observed a pretty big girl, of about twelve years old, very busy in making the others remark – *what do you call it* – took her to a closet just by the school, where she gave her too an excellent whipping. (November 1786, pp. 418-19)

While investigating birching at Eton it often occurred to me that the victim's genitals must on occasions have become visible to the assembled company, thereby adding to the mortification of sensitive boys. Clearly 'Fanny Quintickler' was thinking along the same lines.

The Rambler's was succeeded by the *Bon Ton Magazine*, or *Microscope of Fashion and Folly*, of which Pisanus Fraxi remarked that it 'may be said to occupy for the 'fashion', 'folly' and scandal of the times, the same place as did *The Gentleman's Magazine* for matters of greater and more universal importance'.[2] Among the ribald contributions printed by the magazine during its five years of existence are several flagellant stories, including a serial entitled 'A Modern Propensity', 'The French Governess' and an account of the 'Female Flagellists. A Club, in Jermyn Street' – an early appearance of a hardy troupe of ladies who throughout the nineteenth century would meet, and beat, in the elegant drawingrooms of flagellant pornography. Iwan Bloch swallowed this and other flagellant fictions hook line and sinker and relayed to his German compatriots his findings concerning the sadistic inclinations of Englishwomen: 'In the eighteenth century it is possible to point to regular clubs for female flagellants from which the conclusion may be drawn that the number of women with this tendency had noticeably increased.'[3]

But it was in the flagellant *letter* that the *Bon Ton Magazine* really specialised. Here we have 'A Boarding School Practice Exposed in a Letter to the Editor' (March 1792), the 'Strange Propensity of Boarding-School Governesses' (February 1794), a 'Letter of Miss Birch to the Editor, on the Utility of Birch Discipline' (March 1794), 'Birch Discipline Recommended, in a Letter to the Editor of the *Bon*

---

[2] Pisanus Fraxi, *Catena Librorum Tacendorum* (1885), p.323.

[3] Bloch (1938), pp. 349-50. This is a slightly inaccurate rendering of the original German: 'Jedenfalls steht is fest, dass thatsächlich im 18. Jahrhundert flagellantistische Weiberklubs in London existirten' (1903, p.424).

Ton Magazine' from 'A Female Advocate for Birch Discipline' (December 1795) and, among several other communications, one from the engaging Rebecca Rantipole of York (January 1796) whose girl friend is unfortunate to have 'the proudest and most tyrannical step-mother you ever heard of':

> Petticoats, etc., are then removed, and after a few words of lecture, during which the snowy prominences lie quivering in sad suspense, she applies the rod with such vigour and dexterity to poor Betty's backside, that in less than a couple of minutes her bouncing bum is 'all one red'. (p.419)

Given the compulsively repetitive nature of the flagellant fantasy, it is not surprising that the style in which these communications are expressed should be uniformly flat. The same expressions, images, turns of phrase recur endlessly. It is little wonder that there would be widespread filching of material during the nineteenth century in the search for something a bit different. Flagellant letter-writers would scour the columns of earlier publications and, when they came up with a juicy detail, would incorporate it in their own outpourings. Sometimes an old letter was refurbished and sent off almost in its original form, with only the more obvious inconsistencies or anachronisms ironed out. The first instance I have found of this occurs with a letter originally inserted in the *Bon Ton Magazine* of March 1792. Writes 'A.C.':

> At a house not a hundred miles from Parson's Green, where a board with large gold letters informs the Cit,[4] who mounts his Rozinante on the Sabbath, and inhales the country atmosphere, at the limited stipend of eighteen pence-a-side, that his daughter may there be genteely educated, resides a certain good lady, by the name of –. She has made shift for a long time, by the assistance of her husband, in some of the more *mechanical parts* of her office, to gain a decent livelihood, and to maintain a pretty numerous family in a very comfortable manner. In short, I believe her conduct, in every point of view, except one, may be considered blameless; and it is to give you an account of this very one that I trouble you at present.
>
> Know, then, Sir, that whenever one of the Mademoiselles offend their Mistress, so as to deserve the calling in of a third power, or, to speak more plainly, to need the application of any instrument with which nature has not already provided her, the young lady is conducted by her governess into a closet, set apart chiefly for that purpose, where they immediately proceed to action, after the following manner. First of all, Mr – is called in, and has assigned to him the *enviable* office of holding up those cumbersome

---

[4] That is, the city gentleman.

things called petticoats, etc. which may otherwise prevent the strokes of his *Sposa* from having proper effect; while she, with a strength which may almost be termed Herculean, makes the poor tender Victim acknowledge her transgressions, and solicit a pardon. I feel almost ashamed to tell you, Mr Editor, that I am actually acquainted with some young ladies of distinction, who with regard to virtue and modesty, and indeed everything else, bear an unblemished character, that have several times undergone this most indecent chastisement for the most trifling causes of juvenile transgression. I have so great an esteem, or rather veneration for your character, that I am sure you will agree with me in thinking a behaviour so totally inconsistent with the decency and decorum necessary to be maintained between the sexes, deserves to be properly exposed. (pp. 18-19)

On 6 October 1838 – the year following the accession of Queen Victoria – the *Crim Con Gazette*, a scurrilous weekly specialising, as its title announced, in 'criminal conversation' cases (a current euphemism for adultery) published a word-for-word copy of this letter – with the exception that it was signed 'Constant' and that the school 'not a hundred miles from Parson's Green' was now to be found in 'a house not a hundred miles from Richmond'. Needless to say the 'revelation' made by the *Crim Con Gazette* concerning the indecent whipping of girls in London in 1838 was followed by further letters expressing a similar sense of outrage while, at the same time, providing titillating details of what was going on in other fictitious schools.

I do not wish to make this chapter excessively long, although it is essential to my purpose to demonstrate the extent to which flagellant semi-pornography was allowed to infiltrate the respectable press in the nineteenth century. What I have done, therefore, is to limit my account to the five most prominent flagellant correspondences that have come to my notice during my investigation.

'Family Herald', 1845-67

The *Family Herald* was founded in 1842 and, unlike such journals as the *Crim Con Gazette*, was intended as good clean reading for all the family, including the children. The full title displayed on the first issue of the paper reads: *Family Herald. Or, Useful Information and Amusement for the Million. Interesting to All: Offensive to None. Life Without Mirth is like a Lamp without Oil*. The *Family Herald* was one of the first of the 'penny periodicals' designed to cater for the rapidly-growing middle-class readership of Victorian England, and it quickly built up a wide circulation.

A 'To Correspondents' section was inaugurated in 1843. It

gathered momentum, and by 1845 an annual index to it had been established. The page is more of an editorial answering-service than a correspondence column as we know it; extracts are given from readers' letters (genuine or not as the case may be) and a disembodied editorial expert pronounces judgment – in the royal plural. The correspondents' real names and addresses are not given: we have to take on trust that 'Ermina', 'Caractacus', 'Emily Prudens', 'Chess', 'Anna Jane', 'Aristide', 'A Traveller in Many Lands', 'Diogenes' and the rest of them actually existed and were not merely editorial concoctions. It can readily be appreciated how such a system – general in the nineteenth century – gave carte blanche to both correspondents and editors to parade their own obsessions under the guise of impartiality, seriousness or respect for 'public opinion'.

The range of topics dealt with in the *Family Herald*'s three-column 'To Correspondents' page was wide, and the series as a whole offers a fascinating insight into the preoccupations, anxieties and interests of the English middle class from the beginning of the Victorian period until late into the nineteenth century. The queries reveal in particular a great uncertainty on the part of readers regarding etiquette. At what age is it best to marry? How should one greet a clergyman in the street? Is kissing morally dangerous?

G.S.B. – A gentleman, on entering church with ladies, may either regard the church itself as the pew, and suffer the ladies to precede, or he himself may precede, according to circumstances. When there is a pew-opener, the pew-opener precedes. When there is no pew-opener, the gentleman takes his place. A well-bred gentleman can act either part so well, that, whether first or last, he will appear in his right place. He is where service is required. (24 January 1846, p.600)

A.F.W. writes all the way from Lisbon to ask us what is the correct pronunciation of 'Albert'. He says the English clergyman of Lisbon (Mr Prior) pronounces it '*All*bert'; and moreover, a friend of A.F.W., another Englishman in Lisbon, maintains that Mr Prior is right. Mr Prior is wrong. (*ibid.*)

AUGUSTUS R. – Banish the idea that you are attracting notice, and the blushing will subside; go into society. (19 July 1863, p.188)

A BACHELOR. – Yes, a widower and son may marry a widow and daughter. (3 August 1850, p.218)

Among the topics aired in the *Family Herald* was that of 'scholastic' and 'domestic' corporal punishment, and between 1845 and 1867 the paper published many dozens of entries on the subject. Some of these were undoubtedly genuine, others manifestly not; some were blatantly pornographic. In discussing parental discipline earlier, I pointed out that the *Family Herald* took a consistently Solomonic line, coming down on the side of 'moderate' flogging. Despite its broad acceptance of the corporal punishment of children, however, the paper could not avoid having reservations about the mode of its infliction, and was less than straightforward on the subject. Take girls, for example. The editor could see no reason in theory why they should be treated differently from boys – at least before puberty ('Fourier' is presumably the French philosopher and sociologist, Charles Fourier, 1772-1837):

> There are some who would make an exception in favour of girls, and leave the boys to the old rod, the birch, the cane, or the thong. This is unjust; we see no reason why they should be treated differently. Children are of no sex. Fourier calls them neuters. When the sex is formed, the distinction begins to be admitted. But why a boy of seven should be whipped and a girl of seven not whipped for an act of disobedience, is more than any logic that we are acquainted with can make apparent. (24 November 1849, p.476)

It is clear that the *Family Herald* is uneasily aware of the objections to what was by now widely referred to as 'indecent' or 'indelicate' whipping. This is the arena of shame, coyness, blushes and disguised sexuality, and the *Family Herald*'s editorials on corporal punishment are reluctant to discuss the matter openly: 'If parents are anxious to have their children well educated, they must not be afraid of a little castigation on the place which nature has ordained for the purpose; but suffer no tyrant to strike a boy on the head or the back of the hand, or any of the joints' (24 January 1846, p.600). The language reminds us that the eighteenth century has been left behind and that we have entered the age of euphemism. The bottom has been ordained by nature for the reception of castigation but cannot be referred to directly in polite company. The particular euphemism concerning the buttocks' ordination by nature recurs *ad nauseam* throughout the century – and may still be met with, as we have seen. Since the back, head, back of the hand and presumably the legs were ruled out by the *Family Herald* as suitable parts of the body for the reception of punishment, that left only the palm of the hands and the buttocks. Given the preference of nature for the latter, the subject, it could be argued, was settled.[5]

---

[5] A letter to the *Englishwoman's Domestic Magazine* suggests that the repellent phrase derived from the brother of Harriet Beecher Stowe, a religious author and journalist: 'But I do heartily believe in a system which I rejoice to see is once more being used –

The theme of 'indelicate' whipping, then, was in the air, and it was on this aspect that the vast majority of the communications published in the *Family Herald* between 1845 and 1869 would concentrate. What constituted an 'indecent' whipping? Was it 'indecent' for a man to whip a girl? For a woman to whip a boy? By general consent, or editorial dictation, it was decided that male to male, and female to female, beatings were perfectly respectable, but that no mixing of the sexes was tolerable. This so far as schools were concerned. In the domestic situation, decisions were best left to individual parents.

By 1848 the *Family Herald*'s flagellant column was positively tripping along. The first intimation concerning the possibly sensual implications of flogging had come on 26 February 1848. 'One no longer a Jesuit' wrote:

> My scourgings were invariably done in the privacy of my closet; and hence you may, perhaps, imagine that if I had pleased to punish myself very leniently, no one would have been the wiser. Not so; for the state of my person, when submitted to the examiner, would at once indicate the real amount of the punishment I had undergone; and a severe penalty would have been the infallible result, had I attempted to evade the due quantum of flagellation expected. Anything like serious lacerations of the flesh never occurred. In my case I invariably desisted when the flesh began to break. I have felt the effects of a flogging for weeks. (p.683)

The *Family Herald*'s commentary that followed this 'confession' is worth noting:

> Our correspondent says that flogging is very generally practised in monasteries and nunneries on the Continent, and even in liberal France. He says there probably is not a nunnery in France where the inmates do not mortify the flesh, either voluntarily or in obedience to order, which is imperative. Our correspondent says flogging excites the passions – a well-known fact; yet it is used by monks and nuns on purpose to allay them. The consequences, he says, are such as he cannot describe, and we, of course, could not publish. (*ibid.*)

Someone, it seems, had read his Meibom, Boileau, Thiers, or the large body of pornographic works concerned with the perverted practices of priests and nuns (a constant favourite, almost a genre in itself). There is no prize for the reader who guesses correctly the

---

viz., the sound, hearty flogging that part which Henry Ward Beecher says "was intended by Nature for the purpose" ' (1 January 1869, p.55).

profession of the next correspondent. It was, of course, a nun, or rather 'One who no longer wishes to enter a convent'. Little wonder, if such stories were really believed. Confirmation of the dangers of convent life was soon forthcoming:

> 'One who has fled from Babylon'. – Allow me to substantiate the assertion of your correspondent 'One who is no longer a Jesuit', respecting the use of flagellation in convents generally. I was for two years a sister of a convent on the French coast; but being convinced of the rottenness of Popery, simply from their own authors, I made my escape from this den of superstition, and embraced the blessed Protestant faith, in which I have since remained, in the full conviction of its truth and purity. We were there compelled by the rules of the order to flagellate ourselves at least three times a week. It was generally done on rising in the morning. The instrument used was a common domestic birch rod, such as is used in England; and the locality to which it was applied the same. We generally inflicted on ourselves from twenty to thirty smart strokes of the rod. The superior paid us a visit on these mornings, and examined our persons, to see that the whipping had been duly inflicted; and in case of an omission, she administered a severe correction herself. For various offences, such as omission of duty, corrections were administered in the presence of all the nuns, and not infrequently in that of *some priests*, who were visiting the convent. This latter piece of indecency fully proves the prophecy of the Revelations respecting the Popish abominations. I frequently spoke of this indecency to the other nuns; but the answer was, 'We are dead to the world, and all our passions are dead also.' Pretty sophistry! Many priests visited the convent, and scenes too impure to be mentioned have passed therein. Let those females who wish there were Protestant convents think of the abominations I have mentioned. (18 March 1848, p.729)

This ludicrous fabrication is reproduced here in full, exactly as it appears (without editorial comment) in the *Family Herald*. One has to remind oneself that one is not dreaming, and that this is a family periodical designed to be 'Interesting to All; Offensive to None'. That such a manifest piece of fantasy could be put out as truth is almost unbelievable, and it did not convince 'Agnes Teresa': 'But I would ask you, sir, can you conscientiously insert such things without further proof of their veracity than the bare word of an anonymous correspondent?' (8 April 1848, p.779). Was 'Agnes Teresa' another bit of the editor's head? Was she genuine? We have no way of knowing. And what about 'Nina M.'?

> NINA M. is seventeen, and married. Her husband is 30. They adore each other; but, in one respect, he is harsh. He beats her when she disobeys. He

says she is a child, and requires discipline. The beating is very severe, and is done with a riding-switch; 'yet it seems as if I loved him,' says NINA, 'far better and more passionately after a whipping. He is the tenderest of husbands in other respects, denies me nothing, even heaps presents and luxuries on me. Is not this a curious case, Mr Editor? And yet there may be many such that the world never suspects. What shall I do? I fear it will at last destroy my love, and I cannot bear that, nor would I hear of a separation. (24 August 1850, p.266)

We saw in the flagellant communications published in the *Rambler's* and the *Bon Ton Gazette* at the end of the eighteenth century that one of the main interests there was to promote the idea that (1) women derive sensual pleasure from applying the birch to both boys and girls and (2) that grown girls ('great girls', the Victorians called them) were regularly birched in respectable English schools. The Victorian pornographers exploited this device to the full, despite the fact (as the Schools Inquiry Commission showed) that in such schools there was practically no beating. So too did those whose letters appeared in the publications we are discussing. Schools and severe schoolmistresses were invented and reinvented (boys' preparatory schools were a favourite) but no verifiable details were ever brought forward in support of the allegations made. Nor did papers such as the *Family Herald* make any pretence to have checked the facts. The establishments were habitually situated 'near Edinburgh', or 'five miles from Bournemouth'; if the locality was named the school was sure to have closed down some years earlier. But still its name was never given. The whole thing was so obviously a hoax that one cannot but impugn the editors involved.

One of the oddest of these schools was that of the 'Misses Fulcher at Chiswick'. It makes its appearance in one of the *Family Herald*'s zaniest productions on the subject, on 22 September 1849:

THE FEMALE BIRCH. – We have received several letters respecting punishments at young ladies' schools, some asserting that there is no such thing, others approving, others disapproving. We gave no opinion on the subject. We merely said that discipline must be preserved in a school by some means or other. In the most aristocratic schools the discipline is more severe than in the common schools. We have one letter from a lady who was educated at the Misses Fulcher's school, near Chiswick (who have now gone abroad), where the terms were eighty and a hundred guineas per annum, and she describes the apparatus for chastisement to be a step to kneel on, a cushion to lie on, and a strap to buckle down the body whilst the chastisement was administered. Now, for a girl of nineteen (as our correspondent asserts in one instance) to be so treated

before sixty giddy girls, is a breach of decorum which modern society is not
likely to tolerate. But such cases are very rare, and the subjects in general
very tiresome creatures. The girl alluded to submitted with patience, but
immediately ran away and threw herself into the arms of a solicitor, who
was separated from his wife. She, having a fortune, the solicitor secured it,
and emigrated to Australia with her. In this school at the time were two
lords' daughters, one baronet's daughter, and the daughters of clergymen,
colonels, esquires, etc. The system, in extreme cases, was therefore
approved of by them; and our correspondent says the Misses Fulcher were
very severe, but just mistresses. (p.331)

The mind boggles, and here again it is impossible not to sense that the
editor controlling this correspondence is a party to the mystification.
Near Chiswick indeed! Despite the pleas from readers as to the whereabouts of flogging schools for young ladies, no one ever comes up with
any information. Only Mrs Walter Smith would be real. We are in the
world of pornographic make-believe, bounded by neither space nor
time. Years later the Misses Fulcher turned up again in the same
columns: 'EMILY wishes to find a school where she can place the
daughter of a friend, a spoiled child, where discipline is very strict,
and where flogging is permitted' (5 September 1863, p.300). Emily,
the Editor informs us, 'herself went to the school of the Misses
Fulcher, at Chiswick (they have now for some years gone abroad)
where great severity was kept up'. Emily's request sparked off the
usual dreary responses, one of them from DOMINA who (although
she confesses herself 'one of the most *earnest* advocates of corporal
chastisement, gently and affectionately administered') rejoices
heartily at the departure of the Misses Fulcher from Chiswick (3
October 1863, p.364). The editor informs ECOLIERE that 'the
"stories" you allude to of Miss Fulcher's establishment we fully
credit; and from the numerous letters we receive we believe that the
practice you condemn is not only indulged in, but that it is indulged in
because severe correction is thought necessary' (19 December 1863,
p.540).
    Another favourite joke of the flagellants was to pretend that the
birching of grown girls was widespread in that iniquitous country
France (where in fact it was unheard of). Thus C.H. and AN ENEMY
TO THE BIRCH:

Both write to us about female castigation in French schools. C.H. says her
daughter, aged 19, is just returned from a school in France, where it is the
constant practice to whip the girls for very trivial offences; and gives an
instance of one powerful girl of 19, on whose person the most
unmentionable of all floggings was perpetrated. The French, we believe,

are very indecent in this respect, especially in the interior, far from the neighbourhood of England. (17 August 1850, p.250)

That last joke, it has to be admitted, was a good one. And what a time AN ENEMY TO THE BIRCH has had in France: 'She was flogged innumerable times, during which she was strapped down. Well, English parents who send their children to France must look after these matters. They are French customs, we suppose; and people must all eat maccaroni when they go to Naples, you know' (*ibid.*). FATHER, too, 'has just discovered that his daughter, lately come from a school in France, was, in common with all the other pupils (some of them twenty and twenty-two), subjected to this ancestorial discipline of birching, and that of the severest kind. He considers it the duty of English parents to make inquiry into this subject before they send their children to the French schools' (14 September 1850, p.314).

The choicest piece on the subject of ladies' schools, however, appeared in the *Family Herald* on 20 October 1849. As an illustration of the essentially ritual nature of the flagellant fantasy, this communication could not be bettered. Indeed, for attention to detail, only the real-life Mrs Walter Smith of Clifton could equal these ladies:

A HATER OF THE SYSTEM (our old friend) writes to inform us that even she does not disapprove of flogging, but only indecent flogging; and she says that in the most aristocratic schools flogging is of daily occurrence. She describes the system pursued in one near Edinburgh, where the terms are 120 guineas per annum. 'A book of offences is kept by one of the young ladies, in which every fault is regularly entered. There is a graduated scale of punishments, the highest of which is corporal. When an offence of sufficient magnitude takes place, the culprit enters it in the book herself, and carries the report to the lady superintendent, who writes under it the amount of punishment. For the first offence, the delinquent is prepared for punishment, but generally pardoned. For the second, she is whipped privately. For all subsequent delinquencies the punishment takes place in the school-room, on 'the horse'; and, in addition to the pain it inflicts, it costs in money about 1s., paid in fees. The system is as follows:– 1st. She proceeds to the housekeeper, to procure the rod, a leathern thong. She pays 2d. for the use of it. 2nd. She has then to be partly undressed by the maid; and this costs 2d. 3rd. The culprit has then to walk barefooted to another part of the house, to be robed for punishment, a peculiar dress being used, to add to the disgrace. It is a long linen blouse, short cotton socks, and list slippers, all of which each offender has to provide for herself. The young lady, thus costumed, now proceeds to the drawing-room, to be exhibited to the lady superintendent. Having been approved, she is then conducted to the school-room, when she has to pay 6d. to the governess, who inflicts the amount of punishment awarded. A wooden horse, covered with soft leather, is the medium of castigation. The delinquent subsequently thanks the governess! kisses the rod!! then thanks the superintendent, and retires to her own room, to appear no more until prayer-time the next morning.' Our correspondent says the ceremony has more effect than the punishment. The young ladies are in other respects tenderly dealt with. Even the horse has a soft cushion. (p.394)

But not content to let the communication stand at this, the editorial voice continues:

Our correspondent says the custom is borrowed from Holland – where, a correspondent some years ago told us, they had whipping establishments, to which parents sent out their children to be punished. It seems they do so in Edinburgh also, for our present correspondent says young ladies are sent to this Scotch horse to get their faults whipped out of them. She has seen girls of all ages whipped as if they were children; though in general it is only those between 10 and 15 that are whipped in the school-room. The elder ones are whipped privately. The last aggravated case our correspondent knows of was a case of theft from another young lady's writing-desk! We must reserve any comment on the practice at present, till we know more of the merits of the question. (*ibid.*)

Is it possible to doubt that 'our old friend' 'A Hater of the System' is any other than the editor himself? Even on the basis of the fatuous text one might think not. But there is further evidence to suggest an editorial hoax. On 8 July 1865, almost twenty years later, when the paper's flagellant column was beginning (beginning!) to slow down, the body of this same letter was reprinted, with slight modifications – attributed this time to 'X.X.X.'. In theory this refurbished communication might have been sent in by someone else without the editor being aware that he was being duped. But a careful comparison of the two versions makes such a possibility unlikely. In particular the passage about the 'horse' seems to show signs of editorial tampering. In the 1849 version the passage reads: 'Even the horse has a soft cushion. Our correspondent says the custom is borrowed from Holland – where, *a correspondent some years ago told us* [my italics], they had whipping establishments.' In the 1865 version, 'X.X.X.' speaks in his own, first person singular, voice, but when he comes to this passage he shifts, unaccountably, into the first person plural: 'Even the horse has a soft cushion. The custom *we are told* is borrowed from Holland – where, *as a friend some years ago told us*, they had whipping establishments' [my italics].

Comparison of the two communications makes it extremely likely that they were written in the *Family Herald*'s editorial office, and suggests that the entire correspondence was little more than a confidence trick played on the public, and an open invitation to the flagellants in the community to submit publishable pornography. The inclusion of the occasional genuine letter only served to make the fake ones appear more plausible. In the light of such editorial complicity, the *Family Herald*'s final comment on the second version of the above letter seems a particularly sick joke:

> Correspondents who have plagued us for so many months as to the *modus operandi* of punishment, may now be satisfied. In our opinion the ceremony is ridiculous. A girl who would steal a sovereign would not be humiliated by being well whipped by women, *minus* the ridiculous costume. (8 July 1865, p.156)

And what do we make now of the *Family Herald*'s claim at several moments during the correspondence that, try as it might, it could not hold back the flood of letters that continued to pour into the office?:

> This unpleasant subject of discipline seems to be thrust upon us in spite of all our efforts to have done with it. This shows its importance. It is a source of great anxiety to teachers and parents. (2 November 1850, p.426)

And a source of income to newspapers, the editor might have added. It is also likely that people's anxiety about corporal punishment was increased by the paper's handling of the subject.

As one goes back over the twenty-years' correspondence, the trickery and deceit leap from the page, and it becomes increasingly clear that, like its correspondent 'Eleanor Prudens' (4 September 1852), the *Family Herald* itself is 'painfully excited about the subject of corporal punishment' (p.298). Excited being the operative word.

It is only necessary to refer to one further aspect of this correspondence: the *Family Herald*'s handling of or allusions to the shame component in flogging (which, as I shall attempt to show later, is vital to an understanding of the whole flagellant phenomenon). As a rule this aspect of the matter is avoided in discussions of flagellation, which makes the *Family Herald*'s comments of particular psychological interest. To begin with, it is conceded that the *humiliation* undergone by the recipient of a good 'old-fashioned whipping' is an indispensable part of the punishment, and a most desirable part too: the *Family Herald* knows that there is nothing like humiliation or fear of ridicule to make a child tow the line. Or anyone for that matter:

> The papers lately mentioned, as a remarkable case, the sentence of flogging pronounced on a young hero of romance, for sending poison in a

letter – the revival of an old practice, which sentimentalism had succeeded in getting rid of, except in its horrible and exaggerated form as perpetrated in the army and navy. A good domestic flogging, inflicted publicly on an offender against the peace or the feelings of society, is, perhaps, one of the most efficient of all punishments. We have had no more attempts against the Queen's life since flogging was prescribed for it.[6] There are many who can brave death, who can inflict it on themselves, and who would even pay you money to take away their lives; but there are very few indeed, religious flagellants excepted, who would ask you to be so kind as to give them a good flogging. Moreover, the flogging of a criminal should never lacerate the flesh, never even break the skin. It should always be attended with ridicule, not sympathy. Whenever you create sympathy, you destroy its efficacy. Let the scoundrel get a smack,[7] and then get up, writhe, and rub it, amid the laughter of the spectators. He would feel it for life, not in his flesh, but in his pride; and no public subscription, as in the case of army victims, would ever be raised in his behalf by popular sympathy. The very leniency of the punishment in a corporeal sense, would constitute its efficiency, because the ridicule, which is an important element of punishment, would come in to supply the defect of corporeal severity. (18 September 1847, pp. 315-16)

The *Family Herald* has come close here to Thomas de Quincey's perception that the corporal punishment of the male sex 'is its peculiar and *sexual* degradation', corresponding to the raping of females (1871, p.498). De Quincey admires the person who would rather die than be subjected to such an indignity, whereas the *Family Herald* approves this form of degradation in the interests of promoting conformity of behaviour in others. As will have been clear from earlier chapters, the English nineteenth-century Establishment preferred not to follow De Quincey.

Flogging humiliates, then, and its mental wounds can last for a lifetime, may never heal. This being so one might think that the *Family Herald* would disapprove of the regular use of the birch in the public schools of England for the correction of trivial offences. For might not these inflictions, often imposed in public, also leave permanent marks on the sensibilities of the victims? One of the paper's correspondents made this very point on 13 July 1850, and I give the entry in full, complete with editorial comment, as a final example of the *Family Herald*'s refusal to deal honestly with a subject whose widespread and largely disreputable discussion it promoted for 20 years:

ONE OF THE FLOGGED is a youth who is at home during the summer

[6] Under the Treason Act, 1842.
[7] Note the sickly euphemism.

holidays, and who has been reading back numbers of the *Family Herald*. The articles on corporal punishments inspired him to write. He has been flogged. At his school there are 224 boys; and when a boy misbehaves he is called to the centre of the school, where he is compelled to lie across a desk. The master then comes, cane in hand, and having made a speech to the spectators, he gathers the boy's nether clothes in one hand, and flogs him with the other. For some offences the boy is stripped and whipped with the hand or a birch rod; 'and I am convinced,' says our young *floggee*, 'that the boy rises from either of these punishments ruined for life in his moral feelings.' (p.170)

Which is after all only the point that the *Family Herald* itself makes in the article just quoted: the shame of a public birching is something a victim would feel for life. Here is how this 'respectable' newspaper reacts to the letter:

This accounts for the corruption of the times. Churchmen, ministers, bishops, judges, legislators, parsons, merchants, tradesmen, mechanics, and editors have all been flogged in their young days, and 'ruined in their moral feelings'. When our correspondent becomes a parent himself he must abjure all chastisements whatsoever, feed his children on milk and honey, give them feather beds to lie upon, and never ruffle their tempers nor irritate their skin with any painful excitement whatsoever. Our correspondent is wrong when he says we advocate flogging. We have never done so. We advocate discipline. The subject is one upon which both masters and parents are making experiments all over the country. Some succeed without flogging, and some do not. We have been told by some masters that they abandoned it for years, and lost authority and pupils in consequence, and then returned to it. Others succeeded. We believe that an absolute prohibition of it in all cases would be a very foolish act of popular interference with the law of discipline. It is very easy to escape a flogging at every respectable school. (*ibid.*)

As an example of the *Family Herald*'s speciality in sneering, hypocritical humbug this piece could hardly be bettered, and we should perhaps be grateful to 'One of the Flogged' (who seems to be a genuine correspondent) for calling it forth. And that is enough about the *Family Herald* except to say that, realising that money was to be made from flogging discussions, it issued a selection of its 'best' letters in pamphlet form.

'The Queen, The Lady's Newspaper and Court Chronicle', 1865-66

Between December 1865 and February 1866 this fashionable newspaper ran a column on the corporal punishment of children variously headed 'Discipline for Young Children', 'Discipline of Children' and 'Infant Discipline'.

The letter that initiated the discussion (16 December 1865) has a familiar ring: 'I.M.L.' is hesitant about inflicting corporal punishment on her two young children, Violet and Irene. One of her whipping friends recommends it. This friend 'invariably made the culprit itself go to the drawer and bring the rod to her, as she says it makes the child more humble'. What is 'I.M.L.' to do? 'My heart fails,' she confesses, 'at the thought of whipping my Violet of five'. Her communication ends: 'Will some mother who, like me, remembers the penalty of whipping being inflicted often on herself for trifles, help me to some way of sparing my children, and yet making them good?' (p.419)

Genuine, hoax or editorial concoction, this letter provoked a spate of replies, most of them against corporal punishment. The letter signed 'A Manager of Unruly Little Girls', though, was decidedly flagellant:

> If you can grant me space, I must tell 'I.M.L.' of one child who was sent to me at seven years old as 'incurably disobedient'. I know it will be thought 'too dreadful' by those mothers who, while too tender-hearted to give pain to their children's bodies, leave their future lives to be rendered wretched by evil passions unchecked in childhood, and seem to forget they have the responsibility of training them for eternity. Well, this little Sibyl, when I was distinctly telling her how I punished different faults, said 'I don't care for that, papa often whips me when I disobey him'. I took no notice. The next day, at nine o'clock, I called her to read. Not a word would she utter. Of course, punishment immediately followed. Still not a syllable. So I said, 'Sibyl, that page has to be read. I mean to whip you every half hour till you obey'. It seems incredible a child should willingly undergo so much pain; but she held out for several hours, until, when I was about to inflict the fifteenth punishment [N.B. at the rate of two whippings per hour this would make a session of seven and a half hours!] she read the page, and voluntarily begged my pardon. I never had to punish her for disobedience but once afterwards. Her father had only whipped her as a punishment; it had never occurred to him to compel obedience by that means. (23 December 1865, p.435)

The letters published in *The Queen* reveal, like those appearing in the other flagellant correspondence columns, a positive obsession with the enforcement of obedience upon children. Even the anti-floggers are obsessed by this aspect of the subject, the difference being that they prefer 'moral persuasion' to physical. Three letters published on 23 December 1865, all opposed to beating, harp on the obedience theme: 'Reason with her, and don't leave her, not even if it takes hours, in a rebellious state, but show her you mean to be obeyed' ('Adaugh'); 'A mother should bring up her children from earliest infancy to obey her slightest word, never allowing it to be disputed for a moment' ('A Hater of the Rod'); 'I have brought up several children without either rod or dark closet discipline, and have had the satisfaction of seeing rebellion and deceit strangers to my home ... the child must be taught to fear God and love mamma, and that the love of both will be removed if forgetful of the words in her daily prayer' ('Y.Z.'). A week later, the no doubt well-meaning 'Harrie' sent in a peculiarly stifling programme for the maintenance of domestic discipline:

> I have already begun to take quite an interest in Irene and Violet [she wrote, referring to the letter from 'I.M.L.' that had sparked off the discussion], and I hope about next Christmas I.M.L. will let us hear from her again, mentioning whose advice she followed and how it has succeeded. I predict that if she follows the plan recommended by the 'Manager of Unruly Girls', some forty years hence will see her dear girls crabbed old maids, instead of the happy mothers of happy children. I would not be understood to include in the term 'crabbed old maids' those gentle, sympathising, loveable, single ladies who are an ornament and a blessing to society. I.M.L. cannot do better, while her little girls are so young, than follow the advice given by Y.Z. When they are a little older she will probably find the following plan beneficial. Procure a small book, and rule each page with seven perpendicular lines, thus:

	S.	M.	T.	W.	T.	F.	S
Bible reading	Y.						
Prayers	Y.						
Truth	Y.						
Obedience	N.						
Temper	N.						
Obstinacy	Y.						

> The letters at the top standing for the days of the week, the words referring to questions written out on the first page of the book, which the child will ask itself; and the Y. and N. standing for Yes and No, which the child will fill in with pencil every night, according as it can satisfactorily to its conscience answer the questions. The mother can allow the book to be entirely private between the child and its God, or can examine it occasionally, according to the character of the child and inclination of the parent. (30 December 1865, p.458)

As the pro-floggers were quick to point out, anything, including a good birching, would be preferable to *that* method.

Among these advocates of the rod, two communications stand out by their notably flagellant tone. 'Virgo' has been speaking to 'a mistress of a preparatory boys' school of fifteen years' standing'. This lady, whose experience of corporal punishment 'extends to both sexes', is clearly something of a psychologist: 'She is satisfied that boys mentally suffer more from punishment than girls – the bodily pain is the only inconvenience the girl suffers, but the deep shame and mortification which invariably attend the punishment of a boy make his sufferings more acute.' 'Virgo' (whose understanding of the shame element in flagellation comes close to that of the editor of the *Family Herald*) states in conclusion that 'she would earnestly advise "I.M.L." to send her little girls to the "Manager of Unruly Little Girls" ' (13 January 1866, p.27).

But it was the communication from 'A.F.W.' that attracted most attention. Here again was that perennial flagellant chimaera, the full-blown whipping establishment for girls:

> Some time ago, in consequence of an advertisement in the London *Times*, I opened up negotiations with a lady who keeps a large school in the vicinity of London, and which resulted in my placing my daughter, now just turned fifteen years of age, under her care. My wife informs me that since her return from school this Christmas, the first holiday since joining the school, that my daughter has had to submit on one or two occasions to the application of the old-fashioned birch in the presence of her schoolfellows, and that, too, in not the most delicate fashion. My wish is to know whether this custom still obtains at other boarding-schools besides this one, and up to what age the pupils have to submit to this style of correction? (13 January 1866, p.27)

A week later 'A.F.W.' had his answer, when *The Queen* distinguished itself by publishing a similarly ludicrous letter from 'Florence R.':

> As I am writing anonymously, I have no objection to informing 'A.F.W.' that at a great many ladies' boarding-schools the birch is very extensively used. I was myself for four years at a strict boarding-school at Bath, until I was seventeen, and for certain offences we were most severely whipped by the mistress, but privately in her own room. I know several of my friends who have been at other schools, and I have always heard that whipping is inflicted for some offences. I remember a case of a girl of over sixteen who refused to submit until her parent (mother) was written to, but the end of it was, that she received twelve most severe strokes. No one can conceive the strictness of a large boarding-school and the tyranny of the governess. (20 January 1866, p.44)

In the same issue, 'Solomon Slow' doubted the authenticity of

'A.F.W.' 's communication, which had made him 'blush with shame and indignation', and put the usual question, which always went unanswered:

> As one having a large interest in girls, who may one day be fifteen years old, I ask 'A.F.W.' to give us, by way of caution to parents and guardians, the address of this model establishment for young ladies.
> I should like to be told also by whom, or what, this punishment is inflicted. Surely no woman worthy the name can be found in civilised England capable of so unsexing herself and brutalising and degrading those entrusted to her charge, unless indeed your strong-armed correspondent 'Virgo' (who has surely omitted an *a* in writing her signature) be retained on the establishment.[8] (*ibid.*)

'Florence R.' also received her reply some weeks later when 'Emilie J.C.', claiming to be a French teacher, wrote in from Bath. 'Emilie' has been 'hardly able to credit' the revelations made by 'Florence':

> Having been connected with this city for now nearly ten years, I must say that I am inexpressibly surprised by the statement which she makes as to the discipline to which she has had to submit at a school in this place.
> My object in writing this note is to say that at several of the leading schools at which I have the honour of being the teacher of my native language, no such system prevails as that of which your correspondent speaks. I would willingly believe that I have misunderstood the purport of her letter, and that she had merely to submit herself to a punishment with the cane, which alone is used, I know, but *on the hand*, for several offences at some schools, and that only in exceptional cases. (27 January 1866, p.65)

'Y.Z.' is similarly outraged, and points out that 'A young person beaten into submission will secretly dislike the inflictor, and deceit will usurp the place of sincerity, and probably of every other noble feeling'; while another alleged schoolmistress wrote:

> I have been a teacher of children and kept a school together for ten years and I never before heard of whipping being practised or allowed either by schoolmistress or governess ... There is something so disgustingly revolting in the idea of their receiving such treatment, that words cannot embody my own feeling about it. (*ibid.*)

In commenting on the flagellant correspondence in the *Family Herald* I quoted a letter from 'A Hater of the System' (20 October

---

[8] i.e. she should more properly be called Virago.

1849). The reader may recall that in that communication there was given a detailed description of the flogging activities at a ladies' school 'near Edinburgh'; the letter, as we have seen, was reprinted with some slight modifications in the same newspaper on 8 July 1865, and it has been argued that it provides evidence of the *Family Herald*'s editorial intervention. It is amusing, therefore, to find that this selfsame letter reappears in *The Queen* on 20 January 1866, quoted by 'A Reader of your Journal from its Commencement' as corroboration of 'A.F.W.' 's contentions concerning the prevalence of birching at girls' schools! The same correspondent's introductory note is as obviously flagellant in character as the *Family Herald* letter which had rendered such service to the pro-floggers:

> Our school, which was conducted by two ladies, consisted of about forty-five boys, varying from five to twelve years of age; terms, 50 guineas a year. But two sorts of punishment were resorted to in our school – first, for minor offences, being placed in a corner of the room, with a birch-rod in the hand; and, second, a whipping in the real public-school fashion; and as the schoolmistress was a very fine, powerful woman, I assure you it was no joking matter. (p.44)

Only one other letter deserves mention. It appeared on 27 January 1866 in the issue that marked the high-point of *The Queen*'s 'inquiry' into corporal punishment, no less than eight communications being printed on that date. The letter comes from 'B.', who claims that he is an Old Etonian whose niece has recently been punished by the headmistress of her school in 'the old-fashioned style'. Why? For putting a visiting English Literature lecturer out of countenance over a line of verse by Matthew Arnold which he had wrongly attributed to Alfred Tennyson:

> Her resistance was useless against force; she was held across a desk, the clothing was completely removed from the lower part of her person, and the lady principal gave her twelve sharp cuts with a birch. No Etonian was ever so indecently and cruelly treated.

And 'B.' should know, for, as he tells us, he attended the Queen of Schools under the venerable Dr Keate. Infuriated by the birching imposed on his niece ('I am an Irishman, and you may imagine my indignation'), 'B.' has decided to avenge the family honour – by subjecting the offending mistress to a taste of her own medicine. He has carried out his plan in the approving presence of 'the wives of three of my friends':

I had ridden over to Eton and got a good stout birch rod from the man who makes for college – it is a good appointment. It is only necessary to add that she was treated as my niece had been in the matter of apparel, and that I gave her twenty strokes, whose severity the state of her cuticle plainly attested. (p.65)

This letter is so obviously farcical that one wonders why the editor decided to insert it in the midst of what the newspaper claimed was a serious discussion of a topic of widespread interest. Winding up the debate on 3 February 1866, the editor stated that 'in the performance of what we regarded as a public duty which might lead to social benefit, we have persuaded ourselves to permit our correspondents to go to the utmost verge and limit'. The limit of what, exactly, the editor did not say, but the reference to indecency is obvious. The editor insists, moreover, that *The Queen* disapproves almost completely of corporal punishment; and feels that the publication of the unpleasant, pro-flogging letters may have been beneficial in this respect by turning people against the practice. There is no indication whatsoever in this article that the editor is prepared to doubt the authenticity of the letters he has published:

And although we confess that we have perused with no small nausea and abhorrence some of the letters we have printed, we are sure that right-hearted and strong-minded readers will only be disgusted by them and that none will be weak enough to regard them with satisfaction. (p.88)

One cannot but reflect that, if the editor of *The Queen* was sincere, he might have taken more trouble to check up on the genuineness of the letters he published. But was he sincere? It is difficult to believe it, especially in view of the ludicrous communication attributed to 'B'. It looks very much as if the mind behind this correspondence was as flagellant as that of the *Family Herald*.

'Notes and Queries', 1852-76

The flagellant communications published sporadically over a period of twenty-five years in this erudite journal have a dotty charm all of their own: scholarly, whimsical, at times provocative and almost always anonymous, they are mainly concerned with bibliographical niceties and the pursuit of documentary evidence for the infliction of the rod.

The discussion got under way in 1852 with an enquiry concerning Henry Layng's satirical poem *The Rod*, published in the eighteenth century. This elicited a reply from a happy owner of the volume, who offered 'to forward the poem to your correspondent, if he wish to see it' (20 November 1852). Writers to *Notes and Queries* watch their subjunctives carefully, and everything is done in a gentlemanly fashion. 'Balliolensis' came next (12 February 1853), contributing a copy of an MS poem in his possession, 'The Birch: A Poem. Written by a Youth of Thirteen'. 'Perhaps the following lines,' he wrote, 'may be received as germane to the subject.' Germane they certainly were. The composition is predictable, a variation on the public-school effusions which were common enough at the time and at which Swinburne excelled:

> Here dwells strong conviction – of Logic the glory,
> When applied with precision *a posteriori*.
> I've known a short lecture most strangely prevail
> When duly convey'd to the head through the tail;
> Like an electrical shock, in an instant 'tis spread,
> And flies with a jerk from the tail to the head;
> Promotes circulation, and thrills through each vein,
> The faculties quickens, and purges the brain.
> By sympathy thus, and consent of the parts,
> We are taught, *fundamentally*, classics and arts. (p.159)

Another reader sent in an enquiry concerning one of the flagellants' favourite topics, the alleged birching of Cupid by Venus:

> There is a curious subject frequently met with in medieval art, both carved and painted, namely, 'Venus Chastising Cupid'. I have met with it treated in different ways; in one, Cupid is 'horsed' on the back of another Cupid, in the orthodox scholastic fashion, and in another he is undergoing the birch, being laid across Venus's knee, after the usual manner of mammas in general. I should feel obliged if one of your numerous correspondents could furnish me with the classical authority for this very eccentric subject. (3 May 1856, p.355)

None of these numerous correspondents came forward with an answer to this query. A few years later, however, 'Antibirch' expressed his perplexity over an analogical case:

> In a cathedral in Italy there is a picture of the Virgin Mary whipping the child Jesus in our ordinary nursery fashion. Is there any legendary authority for such a painting? ... a similar question, unanswered, was put as to representations of 'Venus chastising Cupid'. Is there any classical authority to show to what part Greek and Roman mothers applied the rod? (13 September 1862, p.212)

Given the similarity of expression between these two letters it seems fair to surmise that the author was the same person. It is perhaps worth noting that there is a modern representation of this subject, Max Ernst's *The Blessed Virgin Chastising the Infant Jesus Before Three Witnesses* (1926).

Other flagellant interests were covered by a series of communications entitled 'Husbands authorised to beat their Wives' (1856), 'Grown Daughters Whipped' (1866), 'The Rod in the Middle Ages' (1862, 1863, 1864), 'Whipped Apprentices' (1869) and 'The Ferula' (1876). These anonymous, learned contributors were determined to leave no bottom unwhipped, and the bring-back-the-rod voice was much in evidence. Several correspondents recounted their own experience of the birch, or that of people known to them, and these letters are indistinguishable from their fellows published in the *Family Herald* and *The Queen*. Wrote 'W.D.':

> I have heard an ancient relative of mine, now deceased, say that when she was at school at Salisbury (a first-rate establishment), she saw two young ladies, aged respectively seventeen and eighteen, undergo a severe whipping before the whole school for some act of impropriety. The mistress herself officiated, 'assisted' by two of her subordinates. (30 May 1863, p.436)

Some years later (25 August 1866) the same letter was reprinted in *Notes and Queries* in an expanded form, now signed 'Betula' (Latin for birch). The 'ancient relative of mine' had become 'a near relative of mine', and the 'first-rate establishment' at Salisbury was now 'one of the most fashionable and expensive in Westbournia' (pp. 155-6). How such tricks deceived the editor of *Notes and Queries*, an undeniably serious publication, one cannot imagine. Or did he too have a flagellant 'penchant'?

Our erudite flagellants were naturally aware that similar debates were being carried on elsewhere; indeed they had probably contributed to them. Thus 'Virga', all innocence, quotes excerpts from the *Family Herald* and informs readers of *Notes and Queries* that they 'will be surprised to hear' that birching in girls' schools 'is not only not obsolete, but actually practised at the present day' (5 March 1864, p.203). If it is in the newspaper correspondence columns it must be true!

Along with their interest in the use of the rod in the Middle Ages, these contributors take much pleasure in the study of flagellant carvings on mediaeval misericords. It is a fact that these ingenious hinged seats are notorious for their bawdiness, whether expressed in the person of the farting juggler at Vence (who watches your response from between his legs), the enema scenes in Zamora Cathedral or the extraordinary fifteenth-century misericord in Holy Trinity Church, Stratford-upon-Avon, which represents (notes 'W.C.B.') 'a man administering somewhat more than *modicam castigationem* to his wife, who is in a very novel and uncomfortable position' (8 September 1866, p.195). She is indeed, and an observant visitor to the church will notice that the penis of the grotesque hooded figure who is applying the birch to the inverted posteriors of the lady is uncovered.

Other contributors pointed out that similar misericords can be seen at Whalley Church, Lancashire; Manchester Cathedral; Sherborne Abbey; and Henry VII's Chapel in Westminster Abbey. One is tempted to conclude, since some of the splendid seats in Zamora Cathedral depict similar scenes, that there was at the time roaming around Europe a hitherto unrecorded sect of flagellant misericord carvers.

There is no need to quote further from these bizarre communications. What really matters about them is the fact that they were actually published, and in a journal which one might have thought would have been proof against such silliness.

'The Englishwoman's Domestic Magazine', 1867-1870

The last communications on the corporal punishment of children published by the *Family Herald* appeared on 30 March 1867. No explanation was given for the brusque termination of a debate that had been carried on in the paper's columns for twenty years.

The flagellants, looking around for another outlet, turned to the *Englishwoman's Domestic Magazine*, a monthly family journal with its own substantial advice and correspondence page, 'The Englishwoman's Conversazione'. The magazine had been founded by Samuel Beeton (husband of the celebrated Mrs Beeton of cookery fame) in 1852, when it proclaimed itself dedicated to 'the improvement of the intellect, the cultivation of the morals and the cherishing of domestic virtues'.[9] It was a better-quality *Family Herald*, in fact, appealing to the same sort of people and covering the same sort of topics. It was hardly surprising that when the *Family Herald*'s flagellant column was shut down the *Englishwoman's Domestic Magazine* should have taken it over, the more so since its own highly dubious debate on corsets ('tight-lacing') was slowly throttling itself to death. According to Fernando Henriques (1969, p.237) this tight-lacing

[9] J.B. Priestley, *Victoria's Heyday* (1974), p.165.

correspondence was so popular that it resulted in the publication of a book, *The Corset and the Crinoline*.

The magazine's first flagellant communication appeared on 1 September 1867, and in it the editor proffered some advice very much in the style of the *Family Herald*:

> AN ENGLISH MAMMA. Many naughty children are only to be startled into better conduct by sudden corporal punishment. In your case, we advise you at the first act of disobedience to administer a sharp box on the ear or *hard* slap; if this fails, have recourse to the remedy you propose, but be sure it is severe, and in the old-fashioned style; a good birch of twigs hurts more and injures less than the hand or a rod. If a 'good sound whipping' fails, you are in a worse plight than before, and school is the only chance of breaking in the troublesome girl. Absence from home, and school trials and hardships have wrought wonders. The whipping ought to be managed by yourself alone, without help or witnesses. (p.503)

It seems likely that the editor of the magazine deliberately inaugurated a debate on corporal punishment by the insertion of this unpleasant item. Because he knew that it would boost sales?

It was not until 1868 that the debate, which would run for two years, really got under way. On 1 March of that year 'Pater' wrote in to say that he was having trouble in controlling his daughters. The same old ploy. 'A lady, an intimate friend, whom my wife consulted on this subject,' he wrote, 'strongly recommends personal chastisement' (p.166). 'Pater' would like to hear the opinions of the magazine's readers. He did not have long to wait, of course. The first really nasty communication appeared on 1 October 1868, purporting to come from 'A Lover of Obedience':

> As the mother of a large family, my experience is in favour of whipping children, beginning as early as possible, say a year and a-half old, and continuing it when required up to fourteen or fifteen. I dislike all prolonged punishments, such as sending to bed, shutting up in a room, and depriving a child of its usual food, as I think they are injurious to the health, and really do little good. I object to the rod as unfeminine, so, up to ten or twelve years old, I whip all my children, boys and girls alike, with my slipper; it punishes quite as much as a birch, and leaves no marks behind. I make it a rule never to whip a child at the moment, but wait till I am cool and collected. (p.221)

Following this letter came a further communication from the 'English Mamma' whose plea for help in September 1867 had been the first intimation that the magazine was preparing to launch a corporal punishment column. Has this lady adopted the editor's advice in the matter of flagellation? Indeed. She now has '*personal* experience' of domestic whipping:

> That very morning, when my daughter was disobedient, I gave her a box on the ear. This seemed to have little or no effect. In the evening she was just as obstinate as ever, so I took her into my room and just raised her dress, and gave her three or four smart slaps, which, through her under-clothing, she could hardly feel, but, having the semblance of a 'good sound whipping', I thought it might frighten her into obedience, and so it did for a day or two, but after that she became just as bad as ever. I then obtained a 'good birch of twigs' and showed it to her, and told her that she would be soundly whipped with it if she continued her disobedience. The next day, forgetful of the warning, she was as bad as ever. I told her to go to her room and wait till I came. I waited for about half-an-hour, as I had no wish to punish her in anger, but wished to think over the matter coolly. I made her take off her trousers in order that she might feel the chastisement sharply. I then put her across my knee in 'the old-fashioned style', and gave her about twenty sound strokes with the birch, and then told her to dress herself, said the punishment was at an end, and there would be no further disgrace. (*ibid.*)

This letter may be taken as a typical 'soft core' example of the genre. We have seen similar entries in the *Family Herald* and elsewhere. An editor could argue that there was nothing 'indecent' in publishing such accounts. As the magazine's flagellant column warmed up, however, the communications became increasingly indelicate, going finally far beyond anything that had appeared in other publications, 'respectable' publications, that is. The trick lay in *suggesting* as much sexuality as possible without incurring the charge of obscenity.

An examination of the correspondence as a whole shows that it was motivated by two main aims – to hoodwink the reader into believing that 'English mammas' frequently applied the birch to the posteriors of their children, boys and girls; and to prove that the birch was in daily use in schools for the daughters of the well-to-do classes. As in all flagellant material, the interest is always centred on naked bottoms.

Along with the constant requests for the names and addresses of birching schools, goes what one is tempted to call a supplication for information as to where the instruments themselves can be purchased:

> A MOTHER is greatly rejoiced at hearing an ENGLISH MAMMA'S opinion as to the usefulness of the rod, as she herself has a very disobedient daughter, and would be glad to know where a birch rod could be obtained, or how made. (1 November 1868, p.280)

I should feel greatly obliged to any of your readers who would kindly let me know through your valuable Magazine of a shop where I could get good birch-rods from in London. ('Mrs L. Gray', 1 March 1870, p.190)

Nobody could actually come up with the name and address of a complaisant birch supplier, any more than they could with that of a flogging school for unruly girls, but there was no shortage of advice on the *modus operandi* of birching. It was here, of course, that the flagellants concentrated their attention. Any number of examples could be given. 'Paterfamilias' had been at Eton, so was experienced in the matter:

It was his duty as junior king's scholar to purchase and apply all the birch rods of the college. He can assure A PERPLEXED MOTHER that the birch was always the most effective instrument of punishment and much dreaded, but must add the warning that any interposition of underclothing materially interferes with the efficiency of the operation. Birch rods are obtainable at most basket-maker's, but to render the discipline salutary, care should be taken to purchase rods with *good buds*, the handles being about the thickness of the wrist. PATERFAMILIAS would *not* recommend the application to the shoulders, as it might interfere with the free action of the arms, so necessary to growing girls. (1 January 1869, p.56)

Let the girls receive the birch on their naked bottoms, therefore, just like their brothers. And why should girls not be treated in this respect like boys? The question had been asked in the *Family Herald* – and answered by the editor. 'A Rector' agreed:

Nor could I ever understand why girls should not be whipped just as much as boys, if they deserved it. If the good old custom had not been allowed to go out, there would not have been so many 'girls of the period' at the present day. (1 January 1870, p.63)

By December 1868 the magazine was printing six dense columns of flagellant material per issue – most of it from 'birching mammas' or fathers who support (and describe in detail the methods of) their disciplinarian wives or, even better, governesses. 'A Lover of Discipline' (of the 'lower' variety, of course) is pleased with the governess he has appointed for his girls:

The eldest was first taken to her dressing room and prepared for the rod, and then conveyed to the boudoir by the governess, who at once administered the discipline. The younger one was then prepared, and received a wholesome flagellation. These whippings were administered *sopra* [sic] *dorsum nudum,* the delinquents being tightly strapped to an ottoman during the castigation, at the conclusion of which they had to kiss the rod and thank the governess, when they were permitted to retire. (1 December 1868, p.326)

As one would expect, a ubiquitous contributor to these discussions is 'An Old Teacher', 'A Schoolmistress' or 'A Teacher of Twenty Years' Experience'. Who better to provide authentic descriptions of the art of birching? 'A Schoolmistress' showed herself a genuine professional in the art of whipping:

I object to striking on the head, or beating them through their clothes. Serious harm may thus be done. It is better to apply the correction to the lower part of the back, which should be *uncovered.* You can thus fix exactly the amount of suffering which you may wish to inflict, and run no risk of injuring ... These means may be applied with great advantage and propriety both in boys and girls up to the age of 12 or 14 years. But afterwards they are certainly inapplicable for reasons which will occur to most if not all mothers. (1 January 1869, pp. 55-6)

On 1 January 1869 the *Englishwoman's Domestic Magazine* published an editorial on the whipping letters. It claimed that these were pouring into its office in an ever increasing volume (the *Family Herald* had made a similar claim at the end of *its* debate); and announced that it was printing a final selection of communications before bringing the subject to a close. It proceeded to publish a group of seemingly genuine letters opposed to beating – some of them from aristocrats, 'members of the Upper Ten Thousand', who expressed their disgust with the whippers and insisted that in the higher reaches of British society girls were never subjected to such indignities. After this group came that of the moderates, followed by the pro-birch brigade. Since there is a dearth of wit among these letters, I cannot refrain from quoting one exception. This nutty contribution is attributed to 'A Happy Mother':

H.M. has always found that the birch has answered capitally for disobedience, but has never put her children across the knee or across the chair, as it was never wide enough. H.M. invariably takes her's to Birch's, in Cornhill, and lays them across the counter, where they receive it hot and strong. H.M. never leaves any underclothing on, but puts a layer or two of cream, and naturally when she whips them it is a case of I scream – Ice cream. The white of eggs well beaten up can be used instead of cream. H.M. never whips children across the shoulders, but always on the 'elsewhere', as PERPLEXED MOTHER politely terms a certain part of the body. H.M. does not know why, as only ladies read this Magazine, there should be anything hidden. (p.55)

That last quip deserves a prize.

Shortly after the *Englishwoman's Domestic Magazine* brought this part of its flagellant debate to a close, three well-known London papers published editorials expressing their dislike of its contents.

On 18 January 1869 the *Daily Telegraph* quoted excerpts from the 'abominable letters', the 'detestable confessions', of the pro-flogging mammas of England, and noted with approval that the majority of the correspondents 'hurl contempt and anathemas at these cold-blooded "Lovers of Obedience"', preferring themselves to use the 'moral system' with their own children. The writer of the editorial seems not to have suspected a hoax: 'This correspondence is a serious thing; it reveals the existence of a whole world of unnatural and indefensible private cruelty, of which the law ought to have cognisance'. Although the *Daily Telegraph* makes the point that, in the Army and Navy, flogging is on the wane, there is no reference to the severe birchings that were still being inflicted in the public schools.

The Saturday Review, in a scathingly ironic article ('The Birch in the Boudoir'), alluded on 30 January 1869 to the new sect of Female Flagellants that had apparently arisen in the land to swell the numbers of those liberated ladies 'who are assailing man's empire'. The writer begins by asserting that the existence of these floggers is 'amply proved' by the letters published in the *Englishwoman's Domestic Magazine*, many of which evince 'that graphic force which some women exhibit when writing on a subject which powerfully interests and excites them'. This flogging phenomenon 'must appear to foreigners simply incredible, to most Englishmen very queer'. The journal, citing one of the letters, notes that it 'occasionally employs a phraseology which is a little too highly spiced to be quoted here', despite which the passages cited must have shocked many a reader of this conservative publication. Towards the end of the leader the writer becomes somewhat less certain of himself. Suggesting, rather naïvely, that the birching of boys at public schools may be drawing to a close, he asks:

Is it possible that before long the only creatures in Europe, besides cattle, that are flogged will be English criminals and English girls? Or is the whole of this amazing correspondence fictitious? Is it nothing more than an elaborate and vulgar hoax? Have 'Materfamilias', the 'Marchioness', the 'Perplexed Mother', and the other 'Lovers of the Rod' no existence out of the fertile brain of the conductor of the *Englishwoman's Domestic Magazine*?' (p.144)

Punch, in an article wittily entitled 'The Englishwoman's Domestic Brownrigg' (an allusion to Elizabeth Brownrigg, who was executed at Tyburn in 1767 for whipping a female apprentice to death), referred on 13 February 1869 to the 'series of vile letters' published in the *Englishwoman's Domestic Magazine* and showed that it, at any rate, had no doubt that the whole thing was a hoax:

> The writers of these foul, if feigned, articles enter into minute details on the choice of instruments of torture, and on devices for inflicting on young ladies a combination of 'shame and pain'. Over these some of them appear to gloat in such a way as almost to persuade one that they are in earnest, and write under the influence of feelings which have been engendered, or aggravated, in Ritualist confessionals. (p.63)

Mr Punch fears that, while the letters 'may be mere inventions', they could none the less 'produce the effect of inflaming the morbid cruelty and malice of some depraved female'. There is no overt reference to morbid *sexuality* here, but *Punch* is not far from the mark. With its customary alertness it has suspected the real motives underlying the whole correspondence. *Punch*, moreover, took a strongly anti-flogging line throughout the century and made no bones about its views on the origin of the sickness: 'When we find a manly sentimentalist advocating the rod, we generally discover that he has been at a public school; and we see pretty clearly that his eulogy of flogging proceeds from an opinion that it has made an exceedingly fine and clever fellow of himself; an opinion sometimes very erroneous.'[10]

Perhaps the oddest commentary on the correspondence was that which appeared on 6 February 1869 in *The Lancet*, in an editorial entitled 'Flogging Girls'. In the view of the writer (who does not doubt the genuineness of the letters), 'women, like other feeble creatures, are naturally and instinctively cruel, especially to their own kind'. Let us be in no doubt about it, or deceived by 'the customs of drawingrooms' which 'rather interfere with the general recognition of this tendency'. Women are cruel by nature; and now that they are seeking to engage 'in many masculine callings', they need to be watched carefully. Moreover, the medical mind behind the editorial feels that the dangers of flagellation must be mentioned. *The Lancet*, as one would hope, was aware of Meibom:

[10] Quoted by Pearsall (1972), pp. 409-10.

A painful and degrading punishment would be certain, in most cases, to change a girl's whole moral nature for the worse; and there are grave medical reasons against the infliction of floggings at the period of puberty. We trust that some of the doctresses of the present day will be good enough to enlighten their sex upon this part of the question. (p.203)

Here again we see the belief, expressed in the country's leading medical journal, that sex only begins at puberty. But at least *The Lancet* had alluded to the real problem.

The *Englishwoman's Domestic Magazine* replied to its detractors on 1 March 1869. Or rather attacked them. Predictably it rejected outright the allegation that the 'pro-rod' letters were not genuine: '*All the correspondence is genuine* [it insisted in italics], *absolutely and without reserve of any kind*'. It pointed out that the discussion had been carried on fairly, with all parties being given an equal opportunity to express their views; and invited the gentlemen of the press to come and inspect the letters for themselves, many of which, moreover, are 'infinitely more suggestive and telling' than the ones published – an interesting concession, this, which shows that, in treating so openly of 'lower discipline', the editor knew that he was sailing close to the wind.

One would have thought that after this the *Englishwoman's Domestic Magazine* would have allowed the matter to drop. Not at all. On 1 November 1869 its whipping column was thrown open again, by the insertion of two 'enquiries':

WHIPPING. – J.H. asks – 'Would you be kind enough to inform me, through the medium of your magazine, whether the subject of whipping children was ever discussed before in your journal and, if so, in what year?' (p.279)

The editor's answer deserves to be noted:

The subject of personal chastisement was never discussed until last year – 1868. (*ibid.*)

This looks like a lie, since the first whipping entry had appeared in September 1867, and contained (as we have seen) a nasty piece of editorial advice calculated to spark off a flagellant debate.

The second enquiry read:

MATERFAMILIAS writes – 'Permit me to ask, through the medium of your columns, one who styles herself A PERPLEXED MOTHER, in your September number for last year, what course she has adopted for the correction of her three refractory daughters, and whether the plan pursued has been successful? By giving the result of her experience in this matter she will be giving practical advice to myself and others, who are at present undecided as to the right measures to be adopted in such cases. The circumstances of the case being so similar to my own, and I may say to many others also, is my only apology for asking the question.' (*ibid.*)

It is impossible to doubt that this was an editorial fabrication. Between November 1869 and April 1870 the *Englishwoman's Domestic Magazine* published monthly a series of detailed whipping letters which, in indecency, far surpassed their predecessors in the same journal. The editor was nothing if not brazen. Finally in April 1870 it was announced that, in view of the increasing number and length of whipping letters pouring into the magazine's office, a separate monthly supplement of from eight to sixteen pages would henceforth be issued, price twopence, 'for those who are anxious to support or follow a discussion which possesses extraordinary interest for so many persons' (p.256). In this the magazine was following the example of the *Family Herald*, which had inaugurated a similar supplement a few years earlier. From April 1870 until the following December, the magazine regularly advertised this whipping supplement, naming the contributors to each month's number – 'Philalethia', 'An Old Boy', 'Satin Shoes', 'An Anxious Mother of Two Ungovernable Boys', 'Modesta', 'Didasculus', 'A Lady Principal', 'A Rejoicer in the Restoration of the Birch', 'R.O.D.', 'One who Practises what he Preaches', and many others who brought their doubtless valuable experience to the discussion. It seems that the Supplement (which I have been unable to see) contained many of those more 'suggestive' letters to which the editor of the magazine referred in his reply to his critics. It seems, too, that the Supplement was a financial success. One understands the relief expressed by two regular readers of the *Englishwoman's Domestic Magazine* when the flagellant letters were banished from its pages – or is this another editorial joke?:

A MODEST WOMAN writes to express the extreme pleasure she and her friends feel at knowing for the future all letters on the Chastisement of Children (which have for so long appeared in and spoiled the ENGLISHWOMAN) will be printed on a separate sheet. Those people who are such advocates for the rod, and who certainly have not scrupled in giving exact directions as to its use, cannot complain of the step now taken by the Editor; whilst, on the other hand, many subscribers, to whom the subject has been a most repulsive one, and who have not troubled to express their contrary opinion, can now once more read the interesting periodical through with pleasure, and not have their womanly feelings shocked. (1 May 1870, p.320)

'Olivia' is of a similar view and

> begs to congratulate the Editor on the very happy idea suggested by him; viz., having all letters on the subject of Corporal Punishment published apart from the Magazine. It is a perfect treat to see the 'Conversazione' once more free from those disgraceful letters by the users of the rod. Let those who support it buy the Supplement, and peruse its pages to their heart's content. (*ibid.*)

Disgraceful letters they had certainly been, and disgraceful, one may think, the editor for publishing (and writing?) them. The *Englishwoman's Domestic Magazine* had made an outstanding contribution to national flagellomania.[11]

'Public Opinion' (1868)

A brief correspondence about the corporal punishment of children began in this newspaper on 18 April 1868, with the insertion of the following item.

> *Whipping in Schools.* – 'A.Z.' wishes to know if a governess has not rendered herself liable to an action for assault, for twice whipping a girl nearly fifteen years of age, with a cane and a birch rod, in a most indelicate manner. (p.401)

Was this a genuine enquiry? It is unlikely. 'H.F.L.', 'a member of the legal profession', replied to point out, quite correctly, that

> the governess standing *in loco parentis* had a right to use such means of correction as in her discretion she thought necessary; and the punishment not appearing to be other than moderate and reasonable, she is not liable to an action for an assault. The fact of its being indelicate is immaterial in a legal point of view. (25 April 1868, p.428)

On 6 June 1868 'Parens' sent in a communication expressing the 'keep-the-children-down' attitude so inevitable whenever these correspondences got under way:

---

[11] The letters published in the monthly supplements, or a selection of them, were issued in a single volume when the correspondence came to an end (Pisanus Fraxi, *Index Librorum Prohibitorum*, p.xli, note 60).

Sir, childhood is now considered to cease at or before twelve years of age. Rebuke from parent or teacher is after that hardly tolerated, and actual discipline there is next to none ... The truth is, that the reins of loving, yet judicious, discipline want tightening both by parents and teachers. I am no advocate for a return to the olden days, when the birch rod was the terror of well-grown youths, and girls were subjected to it until their marriage-day. I think that in well and wisely-trained families corporal punishments are almost entirely unnecessary. But I confess it seems to me that such a chastisement as your schoolgirl received is the fitting corrective of that pert precocity which we see everywhere developing into the fast young man or the 'girl of the period'. Some of my lady friends assure me that it is now employed as such at several schools. I know not whether any of your lady readers will confirm this ['Parens' adds, wishfully]. But, however produced, it is certain that we greatly need in the present day some of that reverence for age and obedience to authority which distinguished Sparta in ancient time, and England in her bright days of old. (p.585)

The corporal-punishment brigade, it may be noted, whether writing in 1868 or 1977, always express nostalgia for the good old whipping days when children showed a proper respect for their elders. The flagellant paradise, like all paradises, is a lost one.

There were protests against the publication of this sort of letter in *Public Opinion*. 'N.C.' (13 June 1868) felt that such a topic 'ought not to be discussed in any public journal', a point of view shared by 'A Married Man' (27 June 1868) for whom 'corporal punishment is disgusting and degrading' and by 'Hy. Clark' (11 July 1868) for whom 'the whipping of children develops combativeness, destructiveness, hypocrisy, anti-socialness, irreverence and fear'. There were still some sane people around, it seemed. But also some out-and-out flagellants, among them 'A Constant Reader'. According to the editorial paraphrase of the beginning of this communication, the correspondent claims 'that for nearly forty years he and his wife have had the care of children. They reared their own seven children and educated some thousands of others'. People of experience, clearly:

During that period we never spared the rod – the chief punishment of the school, for girls as well as boys, was 'whipping'. Yet our school was always full, and both our own children and the others educated by us admit, now that they are grown up, that we acted most rationally – never cruelly – and that corporeal punishment must often be resorted to in order to bring up the young properly. (4 July 1868, p.15)

One other entry may be noted – the editor's paraphrase of two obviously flagellant communications concerning the birching of girls:

'Euphemia Wilmot' is a married woman of some experience, and when she administers punishment to her daughters (grown-up girls) – which is required but seldom – she locks the offender up in a private room, and proceeds, after explaining the nature of the offence, 'to the most motherly of all chastisements, with the birch rod', and the result is eminently satisfactory. 'Georgina' believes that the birch for some young ladies is a very useful punishment, though she cannot help acknowledging, from her own experience, that it is a very horrid and painful one. Companion governesses administer this punishment as frequently as schoolmistresses. (20 June 1868, p.639)

This item was quoted by 'J.K.' in the *Englishwoman's Domestic Magazine* (1 December 1868) in the midst of that journal's disreputable flagellant debate, in support of his own professed view that 'where the stubborn will of a girl requires to be brought into subjection, no means are so efficacious as the judicious use of the birch' (p.327). As we have seen, one of the stock techniques used by the writers of flagellant letters was that of referring to other similarly dubious correspondences as if they were authentic.

It seems possible that the editor of *Public Opinion* realised the dangerous direction the discussion was taking. The 'Home and School Discipline' column was closed on 11 July 1868, and gave way to passionately argued debates on 'Shall Women Vote?' and 'Private Executions'. The latter was followed by an interesting discussion about the question of anonymous correspondence columns in the popular press, *Public Opinion* suggesting that it might be preferable if all letters to the editor were signed and authenticated, and pointing out that *Good Words* and the *Fortnightly* had already 'tried the experiment with success' (28 November 1868).

It can safely be said that, so far as the nineteenth-century discussions of corporal punishment were concerned, such an innovation would have immediately silenced the voices of the flagellants. For, as our analysis of the correspondences has shown, anonymity was essential to the whole game.

Conclusion

Given the widespread existence of 'old-fashioned whipping' in the well-off homes and schools of England, it was possible for the flagellant letter writers to go a long way without incurring the charge of either exaggeration or obscenity. If the beating of children was respectable, and had been ordained by God, what was wrong with discussing it in public? With giving detailed accounts of its efficacy? With swapping hints on technique? The skill lay, as I have said, in suggesting as much excitement as possible under a camouflage of moral concern for the young.

The distinction between a flagellant and a genuine communication is, admittedly, not always easy to make out, and it may be that some readers of this book would still wish to deny the sexual component in the letters that have been quoted. Such readers would have no doubts if they were to peruse the outrageous flagellant communications that appeared in the weekly magazine *Town Talk: A Journal for Society at Large* between 1896 and 1898, or in another similar weekly, *Society*, between 1896 and 1900.

Town Talk and *Society*, while pretending to be concerned with the exposure of scandals and abuses, were in fact devoted to pornography. Between them they published many hundreds of flagellant letters of the most lurid kind, as well as advertisements for flagellant books and brothels (see Plates 24 and 25). The letters concentrate more unashamedly than those we have seen on the naked buttocks, and there are frequent allusions to sexual birching:

> SIR – May I ask whether you or any of your readers have ever heard of a vile practice of birching of men by women who have been paid for their services? I am led to believe that this is now in vogue. If it is, it is a form of vice which should be speedily stamped out. – Yours, etc. TRUTH. (*Town Talk*, 22 March 1884)

> I think many women will agree with me that there is pleasure in being tightly laced by one's husband. Once my husband asked me to whip him, which I did, severely, having first laced him in a pair of my stays. We have been great friends since, but one of us is sure to get a whipping before long. WASP-WAIST. (*Society*, 23 September 1899)

> I was made to kneel on a low deal table on my knees and elbows, with my face against the table, and my back quite arched in – to give proper prominence to the part to be chastised. My skirts were then drawn over my head and my flesh bared. I was told that if I moved I should receive an additional six cuts; but as this was my first I should only receive eight. (*Society*, 10 October 1896)

> Some lad, who has forgotten any childish spanking he has had, thinks little of the warning, but when he sees some older companion kneeling with back bared, twisting and crying as the whip marks his hips, he sees that the pain is severe and determines to avoid such a punishment. A light riding whip, the cuts given down each below the last, does not cut the skin, but each cut causes a stinging pain and marks the body with red lines, such as to evidence the sharpness of the strokes ... (*Town Talk*, 4 July 1885)

> Should, however, the reprimand not have the desired effect and the girl

again misconducts herself, then the punishment is inflicted – the young delinquent being laid across the knees, her petticoats taken up, drawers unfastened and lowered, and the open hand or birch smartly applied to the lower part of the back ... There is no needless severity – only about ten or twelve strokes of the birch being given or, if the open hand is used, the spanking may be continued until the person is well reddened ... Everything, however, depends upon the baring of the whipped parts – and to attempt to give the punishment without putting down the drawers would be perfectly useless. (*Town Talk*, 4 July 1885)

Town Talk, following the example of the *Family Herald* and the *Englishwoman's Domestic Magazine*, was quick to seize the opportunity to issue a selection of flagellant letters in profitable, pamphlet form.

Like the latter two publications, *Society* claimed that it had been 'shocked' by the communications it had received during its long investigation into 'indecent whipping'. Winding up the debate on 21 November 1896 (it began again shortly afterwards, predictably), the editor referred to what he called 'the extraordinary revelations of brutality, callous cruelty, and obscene gloating over details, together with gross and revolting religious superstitions, which certain letters disclose'.[12]

Town Talk and *Society* attracted the attention of two foreigners who were much interested in English sexual mores: Hector France and Iwan Bloch.

In the Parisian journal *Le Réveil*, Hector France published in translation a selection of flagellant letters from *Town Talk* dealing with the birching of fully-grown girls in English schools. He even claimed that he had witnessed one of these wholesome corrections himself (through a key-hole). Much of this material he reprinted in his book *La pudique Albion: Les Nuits de Londres* (1885).[13] It is difficult to believe that Hector France was writing other than tongue in cheek (he knew England well), although he never lets on; and there is no doubt that his accounts were widely believed in his native country.

Iwan Bloch, who became a well-known writer on sexual matters, drew the attention of German readers a few years later to the flagellant letters and advertisements appearing in *Society*. Bloch seems to have accepted their authenticity in good faith and to have believed that the accounts of birching in English girls' schools were genuine. He deduced from these communications that Englishwomen were

---

[12] The British Library copies of *Society* have been badly mutilated, many of the flagellant letters having been cut out (apparently with a razor).

[13] See especially the chapters 'Filles fessées' (pp. 203-15), 'La dompteuse de filles' (pp. 217-25) and 'Lettres édifiantes' (pp. 233-44).

strongly addicted to active flagellation – and was not alone in that belief.[14]

Given the fact that beating was widespread in Britain, foreigners could be forgiven for failing to distinguish between flagellant reality and flagellant fantasy where the correspondence columns of such publications as we have been considering were concerned. But it is odd to observe the apparent acceptance, by a *modern* sexologist, Fernando Henriques, of the authenticity of the communications published in *Society*. 'What is not so readily appreciated', writes Henriques in *Modern Sexuality* (1969), 'is the fact that discipline in girls' schools was quite commonly exerted by whipping. The London magazine, *Society*, which existed towards the end of the century, had a long correspondence regarding this' (p.235). The letter from *Society* quoted by Henriques is a manifest hoax.

In our own day the flagellant correspondence column would no longer be tolerated in a serious newspaper or magazine, but a glance at *Forum*, *Penthouse* and similar journals is enough to show that there is still a demand for the genre, on both sides of the Atlantic if not on both sides of the English Channel.

[14] Bloch (1903), p.441; (1938), p.357.

6

Flagellant Prostitution in Victorian England and After

There are two areas of human experience in which it is impossible to deny that beating and sexuality are intertwined – flagellant pornography and flagellant prostitution.

The nineteenth century was extraordinarily prolific of both, and they are still with us today. The endless discussions about corporal punishment that filled the columns of the respectable (more or less) newspapers and magazines were paralleled by a spate of out-and-out flagellant pornography; while brothels devoted to the rod flourished. 'I am almost ashamed to say,' wrote William Acton in a passage quoted earlier from *The Functions and Disorders of the Reproductive Organs* (1857), 'there are vile wretches who, to excite emission, have recourse to this means of stimulating their flagging powers' (p.60). Acton, who was an expert on prostitution, must have come across many a flagellant brothel during his researches. Perhaps, moreover, he had seen the 1718 London edition of Meibom, the frontispiece to which represents a scene in such an establishment (see Plate 1); perhaps, too, he knew Hogarth's famous etching (number 3 of the series 'A Harlot's Progress') in which a birch is shown hanging on the wall of Moll's wretched room in Drury Lane, a sign that the 'English Vice' had its roots in the eighteenth century (see Plate 21). And it is possible that he had read the brothel scene in *The Virtuoso*, which we saw earlier, not to mention the many other references to the subject in English and European literature.

As regards flagellant pornography, all those who have studied Victorian sexuality are agreed that the volume of material produced during the century was immense. Steven Marcus, for instance, begins his chapter 'A Child is Being Beaten' in *The Other Victorians* thus: 'My title is from Freud. My text is the vast literature of flagellation produced during the Victorian period' (p.255). Earlier in his book Marcus refers to 'the veritable flood of publications during the Victorian period of works devoted to describing the experience of flagellation'. My own research confirms the findings of Marcus and others in this respect. Having been granted admission in the spring of 1975 to the British Library's Private Case, I spent six months wading through a mass of nineteenth-century flagellant pornography, and came to realise that I was only seeing the tip of a huge iceberg. Moreover, it became apparent to me that, quite apart from the works dedicated exclusively to flagellation, few pieces of Victorian pornography felt themselves complete without the inclusion of at least one beating episode. There could be no doubt that flagellation was the 'English Vice' not only in real life but in pornography as well.

At this point it must be explained that the British Library has a large collection of Victorian pornography, much of it bequeathed by the great bibliophile, traveller, scholar and bibliographer of erotica, Henry Spencer Ashbee (1834-1900), who devised for himself the witty pen-name of 'Pisanus Fraxi'.[1] Ashbee had assembled one of the finest libraries in the world of books by and about Cervantes, and offered this to the British Museum in his highly eccentric will along with his unique collection of erotica. Happily the Museum authorities decided to accept the bequest. Had Ashbee not made these provisions, his library of erotica would undoubtedly have been dispersed, and perhaps part of it would have been destroyed by his family. In this latter connection I came across a fascinating entry in the unpublished diary of Ashbee's son, C.R. Ashbee, dated Christmas Day, 1901: 'Going through the library the other day at the Museum where it had been collected for cataloguing before distribution, was like reviewing an army of ghosts ... Here were all the books that my father had collected with a refined bibliomania and my grandfather before him over a period of some 70 years ... The British Museum ... had kept some 8,000 volumes of which it had no duplicates, and let us hope will destroy a certain number which can be of no service to anyone on this earth'.[2]

Until quite recently, access to the Library's 'Private Case' (comprising, in fact, many different cases located in different parts of the building) was restricted, and there were no P.C. entries in the General Catalogue. Unless you knew exactly what you were looking for, you were lost, or almost so.[3] It was a most unsatisfactory situation. About eight years ago, however, things started to look up when the authorities

---

[1] A rearrangement of the letters in the Latin words 'apis', bee, and 'fraxinus', ash. 'Pis' and 'anus' speak for themselves.

[2] The diaries of C.R. Ashbee are in King's College Library, Cambridge.

[3] The *Registrum Librorum Eroticorum* compiled by Rolf S. Reade (an anagram of Alfred Rose) was useful in this respect, as it gives many Private Case press-marks. It is, however, extremely inaccurate. There is a recent reprint, in 2 volumes, published by Jack Brussel, New York, 1965.

decided to begin entering the P.C. press-marks in the General Catalogue. This process has now been almost completed. Anyone with a valid reader's ticket can apply for a P.C. book on the special form provided, and, as a rule, no objections are placed in his way. There is apparently no intention at this stage, however, of issuing a separate catalogue to the Private Case, which is a pity (I suppose one could, in theory, go through the entire General Catalogue in search of P.C. press-marks and compile one's own catalogue, but it would be an enormous task). One consequence of the unavailability of the Private Case catalogue is that it is almost impossible to gauge what proportion of Victorian pornography may have been flagellant in character. All we can be sure of is that the genre pullulated.[4]

Ashbee's three descriptive bibliographies of English, French, German, Italian and Spanish erotica are the indispensable starting point for an exploration of Victorian flagellant pornography and prostitution. It must be stated categorically, however, that these compilations (of which there have been some modern editions[5]) are not to be taken as a catalogue to the British Library's Private Case, since Ashbee was frequently working with copies of books belonging to other people. Published under the pseudonym of 'Pisanus Fraxi', these extraordinary volumes are:

Index Librorum Prohibitorum: Being Notes Bio- Biblio- Icono- graphical and Critical, on Curious and Uncommon Books. London: Privately Printed, 1877. (Henceforth: *Index*)

Centuria Librorum Absconditorum: Being Notes Bio- Biblio- Icono- graphical and Critical, on Curious and Uncommon Books. London: Privately Printed, 1879. (Henceforth: *Centuria*)

Catena Librorum Tacendorum: Being Notes Bio- Biblio- Icono- graphical and Critical, on Curious and Uncommon Books. London: Privately Printed, 1885. (Henceforth: *Catena*)

The mind behind these bibliographies has been perceptively analysed by Steven Marcus in *The Other Victorians* ('Pisanus Fraxi, Pornographer Royal'), and it is not my intention to discuss the

---

[4] For a witty, angry and readable account of the British Library's procedure regarding its collection of erotica, see Peter Fryer's *Private Case – Public Scandal* (1966).

[5] Notably those issued in a splendid facsimile edition in 1960 by Charles Skilton Ltd., London. See also Peter Fryer's *Forbidden Books of the Victorians* (1970), an abridged and edited version of Ashbee's bibliographies.

volumes in detail here. Pisanus Fraxi insists that all his information is scrupulously accurate but, as Marcus has shown, there are moments in which it is impossible to distinguish between the scholarly bibliophile and the pornographer. As regards Ashbee's descriptions of the contents of the books that have come to his notice, however, there is no doubt that he is indeed reliable. As a result, it is possible to have a clear enough idea of the general drift of a book which it may not be feasible to consult at first hand.

Ashbee's three volumes confirm that a high percentage of nineteenth-century English works of pornography were concerned with beating; they also show, as we shall see in the next chapter, that he himself was interested in the subject, and not only as a bibliographer. As well as providing detailed information about flagellant pornography and the publishers who produced it, Ashbee is also a useful source of knowledge about flagellant prostitution in London.

According to Ashbee, George Cannon, a notorious London publisher of flagellant material, was active in that capacity between 1815 and his death in 1854.[6] Ashbee lists and describes several of Cannon's volumes, including his edition of *Venus School Mistress; Or, Birchin Sports*. Ashbee quotes liberally from Cannon's Preface to this book (which, unfortunately, has 'disappeared' from the British Library's Private Case).[7] Flagellation, says Cannon

> is, however, a *lech*, which has existed from time immemorial, and is so extensively indulged in London at this day, that no less than twenty splendid establishments are supported entirely by its practice: nor is there amongst the innumerable temples dedicated to the Paphian Goddess, which adorn this immense metropolis, any one, in which the exercise of the rod is not occasionally required. (*Index*, p.399)

Cannon's Preface shows considerable insight into the flagellant

---

[6] Pisanus Fraxi, *Index*, p.114.

[7] According to Peter Fryer (1966, p.133), the theft of this volume was recorded on 26 November 1965. Ashbee believes (*Index*, p.397) that the first edition of *Venus School Mistress* probably appeared between 1808 and 1810. Since, in Cannon's edition of the book, the preface contains a description of Theresa Berkley's flagellant activities and refers to her death in September 1836, the volume is likely to have appeared in 1837, and not 'about 1830' as Ashbee states (*ibid.*). Cannon ascribes the preface of his edition to one Mary Wilson, often referred to in the pornographic literature of the time as a notorious flagellant in the dual capacity of governess and writer. Ashbee, however, clearly doubts that she was active in the latter capacity; and I take it, therefore, that the preface was composed by Cannon himself.

phenomenon, and knowledge of its professional practitioners. The author recognises, for example, that it is not only old debauchees who have recourse to the rod:

> Many persons not sufficiently acquainted with human nature, and the ways of the world, are apt to imagine that the *lech* for Flagellation must be confined either to the aged, or to those who are exhausted through too great a devotion to venery: but such is not the fact, for there are quite as many young men and men in the prime and vigour of life, who are influenced by this passion as there are amongst the aged and debilitated. (*ibid.*, p.400)

We recall Fanny Hill's surprise on discovering that Mr Barville was a flagellant of such tender years.

Cannon feels quite sure, moreover, that the taste for the rod derives from school experience: 'it is equally true, that hundreds of young men through having been educated at institutions where the masters were fond of administering birch discipline, and recollecting certain sensations produced by it, have imbibed a passion for it, and have longed to receive the same chastisement from the hands of a fine woman' (*ibid.*). Many 'fine women', indeed, realising the extent of the demand for flagellation, have acquired excellence in the art. The successful exponent will have passed through an exacting apprenticeship:

> Those women who give most satisfaction to the amateurs of discipline are called governesses, because they have by experience acquired a tact and a *modus operandi* which the generality do not possess. It is not merely keeping a rod, and being willing to flog, that would cause a woman to be visited by the worshippers of birch: she must have served her time to other women who understand her business, and be thoroughly accomplished in the art. (*ibid.*, p.401)

Among the 'governesses' known to Cannon are Mrs Chalmers and Mrs Noyeau ('two of the most experienced', but now retired from business); 'the late Mrs Jones, of Hertford Street and London Street, Fitzroy Square'; 'the late Mrs Berkley'; and two contemporaries, 'Betsy Burgess, of York Square and ... Mrs Pryce, of Burton Crescent' (*ibid.*).

Of these ladies, Mrs Theresa Berkley (sometimes spelled Berkely or Berkeley) seems to have been the most proficient – and imaginative: a legendary figure among flagellant 'governesses'. If we are to believe

Cannon's account in *Venus School Mistress*, as quoted by Ashbee, she operated at 28, Charlotte Street, Portland Place:[8]

> Her supply of birch was extensive, and kept in water, so that it was always green and pliant: she had shafts with a dozen whip thongs on each of them; a dozen different sizes of cat-o'nine tails, some with needle points worked into them; various kinds of thin bending canes; leather straps like coach traces; battledoors, made of thick sole-leather, with inch nails run through to docket, and currycomb tough hides rendered callous by many years flagellation. Holly brushes, furze brushes; a prickly evergreen, called butchers bush; and during the summer, glass and China vases, filled with a constant supply of green nettles, with which she often restored the dead to life. Thus, at her shop, whoever went with plenty of money, could be birched, whipped, fustigated, scourged, needle-pricked, half-hung, holly-brushed, furze-brushed, butcher-brushed, stinging-nettled, curry-combed, phlebotomized, and tortured till he had a belly full. (*Index*, pp. xliii-xliv)

Cannon explains that, in 1828, Mrs Berkley caused to have built a 'flogging machine' which came to be known in the trade as the 'Berkley Horse'. An illustration of this contraption was published in Cannon's edition of *Venus School Mistress* and reproduced by Ashbee in the *Index Librorum Prohibitorum* (opposite p.xliv), whence I have taken it (see Plate 26). As can be seen, the 'Berkley Horse' was in fact not a machine but a folding ladder, fully padded, with holes in the relevant places, to which flagellants could be affixed to receive their whippings at whatever angle they found most titillating. According to Iwan Bloch, the prolific German sexologist, Ashbee's plate was reproduced in D. Hansen's *Stock und Peitsche in XIX. Jahrhundert* ('Rod and Whip in the Nineteenth Century') (Dresden, 2 vols., 1899)[9]; it also appeared in Albert Eulenburg's *Sadismus und Masochismus* (Wiesbaden, 1902). The Germans, themselves addicted to flagellation, were no doubt fascinated by Mrs Berkley's inventiveness.

The 'Berkley Horse', in point of fact, was but a luxury model of a gadget apparently in widespread use in flagellant brothels, and often referred to by the French word *chevalet* (easel or folding ladder). As we shall see from the account of the Sarah Potter case in a moment, that lady certainly had one at her premises in Wardour Street. Dr Ryan also refers to a similar contraption in his book on prostitution, mentioned earlier: 'Mr Talbot assured me that he saw a most

---

[8] Not to be confused with the Charlotte Street that runs close to and parallel with the Tottenham Court Road. Teresa Berkley's Charlotte Street is now named Hallam Street.

[9] Bloch (1903), p.433, note 1.

extraordinary machine for this purpose, in a certain brothel suppressed by the London Society for the Suppression of Juvenile Prostitution' (p.381).

Cannon tells us that Mrs Berkley made £10,000 from her invention before she died in 1836, an incredible sum.[10] If he is right, one can imagine the number of passive flagellants there must have been in London at the time.

It seems that Richard Monckton Milnes's friend, General Studholme Hodgson (about whom I have been able to discover very little) knew Mrs Berkley, for I found the following entry in the one of Milnes's commonplace books:

> Mrs Berkeley of Charlotte Street telling Hodgson that a dignitary of the Irish [Caths?] (not Jocelyn) had an invincible desire to be 'enculé' and gave her a large sum for that purpose. The ceremony was performed by a confidential ruffian – he tied up and resisting and screaming and, as far as she knew, never having any inclinations of the kind again.[11]

Further evidence about the flagellant brothels of London in the nineteenth century comes from the eccentric Frederick Hankey (1828?-1882). Hankey was the son of General Sir Frederick Hankey, 'Governor' of Malta. Having become a captain in the Guards, he retired from active service and settled in Paris in the 1840s where he immersed himself in the world of pornography, prostitution and book collecting. 'If ever there was a bibliomaniac in the fullest sense of the word', wrote Ashbee, 'it was Frederick Hankey' (*Catena*, p.l). In Paris Hankey was well known, too, as the 'type' of the English sadist: 'He had fair hair, blue eyes, and an almost feminine expression, and answered in many respects to the descriptions which have reached us of the Marquis de Sade, his favourite author. He told me he had on one occasion recovered from a serious illness by suddenly obtaining an edition of *Justine* which he had long sought in vain' (*Catena*, p.li).

Hankey became acquainted with Milnes, himself a fanatical collector of erotica – his country home, Fryston, was known to his

---

[10] Pisanus Fraxi, *Index*, p.xlv.

[11] Hodgson figures several times in Milnes's unpublished commonplace books. This reference, Houghton 213 (1860-61-62-63-64), p.68. That Hodgson was a flagellant there seems to be no doubt. One of Milnes's entries reads: 'Burton says "he has remarked several men with the vice of Studholme Hodgson ... and they were all men delighting in cruelty – what a sheik he wd. have made! Which refinement of torture and pleasure he would have invented!"' (Houghton 212 (1857-58-59-60), p.158). Hodgson was a friend of the Hankeys. 'Jocelyn' seems to have been Percy Jocelyn, Roman Catholic Bishop of Clogher, who was accused in 1822 of committing sodomy with a soldier (Pisanus Fraxi, *Centuria*, p.48).

friends as Aphrodisiapolis – and by 1857 was acting as his 'dubious' books agent in Paris.[12]

Milnes arranged an introduction between the explorer Richard Burton and Hankey, and on 22 January 1860 Burton wrote to Milnes from Boulogne announcing that the meeting had taken place – at Hankey's Paris flat at 2, rue Laffitte.[13] This passage (which, to my knowledge, has not been published in full before) deserves quotation:

> Since we met I saw Hankey. The 'sisters' are a humbug – Swiss women, cold as frogs, and thorough mountaineers, a breed as unfit for debauchery as exists in this world. I told Hankey so and he remarked philosophically enough that they were quite sufficiently good for the public of postcards. He showed me also a little poem entitled the Betuliad. I like very much every part of it except the name – you are writing for a very small section who combine the enjoyment of verse with the practice of flagellation and the remembrance that betula is a birch. Why not call it the Birchiad? If you want it corrected here I can do so. Hankey and I looked over the copy at Paris and corrected the several errors.[14]

It seems beyond doubt that Milnes's flagellant poem to which Burton refers here was that published in 1871 by John Camden Hotten as *The Rodiad* (the title achieving a nice compromise between *Betuliad* and *Birchiad!*). Hotten ascribed the work, which was falsely dated 1810, to George Colman the younger (1792-1836). On 21 October 1876 a letter, almost certainly from Ashbee, appeared in *Notes and Queries* (to which he was a regular contributor in his own name). 'This poem,' wrote APIS, 'which is by no means devoid of merit, was not written by George Colman the younger. I do not know who was the author, although I possess the original MS, and could

---

[12] In the Trinity College, Cambridge, collection of Houghton Papers there is a letter from Hankey to Milnes dated 4 April 1857 (Supplementary List no.44). It is clear from this that by that date Hankey was already hard at work in Paris winkling out new books for his patron.

[13] The building in which Hankey lived is no longer standing. The site is now occupied by the headquarters of the Banque Nationale de Paris.

[14] The letters from Burton to Milnes to which I refer here are also part of the Houghton Papers in Trinity College Library, Cambridge. Inserted into one of Milnes's commonplace books (Houghton 212 (1857-58-59-60), p.60) is a manuscript note from Hankey in which he too refers to this flagellant poem. He has sent Milnes a copy of an item (dated 1 December 1859) from a French newspaper concerning a recent 'attentat à la pudeur': two boys aged 12 and 11 have apparently tried to rape a girl of 8, and been committed to a House of Correction. 'I wonder,' muses Hankey, 'whether "the Betuliad" is known in the above establishment, "the maison de correction". *How well* it might have been brought to bare [sic] when they were caught in the act.'

give its history. J.C. Hotten printed *The Rodiad* in a neat little volume, which did not of course get into the hands of the trade generally; but curiously enough he misspelt the author's name, giving it as Coleman instead of Colman. The whole thing then is a *supercherie'* (p.336).

At this time Ashbee had not yet met Milnes, and it may well be that he was indeed ignorant of the identity of the poem's author. According to Pope-Hennessy, an entry in Ashbee's diary recorded that he met Milnes for the first time in 1878. Ashbee had dined that evening in the Albany with Hankey and his French mistress at the rooms of one of their acquaintances, and after dinner Milnes joined the company.[15] Ashbee and he became friends, and Milnes was soon a frequent visitor at the former's splendid corner house at 53 Bedford Square (which is still standing). It was not surprising that the two men got on well together, in view of their shared interest in travel and erotic literature. In such circumstances it is unlikely that Milnes would have for long concealed from Ashbee his authorship of *The Rodiad*.[16]

In the *Centuria Librorum Absconditorum* (1879), Ashbee allowed himself to assert that *The Rodiad* was written 'by one of the clients of the notorious Sarah Potter, alias Stewart, from whom it was obtained by a well known London collector; he lent the MS to Hotten who printed it *without* permission' (p.472). The syntax of the sentence is ambiguous, and it is not altogether clear whether the collector (Ashbee himself?) obtained the MS from Sarah Potter or from her author-client. Perhaps Ashbee was being intentionally vague, given that Milnes was still alive (he died in 1885). As we shall see in a moment, there is evidence that Milnes may indeed have been a client of the lady in question, which makes his authorship of *The Rodiad* even more plausible.[17]

[15] Pope-Hennessy (1951), p.120.

[16] There are four cordial letters from Ashbee to Milnes among the Houghton Papers in Trinity College Library, Cambridge. In the first of these, dated 7 October 1878, Ashbee invites Milnes to dinner and says 'the M.S. which you left in my hands is very curious and interesting. I hope to make good use of it'. In the second, dated 24 July 1880, Ashbee provides Houghton with the names of some of his Paris acquaintances. Of a certain Major Ricketts, Ashbee warns 'do not speak of him to Hankey as they are not friends'. The third letter is from Java, and dated 18 February 1881. In it Ashbee expresses his gratitude to Milnes for proposing him for the Geographical Society. In the fourth letter, dated 23 May 1884, he looks forward to seeing Houghton again. Ashbee's son, C.R. Ashbee, remembered seeing Houghton on several occasions at their Bedford Square house (*'Grannie': A Victorian Cameo*, 1939, pp. 54-5).

[17] It is possible that the 'collector' was Ashbee's friend and fellow bibliographer of erotica, James Campbell Reddie.

But perhaps the strongest evidence that Milnes composed the poem comes in the letter to him from Swinburne to which attention was drawn earlier (pp. 123-4). In this letter (dated 1863) Swinburne, referring to his birchings at the hands of his tutor, says 'I should have been thankful (barring the *insult* which we should have resented) for the *diversion* of a box on the ears, such as Rodin's superincumbent John "bestowed" ' (Lang, I, p.77). Rodin, the flagellant surgeon-schoolmaster in *Justine*, has no servant going by that name.[18] The suspicion that Swinburne is referring to Milnes as Rodin (a trick he uses frequently in these letters) is confirmed by *The Rodiad*. For in the poem, the schoolmaster (who speaks in his own voice throughout) is indeed assisted by a servant called John, who hoists the victims on his back while his master flogs them with the birch:

> But now for years my chief delight has been
> To scourge the obnoxious stripling of sixteen –
> Horsed at nice angle on the sturdy back
> Of one whose faithful aid I never lack,
> My John, who, with his grip and grin, enjoys
> The bounds and twisting of rebellious boys.

All in all, it seems that the textbooks should no longer ascribe *The Rodiad* to George Colman the younger but to Richard Monckton Milnes, Lord Houghton.[19]

It is clear from Burton's letters to Milnes that he had a soft spot for Hankey, after whom he makes frequent inquiries. 'Give my love to Hankey when you see him,' he writes in an undated letter; 'Remember me with love to the amiable trio Hodgson, Bellamy[20] and Hankey – when shall we all meet again?', he wrote from Fernando Po on 26 April 1862. 'Anything of Hankey?' he asked on 29 March 1863, and 'Any news of Hankey?' in 1871. On 5 November 1873 he wrote to Milnes from Trieste: 'Fred Hankey must nearly have been burnt out' (a reference which I have not been able to clarify). Burton was evidently fascinated by Hankey's sadistic obsessions. An entry in one of Milnes's commonplace books for 1860 reads:

> Burton of Hankey: 'There is no accounting for tastes in superstition. Hankey would like to have a Bible bound with bits of skin stripped off live

---

[18] He does, however, have an assistant surgeon, Rombeau.

[19] According to Fuller (1968), p.68, note – who also suspects that Milnes may have been the author of *The Rodiad* – Professor Wilson Knight ascribed the poem to Colman in his book *Lord Byron's Daughter*.

[20] Bellamy also appears in Milnes's commonplace books. I do not know his identity.

from the cunts of a hundred little girls and yet he could not be persuaded
to try the sensation of f . . g a Muscovy duck while its head was cut off.

Milnes goes on to observe: 'Hankey's line of cruel enjoyment and his
strong sense of the wickedness of killing animals for food. His extreme
desire to see a girl hanged and have the skin of her backside tanned to
bind his "Justine" with.'[21]

Burton, in fact, as he was passing through Paris in 1862 on the way
to Africa had promised to do his best to procure for Hankey a human
skin stripped from a sacrificial victim. A few days after his departure,
on 7 April 1862 to be precise, Hankey received the visit of those two
indefatigable chroniclers of Parisian literary life, the Goncourt
brothers. In their diary the Goncourts recorded their impressions of
the English eccentric (they wrote in the singular):

> Today I visited a madman, a monster, one of those men who live on the
> edge of the abyss. Through him, as through a torn veil, I had a glimpse of
> an appalling aspect, a terrible side to a wealthy, blasé aristocracy – the
> English aristocracy – who bring ferocious cruelty to love and whose
> licentiousness can only be aroused by the woman's sufferings.[22]

When the entry which this passage introduced was published in 1887
it was, however, severely curtailed, despite the fact that Hankey had
died in 1882. His name does not appear, although it was no secret in
Paris that the 'monster' was none other than the English erotomaniac
living at 2, rue Laffitte. The full version of the entry can be read in the
1957 Monaco edition of the diaries (V, pp. 89-93), where Hankey's
name appears (misspelt Henkey).

In this unexpurgated edition of the diaries another personage
makes an unexpected entrance: Richard Monckton Milnes. Hankey
had told a friend of the Goncourts about a flagellant brothel in
London run by a certain 'Mrs Jenkins'. This establishment, he
claimed, he had often visited 'with some horseguards and my friend

---

[21] Houghton 212 (1857-58-59-60), p.160.
[22] 'Aujourd'hui j'ai visité un fou, un monstre, un de ces hommes qui confinent à
l'abîme. Par lui, comme par un voile déchiré, j'ai entrevu un fonds [sic] abominable,
un côté effrayant d'une aristocratie d'argent blasée, de l'aristocratie anglaise
apportant la férocité dans l'amour, et dont le libertinage ne jouit que par la souffrance
de la femme.' In the 1957 version this passage reads: 'J'ai vu aujourd'hui un type, un
fou, un monstre, un de ces hommes qui confinent à l'abîme, qui avouent dans leurs
excès les mauvais instincts de l'humanité. Par lui, comme par un voile déchiré, j'ai
entrevu un fond abominable de l'homme, un côté effrayant d'une aristocratie
d'argent blasée, l'aristocratie anglaise: la férocité dans l'amour, le libertinage qui ne
jouit qu'à la souffrance' (V, p.89).

Milnes' (1957, V, p.89). It was little wonder that the Goncourts suppressed Milnes's name in the 1887 edition, for, although 'Dickie' had died in 1885, his many friends in high French places might have made trouble for the diarists. According to Hankey (and this passage *did* appear in 1887), the brothel in question provided facilities for flogging girls of the age of 13 or so 'whom first we made sit in class and then whipped – the little ones not too hard but the big ones very hard indeed. We could also stick needles into them, not very long needles – only as long as this – and he showed us the tip of his finger' (1887, II, p.27).[23]

Hankey could not help boasting to the Goncourts about Richard Burton's fantastic offer, showing them an unbound book lying on the table:

> Yes, I'm waiting for a skin for this volume, a young girl's skin ... which one of my friends has procured for me ... it's being tanned ... the tanning takes six months ... You'd like to see my skin? ... It's hardly of interest ... It ought really to have been stripped from a living girl ... Luckily I have my friend Dr Bartsh [sic] ... you know, the one who travels in the depths of Africa ... well, in the massacres ... he has promised to get me a skin like that ... from a living negress. (*ibid.*, pp. 28-9)[24]

Hankey never got his skin, however. On 31 May 1863 Burton wrote to Milnes from Dahomey: 'I have been here 3 days and am generally disappointed. Not a man killed, not a fellow tortured. The canoe floating in blood is a myth of myths. Poor Hankey must still wait for his peau de femme.'

In *The Romantic Agony*, Mario Praz has studied the development of that stock figure in French novels of the nineteenth century, the English sadist. Hankey was not the prototype of this figure, but that he influenced it there can be no doubt.[25]

We do not know exactly when Swinburne met Hankey, nor whether

---

[23] 'Auxquelles d'abord on faisait la classe, puis qu'on fouettait, les petites, oh! pas très fort, mais les grandes tout à fait fort. On pouvait aussi leur enfoncer des épingles, des épingles non pas très longues, longues seulement comme ça, et il nous montrait le bout de son doigt.' In the 1957 edition the reference to the digital measurement makes more sense: 'et il montre la moitié du doigt. On voit le sang ... Il y a des matelas, si elles crient ...' (V, p.89).

[24] 'Oui, pour ce volume j'attends une peau, une peau de jeune fille ... qu'un de mes amis m'a eue ... On la tanne ... c'est six mois pour la tanner ... Si vous voulez la voir, ma peau? ... Mais c'est sans intérêt ... Il aurait fallu qu'elle fût enlevée sur une jeune fille vivante ... Heureusement, j'ai mon ami le docteur Bartsh ... vous savez, celui qui voyage dans l'intérieur de l'Afrique ... eh bien, dans les massacres ... il m'a promis de me faire prendre une peau comme ça ... sur une négresse vivante.'

[25] See Praz's appendix 'Swinburne and "le vice anglais" '.

that meeting took place in Paris or during one of Hankey's frequent visits to London. Swinburne had been invited to Milnes's house in Brook Street for the first time in May 1861,[26] and a month later he met Burton at one of Milnes's famous breakfast parties.[27] Given the close friendship that immediately sprang up between Burton, Swinburne and Milnes, there can be no doubt that the poet was soon apprised of the existence of Fred Hankey; the more so in view of Swinburne's passionate desire to get hold of a copy of Sade's *Justine*, one of Hankey's favourite books, as Milnes well knew. Perhaps the poet met Hankey at Paris in March 1863 during a brief visit to that city;[28] or in February-March 1864 when he and Milnes coincided there.[29] Certainly it seems inconceivable that by 1864 they had not become acquainted.

Swinburne never mentions Hankey by name in the letters that have been published to date, but there is one clear reference to him. Writing to George Powell on 29 July 1869, the poet expressed the wish to introduce him in Paris to a friend who is

> *the* Sadique collector of European fame. His erotic collection of books, engravings, etc. is unrivalled upon earth – unequalled, I should imagine, in heaven. Nothing low, nothing that is not good and genuine in the way of art and literature is admitted. There is every edition of every work of our dear and honoured Marquis. There is a Sapphic group by Pradier of two girls in the very act – one has her tongue up où vous savez, her head and massive hair buried, plunging, diving between the other's thighs. (Lang, II, pp. 19-20.)

Hankey was proud of his Pradier, and showed it to the Goncourts – who were not so impressed: 'Then he opened a big box. A marble which he says is by Pradier. A tribadism scene, very bad, feeble and weakly designed, the only bit of Pradier in it a woman's hand, charmingly and softly contracted by pleasure' (1957, p.93).[30] Ashbee, too, saw the Pradier group some years later: 'Among others may be mentioned what he was pleased to call the sign of his house, *viz*, a most spirited marble by Pradier representing two tribades' (*Catena*, p.l, n.75).

---

[26] Lang, I, p.44.

[27] Pope-Hennessy (1951), pp. 127-8; Henderson (1974), p.53; Brodie (1971), p.247.

[28] Lafourcade (1932), p.111.

[29] *ibid.*, pp. 118-19; Pope-Hennessy (1951), pp. 137, 181.

[30] 'Puis il ouvre une grande boîte. C'est un marbre qu'il dit être de Pradier, une scène de tribauderie, très mauvaise, veule et mal dessinée, où il n'y a guère de Pradier qu'une main de femme, gracieusement et mollement infléchie par la jouissance.'

There can be no doubt, then, that Swinburne knew Hankey. Given the fact that Hankey was an expert on flagellant brothels in London it seems quite possible that he may have passed on information on the subject to Swinburne – who anyway had Milnes for a guide.

When Ashbee met Hankey for the first time at Paris in 1875 he immediately recognised him as an authority on flagellation.[31] Bound into Ashbee's interleaved copy of the *Index Librorum Prohibitorum* (opposite p.xlvi) in the British Library is the manuscript communication from Hankey, dated by Ashbee 26 May 1875, which served as the latter's principal source of information concerning nineteenth-century flagellation brothels in London. Ashbee had incorporated this document almost word for word in the *Index Librorum Prohibitorum* (pp. xlii-xliii and xlv-xlvi) but, since Hankey was still alive in 1877, did not ascribe the information to him (Hankey is referred to as 'a gentleman still living, a passionate devotee of the birch, and one who is worthy of all confidence in matters connected with flagellation', *Index*, p.xlvi, n.66). Various writers on Swinburne have quoted from this document, usually rather inaccurately and always incompletely, so I think it worthwhile to give it here in full:

Mr F. Hankey of 2 rue Laffitte Paris has requested that the following details might be sent to Mr Ashbee.

The first establishment known by me [over?] the last fifty years where the practice of the rod was carried on to a great extent, was held by Mrs Collett in Tavistock Court Covent Garden, from whence she removed into the neighbourhood of Portland Place – and then to Bedford St, Russell Square, where she died – George the 4th is known to have been in her house – she brought up her niece in the same line, and who as Mrs Mitchell carried on a great business in the same line, in various places, and finally in St Mary's Square, Kennington, where she died –

Then came Mrs James who had been maid in the family of Lord Clanricarde – she had a house in Carlisle St but eventually retired from business with a good fortune, a villa at Notting Hill, and a house in Quebec Street – with pictures and jewels without end. No one ever surpassed in this particular line Mrs Theresa Berkley who lived and died in Charlotte St, Portland Place, no.28 – A few days after her death her brother who had been a missionary for 30 years in Australia arrived, and found she had bequeathed to him £12,500 in the funds, besides other property – but when he learnt the source from which it had been derived he renounced all claim and immediately went back to Australia – In default the property was to go to Dr Vance of Saville [sic] Row, her medical attendant, but he also refused to administer, the whole was escheated to the crown – She never destroyed a letter, and Dr Vance as

[31] Pope-Hennessy (1951), p.119.

executor received several boxes full, which he allowed the writer of this to examine. They were of the most extraordinary character, from the highest personages, male and female, in the land –

Mrs Potter carried on a good business a few years ago near Tottenham Court Road, but being sentenced to imprisonment for getting some young girl birched by one of her customers was ruined –

There were several others whose names and addresses I forget – all made fortunes –

The only establishment I know of now is in the Regent's Park, a lovely little villa presided over by a well-educated lady, well versed in the birchen mysteries.

Her clientele is small but select, consisting of a few persons belonging to the higher order of society –

The birch at most of these places was provided by one Mrs Potter, living at Walworth –

In my experience I have known personally several ladies of high rank who had an extraordinary passion for administering the rod, and that too with merciless severity – I knew too the wife of a clergyman, young and pretty, who carried the taste to excess – I have known only one who liked to receive it, and she was quite of the lowest order – when excited by drink she would allow herself to be birched until the bottom was utterly raw, and the rods saturated in blood, she crying out during the operation, 'Harder, harder', and blaspheming if it was not well laid in – At the establishment I have named in Regent's Park, there come two very young girls who go through all the phases of a schoolmistress and whip fearfully severely –

The programmes sent by 'pupils' are extraordinary – some like to be whipped as children across the knee – some on the back of a servant, others to be strapped down –

A friend of Hankey who had been a governess in a [?] family in England, used the rod most cleverly – she is French, but is going to be married next week, and to the loss of the lovers of discipline.

I could give many anecdotes connected with this business.

I write in poste haste, starting today for Paris.

As regards the activities of Mrs Sarah Potter (referred to by Cannon, Ashbee and Hankey), the press of the period provides detailed information, suggesting that Hankey's comments on other 'governesses' may be substantially accurate. On 6 July 1863 *The Times* reported that 'Sarah Potter, *alias* Steward, a married woman, respectably connected' had been charged the previous day at Westminster Police Court with assaulting a young girl, Agnes Thompson. A close account of the court proceedings followed:

Previous to the evidence being taken Sergeant Beach, assisted by other officers of the D division, brought into the court a number of birch rods, two bunches of dried furze, and other articles.[32]

The complainant, a good looking girl, who gave her evidence quietly, said that she is 14 years of age. She has a father and mother, who are living in Middlesex-street, Somers-town. About 12 months ago she was walking in the street when she was spoken to by a gentleman, who ... effected her ruin. In about a week afterwards she met a woman, who took her to a house in Wardour-street which was occupied by the prisoner. She was there about seven months, and led an immoral life. She wanted to leave, but was not allowed to do so. She was beaten by a man with birch rods on her naked body. The prisoner was down stairs; she told her to go upstairs. She went there and was followed by the man into a room. The servant was sent up with the birch rod. After this the man locked the room door and beat her. She cried out, when the prisoner called out to her and said 'If she was not quiet she would send Mr Steward to her.' She said to the prisoner when she saw her, 'You did not tell me when you sent me to the room what was going to be done.' She replied, 'Oh, never mind. He did not hurt you.' She could not make her escape out of the house. She tried to do so, but whenever she went out the prisoner went with her. She was also beaten by a person who goes by the name of Sealskin, and by another who is known by the name of the Count. Other girls were treated in the same way. The servant in the house had been beaten more than once. She was in the room once when the servant was being beaten by a man. She was once beaten by the prisoner while a man was in an adjoining room which had a folding door. This was about a month ago. Prisoner always used to send her up and send up the rods afterwards. She had told the witness that if she went away with the clothes she had on she would lock her up. She had been strapped to some steps while being beaten, so that she could move neither hand nor foot, nor could she call out, as a towel was forced into her mouth. (The steps and four straps were produced.) The servant was treated in the same way. She had seen blood flow from the wounds inflicted on the servant. Last Monday week the prisoner turned her out without any breakfast. She then went to the house of a woman living in the same street. She interested herself in her behalf, and got her a doctor, as she was very ill. (p.11, col.5)

Further reports in *The Times* revealed that Agnes Thompson was not exaggerating when she said that other girls were similarly whipped at the Wardour Street and Albion Terrace, King's Road, Chelsea brothels of Sarah Potter. On 11 July 1863 two more witnesses testified:

Catherine Kennedy, about 17 years of age, was next examined. She entered the prisoner's house in Wardour-street about January last. For

---

[32] Among the 'other articles' was a folding ladder.

about three days she was asked by the prisoner to allow herself to be flogged with birch rods by gentlemen. She was in want of money and submitted. She was strapped to a folding ladder, without any clothes on. After she was flogged the gentlemen gave the prisoner some money. She did not see how much. The prisoner gave her a sovereign. The room in which she was flogged was called the 'schoolroom'. She was flogged on a second occasion for about ten minutes very severely. She received half a sovereign for that flogging, and left the next day.

Alice Smith said that in February she was first introduced to the prisoner in Wardour-street. She had not long been there before she was told by the prisoner to go into the schoolroom. She found there a short, fat gentleman. He was standing by a ladder, and there were rods lying on a sofa. She was fastened to a ladder with straps, and then flogged. The prisoner was in the room standing by the door. The lashes were very severe, and she screamed. She asked them to let her go, and called out 'Police!' and said that she could bear it no longer. The flogging brought blood from her person. She had no power to release herself, as she was tied to the ladder. She got no money on that occasion. (p.13, col.5)[33]

The Potter case was brought to a close soon afterwards, with the requisite expressions of disgust from the prosecution and magistrate. *The Times* reported on 20 July 1863:

> Mr Sleigh then said that for the ends of public morality, and to prevent a repetition *in extenso* of the disgusting disclosures which had been made in that court before the Sessions, he would respectfully ask the magistrate to dispose of the case summarily, and proceedings could otherwise be taken for the indictable offence of procuring indecent prints and photographs with intent to publish them. (p.11, col.6)

One has the strong impression that pressure was being brought to bear on the prosecution to have the case hushed up. Be that as it may, matters were quickly terminated. The magistrate observed that

> He was sensible that the punishment he could inflict was not commensurate with the enormity of the offence, but he felt with Mr Sleigh that it would be best for the public morals that the case should be closed as soon as possible. He had to express his regret that the wretches who had misused the wealth bestowed upon them for better purposes than to stimulate their passions should have escaped the just punishment of their revolting conduct. (*ibid.*)

---

[33] It is clear that these girls were able to get their own back on their clients from time to time. Another of Sarah Potter's girls, Emma Wilmot, stated that she had birched men (*Reynold's Newspaper*, 26 July 1863).

Mrs Potter got six months with hard labour, and the magistrate 'required her at the expiration of that time to find two sureties in £100 each for her good behaviour six months longer'.

It seems very likely to me that Richard Monckton Milnes was involved with Sarah Potter. To start with there is the fact, as we have seen, that Hankey was telling people in Paris in 1862 that he, Milnes and some horseguards used to frequent the flagellant brothel of a certain 'Mrs Jenkins' in London, where they whipped young girls 'whom first we made sit in class'. Mrs Potter's establishment had a flogging apartment called the 'schoolroom', as we have just seen, and the revelations of Agnes Thompson and Catherine Kennedy conjure up a picture similar to that conveyed by Hankey to his French acquaintances – the discrepancy between the names Potter (or Stuart) and Jenkins need not bother us, since most of these people operated under aliases. The dates, moreover, coincide closely. As well as this we have the evidence from Ashbee that *The Rodiad*, which was almost certainly written by Milnes, was composed 'by one of the clients of the notorious Sarah Potter, alias Stewart' (*Centuria*, p.472). Finally, there are allusions to Sarah Potter in two letters to Milnes from Richard Burton which indicate that both men knew this flagellant madame personally. On 29 March 1863, Burton inquired from Tenerife: 'Anything of Hankey? I suppose Bellamy is still fencing off the angry fiend. The [good?] Stewart? – I had no time to *confectionner* an *orgie chez elle*. I left Hodgson the Genl. sweating under the pangs of a balked ambition and should be glad to know that he has ejected the irrelevant matter.' Ten years later, on 5 November 1873, Burton asked from Trieste: 'What is become of ... Hodgson? Of Stuart alias Potter?'

Could it be that Milnes was 'The Count' or 'Sealskin'? Or that 'short, fat gentleman' whom Alice Smith had found standing by the folding ladder one day, waiting to birch her? We cannot know for sure. Certainly *The Rodiad* expresses the pleasure to be found in beating rather than in being beaten, which seems to correspond to what went on most of the time at Mrs Potter's establishment. Taking all the evidence together it seems probable that Milnes was indeed one of her clients.

The Potter case produced much excitement in the porno-flagellant circles of London; and at the same time made it difficult for the hypocrites and puritans to deny the connection between birching and sexuality. Shortly after the court case, the underground press brought forth a pamphlet arising from the Potter revelations and drawing attention to other similar brothels, real or imaginary:

Mysteries of Flagellation or, a History of the Secret Ceremonies of the Society of

Flagellants. The Saintly Practice of the Birch! St. Francis whipped by the Devil! How to subdue the Passions, by the Art of Flogging! With many Curious Anecdotes of the Prevalence of this Peculiar Pastime in all Nations and Epochs, whether Savage or Civilized. Printed by C. BROWN, 44 Wych Street, Strand. Price 2d.

According to Ashbee, who describes the pamphlet, it 'notices more particularly some of the noted establishments of London, among them the "White House", the "den of Mother Cummins", the "Elysium in Brydges Street", etc.' (*Index*, p.312). Judging from the excerpts printed by Ashbee, the activities that went on at the Potter Brothel in Wardour Street were indistinguishable from those recorded in hundreds of nineteenth-century flagellant stories.

Mrs Potter survived her time in the House of Correction. Ashbee records, however, that she was soon imprisoned again, for selling indecent books.[34] When Burton wrote to Milnes on 5 November 1873 enquiring after acquaintances including 'Stuart alias Potter', the notorious brothel-keeper was no longer of this world. Her death certificate shows that she died on 24 February 1873 of cancer of the uterus, at 3 Lavinia Grove, Islington. Her husband is named as 'Charles Potter, silversmith'. She was 41.[35]

Immediately following Fred Hankey's manuscript document concerning flagellant brothels in London, Ashbee has bound into his copy of the *Index* an unusual letter. It is written in a clear but uneducated hand, and purports to come from the 'governess' of a whipping establishment. Whether this is a spoof letter or one really written by a 'governess' according to a prescription laid down by one of her clients, it is impossible to say. I quote it because it exactly captures the infantile, school-room world of the flagellant imagination. A few years ago, when T.E. Lawrence's whipping obsessions were revealed to the world, similar documents came to light.[36]

Dear Sir,
I received your letter informing me of your nephew's bad conduct. And so he stayed out all night and was afraid to return home. In the morning set off for Paris – What a fearful state of mind you must have been in – What a lucky thing your friend met him and sent him back. Now dear sir I hope you will not pardon such bad conduct – if you do depend upon it he will do it again.

[34] *Index*, p.313.
[35] Death certificate extracted by the author at Somerset House.
[36] For a detailed but not very perceptive consideration of Lawrence's flagellomania, see John E. Mack, *A Prince of our Disorder: The Life of T.E. Lawrence* (1976).

I have a new governess she is tall and very severe, she will not be trifled with – she will attend on Sunday morning. There are other boys to be punished that day, so I shall rely upon your sending him at 2 p.m. and if I do not have him punished as he never has been before never trust me again.

The daring young rascal called upon me the other day with a present from Paris – he said that you had sent him to see a sick Aunt who was ill and wished to see him very much. I thought the young gentleman was telling the truth, and felt so pleased with the present he so kindly brought me and now to think that I must have him punished and that very severely.

I promise you.

This is waiting for him

[ink sketch of a birch rod]

The gate will be open at 2.

Charles can go at once to the schoolroom.

It will be recalled that Hankey, in his flagellant communication to Ashbee, wrote that 'the only establishment I know of now is in the Regent's Park, a lovely little villa presided over by a well-educated lady, well versed in the birchen mysteries'. Swinburne scholars are agreed that this loosely and improbably located establishment may be identified with one a stone's throw from the Park at 7, Circus Road, St John's Wood, which it seems the poet began to frequent in the 1860s. Perhaps the letter just quoted emanated from this house, the reference to the 'gate' being consistent with a villa in the leafy quarter of St John's Wood, a district notorious in the nineteenth century for its artists, bohemians and high-class tarts.[37]

In the early summer of 1865 Swinburne had moved into rooms at

[37] Professor Lang has reminded us (VI, p.245) of the passage in *The Forsyte Saga* in which we find Old Jolyon in St John's Wood: 'He looked about him with interest,' writes Galsworthy, 'for this was a district which no Forsyte entered without open disapproval and secret curiosity' (*The Man of Property*, Ch. 7). A.M. Eyre relates the following story in his book *Saint John's Wood* (1913): 'When it was announced that Herbert Spencer had taken up his residence there, "Really," exclaimed a bishop to Mr Charles Brookfield, "and who is the lady?"' (p.145). On 26 April 1884, *Town Talk* published a witty leading article entitled 'Decay of St John's Wood: Rise of Pimlico'. 'One by one, slowly but surely,' the article began, 'the prostitutes are turning their back upon St John's Wood. The district which has but to be named, and visions of bloated land-ladies, bejewelled harlots, and champagne at a guinea a bottle arise before the mind, will ere long be associated with everything that is nice, respectable, and proper. When a man tells you that he lives in St John's Wood you will no longer wink your eye and smile a wicked smile ... In the St John's Wood district I have seen hundreds of the monster furniture removal vans ... Pounds are no longer to be made in the shady groves of the Evangelist, and Aspasia must now content herself with the shilling of plebeian Vauxhall ...'

22a Dorset Street, just behind Marylebone Railway Station.[38] In July of that year we find him writing to Milnes:

> As my tempter and favourite audience [Richard Burton] has gone to Santos I may hope to be a good boy again, after such a 'jolly good swishing' as Rodin alone can and dare administer. The Rugby purists (I am told) tax Eton generally with Maenadism during June and July, so perhaps some old school habits return upon us unawares – to be fitly expiated by old school punishment. (Lang, I, p.124)

Jean Fuller wonders in her book on Swinburne if this reference to the birch may not suggest that the poet was already by 1865 attending a flagellant brothel.[39] It is a plausible hypothesis, although it seems to me more likely that the poet is alluding to Milnes's own apparent willingness (in the guise of Rodin, again) to apply the occasional fustigation to his young friend. At all events, in view of Swinburne's friendship with Milnes and Hankey, we can be sure that by 1865 he was acquainted with the whereabouts of these establishments.

The first explicit allusion to a flagellant brothel occurs in 1868 (in the letters that have so far come to light, that is). On 28 July 1868 Swinburne wrote to Powell: 'My life has been enlivened of late by a fair friend who keeps a maison de supplices à la Rodin – There is occasional balm in Gilead' (Lang, I, p.305).

From September to mid-October 1868 Swinburne stayed with Powell at the latter's cottage at Etretat in Normandy (later baptised 'Chaumière Dolmancé' in honour of the Marquis de Sade[40]), and back in London he wrote to Milnes, on 9 November 1868: 'Our fair friend of the grove of the Beloved Discipline [that is, St John's Wood] has also returned from France and is in high feather. I always find her

---

[38] Fuller (1968), p.146.

[39] *ibid*.

[40] By Powell, independently it seems of Swinburne (despite what the Swinburne scholars have said). Among the Powell letters to Swinburne in the Brotherton Library, Leeds University, collection is one from Etretat dated 12 December 1868. The notepaper is headed 'Chaumière Dolmancé', and the Welshman explains: 'I have, in honour of the Marquis, as you know, and in remembrance of our walk there, called the avenue in my garden the '*Avenue de Sade*' wh. name shall cleave unto it. What further can I do save call this cottage (on a board nailed on to the gate post, or on a brass plate) 'Chaumière Dolmancé'. Would this please the soul of the Marquis or would it (on your letters to me) shock the sensibilities of the post-office officials? I will abide by your judgement.' For a Frenchman's view of the Powell-Swinburne ménage at Etretat, see Maupassant in the Bibliography. Maupassant described his visit to Powell's cottage to the Goncourts and, as Praz has pointed out, George Selwyn, the English sadist in Edmond de Goncourt's novel *La Faustin* (1882), inhabits a 'petite maison sur les côtes de la Bretagne ... la *Chaumière de Dolmancé*' (Goncourt, *La Faustin*, p.328).

delicious dans son genre' (Lang, I, p.310). On the same day he told
Powell: 'I have found far from dry or chilling the Sadice-Paphian spring
of St John's Wood whereof I once spoke to you' (Lang, I, p.311).

These allusions show that the 'fair friend' in question was also
known to Milnes, and suggest that the latter was another habitué of
the St John's Wood establishment.

It has been stated by Gosse, in his paper on Swinburne's 'moral
irregularities',[41] that the poet was introduced to the brothel by the
journalist John Thomson, who later became his secretary:

> John Thomson had an interest (Sims tells me that it was perhaps a share)
> in a mysterious house in St John's Wood where two golden-haired and
> rouge-cheeked ladies received, in luxuriously furnished rooms, gentlemen
> whom they consented to chastise for large sums. Thomson introduced
> Swinburne to this establishment and he became a regular visitor. There
> was an elder lady, very respectable, who welcomed the guests and took the
> money. Swinburne very much impoverished himself in these games, which
> also must have been very bad for his health. (Lang, VI, p.245)

Gosse, one may say at this point, was a prude, and had no
understanding of Swinburne's flagellant problem. Perhaps the house
to which he refers was the same one mentioned by George R. Sims
(the Sims in the quotation) in his memoir, *My Life: Sixty Years
Recollections of Bohemian London* (1917). It was the indefatigable
Professor Lang who first drew our attention to the relevant passage in
this book. According to Sims, John Thomson 'lived in one of the side
roads of St John's Wood, then playfully referred to as 'the Grove of the
Evangelist', and the house in which he lived was rather sumptuously
furnished' (p.44). Sims, one of the best-known residents of the quarter,
was not likely to get his facts about John Thomson's house wrong.[42]
Following up these clues, Lang found that John Thomson's address
was listed by the *Post Office Directory* as 7, Circus Road, St John's
Wood.[43]

A plan of St John's Wood dating from this period shows that no. 7
Circus Road stood at the corner of Cavendish Street (now Avenue).[44]
The house occupying the site today is no. 31, and it is hardly a 'lovely

---

[41] This document was first published by Professor Lang, VI, pp. 233-48.

[42] A.M. Eyre, in the work quoted, writes 'perhaps no contemporary journalist has
longer and better known the Wood of Saint John than Mr G.R. Sims' (p.282).

[43] Lang, VI, p.245. Lang had looked at the 1876 edition of the *Post Office Directory*. In
fact, as the same annual publication shows, Thomson first began to live at this
address in 1857.

[44] This and other plans of the area may be consulted at the Marylebone Public
Library.

little villa' – Hankey's description of the flagellant establishment 'in the Regent's Park'. However, there are indications in the *Post Office Directory* that, after John Thomson left 7 Circus Road in the early 1880s, the house was demolished and a new building erected in its place. Certainly the present house seems, to my eye, to be late Victorian.

Hankey's adjectives can still be applied, however, to the charming, walled villas of Elm Tree Road, just around the corner from Circus Road. Elm Tree Road is one of St John's Wood's most attractive, secluded streets, and it takes little effort of the imagination to picture what it must have looked like in the 1860s. It is of interest to note that the *Post Office Directory* of 1863 records that a 'Mrs Stuart' had taken up residence there, at no. 18. Could this perhaps have been the notorious Sarah Potter, under her alias of Stuart? Might she and Thomson have been somehow involved in the flagellation business together? This is pure speculation, although it is true that Mrs Stuart had disappeared from 18, Elm Tree Road by 1864. We recall that she was imprisoned after the flagellant brothel scandal in July 1863, so the dates seem to coincide.

There is no evidence that Gosse had seen the flagellant information sent by Hankey to Ashbee, which makes the agreement between his and Hankey's details the more striking: it seems quite possible, in fact, that they had the same establishment in mind, wherever, exactly, it may have been situated; and that the 'elder lady, very respectable' (Gosse) and the 'well-educated lady, well-versed in the birchen mysteries' (Hankey) were one and the same person.

Gosse is of the opinion that Swinburne quarrelled with the flagellant ladies of St John's Wood, probably over money; and has been unable to find evidence for Swinburne's attendance there after 1869.[45] Lafourcade, however, wrote that the poet continued to satisfy his tendencies until 1895 at least in 'special establishments' (1928, I, p.265, n.109). Whether this date is a misprint, and what was the source of the French scholar's information, I do not know. It would come as a surprise to learn that, during the Putney period, Swinburne managed to evade the attentions of Watts-Dunton and escape to a brothel, but such may have been the case. It seems unlikely, on the face of it, that in 1879 Swinburne could have suddenly abandoned for ever the pleasures of those flagellant establishments to which he had become accustomed. We know, moreover, that while in Putney he was not above engaging from time to time in a little composition of birch-orientated pornography.[46]

[45] Lang, VI, p.247.
[46] For details of Swinburne's contributions to *The Pearl* (1879-1880) and *The Whippingham Papers* (1888), see Swinburne in the Bibliography.

In a later book Lafourcade revealed that he had received information about another flagellant brothel visited by the poet in the Euston Road; and drew the reader's attention to two further documents of interest: 'In an undated letter Swinburne mentions a "Mrs A." who was perhaps connected with it. See also the reference to "Florence" in Nichol's letter to Swinburne' (1932, p,196, note).

The reference to 'Mrs A.' comes in an undated letter to George Powell:

> A word of good news which I know you will be glad to hear. Dr Duncan tells me that the awful Mrs A. is all right – he found her in a state of melting ecstasy over one of my works (qu. Anactoria – with an eye on the maid? The nice little one might serve – in any sense of service – at a pinch) and speaking of me personally 'in terms of regard' – so he of course made no reference to any past threat or quarrel, but took the best for granted. So that episode is closed. Laus Deo – also to you – also to Duncan. (Lang, VI, p.250)

The second reference is more interesting but equally enigmatic. Another friend, John Nichol, has just read the manuscript of Swinburne's *A Year's Letters* (his communication is dated 22 January 1877):

> Not having been a public school boy I was never properly flogged, only cuffed and caned, and so have no experience. With this apology for ignorance I would be in favour of excising the passages I have marked in, I trust, erasible green pencil. Besides I think it inadvisable to mislead, possibly, the reader at starting into a hope or fear of a flagellation novel. Florence told me that a clergyman once came asking for a swishing, and that with twigs she flogged him (having muscles that have knocked down two men and horse-whipped other two [sic]) till he roared for mercy.[47]

Who was 'Mrs A.'? And who Florence, whom Nichol takes for granted is known to Swinburne? That Florence was a flagellant 'governess' there would seem to be little doubt from the details of her activities provided by Nichol. Perhaps some future Swinburne scholar will be able to answer these questions for us.[48]

Whoever Swinburne's flagellant ladies were, it is legitimate to assume that, having helped the poet to erection by acting out his fantasies for him, they proceeded to assuage his desires in a more

[47] Printed by T.J. Wise (1925), VI, p.208.
[48] On 29 December 1876 Nichol had written to Swinburne in a P.S.: 'I saw poor Florence lately. She is drinking herself to death yet still sings like an angel' (British Library, Ashley 5752).

conventional manner. The evidence is conclusive that passive flagellants would prefer not to have their compulsive *lech* and to be able to become sexually excited in a more normal way; but that, despite themselves, they can only achieve erection by having recourse to their fantasies. I see no reason to think that Swinburne was any different, Swinburne who loved women and was of a passionate temperament. We might note that the poet refers to the St John's Wood establishment as a 'Sadice-Paphian' spring and not merely as a *sadique* one, suggesting that after the birch came the bed. Swinburne's problem must have been that, like Rousseau, he could never bring himself to confess the truth about his inner life to a 'decent' woman. The nearest he came to doing so seems to have been to his cousin, Mary Gordon. She, without his having to explain, shared his interest in the rod, although it is most unlikely that she would have understood how overtly sexual the whole business was for Swinburne. In his imagination the poet may have attributed to Mary sadistic qualities which she did not really possess; and, after her marriage in 1865 to her military hero Colonel Leith, many years her senior, it must have increasingly seemed to Swinburne that he had lost the one person to whom, eventually, he might have been able to confide the whole truth.

I have spent some time in seeking to analyse the relations that existed between Hankey, Milnes, Burton, Swinburne and Ashbee because it seems to me that this group offers us a unique insight into the 'sado-masochistic' side of Victorian England. All of these men felt themselves to be in rebellion against the Establishment of the day in matters of sexual morality, and greatly disliked its hypocrisy and puritanism; all were travellers, linguists and students of foreign literatures, erotic and otherwise; and all of them were obsessed with sexual perversion. As regards flagellation, the documentation which it is possible to put together concerning this group's activities shows that they were far from being unique in their interest in the subject. We can be absolutely certain that their tastes were shared by a great many men from similar backgrounds.

In Chapter Two reference was made to the dubious advertisements concerning the birch which appeared from time to time during the nineteenth century in respectable publications. If such advertisements could be inserted in a religious journal as impeccable as the *Guardian*, one can imagine what the situation was like in the gutter press. During the 1880s *Town Talk* did a special line in flagellant insertions:

THE ROD. – Ladies resident in London interested in the above subject are invited to communicate with L.J., 2 Vigo Street, Regent Street, when he will be happy to arrange an interview. (14 April 1883)

TO LADIES. – Lady wanted to teach French. Birching necessary. Address Z.Z., care of Mr W. Polden, 18 York Road, S.E. (21 April 1883)

'INDECENT WHIPPING' ADVERTISEMENTS

In reply to numerous inquiries, the manager of *Town Talk* begs to state that advertisements having reference to the infliction of corporal punishment in schools can be inserted at FIVE SHILLINGS each for five lines and under. Every additional line ONE SHILLING. (26 April 1884)

W.T. Stead, during his researches on child prostitution in London, found that flagellation was common in brothels. Among the other scandals revealed in his famous series of articles published in the *Pall Mall Gazette* under the title 'The Maiden Tribute of Modern Babylon' in July 1885, there figured the following revelation:

> Flogging, both of men and women, goes on regularly in ordinary rooms, but the cry of the bleeding subject never attracts attention from the outside world. What chance is there, then, of the feeble, timid cry of the betrayed child penetrating the shuttered and curtained windows, or of moving the heart of the wily watcher – the woman whose business it is to secure absolute secrecy for her client. When means of stifling a cry – a pillow, a sheet, or even a pocket handkerchief – lie all around, there is practically no danger. To some men, however, the shriek of torture is the essence of their delight, and they would not silence by a single note the cry of agony over which they gloat. (6 July 1885, p.5, col.2)

'The Maiden Tribute of Modern Babylon' caused a sensation, and was widely reported in the foreign press, especially in France where a full translation was issued in book form in the same year.[49] As Stead's revelations showed, London's flagellant establishments had not disappeared with the death of Sarah Potter in 1873. Elsewhere Stead was more specific about one of the brothels which he had investigated (Henriques, 1969, p.239):

> Flogging or birching goes on in brothels to a much greater extent than is generally believed. One of Mrs Jeffries' rooms was fitted up like a torture chamber (in a street leading off Gray's Inn Road). There were rings in the ceiling for hanging women and children up by the wrists, ladders for strapping them down at any angle, as well as the ordinary stretcher to

---

[49] *Les Scandales de Londres dévoilés par la Pall Mall Gazette*. Traduction littérale des articles de ce journal, Dentu, 1885. Praz has traced the influence of this translation on the *fin de siècle*, 'decadent' novel.

which the victim is fastened so as to be unable to move. The instruments of flagellation included the birch, whips, holly branches and wire-thonged cat-o'-nine-tails.

In 1898 there was a famous 'massage scandal' at Marylebone Police Court, when the first prosecution was made under the provisions of the new Vagrancy Act. The reader may recall that, under this Act, any person convicted of living on the earnings of prostitution, or soliciting for immoral purposes, might be sentenced to a whipping on a second or consequent conviction of the offence. Only George Bernard Shaw, as has been said, was prepared to refer at the time in public to the fatuity of a whipping Act intended to put down prostitution, a prostitution that often itself catered for whipping.

In court it was revealed that at 120 Marylebone Road there was a 'massage establishment' described as 'The Balneopathic Institution for the treatment of rheumatism, gout, sciatica, and 'neuralgia, by dry hot-air baths, massage and discipline, etc.' (*Daily Telegraph*, 17 October 1898, p.9). This establishment had been advertising its services openly in the press, as was common at the time (see plates 24 and 25, which reproduce parts of pages of such advertisements from the scabrous journal *Society*). The prostitutes in the 'Balneopathic Institution' were dressed as, and called, 'nurses'. Fees were high: those 'charged for massage ranged from 10s.6d., but the witness would tell the court that stockbrokers and rich gentlemen often came, who paid as much as £3 or £4' (*ibid.*). The police found (as they always did on such occasions) bundles of letters from 'patients', one of which read: 'I cannot come today, as I have an engagement. I was sorry I was out when you called. I should like to see you, so will you pop down at 4.30 and bring the birch with you?' (*ibid.*). Maud Edwards, one of the 'nurses' (described by the reporter as a 'stylishly-dressed blonde') explained how the Institution worked:

Cross-examined by Mr Freke Palmer: She was not living with her husband. She did not live at Marylebone-road, but visited there.
Are you one of the nurses? – No.
What do you go for, then? – When they are short of nurses.
When they are short of a lady, I suppose? – Yes.
You go there to meet gentlemen? – Yes, if a patient comes for a hot-air bath.
You meet gentlemen there for the purpose of immorality? – No.
The Magistrate: Never? Now be careful. – Witness: No, never.
Mr Freke Palmer: What do you know about massage? – Nothing.
What is the discipline you give? – Well, it is a treatment.
Yes, but what is it?

Mr Curtis-Bennett: Come on, out with it.

Mr Freke Palmer: Is it the birch? – Yes, it is flagellation, of course. (Sensation.)

Mr Curtis-Bennett: Ah, you need not go any further. (*ibid.*)

As the court soon realised, the 'hot-air baths' were – a lot of hot air.[50]

In 1904 there were similar revelations concerning a flagellant brothel in Elm Tree Road, St John's Wood (ever a haunt of the brethren of the birch, it would seem). Sophia Mabel Pearse, appearing at Marylebone Police Court, 'aged 45, described as of independent means', was charged with using her premises for 'improper purposes'. Chief Inspector James Cameron and other officers had visited the house unexpectedly one night. It was strictly a high-class establishment:

> Sub-divisional Inspector Roberts said the place was furnished in the usual way of a disorderly house. It consisted of twelve rooms, seven of which were furnished as bed-rooms. They found in a studio on the ground floor – which was arranged as a bed-sitting room – a lady and gentleman in evening dress, who gave their names and addresses. Having explained how they came to be there, the gentleman said that if anything came of this he would get into frightful trouble. From there they went to a bedroom on the first floor, which was occupied by a lady and gentleman, who gave their names and addresses. The gentleman said the meeting took place by arrangement through the post. He had been there before. The inspector then described what he found in the house. In the centre of the studio was a large arm-chair, with brass rings fixed to the top of the frame. In a wardrobe he found two birches and several wrist and ankle straps, which could be fixed to the chair; in a room on the second floor another birch; and in a box in a lumber-room two other birches or flagellettes. ('Raid on a Mansion', *Daily Telegraph*, 28 July 1904)

Sophia Mabel Pearse sounds as if she might have served a double apprenticeship with both Theresa Berkley of Charlotte Street and Mrs Walter Smith of Clifton.

To the revelations periodically offered to readers of the *Daily Telegraph*, *The Times* and other respectable newspapers may be added those published in scandal papers such as *Society* and *Town Talk*, both of which specialised in flagellant material, as we have seen. It becomes increasingly hard to accept that any literate man at the time could

---

[50] Hansen (1899) and Bloch (1903) brought this case to the notice of German readers (Bloch, 1938, pp. 143-4).

have been totally ignorant of the connection between whipping and sex.

One or two further cases will bring us up to our own day.

In 1913, shortly after the passing of the White Slave Act which, as we have seen, introduced new whipping measures for sexual offences, procuration, etc., there was another case involving flagellant prostitution. In this, Queenie Gerald, 26, 'described as an actress', was charged at Marlborough Street Police Court with living on the earnings of young girls. Her flat at Abingdon House, Piccadilly, had been raided by officers of the White Slave Suppression Branch of the C.I.D., who had found a woman dressed as a nurse ('a mental nurse,' she styled herself) and two almost naked girls. 'They also found a whip, a cane, and a birch, and a very considerable quantity of correspondence and "literature", and objectionable photographs' (*Reynold's Newspaper*, 22 June 1913, p.5).

The trial of Dr Stephen Ward some 60 years later revealed that English upper-class males still occasionally need tickling up. On 25 July 1963, a banner headline in *The Times* announced 'Dr Ward Trial: Birmingham girl of 20 tells of caning and horsewhipping men in Bryanston Mews flat'. An excerpt from the previous day's court proceedings read:

'MARKET PRICE £1 A STROKE'

Mr Griffith-Jones continued: 'You told us of the third occasion when you were asked to whip one of the men with the cane. Were you asked to whip other men?'

Miss Barrett. – Yes.

Was it always with a cane? – Not always.

On one occasion you used a whip? – A horsewhip.

Who handed you that? – It was in the bedroom.

Did you whip only one man with the horsewhip or more? – Two or three men with the horsewhip.

Was it the same horsewhip each time? – No.

There were two different men with the same whip? – Yes.

Did the men take their whips, or were they already there? – I do not know.

There were two different men on two different occasions but you used the same whip? – Yes.

Did you beat other men with the cane? – Yes.

Was it the same cane? – Yes.

Asked what sort of age the men were at the flat and she replied that they were middle-aged or elderly.

She said that when she asked Ward how the savings were getting on he said that he had nearly enough but he did not tell her how much.

He did not speak again about a flat and clothes for her but he did buy her a dress and a costume and two pairs of high-heeled shoes.

Mr Griffith-Jones. – With your knowledge of the trade, rather profession, what would be the normal payment for services such as you rendered? How much a time? – £5 in the flat.

And for the whipping, what is the market price? – £1 a stroke. (p.5)

The revelations concerning the proclivities of Lt-Colonel John Brooks, 'the Spanking Colonel', hit the national newspapers in November 1974. Neither the press nor the military gentleman himself seem to have been aware that, in Victorian pornography, he had an illustrious predecessor called Colonel Spanker. Brooks, it transpired, liked smacking girls' bottoms, particularly the bottoms of girls crewing for him on his boat on the Thames. What was remarkable and refreshing about Brooks was his complete openness in court about his interest in flagellation, and his refusal to consider such an interest abnormal (at least for him). Perhaps the fact that, apparently, he only specialised in the active variety of beating is relevant, for it seems that not so much guilt and shame attach to this manifestation of flagellomania as to the passive form. It was odd to travel on the London underground at this time and to see the headlines blaring from the front pages of the newspapers: 'Girl Student tells of an Encounter on the Thames. My trip with the Spanking Colonel' (*Evening Standard*, 21 November 1974); 'I Shall Spank On, promises the ½p Colonel' (*Daily Telegraph*, 26 November 1974); 'Bottoms Up, says the ½p Colonel' (*Guardian*, same date).

It seems that the upper-class and affluent English, in prostitution as in their preparatory and public schools, have just not been able to get on without 'lower discipline'. Like Snarl in *The Virtuoso*, they have found it difficult, if not impossible, to 'leave it off'.

The symptoms of this obsession are all around us, and some of them have been identified already. In August 1976, while working on this book, I happened to see a repeat showing of a 'Monty Python's Flying Circus' programme on BBC TV. One sketch struck me particularly, a brilliant parody of a TV game. In it members of the public are caught 'with their trousers down' in the commission of some shameful, essentially sexual, activity. The money clocks up frenetically on a dial, like a petrol pump, and the victim, apprised that he is being watched, rushes for the nearest telephone and promises the master of ceremonies that he will pay up. Anything to prevent the final exposure. One of these victims is a seedy, rain-coated little man whom we see popping as unobtrusively as possible into an equally banal terrace house, somewhere in London. A moment later, through an upstairs window, we observe him on his knees before the object of his visit, a prostitute dressed in black underwear and boots – brandishing, need one say it, a whip. Somehow that touch could only be possible in England, where such allusions are immediately understood.

That flagellation is common in London's brothels today is evident from the number of advertisements appearing on notice boards and in newsagents' windows in the seedier parts of the city:

Wicker chair seats *Re-Caned*. Ring –
Dominant Ex-Governess Seeks Afternoon Pupils. Ring –[51]

As the *News of the World* revealed (23 January 1977), the demand for flagellant brothels is not restricted to London. Mrs Betteena Vibak runs an establishment in Birmingham that would do credit to Teresa Berkley herself.

Students of lavatorial graffiti will also be aware of the frequency with which this sort of thing can be seen in mens' conveniences:

I want to feel the hard cuts with a well applied cane across my bare arse – hard until I am yelling for mercy and then more – to bend over with my bare arse exposed to a strong man who will lay it on and on is what I want.[52]

Sometimes the different handwriting shows that the question and answer technique is not simply the product of one mind:

I'm wearing tight white shorts and need cane on them.
Lovely. 12 HARD CUTS then 12 on each buttock with slipper.[53]

Read the leading English newspapers attentively for a week and you are sure to come across a reference to some aspect of flagellation. Perhaps I may be allowed to refer to two recent examples. On 28 November 1976 the *Sunday Times* carried a review by Colin Nears of a book by John Bird, *Percy Grainger*. I read: 'It's good ... on Percy behind the scenes: flagellation (he always toured with whips) and he didn't tell his wife till they were married. Mother knew. Maybe she was responsible, chasing his alcoholic father with a horsewhip and using it on Percy himself till he was 16' (p.40).

---

[51] Transcribed by the author from a notice board in Notting Hill Gate, London, January 1977.
[52] Transcribed by the author from a lavatory wall at Waterloo Station, London, January 1977.
[53] *ibid.*

On 26 October 1977 the *Daily Telegraph* informed its readers that ' "Chest Sale" led Police to Vice Flat'. There the officers of the law found – guess what? – 'a collection of whips, ropes, canes and various kinds of clothing' (p.19).

We know that flagellant fantasies are rooted in early childhood. We know that they arise in the context of domestic and school beatings and that, where the latter are concerned, the preparatory and public schools have been the main culprits. But what are the components of the fantasy? How can it come about that beating, or the idea of beating, can be sexually exciting? In the next chapter we must begin to move in an interpretative direction and pick up from where we left off with Krafft-Ebing. As a start we may begin by attempting to separate out the principal elements of the flagellant fantasy as it finds expression in pornography.

7

The Flagellant Fantasy

It is well known, as I said at the beginning of the last chapter, that a vast amount of flagellant pornography was generated during the nineteenth century. It is not my purpose in this book, however, to provide a bibliography of such works or an account of their fortunes (which anyway, for reasons already given, would be extremely difficult to achieve). Anyone desirous of entering the Victorian flagellant labyrinth should begin by acquiring or obtaining access to Ashbee's three bibliographies, which contain much information on the subject and many clues which could be followed up. What I wish to do is to use a selection of flagellant pornography, mainly from the nineteenth century, as source material for an examination of the fantasy itself. For, after all, it is the fantasy which interests us.

The buttocks

Flagellant fantasies as we find them expressed in pornography – whether Victorian or modern – concentrate exclusively on the buttocks. It is clear that floggings inflicted on other parts of the body – shoulders, back, palms of the hands – would not be felt to be sexually stimulating. The pornography confirms Meibom. It is true, of course, that in some modern pornography lacerations of the back are recorded along with other mutilations, but here the interest is of a broad sadistic kind and not specifically flagellant.

Where Victorian pornography is concerned the reader has little option but to accept the truth of this general assertion, since reprints of nineteenth-century flagellant material are not generally available (that of *The Pearl* is an exception[1]). But it is easy to check on current practice. The porn marts of Soho today, like their Victorian

---

[1] *The Pearl. A Journal of Facetiae and Voluptuous Reading* (1879-80). Reprinted in reduced facsimile by Amour Publications, London, 1975.

predecessors in Holywell Street near Drury Lane, do a busy trade in 'fladge'. Many of these publications are profusely illustrated with photographs and drawings. Now as before interest is centred on the naked buttocks, as even a cursory glance at such magazines as *Janus*, *Martinet*, *Spank*, *Sting* (imported from California), *Victorian Erotica* and *Spanking* demonstrate. Commenting on the prevalence of such material in London today, Gillian Freeman observes in her book *The Undergrowth of Literature* (1967): 'The sheer volume of sado-masochistic literature available makes one wonder just what percentage of the male population can only contemplate sexual relationships which have their basis in the wielding of a whip' (p. 90).

As regards the primacy of the buttocks in the flagellant fantasy, some further observations may be made at once.

First, in all representations of the fantasy the *uncovering* of the buttocks by the dominant figure forms an absolutely indispensable part of the ceremony. Dr Michael Ryan had written in 1837, as we have seen, that 'flagellation and denudation are inseparable, and often excite erection even in children'. Ryan was on the right track, but did not develop this insight. In the flagellant fantasy the baring of the buttocks is carried out with deliberate ritual, the details of which vary very little from book to book, case history to case history, year to year. We have seen instances of this insistence on ceremonial uncovering in some of the letters quoted in the chapter on the flagellant correspondence column. After the preliminaries have been completed, the exposure of the buttocks (there is a carefully-orchestrated build-up to this moment) is described with precision: there is obsessive interest in the 'pinning up', 'fastening up', 'turning up', 'taking up' or 'tucking in' of shirts, chemises, shifts, petticoats and other encumbrances; delight at the 'letting down', 'lowering', 'unfastening' and 'unbuttoning' of drawers, trousers, knickers and other nether garments; ecstasy and fascination when the final revelation takes place.

It is clear that beating applied to an already naked body would be a much less effective turn-on, as an acquiescent and practised floggee in the *Fashionable Lectures* (1872) well knows: 'Just as he heard them at the door, he jumped out of bed, and slipped on his breeches, that he might have the pleasure of her taking them off' (p. 103). As a rule, moreover, only the buttocks themselves are bared, their nakedness and uniqueness being heightened by the fact that, during the beating, the rest of the body remains clothed. 'Nakedness must always in these matters be partial, to give the highest degree of satisfaction,' observes the aptly-named 'Philopodex' in *The Exhibition of Female Flagellants* (1872), and flagellant pornography is almost always true to this dictum. When a female is being beaten in modern pornography, the rest of her body is frequently clothed in black (black stockings seem to be an indispensable prop), the *chiaroscuro* thereby produced stressing further the pre-eminence of the buttocks. The fact that the beater is usually fully clothed also serves to emphasise the nakedness of the victim.

The parallel between this aspect of the flagellant ceremony and conventional strip-tease is obvious: the technique of denudation is exactly similar except that here, instead of breasts and genitals, it is the buttocks that are exposed:

> I assisted to tie her up, and unfastening her drawers Jane drew them well down, whilst Mrs Mansell pinned up her chemise, fully exposing the broad expanse of her glorious buttocks, the brilliant whiteness of her skin showing to perfection by [sic] the dazzling glare of the well lighted room.[2]

The second observation grows out of the first. It is that, in flagellant pornography as in the traditional beatings inflicted in the private schools of England, the buttocks of the culprit are habitually disposed by the active partner so as to accentuate their roundness, submissiveness and vulnerability. Just as in these writings flagellation is rarely, if ever, inflicted on an already naked body, or on a fully clothed one, so it is unusual to find it applied to the buttocks of a person standing upright. All flagellants, it seems, would agree with the wit who remarked in the *Gentleman's Magazine* of January 1735 that the rod should be applied 'in an Angle of about 45 Degrees. For it is a Maxim that this does the Business far more effectually than the most violent Perpendicular Impression' (p.17). The bent-over position is always insisted upon in flagellant pornography, whether the victim be forced to touch his or her toes, bend over an Etonian-style flogging-block, a stool, table or chair, or adopt the over-the-knee posture. Sometimes mechanical means are used to secure the victim, thereby emphasising his or her powerlessness (we saw an elaborate example of this in the real-life methods described by Mrs Walter Smith of Clifton). Countless instances could be given of this fascination with the bent-over position:

> In the [victim's] act of kneeling, Mama whisks up her skirts behind, packs them tight-drawn beneath the captor's hands, lifts and tucks in the pendant front, and moulds the doomed posteriors to a crescent form.[3]
> (*The Romance of Chastisement*, 1866)

[2] 'Miss Coote's Confession', in *The Pearl*, no.1. August 1879.
[3] Quoted by Pearsall (1972), p.414.

During this interval a kind of ottoman, called by the pupils the 'block', had been wheeled up to the head of the room. This was covered with a dark red baize, and was so constructed that the head and shoulders and part of the back were so slanted as to be nearly concealed from view, while the lower part of the back and legs were fully exposed. (*Town Talk*, 15 March 1884, p.3)

I was made to kneel on a low deal table on my knees and elbows, with my face against the table, and my back quite arched in – to give proper prominence to the part to be chastised. My skirts were then drawn over my head and my flesh bared. (*Society*, 10 October 1896)

The third point is that almost all flagellant literature stresses the *reddening* of the buttocks that takes place during whipping. At one end of the spectrum there is ecstasy at the sight of the lacerations and bleeding produced by vigorous applications of the birch rod (Swinburne is the great authority here); at the other, a more moderate delight with the prospect of those 'snowy prominences' which 'in less than a couple of minutes' become 'all one red' (*Bon Ton Magazine*, January 1796, p.419).

Current American magazines such as *Sting* emphasise this redness by applying ludicrous patches of rouge to the bottoms of the models who pose for the colour photographs that accompany the texts – patches rather than stroke-marks because, it seems, in America table tennis bats and 'paddles' are the preferred instruments of castigation. In modern England the cane holds pride of place in flagellant pornography; and its marks are frequently represented by lipstick strokes laid across the buttocks.

Along with the interest in the reddening of the victim's buttocks goes a fascination on the part of both beater and audience with the twitchings and writhings of the flagellated part. Open any flagellant story at any page and you are bound to come across this sort of description:

Mademoiselle makes desperate efforts to release herself, but Lady Clara and Cecile also help to keep her down, all apparently highly excited by the sight of her excoriated blushing bottom, adding their remarks, such as, 'Bravo, Bravo, Rosie, you didn't think she would catch it so, how delightful to see her writhe and plunge in pain, to hear her scream, and help to keep her down,' till at last the surprised victim begs and prays for pardon, crying to be let off, with tears in her eyes. (*Miss Coote's Confession*, *The Pearl*, no. 4, October 1879)

Finally, it can be stated with confidence that, in stressing the buttocks, flagellant pornography regularly avoids or plays down awareness of the genitals, whether male or female. When we consider that, if a woman is in the bent-over position, the vulva protrudes noticeably, and that the uncovering of the male buttocks automatically involves some baring of the genitals, the omission can be seen to be significant. Modern flagellant magazines confirm the Victorian material: in these publications, photographs portraying female posteriors tend to be taken from the side. Direct visual contact with the genitals and pubic hair is thus largely obviated; and when a view from behind is provided, the genital area is often shaded or indistinct.

The fact that the writers of beating stories do not dwell on the female genitals does not mean, of course, that in flagellant pornography there is no sexual intercourse. On the contrary, the whole point of the exercise is to overcome impotence and, having been whipped to erection, the 'victims' are as a rule only too happy to effect penetration of the nearest complaisant vagina. But the genitals, of themselves, do not excite the sexual appetite of the flagellant. He does not enjoy looking at them (remember Rodin) or presumably even thinking about them. But once he is erect and 'a man again', he is extremely anxious to prove that he is potent.

The flagellant ceremony

The beatings described in pornography are, invariably, ritualistic in character. Nothing unforeseen is ever allowed to happen, and the ceremony, carried out with great solemnity, proceeds according to a set plan, any variation in which would result in a loss of meaning, power and effectiveness: the spell would be broken, the magic dispersed. Spontaneity is totally absent from these performances.

The officiant in the flagellant ritual tends to be specially dressed for the occasion. We have seen that, in Victorian brothels, the fair disciplinarians were often called and dressed as 'nurses' or 'governesses' (the birching madame in *My Secret Life* is referred to as the 'abbess').[4] The pedagogue's gown and demeanour are, of course, the requisite props when the setting is the schoolroom (which it very often, perhaps usually, is), and the gown may be worn by both men and women. With the donning of this official garb the person often changes or is felt to change from a normal human being into some sort of almost supernatural figure. The Rev. A.G. L'Estrange's description of an Eton birching, which we saw in Chapter Three, exactly captures

---

[4] This enormous Victorian work was issued in a complete, unexpurgated edition by the Grove Press, New York, in 1966 with an introduction by G. Legman.

this aspect of the fantasy, and I hope I may be forgiven for repeating part of it here:

> The block, with all its appalling associations, had been drawn forth, and beside it stood two collegers in their long black gowns, as if about to assist at a real execution. The centre of the scene was formed by the doctor himself; but how changed from the obsequious courtier of yesterday! There he stood, stern and statuesque, with his nose sublimely elevated, and the birch rod in his hand – eternal thunder 'settled on his head'. (pp. 17-18)

Here Hawtrey, the man, has become something else – almost a medium through whom the God of Flagellation (we recall that Hawtrey was a doctor of divinity) immolates his victims.

When the beater is female, and not in the guise of a strict schoolmistress, she is usually decked out in aristocratic finery as befits her station. Riding gear is another favourite, as James Joyce was not unaware. The Honourable Mrs Mervyn Talboys in *Ulysses*, from whom Bloom tinglingly awaits a 'refined birching to stimulate the circulation', is lovingly described as: 'In amazon costume, hard hat, jackboots cockspurred, vermilion waistcoat, fawn musketeer gauntlets with braided drums, long train held up and hunting crop with which she strikes her welt constantly'.[5]

Occasionally, too, the person beaten may be got up in a special costume. Mr Barville requires Fanny Hill to be dressed 'all in the finest linen and a thorough white uniform: gown, petticoat, stockings, and satin slippers, like a victim led to sacrifice' (p.174). The flagellant ritual is indeed a form of sacrifice, as is the Mass, and this aspect is made explicit in its Etonian version, the 'execution' at the 'block'. A sacrifice demands, by definition, a god or supreme authority who demands it or may be propitiated by it, and in the next chapter we shall inquire into the identity of this deity. Also into the nature of the crime committed by the victim.

Another point of contact between the flagellant and religious rituals is that there are always spectators present. Sometimes, it is true, the scene is enacted between only the beater and the victim, but even then the eye of the fantasy-producer is present. Usually, as well as the eye of the narrator, there are other witnesses. Invariably these spectators follow the proceedings with rapt attention. Nothing escapes them,

---

[5] *Ulysses* (The Bodley Head, 1955), pp. 444-5. Mrs Talboys is accompanied by two other aristocratic ladies whose names might have been taken from any Victorian flagellant story: Mrs Bellingham and Mrs Yelverton Barry (Swinburne's *The Flogging-Block* is ascribed to Bertram Bellingham).

every detail is noticed. The spectators never show pity for the victim, and indeed often express their pleasure quite openly. As one character under the rod in Swinburne's *The Flogging-Block* puts it, accurately enough: 'Each Pang that thrills my Buttocks through and through/Torture to me, is Ecstasy to you.' While the victim may on occasion show pleasure, the spectators are all like the boy referred to in Swinburne's piece 'Reginald's Flogging', published in *The Whippingham Papers*:

I never knew anyone take such delight
When a schoolfellow has to·be whipped, in the sight.
I believe – his delight is so frank and explicit –
He would rather himself have a whipping than miss it.

There can be no doubt – and this ties in with what was said earlier about the insistence on the buttocks – that the flagellant fantasy has a very strong voyeuristic component.

What is said by victim and beater during the ceremony is also important. And if the spectators are as a rule silent during the scene it is partly because they wish to hear these exchanges. Indeed, one is tempted to call the spectators the congregation, for they are certainly not passive witnesses. The language of the ceremony tends to be stereotyped, liturgical, with commands and responses of an almost antiphonal quality. Here again the influence of actual practice at the preparatory and public schools seems undeniable. The usual pattern of language is: command (to remove or lower trousers, etc., to bend over); response of the victim (hesitation, resistance, request to be let off, etc.); second command (more stentorian this time). The second command is invariably obeyed. The continuation of the L'Estrange passage just quoted exactly captures this aspect of the ceremony:

'Go down!' commanded the doctor airily.
'Please, sir, it's my first fault,' urged Spratt, in a tone of injured innocence.
'Why, you were here last week!' replied the doctor indignantly.
'No; please, sir, that was my major' (elder brother).
'I know your face perfectly,' insisted the doctor.
'And more than his face,' suggested a boy behind him.
'At all events,' concluded the doctor, 'I only allow first fault for lesson. Go down!' (p.18)

All the flagellant works I have read stress the importance of this command that brooks of no resistance. It is clearly vital to the whole phenomenon.[6] Swinburne again:

'What made you late, Sir?' with a smile and frown
  Of outward wrath and cruel inward joy,
Replied the master, 'Were you not up town
  On some vain errand for some foolish boy?'
No answer. 'Clifford, take your trousers down.'
  With piteous eyes uplifted, the poor boy
Just faltered, 'Please, Sir,' and could get no farther.
  Again, that voice, 'Take down your trousers, Arthur.'
('Arthur's Flogging', in *The Whippingham Papers*)

The ceremonies represented in the flagellant fantasy fall into two well-defined categories – that in which the events are described as really happening, with no acknowledged 'pretence', and that in which the characters are aware that they are acting out a fantasy in order to excite themselves sexually.

Let us look to begin with at the first, and much larger, category. Here the victim, in nine cases out of ten, is a child and the beater an all-powerful adult whose authority cannot be questioned: typically a schoolmaster acting *in loco parentis*. Precisely because such whippings have been common in England, no 'acting out' is necessary in this fantasy. Verisimilitude is complete. The same holds true of those scenes depicting 'old-fashioned' nursery whippings. There are any number of texts describing such inflictions, and we have seen some of them already in the chapter on flagellant correspondence columns. In pornography, as in these 'respectable' accounts, the pattern is always the same: a warning is given, a misdeed is committed, sentence is pronounced and, at a specified time, the execution takes place. In line with the ritual nature of flagellation, the punishment is never meted out spontaneously. The real-life beaters and upholders of the rod, fully aware of the stimulating suspense-element in flagellation, have always been able to justify the time-lapse between crime and retribution on the grounds that it is morally wrong to punish in anger. We see this ploy used *ad nauseam* in the flagellant correspondence

---

[6] Compare Reik (1962): 'Dialogues during the masochistic phantasy are pretty frequent. Certain accents or expressions are then deemed very important, the cadence of a certain sentence is tasted voluptuously ... In one case a sentence used by the patient's father – "Be careful you don't do it again" – became the content of such a phantasy scene and had to be repeated again and again with a definite melody. The son, who had to be on his knees, would ask with a certain fearful expression, "May I get up?" ' (p.53).

columns of the nineteenth century. '*Never birch when angry,*' Mrs Walter
Smith emphasised, and the cry was repeated on all sides.

Sometimes Victorian flagellant pornography is explicit about the
sexual response of the 'victim', and one is reminded of Rousseau[7] and
those cases in Krafft-Ebing in which patients admitted that their first
sexual feelings had manifested themselves while being beaten on the
buttocks as children. The following passage from *The Romance of Lust*
(1873-6) is one of the most acute I have come across, and can serve as
an example of the first category of fantasy in which the ceremony is
played straight, without 'pretence'. The flagellator is Miss Evelyn,
aged 22, who is governess to Mary (aged 14), Eliza (13) and the
narrator, Charles (15). The passage deserves quotation in full, for it
contains almost all the elements essential to the flagellant fantasy:

'Now, Charles, I give you ten minutes longer to finish that sum, if not
done in that time I shall whip you; you are exhibiting the mere spirit of
idleness. I do not know what has come over you, but if persisted in, you
shall certainly be punished.'

The idea of the beautiful Miss Evelyn whipping my bare bottom did not
tend to calm my excitement; on the contrary, it turned my lewd thoughts
upon the beauties of her person, which I had so often furtively gazed upon.

It was close upon four o'clock, at which hour we always broke up for a
run in the garden for an hour, and during this period I had resolved to
begin instructing Mary in the secret mysteries [of sex] I had so lately been
a witness to. But fate had ordered it otherwise, and I was to receive my
first practical lesson and be initiated on the person of a riper and more
beautiful woman. At four o'clock I had done nothing with my task – Miss
Evelyn looked grave –

'Mary and Eliza, you may go out, Charles will remain here.'

My sisters, simply imagining that I was kept in to finish my lessons, ran
into the garden. Miss Evelyn turned the key in the door, opened a
cupboard, and took out a new rod, small, flexible as a whalebone, and
neatly tied up with blue ribbon. Now, my blood coursed through my veins,
and my fingers trembled so that I could hardly hold my pencil.

'Put down your slate, Charles, and come to me.'

I obeyed, and stood before my beautiful governess, with a strange
commixture of fear and desire.

'Unfasten your braces, and pull down your trousers.'

I commenced doing this, though but very slowly. Angry at my delay her
delicate fingers speedily accomplished the work. My trousers fell to my
feet.

[7] In the *Fashionable Lectures* and *Exhibition of Female Flagellants* there are frequent
references to Rousseau. In the former volume the narrator remarks that 'Rousseau,
perhaps, is the only man who has ever made a public confession of this unaccountable
taste' (p.25).

'Place yourself across my knees.'

Tremblingly, with the same commixture of feeling, I obeyed. Her silk dress was drawn up to prevent its being creased – my naked flesh pressed against her snowy white petticoats. A delicate perfume of violet and vervain assailed my olfactory nerves. As I felt her soft and delicate fingers drawing up my shirt, and passing over my bare posteriors, while the warmth of her palpy forms beneath me penetrated my flesh, nature exerted her power, and my prick began to swell out to a most painful extent. I had but little time, however, to notice this before a rapid succession of the most cruel cuts lacerated my bottom.

'Oh, dear! Oh, dear! Oh, dear! Oh, Miss Evelyn. I will do the sum if you will only forgive me. Oh, oh, oh, etc.'

Holding me firmly with her left arm, Miss Evelyn used the rod most unmercifully. At first the pain was excruciating, and I roared out as loud as I could, but gradually the pain ceased to be so acute, and was succeeded by the most delicious tickling sensation. My struggles at first had been so violent as to greatly disorder Miss Evelyn's petticoats, and to raise them up so as to expose to my delighted eyes her beautifully formed silk clad legs up to the knees, and even an inch or two of naked thighs above.

This, together with the intense tickling irritation communicated to my bottom, as well as the friction of my cock against the person of Miss Evelyn in my struggles, rendered me almost delirious, and I tossed and pushed myself about on her knees in a state of perfect frenzy as the blows continued to be showered down on my poor bottom. At last, the rod was worn to a stump, and I was pushed off her knees. As I rose before her, with my cheeks streaming with tears, my shirt was jutting out considerably in front in an unmistakeable and most prominent manner, and my prick was at the same time throbbing beneath it with convulsive jerks, which I could by no means restrain.

Miss Evelyn glared at the projection in naked astonishment, and her open eyes were fixed upon it as I stood rubbing my bottom and crying, without attempting to move or button-up my trousers. She continued for a minute or two to stare at the object of attraction, flushing scarlet up to her forehead, and then she suddenly seemed to recollect herself, drew a heavy breath, and rapidly left the room. She did not return until after my sisters came back from the garden, and seemed still confused, and avoided fixing her eye upon me. (I, pp. 18-20)

The characters in the second category of fantasy are aware that they are acting a part, and are much concerned with points of detail, role-playing and so on. The flagellant scene in *Fanny Hill* exemplifies an early stage in such elaborations. In it the resistance to being flogged, which in real life must often have been expressed in terms akin to those we heard in the passage from L'Estrange, has become a *pretence*: 'I led him then to the bench, and according to my cue, play'd at forcing him to lie down: which, after some little show of reluctance, for form's sake, he submitted to' (p.176).

Among the flagellant books that recognise fantasy for what it is, the two volumes of *The Exhibition of Female Flagellants* (1872) are outstanding. In these collections of flagellant fantasies (the italics are mine) a character 'begged I would suffer her *to represent my niece*' (I, p.11); 'I am afraid I shall be a bungler,' admits a 'blushing charmer', 'I never whipped anyone in my life' (I, p.15). With persuasion a group of inexperienced ladies agree to take part in a flagellant play: 'she instantly, by desire, *assumed the character* of Flirtilla's governess' (I, p.16). The strict governess, of course, is a great favourite with the flagellants. 'You remember my compliment,' someone recalls, 'when you first charmed me with the rod *in the character* of a governess' (I, p.19); another lady is required 'to *assume the character of* my offended governante instantly' (I, p.25). Stepmothers, mothers and aunts are also in demand:

> She would *usurp the character of* a stepmother (a character he was very fond of as there is in general much severity connected with it). (II, p.31)

> She took it up, and, *assuming* a severe look, she, *in the character* of an angry mother, whipped him as severely as she could. (II, p.58)

> He told me I must *act the part of* a mother, and whip him well for not going to school. (II, p.78)

> This lady *used to assume with him the character* of a severe aunt. (I, p.52)

There seems to be no doubt that Swinburne was the author of 'Hints on Flogging ...', published in the anonymous *The Whippingham Papers*. The writer is perceptive on the 'acting out' aspect of the flagellant ritual (the italics are his):

> There should be simulated on the part of the flogger, passionate anger with her subject, and on the part of the floggee or patient, powerless to resist the punishment inflicted, *fear of the operation, and a desire to escape the punishment*.

The author proposes, moreover, that, in order to discover the true desires of the flagellant clients who attend her brothel, the lady should

> keep a small book containing a series of birch scenes, written in a dramatic form, which, when your visitor calls, you should put into his hands, and ask him which of them he would like to enact with you. His part would be got up in a moment, and you, of course, would be up in the ladies' parts of all of them.

These scenes, of which the author provides some examples, will serve 'as plans or outlines of the relations in which you would pretend to stand towards one another during the operation, the style of conversation you should use, and the performance you should go through'. Swinburne, who as we have seen frequented a flagellant brothel in St John's Wood, obviously knew exactly what he was talking about.

Whichever category a flagellant story may belong to, however, is ultimately irrelevant, since they all express the same phenomenon: the fixation of a childhood fantasy and its compulsive re-enactment in later life when the adult finds that, without it, he is impotent. The setting of the ceremony (schoolroom, nursery, boudoir) confirms the infantility of the fantasy, as does the acknowledgment of 'acting out' on the part of many characters appearing in the stories.

Who's who in the flagellant fantasy?

In trying to sort out the identities of the participants in the flagellant fantasy we meet an immediate difficulty; for, as psychoanalysis has shown, the *manifest*, surface content of fantasies, like that of dreams, may not correspond to their *latent* content. This is likely to be particularly so when the fantasy carries a charge of guilt or shame, in which case the person producing the fantasy may be loath to admit, to himself or others, its true significance. This resistance may find expression in the mind's ability to alter the identities of the characters in the fantasy, to mask their true identity. Thus one can imagine that, in the case of a repressed homosexual, for example, a fantasy might contain a girlish figure concealing that of a boy; or that the ashamed masochist might conjure up the picture of someone else being beaten rather than visualise himself or herself in that situation.

The identification of the participants in flagellant fantasies is therefore complicated. In each case numerous questions present themselves. Does the person producing the fantasy identify with the person being beaten, or with the beater? Is he or she, that is, 'masochistic' or 'sadistic'? Or both at the same time, that is 'sado-masochistic'? Is Victorian flagellant pornography predominantly masochistic or sadistic? As regards the latter question, the authorities I have read seem to be at variance. In *The Other Victorians*, Steven Marcus asks 'Why is it that this literature is overwhelmingly masochistic rather than sadistic in its coloration?' (p.267). Peter Fryer, on the other hand, remarks in *Private Case – Public Scandal*: 'So far we have examined fantasies written almost exclusively from the point of view of the sadist or the dominant partner. Surprisingly few

English erotica have been written from the opposite point of view' (p.121). You can hardly get further apart than that; and such divergences, it seems to me, can only be explained by confusion between the manifest and latent meanings of the flagellant fantasy.

In the next chapter we shall enquire into these meanings more carefully. For the moment let us look at the *manifest* characteristics of the partners in the flagellant fantasy.

The principal fantasy of Victorian flagellant pornography is that women positively revel in administering the birch. Not just the occasional woman, we are asked to believe, but all women are potential flagellants.

All those researchers who have written on the subject agree that, in Victorian pornography, the female beaters vastly outnumber the male. When we consider that, in real life, almost all the beating was done by men, this finding assumes the utmost importance.

Ashbee, after asserting that 'the propensity which the English most cherish is undoubtedly Flagellation' (*Index*, p.xl), proceeds to state as a fact (a) that only in England 'can be found men who experience a pleasure rather in receiving than in administering the birch' and (b) that women are especially fond of inflicting flagellation. Talking of some famous flagellant prostitutes in London he says:

Many of these women, there can be little doubt, took an interest, if not a pleasure, in their vocation. It is a well known fact that women are, and always have been, even more fond of wielding the rod than men, and this passion pervades the higher, rather than the lower classes. (*Index*, pp. xlvi-xlvii)

Ashbee himself was surely something of a flagellant, and to read this passage attentively is to observe the pornographic mind in action. Its dishonesty and inaccuracy are transparent, the statement 'there can be little doubt' (that is, there *may* be some doubt), and the hesitation about 'interest' and 'pleasure', leading straight into a totally unjustified assertion ('it is a well known fact') that 'women are, and always have been' (always?) lovers of the rod. In his three bibliographies of erotica, Ashbee has a lot to say about flagellation, and clearly knows his subject well. But at no point does he produce any hard evidence in support of his claim that women derive overt sexual pleasure from inflicting whippings. The truth is that, like most men attracted by flagellation, Ashbee would like to believe that such ladies really exist – but knows in his heart that they don't. He would like us to believe it too:

> Women, as I have elsewhere remarked, delight in administering the birch;
> and innumerable are the tales of schoolmistresses whipping their pupils,
> mothers, and especially mothers-in-law, their children, and taking grim
> pleasure in the operation. (*Centuria*, p.456)

Here again we see the weakness of the reasoning, a general statement
about the whipping proclivities of women being illustrated by nothing
better than 'innumerable tales'.

Whenever Ashbee touches on the subject of flagellation the same
thing happens – unsigned documents are produced, fantasy is
presented as fact, obvious pornography becomes 'an authentic
memoir' serving as 'proof' that women enjoy flagellation. Ashbee's
conclusion?:

> Evidence there is then, more than sufficient, to show that women take
> delight in chastising others, that they are more prone to it, and more
> insatiable and obdurate than the sterner sex. (*Catena*, p.461)

It is difficult not to conclude that Ashbee's propagation of the myth
of the flagellant female was undertaken consciously. Here was a man
of the world with a wide range of acquaintance in many countries,
who must have known that, with occasional exceptions perhaps,
whipping ladies existed only in brothels and the fantasies of men like
himself. Steven Marcus, however, sees Ashbee as a *victim* of his own
fantasies. As regards whipping females: 'There is no evidence in
support of this contention, there never was any, and if Ashbee had
been able to disentangle himself from the material that he reproduces
in his pages he would have been able without much effort to make this
out' (p.61). It seems to me more likely that Ashbee was simply
luxuriating in fantasy – and betraying at the same time his italicised
promise at the beginning of the *Index Librorum Prohibitorum* to give '*facts
and facts only*' (p.xlix).

It is relevant to insist again that, from Krafft-Ebing onwards,
psychiatrists have come across only a tiny number of sadistic female
flagellants. We may agree, I believe, that the whole thing is a male
fantasy. Anthony Storr (1965) puts it thus:

> In clinical practice, at any rate, it is not very uncommon to find intensely
> masochistic women who desire to be subjugated, beaten, and ill-treated
> before they can be fully erotically aroused: but it is rare to find women
> who actually want to beat or ill-treat men in order to obtain erotic
> satisfaction ... Women in top boots cracking whips are generally either
> creatures of the masochistic male's imagination, or else prostitutes
> obliging their clients by trying to fulfil their phantasies. (p.44)

What are the flagellant ladies of Victorian pornography like? Not puny, flat-chested and hesitant, certainly. Without exception those I have come across are well-endowed physically, and Miss Evelyn, whom we met in the passage quoted from *The Romance of Lust*, may be taken as a fair example of the type.

In particular the writers seem to be fascinated by the fullness and beauty of the fair beaters' breasts. A character in the *Fashionable Lectures* recalls: 'She, then, at my request, took her handkerchief from her neck, that I might see her lovely bosom while she was whipping me' (p.47). Jean-Jacques Rousseau admitted that he had a breast fixation,[8] and Gertrud Lenzer has found a similar obsession in Sacher-Masoch: 'Although Sacher-Masoch is fascinated by the female breast, overt genital phantasies are disavowed in his writing' (p.304). Victorian flagellant engravings also stress the breasts (see Plates 27 and 28).

We have already quoted from 'Hints on Flogging ...'. The author, well versed in matters of the birch, knows exactly what sort of body he requires in a flagellant 'governess':

> Your personal qualifications for *une fouetteuse* are excellent. You are just about the right age, for you cannot be more than thirty. Your figure, as it should, inclines decidedly to plumpness, and your arms are strong and finely rounded. With the right sleeve turned up, the movement of the biceps muscle when you are birching must be most fetching to beholders, especially if a good view can also be obtained of the round full breasts while they are heaving with exertion.

But although it is true that 'round full breasts' are an indispensable endowment of the ideal flagellant female, Steven Marcus exaggerates, I think, when he states that the latter is habitually 'an immense female figure' (p.259), a being of 'gigantic size' (p.261). This is by no means usually so. It appears that Marcus is basing his generalisation on passages such as the following (which he takes, without giving the reference, from *The Romance of Chastisement* (1866)):

> Martinet meanwhile had taken off her loose morning wrapper, and armed herself with a rod, formed, not of canes and cuttings like the rest, but of stout birch stems with innumerable branches, like a tree in miniature.
> With this weapon in her hand, how terrible she appeared! Juno

[8] 'Jamais mon coeur ni mes sens n'ont su voir une femme dans quelqu'un qui n'eût pas des tétons' (*Confessions*, II, Book 9, p.163). Mme de Warens ('Maman', as Rousseau called her, significantly) seems to have been well-endowed, as no doubt was the long-suffering Thérèse.

deprived of the apple might have looked like her. Her splendid arms and neck were bare, her cheeks flamed, her huge breasts were heaving. Speech was too weak, the graces of birching were ignored, nothing short of savage *beating* could satisfy her present need of vengeance. (Marcus, p.261)

A fury indeed, but not any more typical of the flagellant females I met in book after book than the ferocious Mrs Trimmer in the passage from *Madam Birchini's Dance* (1872) quoted by Marcus a few pages earlier, or than the redoubtable Lady Termagant Flaybum in *The Sublime of Flagellation* (1872) (see Plate 27). These enormous females, I believe, are the exception rather than the rule: exaggerated versions of the passive flagellant's ideal woman. Far more common is the Miss Evelyn type whom we saw administering her birch in *The Romance of Lust*. Given the huge demand for flagellant pornography that existed in the nineteenth century, it is likely that many hack writers were engaged by publishers to try their hand at the genre, with a view to giving the flagellants what it was thought they wanted. I doubt very much if Martinet and Mrs Trimmer satisfied that demand.

One other aspect of the beater should be mentioned here: her 'countenance'. When the lady is provoked, or simulating anger, she assumes that authoritative, severe expression which flagellants apparently crave. The writers notice especially the look in her eye:

If I was struck with her figure, I was no less so by the haughty severity of her countenance and carriage; her very eyes flashed fire.[9] (*Bon Ton Magazine*, June 1792, p.136)

She had also that haughty and severe look that men delight in who are fond of tasting the rod from the hand of a woman. (*Exhibition of Female Flagellants*, I, p.41)

She approached him with a countenance expressive of the utmost severity, blended with a smile of pleasure. (*Fashionable Lectures*, p.30)

A classical description of such a lady comes in *The Exhibition of Female Flagellants* in a passage quoted by Marcus and which Ashbee also singled out:

Know then thou silly girl, (said Flirtilla) there is a manner in handling this sceptre of felicity, that few ladies are happy in: it is not the impassioned and awkward brandish of a vulgar female that can charm,

[9] In 1909 James Joyce wrote to his wife, Nora Barnacle: 'Tonight I have an idea madder than usual. I feel I would like to be flogged by you. I would like to see your eyes blazing with anger' (*Selected Letters of James Joyce*, edited by Richard Ellmann, Faber and Faber, 1975, p.166).

but the deliberate and elegant manner of a woman of rank and fashion, who displays all that dignity in every action, even to the flirting of her fan, that leaves an indelible wound. What a difference between high and low-life in this particular! To see a vulgar woman when provoked by her children, seize them as a tyger would a lamb, rudely expose their posteriors, and correct them with an open hand, or a rod more like a broom than a neat collection of twigs elegantly tied together; while a well-bred lady, coolly and deliberately brings her child or pupil to task, and when in error, so as to deserve punishment, commands the incorrigible Miss to bring her the rod, go on her knees, and beg with uplifted hands an excellent whipping; which ceremony gone through, she commands her to lye across her lap, or to mount on her maid's shoulders, and then with the loveliest hands imaginable removes every impediment from the whimpering lady's b-e, who all the time, with tears, and intreaties of the sweetest kind implores her dear mother or governess, to pardon her; all which the lovely disciplinarian listens to with the utmost delight, running over with rapture at the same time those white, angelic orbs, that in a few minutes she crimsons as deep as the finest rose, with a well-exercised and elegantly-handled rod! (*Index*, pp. 242-3)

Marcus found that, in Victorian flagellant pornography, 'only rarely is the accuser the mother herself' (p.258). This is also my own impression. In Marcus's view the beater is, however, 'almost always a surrogate from the mother'. Not only this, she is 'also unmistakeably the terrible mother, the phallic mother of childhood' (p.261). Without becoming involved in Freudian theory at this point, we can, I think, agree with Marcus that the beating females of the flagellant fantasy have unmistakeably *maternal* characteristics, in particular full breasts. Whether they are the Freudian 'terrible mother, the phallic mother of childhood' is another matter. Taking the *surface* details of these stories, it seems to me that the typical flagellant lady is hardly terrible, that her anger is largely pretence and that her relationship with the person beaten is a loving one, a sexual one, as is evidenced by the pleasure both parties take in the flogging.

It is well known that psychoanalysis claims that, behind the beating female or fused with her, there is a dominant male figure. Different analysts have looked at this male component from different points of view, but all believe it to be present. We shall need to return to this aspect of the subject in the next chapter.

Given the huge mass of Victorian flagellant pornography, and its difficulty of access, it would be dangerous to attempt a statistical generalisation about the 'manifest' sex of the person beaten in these endless elaborations of a single fantasy. Marcus wisely hasards no such numerical break-down: 'The sexual identity of the figure being beaten is remarkably labile. Sometimes he is represented as a boy, sometimes as a girl, sometimes as a combination of the two – a boy dressed as a girl, or the reverse' (p.262).

As regards the 'latent' sex of the victim, however, Marcus entertains no doubts:

> We know from the actual circumstances of this perversion, from the circumstances in which this literature was produced – its writers and the audience who made up its market – and from the internal circumstances of the literature itself that the figure being beaten is originally, finally, and always a boy. (pp.262-3)

Here, I think, it is impossible to disagree with Marcus.

Discussing the *mises en scène* in which these figures receive their whippings, Marcus remarks that 'Stories about life at school appear frequently, girls' schools, surprisingly, appearing with greater frequency" (p.258). I do not think this is really so surprising, particularly in view of the fact that Marcus believes that flagellation relates closely to homosexuality. What would be most surprising would be to find these fantasies set in preparatory or public schools, for that would mean that there was very little repression going on at all. Guilt and shame no doubt play a role in this transference from male to female establishments, the pretence of the girls' school acting as a form of defence against the recognition of the male component in the beater.

One of the striking features of Victorian pornography, in fact, is the almost complete absence of homosexual material – this at a time when homosexual relationships seem to have been common in the schools favoured by the privileged classes. Only repression can explain this absence, since pornography was free to do as it wished and would have catered for the demand had it existed.

Just as homosexual pornography was extremely rare in Victorian England, so it is very unusual to come across flagellant pornography in which boys are beaten by men. I have found only one or two cases out of the dozens of flagellant books I have read during my research for this study. The one great exception to the rule is Swinburne, whose flagellant writings are exclusively devoted to male-to-male beatings administered in settings of Etonian inspiration. These writings, in consequence, are of extreme interest and relevance to any examination of the male component in the flagellant fantasy.

In this chapter I have tried to isolate the principal characteristics of the flagellant fantasy as seen 'from outside'. What we must now do is to look beneath the surface content of the fantasy in order to inquire into its real meaning. Having a clear idea of what pornography reveals about the fantasy should help us to evaluate the various modern theories which have been elaborated to explain the flagellant phenomenon.

8

Towards an Understanding of Sexual Flagellation

Before we become involved in theoretical considerations, two points must be repeated. First, as we have seen throughout this book, it is clear that sexual flagellation concentrates exclusively on the buttocks. It follows that any investigation of the subject that fails to take this fact into account must be deficient. Secondly, it is equally certain that the flagellant obsession with the buttocks originates long before puberty. Krafft-Ebing provided ample evidence of this before the advent of psychoanalysis in his long section on masochism in *Psychopathia Sexualis*; and Freud's unequivocal assertion in 'A Child is Being Beaten; (1919) that it begins 'certainly before school age and not later than in the fifth or sixth year' (XVII, p.179) has been substantiated by other researchers.

The adult flagellant fantasy, in short, always derives from the infantile one. As with all the sexual perversions, we are dealing with a variety of arrested development, with a 'prephallic' *fixation* that puberty and subsequent experience have been unable to dislodge; and before we can hope to explain the tenacity of the fixation itself we need to examine its roots in childhood.

How, then, at such an early age, can the subject of gluteal flagellation acquire such a strong sexual significance? We have seen in the first chapter that, before psychoanalysis, the phenomenon was habitually explained in terms of 'reflex spinal influence', skin irritation and so on. We have seen, too, that the theory simply did not cover the facts. With the development of psychoanalysis shortly after the publication of Krafft-Ebing's great pioneer work, however, the cracks in the old Meibomian etiology soon became apparent; and it was not long before far more convincing theories were elaborated to explain the dynamics of sexual flagellation.

Flagellation and oral aggression

In 'A Child is Being Beaten' (1919), Freud concluded that, for girls, beating fantasies are primarily sadistic ('My father hates you, beats you and loves only me') and that they only become masochistic through the child's guilt about its aggressive behaviour, a guilt arising from the fear of retaliation by the all-powerful adult. For boys Freud could find no primary sadism, but admitted that he would not be at all surprised to do so at a later date. Freud believed at this time that 'the boy's beating-phantasy is ... passive from the very beginning, and is derived from a feminine attitude towards his father' (XVII, p.198).

In 1938 Edmund Bergler announced that he had 'discovered' Freud's missing, primary sadistic component in the male beating fantasy.[1] He located it in early *oral aggression* directed against the mother's breasts (for denial of milk, weaning, refusal to cuddle and so on). Bergler's formulation went: the child is aggressive towards the breast; the mother punishes it (by deprival, threats of withdrawal of love, slapping, etc.); the child becomes terrified of its aggressive feelings, which threaten to overwhelm it; this aggression is repressed and redirected against the child itself – to be anatomically precise, against its buttocks, 'which are identified with the breasts of the mother' (p.518).

Thus, for Bergler, it is fear of retaliation that lies at the heart of passive flagellation fantasies, both of the male and female variety. The Law of Talion has been recast: not an eye for an eye, or a tooth for a tooth, but 'you attack my breasts and I'll attack your buttocks'. Since the repressed aggression against the breasts continues to be active subconsciously, however, the need for punishment also continues, and so a fixation is established. Sadism, under the pressure of guilt, has been converted into masochism.[2]

It is impossible not to agree with Bergler that the child at the breast can be extremely demanding and aggressive. At times a wild animal. No modern analyst has written with more insight of the early relation of mother and baby than D.W. Winnicott in *The Child, the Family and*

---

[1] Edmund Bergler, 'Preliminary Phases of the Masculine Beating Fantasy', *Psychoanalytic Quarterly*, VII (1938), pp. 514-36.

[2] Compare Freud (1919): 'A sense of guilt is invariably the factor that transforms sadism into masochism' (XVII, p.189). And Reik (1962): 'Where there is no distinct and strong sadism, no masochistic inclination can or will develop' (p.217). In *The Ego and the Id* (1923), Freud drew attention to the paradox whereby 'the more a man controls his aggressiveness, the more intense becomes his ideal's inclination to aggressiveness against his ego. It is like a displacement, a turning round upon his own ego' (XIX, p.54).

the Outside World (1964). Discussing feeding, Winnicott remarks:

> Every function is elaborated in the psyche, and even at the beginning there is fantasy belonging to the excitement and experience of feeding. The fantasy, such as it is, is of a ruthless attack on the breast, and eventually on the mother, as the infant becomes able to perceive that it is the mother whose breast is attacked. There is a very strong aggressive element in the primitive love impulse which is the feeding impulse ... there develops a considerable degree of concern on account of the aggressive ideas as soon as the infant begins to put two and two together, and to find that the breast that was attacked and emptied is part of the mother. (1975, p.53)

If the mother is understanding and patient, all is well. She can help the child to cope with these powerful feelings, and the child will come to realise that, despite its rage, the breast does not disappear: its attacks have not driven the mother away, and love survives. If, on the other hand, the mother is unable to handle the child's aggressive tantrums, serious problems may develop.

In his 1938 paper Bergler did not make it clear why, in flagellation, the buttocks should take the place of the mother's breasts against which the original aggression was directed. It is not too difficult to see, however, that there are obvious similarities between the two parts of the body and that such a symbolic transference might well be feasible. Sadger (1913) observed that some of his patients identified the cleavage between the mother's breasts with the *crena ani*, the buttocks-cleavage.[3] And one of Ives Hendrick's patients 'had repeatedly associated his interest in his mother's buttocks as a child with the idea that they were round and stuck out behind like the breasts in front' (1933, pp. 80-1). In this connection it is also worth pointing out that Desmond Morris, in *The Naked Ape*, expresses the view that full breasts (quite unnecessary for feeding purposes) are imitation buttocks, developed as sexual signs when we became bipeds; and that, not long ago, a Parisian couturier designed a revolutionary garment calculated to give full prominence to the cleavage of the buttocks.

It is also possible, it seems to me, that the uncovering of the buttocks, which we have seen to be an essential feature of the flagellant ritual, might be a reminiscence of the uncovering of the mother's breasts prior to feeding. There might also be a correlation between the whiteness of both sets of protuberances.

In 1944 Bergler produced an article on blushing, the conclusions of which fitted neatly with those of his 1938 beating paper, although,

---

[3] J. Sadger, 'Über Gesässerotik', *Int. Zeitschrift für Psychoanalyse*, I (1913), pp. 351-8.

oddly, he himself was apparently unaware of the fact.[4] Bergler disagrees in this paper with those writers on blushing for whom repressed exhibitionism is the primary cause of the symptom; for him it derives, rather, from the repression of an original voyeurism (and related aggressive activities) directed against the maternal breast:[5]

> All of the child's multiform tendencies of devouring, tearing, biting, handling and gazing at the breast are understandably checked by the mother. This leads to the damming up of the oral component, to aggrievement at the blow to the baby's assumption of omnipotence and to reactive revenge. In boys, one solution of this conflict is a defiant reactive exhibition, somewhat according to the formula: 'I don't want to look at the mother's breast; I want to show myself.' The organ defensively displayed is the whole body ... but particularly the penis, the cheeks, and the buttocks. (p.44)

According to Bergler, this reactive exhibitionism is in turn repressed, to be replaced by the fear of blushing (erythrophobia) 'in which the aggressive and exhibitionistic wishes are no longer conscious' (p.45).

In this article Bergler does not mention flagellation, but its relation to blushing seems obvious. Bergler's passive flagellant and blusher coincide: both sufferers were children whose aggressive impulses towards the breast were punished and repressed; both are weighed down with guilt, even though they may not recognise that this is so; both, deep down, seethe with repressed rage and hatred; and both, especially where males are concerned, are sexually disturbed and more or less impotent.

In 1948 Bergler announced in a further paper that he had found more evidence since 1938 confirming his belief in the original, oral-

---

[4] Edmund Bergler, 'A New Approach to the Therapy of Erythrophobia', *Psychoanalytic Quarterly*, XIII (1944), pp. 43-59.

[5] Bergler's findings were not entirely new. Hitschmann (1943) had reported that the emotional problems of blushers relate more closely to mothers than to fathers, and that in blushing there is a close connection between the cheeks of the blusher's face and the maternal breasts. Hitschmann also pointed out that Benedek (1925) 'was among the first psychoanalysts to show that looking at and biting the mother's breasts can play an important part in the early development of erythrophobia' (p.441). Psychoanalysis tends to see a relationship between 'libidinal staring' and eating (incorporation); and in English we talk of 'devouring with a look', 'feasting the eyes' and so on. On staring and eating see also Fenichel (1937). The most comprehensive recent study of the subject I know is David W. Allen's monograph *The Fear of Looking or Scopophilic-Exhibitionistic Conflicts* (1974).

sadistic component in both the male and female beating fantasy.[6] Strangely, he still seemed not to have appreciated the connection between beating and blushing to which his own work pointed. We shall return to a consideration of this connection in a moment.

Flagellation and anal eroticism

Freud's first reference to sexual flagellation occurs in *Three Essays on the Theory of Sexuality* (1905) in a passage which indicates that, broadly, he was following at this time the Meibomian view recently revived by Krafft-Ebing (whose contribution to the *Three Essays* Freud acknowledges):

> Ever since Jean Jacques Rousseau's *Confessions*, it has been well known to all educationalists that the painful stimulation of the skin of the buttocks is one of the erotogenic roots of the *passive* instinct of cruelty (masochism). (VII, p.193)

In 'A Child is Being Beaten' (1919), Freud did not emphasise the buttocks, despite his comment that 'Now and again another characteristic detail of the content of the fantasy came to light: "A small child is being beaten on its naked bottom"' (XVII, p.181). There is no reference in the paper to that elaborate ritual of uncovering which we have observed to be ubiquitous in flagellant pornography and which is certainly an essential component of the fantasy; nor to the reddening and movements of the buttocks which flagellants evidently prize; in fact it seems that for Freud, at least in this paper, it is the punishment that counts and not its place of application.

Freud's reference to the buttocks in 'The Economic Problem of Masochism' (1924) marks an advance in this thinking:

> The part played in masochism by the nates, too, is easily understandable, apart from its obvious basis in reality. The nates are the part of the body which is given erotogenic preference in the sadistic-anal phase, like the breast in the oral phase and the penis in the genital phase. (XIX, p.165)

Some explanation is needed here. According to the Freudian model, the 'sadistic-anal' phase stretches roughly from the second until the sixth or seventh year of life. This phase Freud first charted in his *Three Essays on the Theory of Sexuality* (1905). Freud found that, while anal

---

[6] Edmund Bergler, 'Further Studies on Beating Fantasies', *Psychiatric Quarterly*, XXII (1948), pp. 480-6.

pleasure is certainly present from the earliest days of infancy, it is particularly marked from the second year, when the erotogenic mucous membrane of the rectum becomes the focal point of the child's sensual feelings. Many children soon discover, Freud observed, that by holding back their faeces a strange mixture of discomfort and pleasure may be produced in the rectum:

> Children who are making use of the susceptibility to erotogenic stimulation of the anal zone betray themselves by holding back their stool till its accumulation brings about violent muscular contractions and, as it passes through the anus, is able to produce powerful stimulation of the mucous membrane. In so doing it must no doubt cause not only painful but also highly pleasurable sensations. (VII, p.186)

In his book *Sexual Deviation* (1965, p.97), Anthony Storr describes the inter-action that may take place between anal and genital stimulation:

> That the anal area is erotically sensitive may not be familiar to everyone; but stimulation of the genitals normally causes contraction of the muscles around the anal orifice, and vice versa, and, after orgasm, the anal sphincter can be seen to open and close convulsively. Both men and women may be capable of reaching orgasm as a result of anal stimulation; and there is no doubt that some people enjoy being penetrated by this route.

Although Storr does not make the suggestion, it seems to me that the contraction of the anus which is bound to occur when the buttocks are whipped, or about to be whipped, is likely to have the effect of stimulating the genitals in the way he has described. Moreover, the flagellant pornographers often show their awareness of this tightening of the buttocks:

> The culprit should be told to relax the buttocks muscles before each stroke is applied, but this requires training and patience which the administrator must attend to. Of course, inevitably, involuntary clenching of the bottom cheeks will occur with most recipients after receiving a sound cut, but experience will minimise this. (*Janus*, vol.5, no.2 [1975], p.49)

Thus what Meibom and others supposed to be the physical effect of beating the *skin of the buttocks* might, in fact, be more correctly related to the tightening of the anus which is automatic when the buttocks are 'clenched'. And here one of Albert Moll's observations on the possible causes of the sexual excitement connected with beating of the buttocks seems relevant. 'It is possible also', wrote Moll, 'that another factor is in operation here, namely, the fact that the child undergoing punishment is commonly placed across the elder's knees in such a way that *pressure upon the child's genital organs* is almost unavoidable' (1912, p.320, Moll's italics).

Also of great importance, as Freud repeated in 'The Economic Problem of Masochism' (1924), is the child's realisation that control of the anal sphincters confers power over adults: withholding may provoke punishment, anger, cajoling, promise of rewards and so forth; giving be received with expressions of praise and love. The child quickly grasps the idea that excrement means power, influence; and for Freud it is at this point that an increase of sadistic aggression may enter into its behaviour. Otto Fenichel (1945) neatly summarised the psychoanalytical view of the relationship between the child and its environment during this critical period of its development:

> The anal-erotic drives meet in infancy with the training for cleanliness, and the way in which this training is carried out determines whether or not anal fixations result. The training may be too early, too late, too strict, too libidinous. If it is done too early, the typical result is a repression of anal eroticism, characterised by a superficial fear and obedience and a deep tendency toward rebellion; if it is done too late, rebellion and stubbornness are to be expected; strictness causes fixations because of the frustration involved; a libidinous behaviour on the part of the mother causes fixation because of gratification; however, such gratification is often a limited one, because the mother excites the child but prohibits gratification of the excitement. Laxatives are apt to increase tendencies toward dependency; enemas create enormous excitation and anxiety at the same time. (1972, p.305)

Of the categories outlined by Fenichel – ways of imposing or encouraging bowel control – that involving excessive strictness seems to be undoubtedly the one most relevant to flagellation. Jonathan Gathorne-Hardy has reminded us that middle- and upper-class Victorians were as unremitting in their insistence upon good behaviour on the chamber pot as they were about polite eating and other forms of obedience. Gathorne-Hardy found, moreover, that the nannies began to impose their toilet disciplines at a very early age. One of the victims told him:

> In some respects Nanny Moore was a fiend. I was never allowed to sit by myself in the lavatory and have a good dream. She always came in with me, and standing beside me holding sheets of Bromo paper, exhorted me to try. I tried until my rectum ached. Whatever turds I had must have

been made of stone. Nothing ever came out. My rectum ached, my tummy ached, with 'trying'. There she stood, a tyrant in her white starched apron, filling the lavatory with terror and misery. After what seemed to me hours of trying I would shuffle off the lavatory seat. Nanny would peer into the bowl: Nothing! I knew I was in for a dose of Gregory Powder or Syrup of Figs. I was the victim of a sort of bowel fever. I went to bed haunted with the guilt of not going and the thought of a dose the following day. (pp. 263-4)

It could hardly have been put better than that – the suppressed fury and rage, the unbearable agglomeration of emotions that could not be expressed. For the children of the well-off English classes, until at least the 1920s and 1930s, there seems to be no doubt that it was often, perhaps habitually, 'done too early' in Fenichel's phrase – and once it had been done the insistence on good bowel control was kept up unremittingly.

For many children the day-time cleanliness anxieties, severe as they were, must have been mild by comparison which those attaching to nocturnal bed-wetting. And it is no wonder that in many cases these anxieties came to adhere to the offending organs themselves; nor that, the organs being the same or in close proximity, sexuality, urination and excretion became inseparably fused in the minds of many children. From such a tangle of prohibitions and conflicting emotions, neurosis was bound to be a frequent way of escape.

Fenichel's reference to enemas in the passage quoted is of particular interest, for there is evidence that, of all the forms of anal meddling by adults, this one causes the greatest resentment. It also appears that enemas and flagellation may be especially related. With enemas may be linked gluteal injections and suppositories, the use of the latter having been frequent in the nurseries of the well-to-do. Nanny Moore's victim told Gathorne-Hardy:

Sometimes she would try to make me 'go' on the pot. If nothing happened she inserted a suppository up my rectum. I remember the horrible sensation of the ice-cold suppository and extreme humiliation to this day; the feeling of having something done to one, an invasion of privacy, was quite horrible. (p.264)

The experience of receiving an enema could be even worse than that, as the case-histories published by psychoanalysts prove – worse and sometimes more exciting. In his clinical practice, Sadger (1913) met many individuals whose interest in the anus and its sensations had been greatly stimulated by the reception of enemas during the 'anal-sadistic' period. One of his patients revealed that, as a child, he had become wildly excited by seeing his sister receive an enema, and proceeded, when they were alone, to place his penis between her buttocks in imitation of the syringe.

Freud, too, was aware of the powerful feelings which enemas can arouse. In 1931 he wrote:

> I believe that ... at the sadistic-anal level, the intense passive stimulation of the intestinal zone is responded to by an outbreak of desire for aggression which is manifested either directly as rage, or, in consequence of its suppression, as anxiety. (XXI, p.238)

Melitta Schmideberg (1948) found that, in some societies, the connection between enemas and punishment has been made explicit:

> Anal elements in beating ideas are obvious. Usually the child gets beaten on the buttocks (hand and cheek are substitutes); he usually first gets beaten for having dirtied himself. In Spain, children used to be punished by being given enemas, and the enemator hung on the wall of the nursery, as the birch rod in other countries.[7] A patient associated being beaten with the fear that the stick would be pushed into his anus. (p.304)

This association of enemas and punishment is also mentioned by Sandor Feldman (1951), one of whose patients, 'a twenty-four-year-old virgin', had a masturbatory fantasy 'in which she is punishing her mother by giving her an enema. In the fantasy her mother does not know that the patient is sexually excited, nor that she has an orgasm' (p.542).

All the papers I have read on anal eroticism and related problems agree that suppressed rage and fury are always present to a very marked degree in the victims of the kind of toilet training we have been discussing. Since, as we know, the Victorians did not tolerate any expression of anger and hatred from their children, we must conclude that, given the toilet disciplines of the day, these children were racked by the guilt deriving from suppressed rage. In many cases anal-erotic guilt must have compacted that already created during the oral phase, and reinforced the need for punishment. And again it may have seemed to such children that flagellation of the buttocks (in this case the directly offending part) was the appropriate atonement, both for aggression and for their forbidden interest in the pleasurable sensations arising in the rectum. Such a punishment imposed by an all-powerful adult would both liberate the offender from his guilt and allow

---

[7] Unfortunately Schmideberg does not give the source of this information concerning the punitive use of enemas in Spain.

him, temporarily, to experience erotic sensations without anxiety.

When one thinks of it, moreover, there are several points of contact between the flagellant ritual and the chamber pot or lavatory one (of which the ceremony of the enema is but a brutal extension). In both the child is dominated by a stern adult; both tend to take place at set times; in both the stress is on the buttocks, which are forcibly bared by the adult; in both there is tension, suspension and (hopefully) release. After the completion of both rituals all should be well – for a time. Melitta Schmideberg's remarks on the connections between beating and anality, while they may go a bit too far, seem nevertheless relevant here:

> For boys at school, it is a point of honour not to show emotion [during beating]; they take great interest in marks left by the beatings, and whether the boy punished shows traces of tears or pain. Traces of tears are a substitute for traces left by urine; dark marks on the buttocks for marks left by excreta. The control over pain and emotion demanded is a substitute for the control over excretions. It is well known that in beating phantasies and rituals, the number of strokes, the frequency of beating, and other obsessional elements play a role, indicative of their anal origin. (1948, pp. 304-5)

In analysing the Nanny's possible effect on the emotional life of the English ruling class, Jonathan Gathorne-Hardy sensed that there might be a connection between toilet training and the national obsession with flagellation, but felt unable to follow up his intuition. I think there can be no doubt that he was right, although other factors certainly contribute to flagellomania. To have had one's bowels under the control of one of those starched viragos must have been an agony, and it is no wonder that many Englishmen have been unable to free themselves emotionally from their early experience in the nursery. It is probably no accident that the nineteenth-century flagellant brothels were often run by 'nurses' whose uniforms assimilated them unmistakeably to Nanny figures. Moreover, there is evidence that some prostitutes today do a special line in the administration of enemas to their clients. And what' of the advertisements for 'high colonics' and 'Victorian enemas and colonics' that appear from time to time in such respectable publications as *The Observer*? Given what we know of anal eroticism, it is not surprising that such services should exist to cater to the sexual victims of faulty toilet training.

In view of the mass of evidence available, then, it seems probable that many people afflicted with passive beating fantasies are unfortunates who were too strictly dealt with at both the oral and the anal-sadistic stages in their development. Having been forced to stifle their aggression and desire for revenge, these people became prey to guilt, which in turn demanded punishment. I have not studied German methods of feeding and toilet training during the nineteenth century, but it would not surprise me to find that they were as rigorous as in England. What is certain is that Germany and England are the only two European countries which have developed flagellomania. In France, Spain and Italy there has traditionally been far more openness about breast feeding, far more tolerance of aggression and a far freer attitude towards defecation than in England. And none of these countries shows much interest in flagellation.

The punishment ritual

At this point I should like to say a few more words about the flagellant ritual which, as has been shown, hardly varies from fantasy to fantasy. Why is it that, for flagellation to be sexually exciting, it has to be carried out ceremonially?

The answer put forward by most analysts seems to be that it is precisely the lack of spontaneity in the ritual, the absence of unexpected violence, that reassures the anxious flagellant that he will not be caught unprepared. The flagellant – and this seems to be true of all masochists – plans his own punishment detail by detail in order to mitigate his anxiety and avert the possibility of being punished unexpectedly by somebody else. In this way he hopes that he may be able to avoid a more terrible retribution, perhaps even annihilation.

It is not surprising that many psychoanalytic writers believe that what the flagellant is really frightened of is castration. Even if one rejects the notion that castration fears are universal in early childhood, one may still accept that, where Victorian England was concerned, explicit castration threats were probably not uncommon. Circumcision, too, must also have seemed a castration threat to many children and been looked upon as a terrible punishment for having a penis.

Now, could it be that flagellation of the buttocks is, among other things, a form of substitute castration, in which the lethal cuts are administered to the buttocks rather than to the genitals? Such a hypothesis does not clash with the oral and anal-erotic explanation of the flagellomaniac obsession with the buttocks, rather it supports them. It should be noted, moreover, that in the beating fantasy the penis, which is hardly ever mentioned, is particularly well protected when the male is placed in the characteristic bent-over position. If flagellation is on one level a substitute for castration, this could be a further explanation of its powerful aphrodisiac effect on the victim; for, after realising that, despite the fact that his genitals have been exposed, they are not to be sacrificed, he may feel such relief that his libido is temporarily freed. The 'execution' is symbolic, and erection would be a natural consequence of the release from sexual anxiety.

From the point of view of the spectators, without whom, as has been noted, no flagellant fantasy is complete, there is little difficulty in understanding why the ceremony should be found exciting, especially in a society as sexually repressed as that of Victorian England. Guilt and shame about the genital and gluteal area, and the knot of emotions connected with the anus and its functions, would be bound to make such performances enthralling: collective guilt being assuaged through the individual sacrifice witnessed by the group. Moreover, there can be no doubt that, in permitting schoolchildren to be present at such ceremonies, the authorities ensured that repressed voyeurism and exhibitionism would find expression. Many writers have commented on the frantic efforts of masochists to be noticed, and it is likely that, in enjoying watching beatings being inflicted on other people's buttocks, the masochist is able to identify vicariously with the victim without being suspected. And even 'normal' boys, as has frequently been pointed out, are excited by witnessing beatings.

As regards the beater, all analytic writers seem to agree, as I have said, that behind the manifest beater – the stern, masterful female – there lurks a father figure. They also agree that, if the adult passive flagellant prefers to imagine himself being fustigated by a female, it is because he is unable to admit to himself that, when he was a child, the idea of being beaten by an authoritative male was sexually exciting to him. Thus Freud, in 'A Child is Being Beaten' (1919) writes: 'The boy evades his homosexuality by repressing and remodelling his unconscious phantasy' (XVII, p.199).

There seems to be no doubt that, in the original fantasy, the beater was undisguisedly male – either the father or a father substitute such as a schoolmaster or senior boy. Since the original object of the child's desires and aggression was largely the mother, however, the beating figure also incorporates certain strongly maternal characteristics, in particular the breasts (the boots and whips are of masculine derivation). As the male flagellant grows older, further female aspects are added, especially after puberty when, in the struggle to achieve genitality, it would be extremely painful to admit the existence of a male component in the beating fantasy. If one has to be beaten in order to achieve an erection, seems to say the flagellant, at least let the beater be a woman.

The rump-presentation theory

In *The Naked Ape* (1967), zoologist Desmond Morris elaborated a fascinating theory which helps to explain the sexual element in flagellation of the buttocks. It is a theory, moreover, which is consistent with the insights of psychoanalysis, although he does not say so. Morris notes that, in certain primates, both males and females may adopt in danger the female rump-presentation posture:

> When it displays towards the attacker in this way, it stimulates a sexual response which damps down the mood of aggression. In such situations, a dominant male *or* female will mount and pseudo-copulate with either a submissive male or a submissive female. (1969, p.138)

The point about rump-presentation, of course, is to offer not the buttocks but the vagina to the aggressive animal. Morris makes an extraordinary connection between rump-presentation and the form of beating with which we have been concerned throughout this book:

> The more specific case of the adoption of the female sexual rump-presentation posture as an appeasement gesture has virtually vanished, along with the disappearance of the original sexual posture itself. It is largely confined now to a form of schoolboy punishment, with rhythmic whipping replacing the rhythmic pelvic thrusts of the dominant male. It is doubtful whether schoolmasters would persist in this practice if they fully appreciated the fact that, in reality, they were performing an ancient primate form of ritual copulation with their pupils. They could just as well inflict pain on their victims without forcing them to adopt the bent-over submissive female posture. (It is significant that schoolgirls are rarely, if ever, beaten in this way – the sexual origins of the act would then become too obvious.) (pp 146-7)

The bent-over position, as readers of this book are aware, is always insisted upon in flagellant pornography – confirming Morris's derivation of the flagellant phenomenon. If Morris is right, both the sadistic and the masochistic components in beating are atavistic throwbacks, and it follows that schoolmasters and boys who are involved in such practices are bound to become excited sexually, no matter how unintentionally in the first instance. It also follows that anyone witnessing such whippings is likely to find his primate depths being stirred.

Morris makes it quite clear that, in his opinion, the instrument used in beating represents the erect phallus: 'The rhythmic pelvic thrusts have become symbolically modified into rhythmic blows of the cane' (p.147). Before him, many more or less psychoanalytic writers had made the same point. And Havelock Ellis wrote that 'the flagellant approaches a woman with the rod (itself a symbol of the penis and in some countries bearing names which are also applied to that organ)' – as in French, where *verge* has both meanings – 'to inflict on an intimate part of her body the signs of blushing and the spasmodic movements which are associated with sexual excitement' (1962, p.166). All flagellant fantasies, whether those expressed in pornography or those recorded by therapists, show a fetichistic obsession with the instrument of chastisement itself.

In 1903, the sexologist Iwan Bloch, noting that in the flagellant ceremony great stress is laid on the reddening of the buttocks, commented:

> When the flagellant brings about a reddening of the nates he is only seeking to produce a natural accompaniment of the *libido sexualis*. Confirmation of this is found in the fact that savage races paint their posteriors red to make them conspicuous, as is the case with apes. Perhaps the contrast of colour between the beaten and unbeaten parts has a sexual effect.[8] (1938, p.328)

Desmond Morris seems to be thinking along the same lines, although he does not mention Bloch:

> It has been imaginatively suggested by one authority[9] that the reason for sometimes forcing schoolboys to lower their trousers for the administration of the punishment is not related to increasing the pain, but rather to enabling the dominant male to witness the reddening of the buttocks as the beating proceeds, which so vividly recalls the flushing of the primate female hindquarters when in full sexual condition. (p.147)

Morris does not mention a possible connection between the blush of shame and the flushing of the buttocks, and we shall return to this aspect of the subject in a moment. What is certainly true is that the

---

[8] The original German (1903) reads: 'Indem also der Flagellant eine Rötung der Nates hervorbringt, sucht er nur eine natürliche Begleiterscheinung der Libido sexualis zu erzeugen. Hierfür spricht auch der Umstand, dass wilde Völker sich die Hinterbacken rot färben, so dass diese wie bei den Affen grell hervortreten. Nach Bloch übt auch der Kontrast der Farben zwischen den nichtflagellirten und den flagellirten Stellen eine sexuelle Wirkung aus' (p.366).

[9] The reference, it seems, is to Alex Comfort who writes in *Nature and Human Nature* (1966): 'Mammalian residues still persist in human sexuality, and we may underrate them. Blushing, and the interest of some individuals in the reddening of the buttocks produced by whipping, may contain echoes of the 'releaser' sex skin of lower primates' (1969, pp. 35-6).

reddening of the buttocks is always stressed in flagellant pornography, as we have seen.

Nor does Morris mention the movements of the buttocks which must inevitably occur during beating. Here, too, may perhaps be found further confirmation in support of the view that flagellation re-enacts rear-entry, primate copulation, or sexual display. As Bloch remarked, following his comments on the flushing of the buttocks in beating:

> A further attraction is provided by the violent movements and twitchings which affect the parts during chastisement, and which may be regarded as the simulation of certain movements during coitus.[10] (1938, p.329)

Flagellation and shame

It seems to me that the shame element in sexual flagellation has not been adequately assessed, either by psychoanalysts or by those who have written on flagellant pornography, Victorian or modern. Yet it is vital to the phenomenon, overlying the original guilt which gave rise to the need for punishment.

It must be obvious, to start with, that in a society in which the exhibition of the buttocks is taboo, their enforced revelation and punishment will tend to produce intense shame in the victim, the more so if the beating is public.

At Eton and other public schools, it must often have happened that innocent boys were birched in front of their fellows, the wrong man having been apprehended by the authorities; and one can imagine that in such cases the shame – and consequent resentment – would have been greatly increased. In the Navy, as has been said, several cadets attempted suicide in order to avoid birching. It was hardly surprising.

'But hast not thou then sense enough to know that thou ought'st to be most ashamed of thyself, when thou hast put another out of countenance?', asks a character in Congreve's *The Way of the World* of a friend who takes pleasure in making the ladies blush.[11] To make someone ashamed may be to make an enemy for life. As Kurt Riezler has written in a perceptive article on the social psychology of shame (1943):

---

[10] 'Die starken Bewegungen und Zuckungen, in welche die flagellirten Teile während der Züchtigung geraten und die ebenfalls als eine Imitation gewisser Bewegungen beim Coitus aufgefasst werden können, bilden einen weiteren Reiz' (1903, p.367).

[11] William Congreve, *The Way of the World* (1700), Act I, sc. 1.

Wise men in all countries and ages have advised their friends never to put a man to shame lest they create a kind of hate keener than the hate from any other source and slower to heal. Man resents being put to shame, being compelled to confront not only others but also himself, bared in all his meanness. There is no doubt about the strength and tenacity of the resentment created. (p.459)

The opponents of corporal punishment, especially of the 'lower discipline' variety, have always stressed the degrading, shame-inducing aspect of the practice; and some of its proponents have been honest enough to recognise the efficacy of the shame as well as the pain of beating. Thus Lord Chief Justice Goddard, addressing his fellow Lords:

> The birch, laid on by a chief warder who knew his job, gave a certain amount of pain while certainly leaving no marks – and I suppose a chief warder can lay it on as well as Dr Busby at Westminster and Dr Keates [sic] at Eton. It gave criminals a taste of something very unpleasant, and very often led to considerable ridicule when they came out. And nothing kills quicker than ridicule. (Hansard, *Lords*, 22 October 1952, col. 851)

The pornographers, too, have frequently made the same point – using it as a justification for applying the rod to the naked and not the clothed buttocks. For, truly, as Lord Goddard said, 'nothing kills quicker than ridicule':

> The old-fashioned whipping is much dreaded, not so much for the pain, as the feeling of shame and humiliation it seldom fails to produce. (*Town Talk*, 4 July 1885)

> The act of removing knickers, trousers and other undergarments induces a highly desirable sense of humiliation in the culprit, which can only enhance the effect of the punishment. (*Janus*, V, no.2 [1975], p.48)

Krafft-Ebing, Freud and other investigators found that their flagellant patients had the greatest difficulty in bringing themselves to confess to their fantasies. Freud wrote in 'A Child is Being Beaten' (1919) that

> It is only with hesitation that this phantasy is confessed to. Its first appearance is recollected with uncertainty. The analytic treatment of the topic is met by unmistakable resistance. Shame and a sense of guilt are perhaps more strongly excited in this connection than when similar accounts are given of memories of the beginning of sexual life. (XVII, p.179)

Those who have written on the emotion of shame – whether psychological investigators or creative writers – have stressed that, by its very nature, shame is related to the impulse to hide, to 'cover up'. As Darwin observed in his chapter on blushing in *The Expression of the Emotions in Man and Animals* (1872):

> Under a keen sense of shame there is a strong desire for concealment. We turn away the whole body, more especially the face, which we endeavour in some manner to hide. An ashamed person can hardly endure to meet the gaze of those present, so that he almost invariably casts down his eyes or looks askant.[12] (1873, pp. 321-2)

Some thirty years earlier, Dr Thomas Burgess, in what was one of the first studies of blushing ever published, observed the 'drooping or downcast aspect of the entire countenance in the blush of guilt' (p.68). 'I defy anyone, in the act of blushing,' wrote Burgess, 'to look at, or stand the glance of another person present' (p.112). In shame the eye of the other person is felt to 'see through' the victim's defences, to pierce through them to his very thoughts.

Shame always occurs in a *visual* context, in fact (or an imagined visual context), and in the face of a threat (or imagined threat) presented by another human being. Erik Erikson has put it thus (1950):

> Shame supposes that one is completely exposed and conscious of being looked at: in one word, self-conscious. One is visible and not ready to be visible ... Shame is early expressed in an impulse to bury one's face, or to sink, right then and there, into the ground ... He who is ashamed would like to force the world not to look at him, not to notice his exposure. He would like to destroy the eyes of the world. Instead he must wish for his own invisibility. (1963, pp. 252-3)

In her book *On Shame and the Search for Identity* (1958) – probably the most profound study of shame ever written – Helen Merrell Lynd has remarked:

> Experiences of shame appear to embody the root meaning of the word – to

---

[12] Compare Havelock Ellis (1900), for whom modesty is 'an almost instinctive fear prompting to concealment' (p.1); and John T. Maccurdy, 'The Biological Significance of Blushing and Shame', *British Journal of Psychology*, XXXI (1930), pp. 174-82. Feldman (1962) lists many ways in which blushers try to conceal their red faces from view (tans, dark glasses, etc.). Mélinand (1893) describes the experience of blushing as being 'unmasked' (*démasqué*): 'Le vrai symbole de la rougeur, c'est la vierge dont on écarte les voiles, l'homme dont on arrache le masque' (p.637).

uncover, to expose, to wound. They are experiences of exposure, exposure of peculiarly sensitive, intimate, vulnerable aspects of the self. The exposure may be to others but, whether others are or are not involved, it is always ... exposure to one's own eyes. (pp. 27-8)

Lynd reminds us that the aspects of the self to which shame attaches vary from culture to culture. In theory, human beings could be made to feel ashamed of almost anything – any form of behaviour, any physical characteristic. It is a question of social conditioning.[13] In the West, shame is particularly connected with the uncovering of nakedness, that is to say of the genitals. The account of the Fall of Man given in *Genesis* states that through their rebellion against Jehovah, Adam and Eve are made aware of their nakedness for the first time – and are immediately ashamed. Their reaction is to cover their genitals:

> And the eyes of them both were opened, and they knew that they were naked; and they sewed fig leaves together, and made themselves aprons. (*Genesis*, III, 7)

Lynd refers to the connection between the experience of shame and the root meanings of the word. The etymology of the English word 'shame' does indeed seem to corroborate the elements of exposure, hiding and concealment always present in the experience. The root of 'shame' and German 'Scham' is the Gothic 'Schama', which signifies 'cover'; the same word is the root of the German 'Hemd', 'shirt' and of the French and English 'chemise'. In some European languages, moreover, the 'shameful' nature of the genitals is explicit in the terms used to designate this part of the body: Latin 'pudenda' means 'shame-producing'; in German the genital region is called 'die Scham' or 'die Schamteile' (literally, 'shame parts', compare 'naughty parts' in English and the French 'parties honteuses'), 'der Schamberg' means 'shame mound', that is the *mons Veneris*, the vulva may be termed 'die Schamlippen' ('shame lips'), while pubic hair is 'Schamhaare'.[14]

It is beyond doubt, then, that one particularly 'vulnerable aspect of the self' that is felt to be exposed in the experience of shame is the

---

[13] In some societies, for example, eating is always done privately, and public 'exposure' leads to shame; in others, defecation is a communal and shame-free activity. Among the Marquesans of the Pacific, 'the decent costume for males was to have the foreskin drawn over the glans [head of the penis] and fastened beyond it with a thread wrapped around and tied. Thus attired, a gentleman was properly clothed, but if the thread slipped, it was a case of indecent exposure' (David Allen, *The Fear of Looking* (1974), pp. 32-3, quoting Ralph Linton).

[14] Helen Merrell Lynd, pp. 23-4; Piers and Singer (1971), p.18.

genitals. If the baring of the buttocks did not involve at the same time the exposure, or partial exposure (in the case of boys), of the genitals, it is unlikely that 'lower discipline' would have such strong sexual significance. I referred earlier to the vital role played in the flagellant ceremony by the command issued by the beater to the victim to lower his trousers, etc. and bend over; it seems to me that, by *ordering* the passive flagellant to reveal those parts which, as a child, he was not allowed to display, the ban on genital exhibitionism is temporarily lifted and the sexual excitement associated with it allowed to reassert itself. At the same time the victim is humiliated by being placed in a passive position by the dominant adult. Thus the flagellant ceremony as described in pornography always contains a mixture of sexual excitement and shame.

Another point about the flagellant ceremony may also be made here: in the ritual the genitals are exposed, to be sure, but never unexpectedly. The victim always has time to prepare, he knows exactly what is going to happen, and when. Thus, once again, the beating ceremony can be seen as a defence against anxiety.

The heart of shame seems to lie in the sudden, unexpected exposure of the quick of the self to other people. Now, as everyone knows, blushing is the most conspicuous manifestation of shame. 'Blushing,' writes Lynd, 'manifests the exposure, the unexpectedness, the involuntary nature of shame. One's feeling is involuntarily exposed openly in one's face; one is uncovered' (p.33). I have already pointed out that flagellant literature is full of blushing, both of the cheeks and of the buttocks, and have drawn the reader's attention to Bergler's 1944 paper in which he explores the relationship between oral aggression at the breast and the fear of blushing.

Bergler failed to make any connection between passive flagellation fantasies and blushing, despite the similarities presented by his patients in both categories. Sandor Feldman, whose three papers on blushing (1924, 1941, 1962)[15] are among the most illuminating I have read, also fails to make the connection, although his diagnosis of the blusher's fundamental problem points in the same direction as Bergler's. The male blusher, Feldman found, was always an aggressive child, desperate for appreciation and a confirmed exhibitionist (Feldman does not wholly accept Bergler's primary voyeuristic component in blushing); these tendencies the future

---

[15] 'Über Erröten. Beitrag zur Psychologie der Scham', *Int. Zeitschrift für Psychoanalyse*, VIII (1922), pp. 14-34; 'On Blushing', *Psychiatric Quarterly*, XV (1941), pp. 249-61; 'Blushing, Fear of Blushing and Shame', *Journal of the American Psychoanalytic Association*, X (1962), pp. 368-85.

blusher has to suppress under parental threats, and becomes a conformist – on the surface, beneath which rages suppressed fury and hatred. Thus for Feldman the male blusher is a man whose self-respect suffered a death blow at an early age and who, through being forced to submit to authority, lost confidence in his masculinity. The blusher is caught between the devil and the deep blue sea: if he expresses himself aggressively, he is ashamed and blushes; if he *fails* to assert himself in company, he is ashamed and blushes. He cannot win, for both aggression and passivity make him ashamed:

> There is anxiety over not being loved or over being killed, or castrated. To avoid these dangers, submission, with shame and blushing, occurs. However, submission means dependence, with accompanying shame because of dependence. Libidinous anxiety is mixed with the social. (1941, p.259)

Several analysts believe that there is a primitive connection between fear of castration and fear of blushing (erythrophobia).[16] Both a blush and a knife can cut deep, keenly, to the quick. If indeed there is a connection between the two, then one can see that flagellation of the buttocks, as a substitute castration imposed by an authority figure, might have the effect of liberating the blusher temporarily from his obsession with the colour of his face, and allowing the blood to flow to the genitals.

I would like to continue this train of thought for a moment. Freud interpreted shame as a *defence* against the urge to exhibit or look at the genitals, that is against exhibitionism or voyeurism;[17] and blushing, the most obvious manifestation of shame, was explained as a 'conversion symptom', a 'hysterical' upwards displacement of sexual excitement from the genitals to the face. A sort of substitute erection. According to this view of blushing, the initial flow of blood to the genitals is checked by the interference of the internalised voice of authority or conscience (super ego) – castration fear may enter in here – and the blood is deflected to the face. In this way some exhibitionism is unconsciously satisfied (the blush draws attention to itself and makes the victim conspicuous) but at the same time punishment is

[16] For Hermann Nunberg (1932), fear of blushing and fear of castration coincide, and the attempts to prevent blushing (the full-time occupation of erythrophobes) are really attempts to prevent the castration which they believed as children would result from genital exhibitionism.

[17] Freud, *Three Contributions to the Theory of Sexuality* (1905): 'The force which opposes scopophilia, but which may be overriden by it ... is *shame*' (VII, p.157).

exacted (some chronic erythrophobes have committed suicide, literally 'dying of shame').

Burgess (1839) believed that the blush is a God-created '*guardian faculty*' (p.78) – a sign to other people that we have sinned. Fear of blushing, of showing shame, is implanted in us by God as a 'check upon the conscience' (p.11). Try as people may to appear calm, the 'eloquent blood' of the blush provides 'external evidence, by the tint of the cheek, of what is going on internally in the *moral sanctuary*' (p.156), enforces 'exposure of their internal sensibility' (p.189). The God-given blush is a form of 'moral atonement' (p.49). As one would expect, Burgess's explanation of blushing was rejected by Darwin and his successors. None the less it is undoubtedly true that fear of blushing does indeed act, and devastatingly, on behaviour, particularly sexual behaviour. Male erythrophobes are almost bound to be sexually impotent, for, if the blood is forever rushing, or liable to rush, to the cheeks in a sexual, or potentially sexual, situation, it can hardly speed to the genitals at the same time. In this respect it is of interest to note that Dr Burgess talks of a blush as a 'vital turgescence' without suspecting that there might be any connection between it and the erection of the penis.

Fritz Perls, the founder of Gestalt therapy, is in no doubt about the connection between blushing and impotence. In *In and Out the Garbage Pail* (1973), Perls comments:

> I still have to read most of Freud's writings. What astonishes me is the fact that with all his preoccupation with sex, he has not seen the relationship of self-esteem to the libido theory ... The similarity of the function of this system to the erection and detumescence of the genitals seems obvious to me. The erection of the total personality glowing with pride contrasts with the abject posture of the one who feels low. The touchiness of the chaste spinster is proverbial. In shame the blood rushes into the head and depletes the genitals. (p.4)

It seems to me that, while not all blushers are passive flagellants, all passive flagellants are likely to be blushers. 'I have found that the repressed desire to assume a feminine role was the key complex in male blushers,' wrote Feldman in a paper that has already been mentioned (1962, p.379). Feldman's patients were all intensely ashamed of displaying feminine behaviour traits that had been imposed upon them in early childhood and had become second-nature through the agency of internalised conscience. 'In order to blush,' writes Feldman, 'a person has to be ordered to be ashamed. At first the shame is imposed upon an individual. If he submits to this imposition, the readiness to be ashamed becomes an inner process' (p.371). Many of Feldman's blushers were compulsive masturbators, but he found that they were ashamed, not so much of the practice itself, as of the passive fantasies and other perverse scenes which they conjured up during it: 'It is the perverse fantasy which is responsible for the shame and blushing, and it is this that the blusher fears the observer will detect' (pp. 375-6).

Now, let us imagine the position of a child who has been made to feel ashamed of its aggression, genitals and excretory functions from a very early age. A child who has been taught that bodily desires may be dangerous. Is it not possible, indeed likely, that he may become a confirmed blusher? And that, whenever there is any danger of being exposed, a blush response may be automatic? Christopher Ricks has noted, in his perceptive book *Keats and Embarrassment* (1974), that 'the hot flush of embarrassment rises with special frequency and centrality in the nineteenth century' (p.2). In England, that is. Ricks limits his attention almost completely to Keats, whose poetry reveals a pervasive concern with blushing, but many other Victorian writers are keenly aware of shame and embarrassment; and advertisements offering to cure blushing appear with great frequency in the newspapers and society magazines of the day. I think we can be certain that one large, perhaps very large, category of Victorian blushers who created the demand for such advertisements was occupied by men who had been beaten into shame as children.

Which brings me back, finally, to Swinburne. Helen Merrell Lynd quotes passages from several nineteenth-century writers in which the experience of shame is described, but there is no mention of Swinburne who, to my mind, has conveyed it with unique skill and insight.

I have mentioned several times that flagellant pornography always stresses the reddening of the buttocks, and we have seen that Bloch and Morris relate this factor to primate sexuality. Swinburne specialises in lurid descriptions of bottoms under the rod, but is unusual in that he almost always points up the connection between the red buttocks and the blushing *upper* cheeks of the victim. In Swinburne's flagellant compositions the latter is never shown as enjoying the birching; whatever the spectators or narrator may feel, the floggee is invariably covered with shame at having to bare his buttocks to the gaze of the assembled company of his fellows. And once he is on the block his one concern is to bear the pain with courage, to 'take it like a man', not to appear a coward. The beatings in Swinburne's flagellant works are habitually so severe, however, that

the boy's stoicism is often broken down, to his own chagrin and the
general amusement of those present:

> Then Reginald no longer durst appeal
>   But reddening to the roots of his red hair
> For shame that cut him to the quick like steel
>   And stung him like a birch, but otherwise,
> Began for flagellation to prepare.

('Reginald's flogging', *The Flogging-Block*)

> They set him on the flogging block,
> They set him on his knee;
> And the flush on his face and the flush on his bum
> Was a stunning sight to see, my boys, was a stunning
>   sight to see.
>
> <div align="right">(<i>ibid.</i>)</div>

> I'm ashamed of you, Frank; yes, I blush for you, Fane,
> You should blush, my boy, deeper with shame than with
>   pain
> To behave like a baby: the shame should be crushing;
> Your cheeks ought to blush as your bottom's blushing.
> There's plenty of blood in your bottom to blush with
> When we've got through some tough birch-twigs to make
>   the blood gush with.
> I look on your blushing posteriors, and wish
> I could see your face blush as your bottom does. Swish!

('Frank's flogging', *The Flogging-Block*)

If the reader can stand an extended example of this sort of thing, the
two flagellant compositions by Swinburne published in *The Pearl*, and
which I reproduce in Appendix C, are eloquent on the connections
between blushing cheeks and bloody bottoms.

It is in his unfinished novel *Lesbia Brandon*, that Swinburne most
convincingly captures the harrowing nature of flogging-induced
shame. Herbert Seyton, who is undoubtedly modelled on Swinburne
himself, is much birched by his sadistic tutor Denham:

> The boy sobbed and flinched at each cut, feeling his eyes fill and blushing
> at his tears; but the cuts stung like fire, and burning with shame and pain
> alike, he pressed his hot wet face down on his hands, bit his sleeve, his
> fingers, anything; his teeth drew blood as well as the birch. (p.32)

Herbert is intensely ashamed of not being able to prevent himself from
crying out under Denham's rod; and he is ashamed, too, of blushing,

which makes his predicament doubly unbearable:

> As his eyes fell on Herbert, the boy felt a sudden tingling in his flesh; his skin was aware of danger, and his nerves winced. He blushed again at his blushes, and gave his small wet hand shyly into the wide hard grasp of the strong and supple fingers that closed on it. (p.16)

Herbert is mercilessly chaffed about his floggings by some of the aristocratic visitors to the house; and even the formidable Lady Midhurst, who prizes herself on her psychological understanding, puts the knife in by noticing his embarrassment:

> 'I hate him,' said Herbert, pricked into candour by the pain of his blushes.
> 'I suppose it's proper,' said Lady Midhurst. 'Having seen you look at him, I needn't ask if he flogs you. Don't colour and shuffle in that way. He is probably right; flogging never did a boy of thirteen any harm, they tell me.' (p.62)

Unlike Lady Midhurst, Swinburne was only too aware of what harm flogging could do to a boy of thirteen; and there is one instance in the novel in which Herbert's feelings of shame about being birched are conveyed with special precision. The company is at dinner:

> Here the Fieldfare of eighteen, who had not left school six months, and had lately assured Herbert that he still tingled[18] at the word 'block', burst into blushing and bubbling laughter as he noticed in his junior opposite a certain shuffle of body and flush of face unmistakeable to any eye trained in a public school. Herbert felt the laughter like a swift lash round the loins, and his cheeks caught fire; his fingers turned to thawing ice, the roots of his hair prickled and burnt the skin; he smarted and sickened with helpless shame and horrible fear of the next word or look. He did not even see how the transgressor for his part turned white and black with horror at himself and made apparently endeavours to get bodily into his napkin. He did not hear Lord Charles ask when he was to be at Eton and whether he liked the prospect of being young Lunsford's fag: also whether he knew what he had to expect at school in case of delinquency. (pp. 51-2)

It would be hard to imagine a more extraordinary description of the experience of shame than that: the sudden exposure of vulnerability, the immediate turmoil into which the body is thrown, the mixed sensations of hot and cold, the panic, the helplessness. But Swinburne

[18] 'Tingling' is a ubiquitous word in flagellant pornography, referring both to genital and gluteal sensations.

is not content to leave it there: he understands shame and knows that it can be infectious. Lord Charles, of course, just blunders on, but Fieldfare cannot fail to observe that his cruel laughter (not a word has been said) has cut Herbert to the quick; he now experiences shame himself, and Swinburne's eye does not miss his attempts to 'cover up'. Both boys would rather be under the table than anywhere else.

'The experience of shame,' writes Helen Merrell Lynd, 'is itself isolating, alienating, incommunicable' (p.67); and there can be no doubt, given what we know of the genesis and development of the flagellant fantasy, that anyone unfortunate enough to be afflicted with the English Vice is bound to feel extremely ill-at-ease in his relationships with other people. Not only is he sexually impotent without having recourse to a fantasy which places him in the position of a naughty child of six or seven, but he has to live with the shame of knowing that he is unable to reveal his true self to other people. We can be fairly sure too, I believe, that the passive flagellant is also a morbid blusher who feels constantly anxious lest he blush and give himself away. Feldman has said that all his male blusher patients were obsessed with the desire to affirm their masculinity, and this reminds us of Swinburne's 'pathetic virility complex' (Harold Nicolson's words),[19] his constant attempts to prove his courage. It is not surprising that masochists, when they drink, can be extremely aggressive (who was it who first defined the super ego as 'the alcohol-soluble part of the psyche'?). Swinburne was no exception to the rule, and during the 1860s his riotous behaviour in London was notorious: when he was drunk his repressed rebelliousness and resentment rose to the surface, and anything could happen.

This hatred and resentment is also very evident in Swinburne's work. It seems clear that, for him as for many masochists, God, as the representative of ultimate authority, was the principal enemy. Swinburne's hatred of Christianity is well known, but it is perhaps not so widely appreciated that it is the Christian denial of the body that he particularly resents. *Poems and Ballads*, which outraged the Victorians on its appearance in 1866, is shot through with the poet's anti-Christian animus ('Thou hast conquered, O pale Galilean; the world has grown grey from thy breath'); but it is in his play *Atalanta* (1865) that, to my mind, we find his most memorable outburst (and most memorable line) on the subject. The Chorus is upbraiding the Deity for his cruelty:

[19] Harold Nicolson, *Swinburne* (1926), p.30.

The lord of love and loathing and of strife
  Who gives a star and takes a sun away;
Who shapes the soul, and makes her a barren wife
  To the earthly body and grievous growth of clay;
Who turns the large limbs to a little flame
  And binds the great sea with a little sand;
Who makes desire, and slays desire with shame;
  Who shakes the heaven as ashes in his hand;
Who, seeing the light and shadow for the same,
  Bids day waste night as fire devours a brand,
Smites without sword, and scourges without rod;
  The supreme evil, God. (1911, p.287)

Whether God is responsible or not, one of the functions of shame is certainly to slay desire – or to turn it into unnatural channels. We can make excuses for the pro-flogging Victorians, but how can we explain that until very recently the British have specialised in a peculiarly obnoxious form of inducing shame in children and encouraging sexual deviation?

9

'It Never Did *Me* Any Harm'

As to severity, I myself have received 15 cuts with a stick, and though I was not particularly strong, it had no more effect on me than to make me fonder of standing up than sitting down for a day or two; and it did me, morally, all the good in the world. 1872.[1]

It is news to me that a schoolmaster may not correct a scholar in a proper way. I have never heard of a summons against the headmasters of Eton, Harrow, or Rugby, or any of those schools for assault. The boys get swished for all sorts of offences at those schools. At least they did in my day, and I hope they do now. 1903.[2]

I know that I was once whipped three times before breakfast, and I do not think I was the worse for it. I can honestly say that it had an extremely deterrent effect in my after career. 1912.[3]

Referring to Gary Paul he said: 'In my view I did my best to strike him on the buttocks where it would hurt but not cause any physical damage. I did not consider I gave him any excessive caning.' Judge Bertrand Richards commented: 'Buttocks were ordained by nature for the purpose.' 1975.[4]

People who have the future of our children truly at heart will agree that there is something to be said for the old adage that if one spares the rod one spoils the child. 1976.[5]

'The phenomenon of the person who can only have sexual intercourse with the aid of a phantasy is a schizoid phenomenon', writes Anthony Storr in *The Dynamics of Creation* (1972, p.64). If that is

---

[1] 'An Old Public School Disciplinarian', *The Times*, 15 November 1872.

[2] The words of a magistrate at Lambeth Court, as reported in the *Daily Mail*, 8 May 1903 and reproduced in *The Humanitarian*, June 1903, p.126.

[3] Mr Edward Wood, M.P., Hansard, *Commons*, 1 November 1912, col. 780.

[4] As reported in the *Daily Telegraph* and reproduced in 'This England', *New Statesman*, 29 August 1975, p.248.

[5] Mr Patrick Cormack, M.P., Hansard, *Commons*, 20 January 1976, col. 1157.

so, then the person in thraldom to obstinate flagellant fantasies must surely qualify for the schizoid category. Forever forced to have recourse to a childhood fantasy in order to achieve erection in an adult situation, the flagellant cannot avoid the constant awareness that he has never matured sexually, has never achieved adequate 'genitality'. He knows that he is sexually fixated at an early age. And he is angry, and ashamed, about it. The position of the *passive* flagellant – and the evidence we have been considering in this book suggests strongly that the addicts of the English Vice are predominantly passive rather than active, although both tendencies are doubtless present in all flagellants – is particularly humiliating. For not only must this victim summon up a fantasy in order to become potent, but in that fantasy he must perforce imagine himself in a submissive, 'unmanly' role. Paradoxically, as it might seem, he must deny his virility in the fantasy in order to achieve erection in relation to his flesh-and-blood partner.

Now, is it conceivable that any parent or teacher would, consciously, wish such sexual unhappiness, frustration and confusion on a child? Surely not. Yet many British parents still appear to believe in the virtues of beating their children into good behaviour, and many still confide their sons to establishments where beating of the buttocks is practised. We have it on the authority of no less a person than the present headmaster of Eton, for example, that boys are even today liable to 'lower discipline' at that most famous of English schools; and there seems little reason to believe that in the last few years the other public schools up and down the country, let alone the preparatory schools, have hurriedly abolished the cane. Moreover, the evidence collected by STOPP (The Society of Teachers Opposed to Physical Punishment), as we have seen, suggests that in State schools beating is far more common than might be believed.

Is all this not, to say the least, extremely odd? How are we to explain the extraordinary adherence of the British to the belief that children are spoiled when the rod, or the threat of the rod, is spared?

It could be maintained, no doubt, that the supporters of beating have simply not been, and are still not, aware of the sexual factors at work in the beating system. This lack of awareness could then be explained as the result of ignorance, or of sexual repression, or of both at the same time. But it is difficult to accept that the more educated upholders of the cane (particularly the teachers themselves) can have been, or are, completely insensitive to the dangers involved. Or of the pleasures – for I believe that 'Y', whose testimony we have seen, is right when he asserts that 'If any man habitually canes without some stirrings of sexual desire, he is not a full man' (p.85). The evidence suggests, I think, that most men would learn without difficulty to appreciate the joys of administering 'lower discipline', and it could be maintained that only hypocrisy, shame and fear of exposure prevent this likelihood from appearing self-evident.

Let us continue this train of thought for a moment. That those who enjoy active beating, in deed or in fantasy, should be loath to admit to their proclivity is quite natural. Nobody wants to be branded as a sadist, and I have yet to hear of a schoolmaster who had admitted publicly that he enjoys caning boys. It is equally understandable that those who are sexually aroused by the idea of being beaten should be resistant to making their private desires known to other people; and one is not surprised to learn from psychiatrists that passive flagellants are intensely reluctant to speak freely of their problem, even in the secrecy of a consulting room. For shame, as Helen Merell Lynd has pointed out, is essentially an 'isolating' emotion, and anyone deeply ashamed of the subject of beating is likely to find it impossible to admit what he really thinks and feels deep down about the practice.

And so it is that, in Britain – until recently a very sexually repressed society – few people have been able to bring themselves to tell the truth about the beating system, even its opponents. One only has to read the Hansard reports of the corporal punishment debates that have taken place in both Houses of Parliament during the last fifty years to see what massive resistances are at work. Nor is it any wonder that, when someone actually dares to suggest that sexual factors are at work in beating, he is attacked as a 'sentimental fool' talking a lot of 'rubbish'.

And here a word should be said about the 'hardening process' whereby boys subject to beating have learnt, and doubtless are still learning, to cope with their feelings of anxiety, outraged modesty and desire for revenge. During the nineteenth century, as we have seen, floggings were often inflicted on children in public, and this made the exposure and shame all the greater. It also meant that the victims felt constrained not to show any semblance of weakness or cowardice while under the rod, for fear of being 'chaffed' afterwards by their schoolmates. As Swinburne put it in the Prologue to *The Flogging-Block*, 'Pain bids cry out but Honour bids be dumb'. As a defence against the inevitable feeling of humiliation involved in being publicly stripped and whipped, the victims were bound to keep that stiff upper lip for which the British ruling class has for so long been famous, bound to affect a lofty indifference. But can we doubt that, beneath the surface, most children forced to undergo such treatment would inevitably feel deep resentment? Or that they would murder their tormentors if they could do so with impunity?

The public schools have traditionally given this desire for revenge opportunity for expression by allowing senior boys, who themselves have been victims lower down the school, to administer corporal punishment to their juniors; and it is not surprising, as *The Edinburgh Review* pointed out as far back as 1830, that these boys have been only too happy to take full advantage of this licence for sadism. Such licence being granted at puberty, we should not wonder that the sexual element has often asserted itself strongly during such proceedings. Moreover, there is ample evidence that, where attendance by other children during beatings is concerned, initial pity and squeamishness can give way to feelings of overt pleasure on the part of the spectators. We can all be 'desensitised' to witnessing the sufferings of others. As Brinsley Richards put it in a passage that has been quoted earlier, 'I gradually came to witness the execution in the Lower School not only with indifference but with amusement' (p.72).

The fact that the rulers of Victorian Britain and her immense Empire came almost entirely from the public schools means that, among them, there must always have been a good, and probably a high, proportion of sado-masochists. It seems to me that it would be impossible to deny that this was the case. Every corner of the Empire must have had its flagellant administrators, and the Empire saw to it that these men should be allowed to continue behaving like so many public school prefects. The figures quoted earlier (pp. 154-5) for judicial floggings in India during the latter half of the nineteenth century must seem to any more or less normal person as staggering; but when we recall the background of the men who imposed them – stern nannies, paternal thrashings, the rigours of prep and public school – they make more sense. For if dukes' sons could be birched in public at Eton on their naked buttocks, why should some young poacher, or sailor, some Indian or Negro, expect that he should escape the lash? And wherever the British Empire spread, the English Vice spread with it. One may be permitted to think that it is a lamentable record; and to wince when, in 1977, a Conservative M.P. rises yet again to plead in favour of the rod.

Henry Salt, seeking sixty years ago for the causes of British flagellomania, came to the conclusion that men trained up in the flogging system were bound to continue it. 'The prevalence of corporal punishment in English homes and schools,' wrote Salt, himself an Etonian, 'is responsible for a tone of mind, at once tyrannical and servile, which prompts men to applaud the infliction on others of what they have themselves undergone in their youth' (1916, p.27). It is hard to argue with that; and in 1977 one can identify the same conditioning process at work.

I should like to make a further point. It is that, in a child-beating society, it is often the children who are never beaten who suffer most. In flagellomania, as we have seen repeatedly, it is the *fantasy* that is all-important; and the fantasy, we know, may as easily arise from seeing, reading or hearing about beating as from experiencing it. Thus it is that the very existence of beating as a potential punishment creates a climate in which flagellant fantasies are encouraged. And as well as the overtly sexual dangers of the practice, the threat of beating may have the effect of terrifying children into mindless submission. As a mother explained to STOPP:

> None of my four children have ever been struck. They are extremely conforming timid children and all four would never have done anything wrong. They love school, but especially as infants, take the threats of caning seriously and are in TERROR (and disgust) of it. It is ironic that it should be for such naturally law-abiding children that the cane looms so large. No one can estimate the harm done to the children who NEVER RECEIVE the cane, but no actual caning could cause my children to suffer more. They've never seen a cane used and none of them are sure that anyone is really caned. It's just the threat that worries them. (*A Last Resort?*, p.138)

In the same publication, a child psychologist comments perceptively on the ways in which the beating system may undermine children's natural urge to independence and self-expression. These words are deserving of attention:

> Studies of family rearing patterns show that when people become parents they deal with (or fail to deal with) their own children in the very same way that their parents dealt with them. Teachers who hit and cane should remember that they will be reinforcing the urge to resort to corporal punishment for generations to come. The child who says he would prefer to be caned may be not only identifying with a caning teacher but also abrogating responsibility for his own self-control. Thus an oppressive regime in a school tends to encourage dependence of a child on adults and stifle the development of self-reliance. (p.102)

We shall never know how many people have been crushed and rendered impotent by the flogging system of which the British preparatory and public school Establishment has been so proud, for the victims have not gone round proclaiming themselves in public. But we can be certain that their name is legion.

It is now 350 years since the publication of Meibom's treatise on the sexual element in flagellation, and nearly 100 since the appearance of

Krafft-Ebing's *Psychopathia Sexualis*. We *know* that beating is sexually dangerous. Yet in Britain the beating of schoolchildren continues, unhampered by government restrictions. In this, Britain (and the countries she has influenced with her flagellomania – see Appendix B) is out of step with almost the whole of the so-called civilised world.

An Act of Parliament making beating illegal in all British schools without exception is long overdue. If the decision continues to be left to individual Local Education Authorities, we can be certain that the process of abolition will be at best protracted.

We can also be certain that the purveyors of flagellant pornography will continue to make a good living at the expense of new victims of the English Vice.

Appendix A

The French text of the two principal quotations from Rousseau's *Confessions* (vol. I, book 1) used in Chapter One. Taken from the Gallimard Folio edition, 1973.

Comme Mlle Lambercier avait pour nous l'affection d'une mère, elle en avait aussi l'autorité, et la portait quelquefois jusqu'à nous infliger la punition des enfants quand nous l'avions méritée. Assez longtemps elle s'en tint à la menace, et cette menace d'un châtiment tout nouveau pour moi me semblait très effrayante; mais après l'exécution, je la trouvai moins terrible à l'épreuve que l'attente ne l'avait été, et ce qu'il y a de plus bizarre est que ce châtiment m'affectionna davantage encore à celle qui me l'avait imposé. Il fallait même toute la vérité de cette affection et toute ma douceur naturelle pour m'empêcher de chercher le retour du même traitement en le méritant; car j'avais trouvé dans la douleur, dans la honte même, un mélange de sensualité qui m'avait laissé plus de désir que de crainte de l'éprouver derechef par la même main. Il est vrai que, comme il se mêlait sans doute à cela quelque instinct précoce du sexe, le même châtiment reçu de son frère ne m'eût point du tout paru plaisant. Mais, de l'humeur dont il était, cette substitution n'était guère à craindre, et si je m'abstenais de mériter la correction, c'était uniquement de peur de fâcher Mlle Lambercier; car tel est en moi l'empire de la bienveillance, et même de celle que les sens ont fait naître, qu'elle leur donna toujours la loi dans mon cœur.

Cette récidive, que j'éloignais sans la craindre, arriva sans qu'il y eût de ma faute, c'est-à-dire de ma volonté, et j'en profitai, je puis dire, en sûreté de conscience. Mais cette seconde fois fut aussi la dernière, car Mlle Lambercier, s'étant sans doute aperçue à quelque signe que ce châtiment n'allait pas à son but, déclara qu'elle y renonçait et qu'il la fatiguait trop. Nous avions jusque-là couché dans sa chambre, et même en hiver quelquefois dans son lit. Deux jours après on nous fit coucher dans une autre chambre, et j'eus désormais l'honneur, dont je me serais bien passé, d'être traité par elle en grand garçon.

Qui croirait que ce châtiment d'enfant, reçu à huit ans par la main d'une fille de trente, a décidé de mes goûts, de mes désirs, de mes passions, de moi pour le reste de ma vie, et cela précisément dans le sens contraire à ce qui devait s'ensuivre naturellement? En même temps que mes sens furent allumés, mes désirs prirent si bien le change, que, bornés à ce que j'avais éprouvé, ils ne s'avisèrent point de chercher autre chose. Avec un sang brûlant de sensualité presque dès ma naissance, je me conservai pur de toute souillure jusqu'à l'âge où les tempéraments les plus froids et les plus tardifs se développent. Tourmenté longtemps sans savoir de quoi, je dévorais d'un œil ardent les belles personnes; mon imagination me les rappelait sans cesse, uniquement pour les mettre en œuvre à ma mode, et en faire autant de demoiselles Lambercier. (pp. 44-6)

Non seulement donc c'est ainsi qu'avec un tempérament très ardent, très lascif, très précoce, je passai toutefois l'âge de puberté sans désirer, sans connaître d'autres plaisirs des sens que ceux dont Mlle Lambercier m'avait très innocemment donné l'idée; mais quand enfin le progrès des ans m'eut fait homme, c'est encore ainsi que ce qui devait me perdre me conserva. Mon ancien goût d'enfant, au lieu de s'évanouir, s'associa tellement à l'autre, que je ne pus jamais l'écarter des désirs allumés par mes sens, et cette folie, jointe à ma timidité naturelle, m'a toujours rendu très peu entreprenant près des femmes, faute d'oser tout dire ou de pouvoir tout faire, l'espèce de jouissance dont l'autre n'était pour moi que le dernier terme ne pouvant être usurpée par celui qui la désire, ni devinée par celle qui peut l'accorder. J'ai ainsi passé ma vie à convoiter et me taire auprès des personnes que j'aimais le plus. N'osant jamais déclarer mon goût, je l'amusais du moins par des rapports qui m'en conservaient l'idée. Etre aux genoux d'une maîtresse impérieuse, obéir à ses ordres, avoir des pardons à lui demander, étaient pour moi de très douces jouissances, et plus ma vive imagination m'enflammait le sang, plus j'avais l'air d'un amant transi. (p.47)

Appendix B

The Use of Corporal Punishment in Schools outside the United Kingdom (as at July 1977)[1]

1. *Countries in which corporal punishment has been abolished*

   Austria 1870
   Belgium
   Cyprus .
   Denmark 1967
   Ecuador
   Egypt
   Finland 1890s
   France 1887[2]
   Germany (West) (quite recently)
   Holland 1850s
   Iceland
   Israel
   Italy
   Jordan
   Luxembourg 1845
   Mauritius
   Norway
   The Phillipines
   Poland 1783
   Portugal
   Quatar
   Sweden 1958
   Switzerland (quite recently)
   USSR (and all Communist bloc countries)

[1] Compiled from documents issued by The Society of Teachers Opposed to Physical Punishment (STOPP). The infomation is reproduced by kind permission of the Society.

[2] As stated earlier in the book, corporal punishment was in fact abolished earlier than this in France, abolition being ratified by the 1887 Act.

2. *Countries in which corporal punishment is still used*

Australia. Subject to regulations. The State of Queensland prohibits the corporal punishment of girls.

Barbados. Subject to regulations; prohibited for physically and mentally handicapped children.

Canada. Teachers' authority to use corporal punishment is established by federal law; teachers' rights are only restricted by common law.

Ireland, Republic of. Use is restricted to specific teachers.[3]

New Zealand. Subject to regulations.

South Africa. Subject to regulations.

Swaziland. Permitted for boys and subject to regulations.

Trinidad and Tobago. Permitted, subject to regulations, but prohibited for girls over 14.

United States of America

United States regulations on corporal punishment vary not o1 ' from state to state but, within states, from city to city. The county or city school boards have jurisdiction on school management provided that their rules are consistent with the minimum standards set by the state.

A *State laws regarding corporal punishment in schools*

Twenty-three states have legislation on corporal punishment in schools. Of these, twenty-one permit such punishment (California, Delaware, Florida, Georgia, Hawaii, Illinois, Indiana, Maryland, Michigan, Montana, Nevada, North Carolina, Ohio, Oklahoma, Pennsylvania, South Carolina, South Dakota, Vermont, Virginia, West Virginia and Wyoming) while only two prohibit it (Massachusetts, 1976-7, New Jersey, 1968). Where there is no specific legislation, the state courts preserve the common law rule permitting teachers to use reasonable force in disciplining children *in loco parentis.*

B *Cities*

Even in states where corporal punishment is permitted, either by legislation or common law (that is to say, in all but two states), some cities – New York City and Pittsburgh, for example – have rules prohibiting corporal punishment in the schools under their control. The District of Columbia has also prohibited it.[4]

[3] During the 1950s, Senator Owen Sheehy Skeffington of Trinity College, Dublin, waged a lone and courageous battle against the Irish variety – largely clerical – of child beaters. His incisive speeches in the Senate and many letters to *The Irish Times* aroused widespread hostility on the part of the Irish teaching profession.

[4] Corporal punishment, then, is widely accepted in the United States as a suitable punishment for children. According to John Holt (1974, p.217), a National Committee to Abolish Corporal Punishment in Schools has been formed, and publishes a newsletter (edited by Donna Hazouri, Emory University, Atlanta, Georgia 30322).

Appendix C

Two flagellant poems published by Swinburne in *The Pearl*[1]

CHARLIE COLLINGWOOD'S FLOGGING
BY ETONIENSIS

Seventeen years of age, with round limbs, and broad shoulders, tall, rosy and
    fair,
And all over his forehead and temples, a forest of curly red hair;
Good in the playing fields, good on the water, or in it, this lad;
But at sums, or at themes, or at verses, oh! ain't Charlie Collingwood bad![2]
Six days out of seven, or five at the least, he's sent up to be stripped;
But it's nuts for the lower boys always to see Charlie Collingwood whipped;
For the marks of the birch on his bottom are more than the leaves on a tree,
And a bum that has worn so much birch out as Charlie's is jolly to see.
When his shirt is turned up and his breeches, unbuttoned, hang down to his
    heels,
From the small of his back to the thick of his thighs is one mass of red weals.
Ted Beauchamp, last year, began keeping a list of his floggings and he
Says they come in a year-and-a-half to a hundred and sixty and three.
And you see how this morning in front of the flogging block silent he stands,
And hitches his waistband up slightly, and feels his backside with his hands.
Then he lifts his blue eyes to the face of the Master, nor shrinks at his frown,
Nor at sight of the birch, nor at sound of the sentence of judgment, 'Go
    down.'
Not a word Charlie Collingwood says, not a syllable, piteous or pert;

[1] Ronald Pearsall, who seems to have been the first to identify Swinburne as the author of 'Frank Fane – A Ballad', published three verses of the composition (1975, p.262). Pearsall does not mention 'Charlie Collingwood's Flogging', however. The punctuation and spelling of both poems are rather erratic, and I have tidied them up where necessary.

[2] There is a reference to Charlie Collingwood in 'Edgar's Flogging', and to an Algernon Collingwood in 'Rupert's Flogging' (both poems are included in *The Flogging-Block*).

But goes down with his breeches unbuttoned, and Errington takes up his shirt.

And again we can see his great naked red bottom, round, fleshy, and plump,

And the bystanders look from the Master's red rod to the schoolboy's red rump:

There are weals over weals, there are stripes upon stripes, there are cuts after cuts,

All across Charlie Collingwood's bottom, and isn't the sight of it nuts?

There, that cut on the fleshiest part of the buttocks, high up on the right,

He got that before supper last evening, oh! isn't his bottom a sight?

And that scar that's just healed, don't you see where the birch cut the flesh?

That's a token of Charlie's last flogging, the rod will soon stamp it afresh.

And this morning you saw he could hardly sit down, or [be] quiet in church,

It's a pleasure to see Charlie's bottom, it looks just cut out for the birch.

Now, look out, Master Charlie, it's coming; you won't get off this time, by God!

For your Master's in, oh, such a wax! and he's picked you out, oh, such a rod!

Such a jolly good rod, with the buds on, so stout, and so supple and lithe,

You've been flogged till you're hardened to flogging, but won't the first cut make you writhe!

You've been birched till you say you don't care as you used for a birching! Indeed?

Wait a bit, Master Charlie, I'll bet the third cut or the fourth makes you bleed.

Though they say a boy's bottom grows harder with whipping, and time makes it tough,

Yet the sturdiest boy's bottom will wince if the Schoolmaster whips it enough.

Aye, the stoutest posteriors will redden, and flinch from the cuts as they come,

If they're flogged half as hard as the Master will flog Charlie Collingwood's bum.

We shall see a real, jolly good swishing, as good as a fellow could wish;

Here's a stunning good rod, and a jolly big bottom just under it – Swish!

Oh, by Jove, he's drawn blood at the very first cut! in two places by God!

Aye, and Charlie's red bottom grows redder all over with marks of the rod.

And the pain of the cut makes his burning posteriors quiver and heave,

And he's hiding his face – yes, by Jove, and he's wiping his eyes on his sleeve!

Now, give it him well, Sir, lay into him well, till the pain makes him roar!

Flog him, then, till he stops, and then flog him again till he bellows once more!

Ah, Charlie, my boy, you don't mind it, eh, do you? it's nothing to bear;

Though a small boy may cry for a flogging, that's natural, but Charlie don't care.

That's right, Sir, don't spare him! that cut was a stinger, but Charlie don't mind;

All the rods in the kingdom would only be wasted on Charlie's behind.

At each cut, how the red flesh rises, the red weals tingle and swell!

How he blushes! I told you the Master would flog Charlie Collingwood well.

There are long, red ridges and furrows across his great, broad nether cheeks,

And on both his plump, rosy, round buttocks the blood stands in drops and in streaks.

Well hit, Sir! Well caught! how he drew in his bottom, and flinched from the cut!

At each touch of the birch on his bum, how the smart makes it open and shut!

Well struck, Sir, again, how it made the blood spin![3] there's a drop on the floor;

Each long, fleshy furrow grows ruddy, and Charlie can bear it no more.

Blood runs from each weal on his bottom, and all Charlie's bottom is wealed,

'Twill be many a day ere the scars of this flogging are thoroughly healed.

Now just under the hollow of Charlie's bare back, where the flanks are aslope,

The rod catches and stings him, and now at the point where the downward ways ope;

Round his flanks, now like serpents, the birchen twigs twining bend round as they bite,

And you see on his naked, white belly, red ridges where all was so white.

Where between his white thighs something hairy the body's division reveals

Falls the next cut, and now Charlie Collingwood's bottom is all over weals.

Not a twig on the rod but has raised a red ridge on his flesh, not a bud

But has drawn from his naked and writhing posteriors a fresh drop of blood.

And the Schoolmaster warms to his work now, as harder and harder he hits,

And picks out the most sensitive places, as though he'd cut Charlie to bits.

'So you'll fidget and whisper in school-time, and make a disturbance in church?

'Can't sit still, Master Charlie, eh, can't you? Well, what do you think of the birch?

'Oh, it hurts you so, does it, my boy, to sit down, since I flogged you last night?

'It was that made you fidget all church time? Indeed, you can't help it, please God –

'By the help of the birch, Master Charlie, I'll teach you to help it, please God –

'If you don't mend your manners in future, it shan't be for want of a rod.

'You're a big boy, no doubt, to be flogged; the more shame for you, Sir, at your age –

'But as long as you're here, I shall flog you;' he lays on the cuts in a rage.

'Aye, and if you were older and bigger, you'd come to the flogging block still –

'Boys are never too big to be beaten!' he lays on the birch with a will.

---

[3] This use of the verb 'spin' is peculiar to Swinburne, and occurs in many of his flagellant compositions. I have not found it thus used elsewhere.

'If a boy's not too old to go wrong, Sir, he can't be too old to be whipped,
'So take that!' and he lays on the rod till the twigs all with crimson are
    tipped.
There are drops of the boy's blood visible now on each tender young bud –
Blood has dropped on his trousers, and Charlie's bare bottom is covered with
    blood.
But I'd rather be shut up for days, in a hole you would scarce put a dog in,
And brought out once a day to be birched, than have missed Charlie
    Collingwood's flogging.
How each cut brings the blood to his forehead, and makes him bite half
    through his lips!
How the birch cuts his bottom right over, and makes the blood spin from his
    hips!
How his brawny bare haunches, all bloody and wealed with red furrows like
    ruts,
Shrink quivering with pain at each stroke, that revives all the smart of past
    cuts!
How the Schoolmaster seems to hit harder, the birch to sting more at each
    blow!
Till at last Charlie Collingwood, writhing with agony, bellows out 'Oh!'
That was all: not a word of petition, a single short cry and no more;
And the younger boys laugh, that the birch should have made such a big
    fellow roar.
For a moment the Master too pauses, but not for a truce or a parley,
Then the birch falls afresh, on the bloody wealed flesh, with 'Take that,
    Master Charlie.'
All the small boys are breathless and hushed; but they hear not a syllable
    come,
They hear only the swish of the birch as it meets Charlie Collingwood's bum.
And the Master's face flushes with anger; he signs to Fred Fane[4] with a nod;
And Freddy reluctantly hands him another stout, supple birch rod.
And again as he flogs Charlie Collingwood's bottom his face seems aflame;
At each cut he reminds him of this thing or that, and rebukes him by name.
Each cut makes the boy's haunches quiver, and scores them all over afresh;
You can trace where each separate birch twig has marked Charlie
    Collingwood's flesh.
Till the Master, tired out with hard work, and quite satiate with flogging for
    once,
With one last cut, that stings to the quick,[5] bids him rise for an Obstinate
    Dunce.

---

[4] Fane is one of the commonest names in Swinburne's flagellant writings, including the letters to Richard Monckton Milnes. It is perhaps significant that three Fanes attended Eton at the same time as Swinburne.
[5] We have noted that, in Swinburne's flagellant compositions, shame, too, 'stings to the quick'.

From the block Charlie Collingwood rises, red faced, and with tumbled red
    hair,
And with crimson-hued bottom, and tearful blue eyes, and a look of 'Don't
    Care'.
And he draws up his breeches, and walks out of school with a crowd of boys
    dogging
The heels of their hero, all proud to have seen Charlie Collingwood's
    flogging.

(*The Pearl*, no.3, September 1879)

FRANK FANE – A BALLAD[6]

The master said to the schoolboy,
    As it fell on a day,
'All the rest are to go,
    Frank Fane is to stay.
I set you all free
    From the birch and the cane,
Not a boy shall be swished,
    Not a boy but Frank Fane.'

Said the Merry Master,
    'Frank Fane is to stay,
To be flogged with a flogging
    As good as your play.
Frank Fane is to stay,
    To be whipped i' the hall,
To be whipped till his whipping
    Atones for you all.

Any boy that enjoys
    A fine flogging to see,
I give leave to stay here
    With Frank Fane and me.
They will see his white bottom,
    When they see it again
I don't think they'd fancy
    It belongs to Frank Fane.'

While the rest went a playing
    In the hall there were four,
Frank Fane and his Master

    [6] The British Library has a manuscript composition, 'Frank Fane: A Ballad of the
Birch' (Ashley 5751) which differs substantially from the version published in *The
Pearl*.

And two fellows more.
There were three there for pleasure
    And one there for pain;
How they giggled and grinned
    At the funk of Frank Fane!

'Now loosen your braces,
    And lower your breeks,
And show your companions
    Your bare nether cheeks.
Make haste to the closet
    And bring a good rod,
Or I'll cut you to ribands,
    You shuffler, by God!'

'O Master! dear Master!
    Have pity for once!'
'What, pity for a truant,
    A thief and a dunce!
For once, and at once,
    You shall smart for all three;
A three-fold example
    Your bottom shall be.'

Now his comrades they took him,
    Each grasping a hand,
And gaily accomplished
    The master's command.
They swayed down his body,
    Rolled up his shirt-tail,
And poised up his buttocks
    That a stroke mightn't fail.

Then they tied down his legs,
    That the skin might draw tight,
That each lash might draw blood
    To the Master's delight;
Then they twitched at his hair,
    And chucked up his chin,
And cried out 'Good Master!
    It's time to begin.'

Now Arthur's and Redgy's
    Own bottoms were sore,
But they knew that Frank Fane's
    Would be terribly more.
And each was too glad
    To forget his own grief
In seeing Frank's flesh

In the state of raw beef.

Said Arthur to Redgy,
    'We've often been stripped,
All three of us together,
    And jollily whipped;
But now we're both masters,
    And, crickey! it's fun
To see Frank Fane catching
    Three floggings in one.'

The first was three dozen,
    Laid in with a will,
'Just enough,' quoth the Master,
    'For a boy in the bill.'
Then he sat down and rested
    His arm for a while
And looked at his work
    With a grim kind of smile.

Then he gave a fresh sentence –
    'So much for the Dunce!
Now five dozen for the Truant,
    But not all at once.
This rod is all splintered,
    Go fetch me two more;
No, two's poor allowance,
    So, Redgie, bring four!'

'There'll be two for the Truant,
    And two for the Thief,
And if that does not bring
    That fat bottom to grief –
Then Keate was a fumbler,
    And Busby a fool,
And I'm not a master
    Of Whippingham School!'[7]

Then the right trusty Master
    Went at him like mad,
And loud were the prayers
    And shrieks of the lad.
Said Arthur, 'You coward!'
    Said Redgie, 'Keep cool!
Your bottom's a credit
    To Whippingham School!'

---

[7] Whippingham, as was said earlier, is a town in the Isle of Wight.

But the Master is pausing!
   Is it mercy or fear?
Ah! no, it's to toss off
   A mug of strong beer.
And refreshed with his tipple
   He's at him again,
He never seems tired
   Of swishing Frank Fane!

He pauses once more – 'Boys!'
   He cries, 'Hold him tight,
I remember I've got
   A short letter to write.
If the creature's rebellious
   Let him taste this sweet cane,
I'll be back in ten minutes
   To finish Frank Fane.'

So the cane on his shoulders
   Went rat-a-tap-tap,
And in turns they examined
   His bum like a map;
Such outlines! Such islands!
   Such mountains of weals!
And such pretty red rivers
   Running down t'wards the heels!

Here's the Master returning,
   A cigar 'tween his lips,
Hurrah! for the Master
   Who smokes while he whips!
He knows how to tackle
   Two pleasures at once –
The taste of the baccy,
   The smart of the Dunce.

So he puffed like a demon!
   And fiercely cut in,
Till you hardly could pick out
   An inch of whole skin.
Then he took a new country,
   And striped the white thighs,
Till the old hall re-echoed
   A tempest of cries.

O! firm was his muscle!
   And supple his wrist,
And he handled the Rod
   With a terrible twist,

But muscles grow weary,
  And arms lose their powers,
There's an end for all nice things,
  For floggings – like flowers.

Shrieks Frank Fane, 'I'm dying!'
  Says Redgie, 'You ai'nt,
And if you go off
  In a bit of a faint,
We'll soon thrash you back
  Into living again,
You've not done with swishing
  Just yet, Master Fane!'

Now the whipping is over,
  And the culprit is free,
I don't think he'll sit down
  This evening for tea!
And when in a fortnight
  He's turned down once more,
I fancy he'll find
  His bottom still sore.

(*The Pearl*, no.11, May 1880)

Bibliography

Note to the Bibliography

Unless otherwise stated, all titles in English were published in London and those in French at Paris. For most titles before approximately 1930 it has not been felt necessary to give the name of the publisher.

This bibliography is not intended to provide an exhaustive list of titles concerned with sexual flagellation. In particular I have refrained from including many more or less psychoanalytic articles on the subject which have proved to be of little interest. For detailed bibliographical information on beating in British schools, the *Students' Reading List* issued by STOPP (see address, p.86) should be consulted.

The places of publication of psychoanalytic, psychiatric, psychological and sociological journals listed in the bibliography are as follows:

American Journal of Sociology, Chicago.
British Journal of Psychology, London.
International Journal of Psycho-Analysis, London.
Internationale Zeitschrift für Psychoanalyse, Vienna.
Journal of the American Psychoanalytic Association, New York.
Journal of Personality and Social Psychology, Lancaster, Pa., and Washington, D.C.
New Behaviour, London.
Pedagogical Seminary, Worcester, Massachusetts.
Philosophy and Phenomenological Research, New York.
Psychiatric Quarterly, New York.
Psychoanalytic Quarterly, New York.
Psychoanalytic Review, New York.
Psychoanalytische Bewegung, Vienna.
Signs: Journal of Women in Culture and Society, Chicago.
Sociometry. A Journal of Research in Social Psychology, Albany, New York.

Other periodical publications to which reference is made in the text are as follows:

Beano, The
Bon Ton Magazine, The
Boy's Own Annual, The
British Medical Journal, The
Brutalitarian, The
Chums
Church Times, The
Coventry Herald and Observer, The
Crim Con Gazette, The
Daily Express, The
Daily Mail, The
Daily News, The
Daily Post, The, Liverpool
Daily Telegraph, The
Dandy, The
Edinburgh Review, The
Englishwoman's Domestic Magazine, The
Evening Standard, The
Family Herald, The
Fortnightly Review, The
Forum
Gem, The
Globe, The
Gentleman's Magazine, The
Good Words
Guardian, The (newspaper)
Guardian, The (religious weekly)
Hansard
Home Chat
Humane Review, The
Humanitarian, The
Humanity
Irish Times, The
Janus
Lancet, The
Law Times, The
Leader and Saturday Analyst, The
Leeds Mercury, The
Magnet, The

Martinet
Morning Post, The
News of the World, The
New Statesman
Notes and Queries
Observer, The
Pall Mall Budget
Pall Mall Gazette
Paris, Le
Pearl, The
Penthouse
Picture Post
Post Office Directory, The
Progrès médical, Le
Public Opinion
Punch
Queen, The
Rambler's, The
Reynold's Newspaper
Réveil, Le
Rock
Saturday Review, The
Society
South Wales Daily News, The
Spank
Standard, The
Star, The
Sting
Sunday Express
Sunday Times, The
Times, The
Times Literary Supplement, The
Topper, The
Town Talk
Truth
Vanity Fair
Victorian Erotica
Where. The Education Magazine for Parents
World, The

Acton, William (1857) *The Functions and Disorders of the Reproductive Organs in Youth, in Adult Age, and in Advanced Life. Considered in their Physiological, Social, and Psychological Relations.*

Adam, Corinna (1968) 'Beating in Britain', *New Statesman*, 29 November 1968, pp. 740-1.

Ainger, Arthur Campbell (1917) *Memories of Eton Sixty Years Ago.*

Alexander, Franz (1938) 'Remarks about the Relation of Inferiority Feelings to Guilt Feelings', *Int. Journal of Psycho-Analysis*, XIX, pp. 41-9.

Alexander, Franz (1963) *Fundamentals of Psychoanalysis*, New York, W.W. Norton. First published 1948.

Allen, David W. (1974) *The Fear of Looking, or Scopophilic-Exhibitionistic Conflicts*, Bristol, John Wright.

Angeli, Helen Rossetti (1954) *Pre-Raphaelite Twilight: The Story of Charles Augustus Howell*, Richards Press.

Anon. (1669) *The Children's Petition; Or, a Modest Remonstrance of that intolerable grievance our Youth lie under, in the accustomed Severities of the School-discipline of this Nation.*

Anon. (1872) *The Exhibition of Female Flagellants, in the Modest and Incontinent World, Proving from indubitable Facts that a Number of Ladies take a secret Pleasure in Whipping their Own, and Children committed to their Care*, etc. 2 vols. Nos. 1 and 2 of John Camden Hotten's 'Library Illustrative of Social Progress'.

Anon. (1872) *Fashionable Lectures: composed and delivered with Birch Discipline ...* No. 7 of John Camden Hotten's 'Library Illustrative of Social Progress'.

Anon. (1835a) 'Flogging and Fagging at Winchester', *Quarterly Journal of Education*, IX, pp. 84-90.

Anon. (1860) *Guide to Eton; Eton Alphabet; Eton Block; Eton Glossary; etc. etc.*

Anon. (1872) *Madam Birchini's Dance. A Modern Tale, with Original Anecdotes collected in Fashionable Circles. By Lady Termagant Flaybum.* No. 5 of John Camden Hotten's 'Library Illustrative of Social Progress'.

Anon. (1879-1880) *Miss Coote's Confession*, serial published in *The Pearl*.

Anon. (1966) *My Secret Life.* Introduction by G. Legman, New York, Grove Press, 2 vols. The first unexpurgated edition of the great Victorian classic.

Anon. (1835b) 'On the Discipline of Large Boarding Schools', *Quarterly Journal of Education*, X, pp. 82-119.

Anon. (1879-1880) *The Pearl: A Journal of Facetiae and Voluptuous Reading.* Reprinted in facsimile by Amour Publications, 1975.

Anon. (1830) 'The Public Schools of England – Eton', *Edinburgh Review*, LI, pp. 65-80.

Anon. (1866) *The Romance of Chastisement; or, Revelations of the School and Bedroom. By an EXPERT.* It seems likely that Swinburne may have written part of this work.

Anon. (1873-76) *The Romance of Lust; or, Early Experiences*, 4 vols. Attributed to Edward Sellon, William S. Potter, etc.

Anon. (1872) *Sublime of Flagellation: in Letters from Lady Termagant Flaybum to Lady Harriet Tickletail.* No. 6 in John Camden Hotten's 'Library Illustrative of Social Progress'.

Anon. (1888) *The Whippingham Papers; A Collection of Contributions in Prose and*

Verse, chiefly by the Author of the 'Romance of Chastisement'. For the contributions by Swinburne, see SWINBURNE.

Arnold, Matthew (1864) *A French Eton; or, Middle Class Education and the State.*

Arnold, Matthew (1866) *Schools Inquiry Commission. Report* [on secondary education in France, Germany, Italy and Switzerland].

Arnold, Thomas, D.D. (1845) 'On the Discipline of Public Schools', in *The Miscellaneous Works of Thomas Arnold*, pp. 363-79. Originally published in the *Quarterly Journal of Education* (1835), signed 'A Wykehamist', as a reply to ANON. (1835a).

Ashbee, C.R. (1880-1941) Diaries, in King's College Library,, Cambridge, England.

Ashbee, C.R. (1939) *'Grannie': A Victorian Cameo*, Oxford.

Ashbee, Henry Spencer *see* Fraxi, Pisanus.

Baldwin, John (1904) 'Flogging in the Navy, By One who has Undergone it', *The Humane Review*, V, pp. 252-6.

Baring, Maurice (1922) *The Puppet Show of Memory.*

'Barry Report, The' see *Corporal Punishment: Report of the Advisory Council.*

Benedek, Therese (1925) 'Notes from the Analysis of a Case of Ereuthophobia', *Int. Journal of Psycho-Analysis*, VI, pp. 430-9.

Benedictus, David (1962) *The Fourth of June*, Anthony Blond.

Benson, A.C. (1924) *Memories and Friends.*

Bergler, Edmund (1938) 'Preliminary Phases of the Masculine Beating Fantasy', *Psychoanalytic Quarterly*, VII, pp. 514-36.

Bergler, Edmund (1944) 'A New Approach to the Therapy of Erythrophobia', *Psychoanalytic Quarterly*, XIII, pp. 43-59.

Bergler, Edmund (1948) 'Further Studies on Beating Fantasies', *Psychiatric Quarterly*, XXII, pp. 480-6.

Bertram, James G. see Cooper, Rev. William *pseud.*

Binet, Alfred (1888) 'Le Fétichisme dans l'amour', in *Etudes de psychologie expérimentale*, pp. 1-85.

Blanch, William Harnett (1877) *The Blue-Coat Boys; or, School Life in Christ's Hospital with a Short History of the Foundation.*

[Bloch, Iwan] Dühren, Dr Eugen *pseud.* (1901-1903) *Das Geschlechtsleben in England mit besonderer Beziehung auf London.*

Vol. I. *Die beiden Erscheinungsformen des Sexuallebens. Die Ehe und die Prostitution*, Charlottenburg, 1901.

Vol. II *Der Einfluss äusserer Faktoren auf das Geschlechtsleben in England*, Berlin, 1903. Chapter 6, 'Die Flagellomanie', pp. 336-481.

Vol. III *Der Einfluss äusserer Faktoren auf das Geschlechtsleben in England. Fortsetzung und Schluss*, Berlin, 1903.

Unsatisfactory translations of this work were published in 1934 (*Sex Life in England*, New York) and 1938 (*Sexual Life in England Past and Present*, London).

Bloch, Iwan (1908) *The Sexual Life of our Time in its Relations to Modern Civilization.* Translated from the sixth German edition by M. Eden Paul, London, Rebman. The same translation was issued by Heinemann in 1924 and 1928.

Boileau, L'Abbé (1732) *Histoire des Flagellans, où l'on fait voir le bon et le mauvais usage des Flagellations parmi les Chrétiens ...*, Amsterdam.

Boileau, Nicolas Despréaux (1969) 'Aux mêmes Révérends Pères sur le livre des Flagellants composé par mon frère le docteur de Sorbonne', *Oeuvres*, Garnier-Flammarion, II, pp. 160-1.

Bourneville, Dr (1899) 'Libéralisme anglais: Saisie d'ouvrages scientifiques', *Progrès médical*, no.52, 30 December 1899, p.503.

Bowlby, John (1971) *Attachment and Loss, Volume I. Attachment*, Harmondsworth, Penguin Books. First published 1969.

Bowlby, John (1975) *Attachment and Loss, Volume II. Separation: Anxiety and Anger*, Harmondsworth, Penguin Books. First published 1973.

'Boy, who was flogged, the', Now a Capt. R.A. (1875) 'Eton Thirty Years Ago', *MacMillans Magazine,* July 1875, pp. 273-4.

Bradley, Ian (1976) *The Call to Seriousness: The Evangelical Impact on the Victorians*, Jonathan Cape.

Bresler, Fenton (1977) *Lord Goddard: A Biography of Rayner Goddard, Lord Chief Justice of England*, Harrap.

Brodie, Fawn (1971) *The Devil Drives: A Life of Sir Richard Burton*, Harmondsworth, Penguin Books. First published 1967.

Browning, Oscar (1910) *Memories of Sixty Years*.

Brunfels, Otto (1534) *Onomastikon Medicinae ...*, Argentorati.

Burgess, Thomas H. (1839) *The Physiology or Mechanism of Blushing; illustrative of the Influence of Mental Emotion on the Capillary Circulation; with a General View of the Sympathies, and the Organic Relations of those Structures with which they seem to be connected*.

Burton, Sir Richard (1850s-1870s) MS letters to Richard Monckton Milnes, Lord Houghton, in Trinity College Library, Cambridge.

Butler, Samuel ['Hudibras'] (1885) *Hudibras*, Routledge.

Butler, Samuel (1963) *The Way of All Flesh*, New York, Signet Classics. First published in 1903.

'Cadogan Report, The', see *Report of the Departmental Committee on Corporal Punishment*.

Campbell, Harry (1890) *Flushing and Morbid Blushing. Their Pathology and Treatment*.

Chakravarti, Hiralal (1908) 'Whipping in India', *The Humane Review*, IX, pp. 172-82.

Cheetham, Anthony, and Parfit, Derek (eds.) (1964) *Eton Microcosm*, Sidgwick and Jackson.

Chesney, Kellow (1974) *The Victorian Underworld*, Harmondsworth, Penguin. First published 1970.

Children and their Primary Schools. A Report of the Central Advisory Council for Education (England) ['The Plowden Report'] (1967), H.M. Stationery Office.

Chitty, Susan (1974) *The Beast and the Monk. A Life of Charles Kingsley*, Hodder and Stoughton.

Christoffel, H. (1936) 'Exhibitionism and Exhibitionists', *Int. Journal of Psycho-Analysis*, XVII, pp. 321-45.

Churchill, Randolph S. (1966) *Winston S. Churchill. Vol. I Youth 1874-1900*, Heinemann.

Churchill Winston S. (1974) *My Early Life. 1874-1908*, Fontana. First published 1930.

Cinglant, Le Colonel, *pseud.* (1866?) *Conférence expérimentale par Le Colonel Cinglant (Col. Spanker's Lecture). Traduit pour la première fois de l'anglais par les soins de la Société des bibliophiles cosmopolites.* Londres, Imprimerie de la Société Cosmopolite, MDCCCLXXX.

'Clarendon Report, The', see *Report of Her Majesty's Commissioners ...*, 1864.

Cleland, John (1974) *Fanny Hill: Memoirs of a Woman of Pleasure.* Mayflower. First published 1748 or 1749.

Cleugh, James (1951) *The Marquis and the Chevalier*, Andrew Melrose.

Cleugh, James (1967) *The First Masochist: A Biography of Leopold von Sacher-Masoch (1836-1895)*, Anthony Blond.

Coelius Rhodiginus, see Rhodiginus.

Coffignon, A. (1889) *Paris vivant: La corruption à Paris.*

Coleman [sic], George, *pseud.* [Richard Monckton Milnes?] [1871] *The Rodiad*, published by John Camden Hotten.

Coleman [sic], George, *pseud.* (1927) *The Rodiad*, Cayme Press.

Coleridge, Arthur Duke (1898) *Eton in the Forties.*

Coleridge, Hon. Gilbert (1912) *Eton in the Seventies.*

Collas, Georg Friedrich [1913] *Der Flagellantismus im Altertum*, etc., vol. I, Leipzig. This work was the first volume of a projected *Geschichte des Flagellantismus* which was not completed.

Collinson, Joseph (1904) 'Flogging in the Navy', *The Humane Review*, V, pp. 123-8.

Collinson, Joseph (1905) *Facts about Flogging*, published for the Humanitarian League.

Comfort, Alex (1968) *The Anxiety Makers: Some Curious Preoccupations of the Medical Profession*, Panther. First published 1967.

Comfort, Alex (1969) *Nature and Human Nature*, Harmondsworth, Penguin Books. First published 1966.

Connolly, Cyril (1948) *Enemies of Promise*, New York, Macmillan.

Cook, Ivor (1967a) Anonymous letters to *The Guardian* concerning beatings at Court Lees Approved School, 2 and 7 March 1967.

Cook, Ivor (1967b) 'Spare the Rod and Save the Child,' *The Observer*, 10 September 1967.

Cooper, the Rev. Wm. M. *pseud.* [James G. Bertram] [1870] *Flagellation and the Flagellants. A History of the Rod in All Countries from the Earliest Period to the Present Time.*

Cooper, The Rev. Wm. M. *pseud.* [James G. Bertram] [1899] *Der Flagellantismus und die Flagellanten*, Dresden.

Corporal Punishment: Report of the Advisory Council on the Treatment of Offenders [the 'Barry Report'], Her Majesty's Stationery Office, Command 1213, 1960, reprinted 1967.

Cotton, Sir Henry (1906) 'Corporal Punishment in India', *The Humane Review*, VI, pp. 215-21.

Cotton, Sir Henry (1910) 'Corporal Punishment in India', *The Humanitarian*, October 1910, pp. 76-8.

Cotton, Sir Henry (1914) 'Whipping in India', *The Humanitarian*, April 1914, pp. 29-30.

Court Lees, see Gibbens.

Covey-Crump, A. (1955) *Naval Information*, type-written pamphlet in Naval Historical Library, Earl's Court.

Craig, Alec (1962) *The Banned Books of England and Other Countries. A Study of the Conception of Literary Obscenity*, George Allen and Unwin.

Croft-Cooke, Rupert (1967) *Feasting with Panthers: A New Consideration of some late Victorian Writers*, W.H. Allen.

Cyclopedia of Education (1911-1913), see Monroe, Paul.

Darwin, Charles (1873) 'Blushing', in *The Expression of the Emotions in Man and Animals*, pp. 310-47.

Davitz, Joel R. (1969) *The Language of Emotion*, New York and London, Academic Press.

Dawes, C.R. (1927) *The Marquis de Sade: His Life and Works*, Robert Holden.

De la Cour, Michael (1977) 'Survey of LEA Regulations on Corporal Punishment', *Where. The Education Magazine for Parents*, no. 128, May 1977, pp. 127-9, 143-4.

Delcourt, Pierre (1888) *Le Vice à Paris*, 5th ed.

Demogeot, J. and Montucci, H. (1867) *De l'Enseignement secondaire en Angleterre et en Ecosse. Rapport adressé à son Exc. M. le Ministre de l'Instruction publique*.

De Quincey, Thomas (1853) 'My brother', Chapter XII of *Autobiographic Sketches*, Edinburgh and London.

De Quincey, Thomas (1871) 'On suicide', in *Works*, vol. XVI, Supplement, Edinburgh, pp. 496-503. The essay was written in 1823.

D'Olbert, Gervas *pseud.?* (1967) *Chastisement Across the Ages: A Scientific Survey*, Fortune Press. First published 1956.

Dühren, Dr Eugen *pseud*. See Bloch, Iwan.

Didier, Béatrice (1976) *Sade*, Denoël/Gonthier, Collection 'Médiations'.

Doppet, François-Amédée (1788) *Aphrodisiaque externe, ou Traité du fouet et de ses effets sur le physique de l'amour. Ouvrage médico-philosophique suivi d'une dissertation sur tous les moyens capables d'exciter aux plaisirs de l'amour, par D****, Geneva.

Ellis, Havelock (1900) 'The Evolution of Modesty', in *Studies in the Psychology of Sex*, Philadelphia, pp. 1-48.

Ellis, Havelock (1942) 'Love and Pain', in *Studies in the Psychology of Sex*, vol. I, part II, pp. 66-188.

Ellis, Havelock (1962) *Psychology of Sex*, Pan Books. First published 1933.

Erikson, Erik H. (1963) *Childhood and Society*, New York, W.W. Norton. First published 1950.

Etienne, Louis (1867) 'Le Paganisme poétique en Angleterre', *Revue des Deux Mondes*, LXIX, pp. 291-317.

Eton Boy (1877) *A Day of my Life at Eton*.

Etonian, An (1870) *Recollections of Eton*.

Etonian, An Old (1829) *A Letter to Sir Alexander Malet, Bart. in Reference to his Pamphlet Touching the late Expulsions from Winchester School*, etc.

Eton Register, The (1903) Part I. 1841-1850, Eton. (1905) Part II. 1853-1859, Eton.

Eulenburg, Albert (1911) *Sadismus und Masochismus*, Wiesbaden, 2nd ed. First published 1902.

Eulenburg, Albert (1934) *Sadism and Masochism. Algolagnia. The Psychology, Neurology and Physiology of Sadistic Love and Masochism.* Translated into English by Harold Rent, New York, the New Era Press.

Eyre, A.M. (1913) *Saint John's Wood. Its History, its Houses, its Haunts and its Celebrities.*

Faber, Richard (1975) *French and English*, Faber and Faber.

Falk, Bernard (1938) 'Tragedy of Simeon Solomon', in *Five Years Dead: A Postscript to 'He Laughed in Fleet Street'*, The Book Club, pp. 311-31.

Feldman, Sandor S. (1922) 'Über Erröten. Beitrag zur Psychologie der Scham', *Int. Zeitschrift für Psychoanalyse*, VIII, pp. 14-34.

Feldman, Sandor S. (1941) 'On Blushing', *Psychiatric Quarterly*, XV, pp. 249-61.

Feldman, Sandor S. (1951) 'Anxiety and Orgasm', *Psychoanalytic Quarterly*, XX, pp. 528-49.

Feldman, Sandor S. (1962) 'Blushing, Fear of Blushing and Shame', *Journal of the American Psychoanalytic Association*, X, pp. 368-85.

Fenichel, Otto (1937) 'The Scopophilic Instinct and Identification', *Int. Journal of Psycho-Analysis*, XVIII, pp. 6-34.

Fenichel, Otto (1972) *The Psychoanalytic Theory of Neurosis*, New York. First published 1945.

Fenwick, Rev. Collingwood F. (1831) *Sermons; Containing a Familiar View and Refutation of Calvinism: in Eight Discourses. A Familiar Exposition of the Morning and Evening Service of the Liturgy of the Church of England: in Four Discourses. Three Discourses on the Sacrament of the Lord's Supper. Three Discourses on the Fall of Man*, Bath.

Féré, Charles (1892) *La Pathologie des Emotions.*

Féré, Charles (1899) *The Pathology of the Emotions*, Paris, Charles Carrington.

Féré, Charles (1904) *The Evolution and Dissolution of the Sexual Instinct*, Paris, Charles Carrington.

Fitzgerald, Percy (1893) *London City Suburbs.*

Fowler, Dr (1907) *Maisons de flagellation. Traité sur les méthodes employées par les Flagellomanes*, Paris-Prague. Not seen: source Eulenburg (1911).

France, Hector (1883) *Les Va-nu-pieds de Londres.*

France, Hector (1885) *La Pudique Albion. Les Nuits de Londres.*

Fraxi, Pisanus, *pseud.* [Henry Spencer Ashbee] (1877) *Index Librorum Prohibitorum: Being Notes Bio- Biblio- Icono- graphical and Critical, on Curious and Uncommon Books*, London: Privately Printed. Facsimile reprint by Charles Skilton Ltd., 1960.

Fraxi, Pisanus, *pseud.* (1879) *Centuria Librorum Absconditorum: Being Notes Bio- Biblio- Icono- graphical and Critical, on Curious and Uncommon Books*, London: Privately Printed. Facsimile reprint by Charles Skilton Ltd., 1960.

Fraxi, Pisanus, *pseud.* (1885) *Catena Librorum Tacendorum: Being Notes Bio- Biblio- Icono- graphical and Critical, on Curious and Uncommon Books*, London: Privately Printed. Facsimile reprint by Charles Skilton Ltd., 1960.

Fraxi, Pisanus, *pseud.* [1970] *Forbidden Books of the Victorians.* Henry Spencer

Ashbee's bibliographies of erotica abridged and edited, with an introduction and notes, by Peter Fryer, The Odyssey Press.

Freeman, Gillian (1967) *The Undergrowth of Liberature*, Nelson.

Freud, Sigmund (1905) *Drei Abhandlungen zur Sexualtheorie*, Leipzig and Vienna. English translation: *Three Essays on the Theory of Sexuality*, Standard Edition of the Complete Psychological Works of Sigmund Freud, Hogarth Press and the Institute of Psycho-Analysis, 1975, VII, pp. 123-243.

Freud, Sigmund (1919) ' "Ein Kind wird geschlagen". Beitrag zur Kenntnis der Entstehung Sexueller Perversionen', *Int. Zeitschrift für Psychoanalyse*, V, pp. 151-72. English translation: ' "A Child is Being Beaten". A Contribution to the Study of the Origin of Sexual Perversions', *Standard Edition*, XVII, pp. 175-204.

Freud, Sigmund (1924) 'Das Ökonomische Problem des Masochismus', *Int. Zeitschrift für Psychoanalyse*, X, pp. 121-33. English translation: 'The Economic Problem of Masochism', *Standard Edition*, XIX, pp. 155-70.

Freud, Sigmund (1931) 'Über die weibliche Sexualität', *Int. Zeitschrift für Psychoanalyse*, XVII, pp. 317-22. English translation: 'Female Sexuality', *Standard Edition*, XXI, pp. 221-43.

Friedjung, Josef K. (1913) 'Über verschiedene Quellen kindlicher Schamhaftigkeit', *Int. Zeitschrift für Psychoanalyse*, I, pp. 362-4.

Frusta, Giovanni (1873) *Der Flagellantismus und die Jesuitenbeichte. Historisch-psychologische Geschichte der Geisselungs-Institute, Kloster-Züchtigungen und Beichtstuhl-Berirrungen aller Zeiten*. Nach dem Italienischen des Giovanni Frusta, Stuttgart.

Fryer, Peter (1966) *Private Case – Public Scandal*, Secker and Warburg.

Fuller, Jean (1968) *Swinburne: A Critical Biography*, Chatto and Windus.

Garmann, L. Christian Friedrich *See* Nesterus.

Garnier, Paul (1885) *Onanisme seul et à deux sous toutes les formes et leurs conséquences*.

Garnier, Paul (1896) *Les Fétichistes*.

Gathorne-Hardy, Jonathan (1974) *The Rise and Fall of the British Nanny*, Arrow Books. First published 1972.

Gibbens, Edward Brian, Q.C. (1967) *Administration of Punishment at Court Lees Approved School. Report of Inquiry by Mr Edward Brian Gibbens, Q.C. Presented to Parliament by the Secretary of State for the Home Department by Command of Her Majesty, August, 1967*, H.M. Stationery Office, Cmnd. 3367.

Goffman, Erving (1972) *Interaction Ritual*, Harmondsworth, Penguin Books. First published 1967.

Goncourt, Edmond and Jules (1877-96) *Journal des Goncourt. Mémoires de la vie littéraire*, 9 vols.

Goncourt, Edmond de (1882) *La Faustin*.

Goncourt, Edmond and Jules (1956-58) *Journal. Mémoires de la vie littéraire ...*, ed. Robert Ricatte, Monaco, 22 vols.

Gordon, Mary Charlotte Jane, see Leith, Mrs Mary C.J.

Gorer, Geoffrey (1955) *Exploring English Character*, Cresset Press.

Gorer, Geoffrey (1964) *The Life and Ideas of the Marquis de Sade*, Panther Books. First published 1934.

Gosse, Edmund (1917) *The Life of Algernon Charles Swinburne*.

Gosse, Edmund (1919) *Confidential Paper on Swinburne's Moral Irregularities*, British Library, Ashley 5753. First published Lang, VI, pp. 233-48.

Gosse, Edmund (1973) *Father and Son*, Harmondsworth, Penguin. First published 1907.

Gross, E. and Stone, G.P. (1964) 'Embarrassment and the Analysis of Role Requirements', *American Journal of Sociology*, LXX, pp. 1-15.

Guénolé, Pierre (1904) *L'Etrange passion. La Flagellation dans les moeurs d'aujourd'hui. Etudes et documents*. Not seen: source Bloch (1908).

Hall, Bradley (1907) 'Flogging at Manchester Grammar School', *The Humane Review*, VIII (1907-1908), pp. 205-18.

Hansen, D. (1899) *Stock und Peitsche in XIX. Jahrhundert*, Dresden, 2 vols. Not seen: source Eulenburg (1911), p.102.

Hardman, William (1930) *The Hardman Papers*, ed. by S.M. Ellis, Constable.

Henderson, Philip (1974) *Swinburne: The Portrait of a Poet*, Routledge and Kegan Paul.

Hendrick, Ives (1933) 'Pregenital Anxiety in a Passive Feminine Character', *Psychoanalytic Quarterly*, II, pp. 68-93.

Henriques, Fernando (1969) *Modern Sexuality*, Panther Books. First published 1968.

Highfield, M.E. and Pinsent, A. (1952) *A Survey of Rewards and Punishments in Schools*, National Foundation for Educational Research.

Hippeau, C. (1872) *L'Instruction publique en Angleterre*.

Hippeau, C. (1873) *L'Instruction publique en Allemagne*.

Hitschmann, Edward (1943) 'Neurotic Bashfulness and Erythrophobia', *Psychoanalytic Review*, XXX, pp. 438-46.

Hughes, Randolph (1952) Commentary and notes to his edition of Swinburne's *Lesbia Brandon*, Falcon Press.

Hughes, Thomas (1974) *Tom Brown's Schooldays*, Harmondsworth, Puffin Books. First published 1856.

Holmes, Thomas (1900) 'Youthful Offenders and Parental Responsibility', *The Contemporary Review*, LXXVII, pp. 845-54.

Holt, John (1975) *Escape from Childhood: the Needs and Rights of Children*, Harmondsworth, Penguin Books. First published 1974.

Houghton, Lord *see* Milnes, Richard Monckton.

Housman, A.E. (1971) *The Letters of A.E. Housman*, edited by Henry Maas, Rupert Hart-Davis.

Isenberg, Arnold (1949) 'Natural Pride and Natural Shame', *Philosophy and Phenomenological Research*, X, pp. 1-24.

Izard, Carroll E. (1973) *The Face of Emotion*, New York, Appleton-Century Crofts.

Johnson, Loren B.T. (1930) 'A Woman is Being Beaten: An Analytic Fragment', *Psychoanalytic Review*, XVII, pp. 259-67.

Joseph, Edward D. (ed.) (1965) *Beating Fantasies*, Monograph I of the Monograph Series of the Kris Study Group of the New York Psychoanalytic Institute, pp. 30-67.

Joyce, James (1955) *Ulysses*, The Bodley Head. First published 1922.

Joyce, James (1975) *Selected Letters of James Joyce*, edited by Richard Ellmann, Faber and Faber.

Kalton, Graham (1966) *The Public Schools: A Factual Survey of Headmasters Conference Schools in England and Wales*, Longmans.

Kingsley, Charles (1885) *Westward Ho!* Macmillan. First published 1855.

Kinsey, Alfred C., Pomeroy, Wardell B., Martin, Clyde E. (1948) *Sexual Behaviour in the Human Male*, Philadelphia and London, W.B. Saunders.

Kinsey, Alfred C., Pomeroy, Wardell B., Martin, Clyde E. (1973) *Sexual Behaviour in the Human Female*, New York, Pocket Books. First published 1953.

Krafft-Ebing, Richard von (1886) *Psychopathia Sexualis*, Stuttgart.

Krafft-Ebing, Richard von (1892) *Psychopathia Sexualis, with Especial Reference to Contrary Sexual Instinct: A Medico-Legal Study.* Authorized translation of the seventh enlarged and revised German edition by Charles Gilbert Chaddock, M.D., Philadelphia and London, The F.A. Davis Co.

Krafft-Ebing, Richard von (1965) *Psychopathia Sexualis. A Medico-Forensic Study.* With an Introduction by Dr Ernest van den Haag. Translation from the Latin by Dr Harry E. Wedeck. First unexpurgated edition in English, New York, G.P. Putnam's Sons.

Kraus, Dorothy and Henry (1976) *The Hidden World of Misericords*, Michael Joseph.

Lafourcade, Georges (1928) *La Jeunesse de Swinburne*, Publications de la Faculté des Lettres de l'Université de Strasbourg, Paris and Oxford, 2 vols.

Lafourcade, Georges (1932) *Swinburne: A Literary Biography.*

Lamb, Charles (1962) 'Christ's Hospital Five and Thirty Years Ago', in *The Essays of Elia*, Dent, Everyman's, pp. 14-26. First published 1823.

Lambert, Royston and Millham, Spencer (1974) *The Hothouse Society: An Exploration of Boarding-School Life through the Boys' and Girls' Own Writings*, Harmondsworth, Penguin Books. First published 1968.

Lang, Cecil A. *see* Swinburne.

Laurent, Emile (1903) *Sadisme et masochisme*, 'Les Perversions sexuelles' no. XI.

Layng, Henry (1754) *The Rod, a Poem. In Three Cantos*, Oxford.

Lecour, C.J. (1882) *La Prostitution à Paris et à Londres, 1789-1870.*

[Leith, Mary C.J.] (1864) *The Children of the Chapel: A Tale. By the Author of 'Mark Dennis'.*

[Leith, Mary C.J.] (1893) *Trusty in Fight; or, The Vicar's Boys. A Story. By the Author of 'The Chorister Brothers', 'Rufus', 'From Over the Water', etc.*

Leith, Mary C.J. (1893) Four MS letters to Swinburne, written in cipher, British Library, Ashley 5752.

Leith, Mary C.J. (1917) *The Boyhood of Algernon Charles Swinburne.*

Lenzer, Gertrud (1975) 'On Masochism: A Contribution to the History of a Phantasy and its Theory', *Signs: Journal of Women in Culture and Society*, I, no.2, pp. 277-324.

L'Estrange, Rev. A.G. (1887) *Vert de Vert's Eton Days and Other Sketches and Memories.*

Lewis, Helen Block (1971) *Shame and Guilt in Neurosis*, New York, International Universities Press.

Lewis, John Delaware (1875) 'Eton Thirty Years Since', *MacMillans Magazine*, May 1875, pp. 42-9.

Livingstone, Shirley (1975) 'Implications of Corporal Punishment', *New Behaviour*, 25 September 1975, pp. 490-2.

Loewenstein, Rudolph M. (1957) 'A Contribution to the Psychoanalytic Theory of Masochism', *Journal of the American Psychoanalytic Association*, V, pp. 197-234.

Lynd, Helen Merrell (1958) *On Shame and the Search for Identity*, New York, Harcourt, Brace and World.

Lyte, Henry Churchill Maxwell (1875) *A History of Eton College*.

Lyttelton, Rev. The Hon. E. (1900) *Training of the Young in the Laws of Sex*, 3rd impression.

Maccurdy, John T. (1930) 'The Biological Significance of Blushing and Shame', *British Journal of Psychology*, XXXI, pp. 174-82.

Mack, John E. (1976) *A Prince of our Disorder: The Life of T.E. Lawrence*, Weidenfeld and Nicolson.

Malet, Sir Alexander, Bart. (1828) *Some Account of the System of Fagging at Winchester School; with Remarks, and a Correspondence with Dr Williams, Head Master of that Public School, on the Late Expulsions thence for Resistance to the Authority of the Praefects*.

Marcus, Steven (1971) *The Other Victorians: A Study of Sexuality and Pornography in mid-Nineteenth Century England*, Corgi Books. First published 1966.

Masters, William H. and Johnson, Virginia E. (1966) *Human Sexual Response*, Boston, Little, Brown, 18th printing.

Masters, William H. and Johnson, Virginia E. (1970) *Human Sexual Inadequacy*, Boston, Little, Brown, 6th printing.

Maupassant, Guy de (1882) 'L'Anglais d'Etretat', *Le Gaulois*, 29 November 1882. Reprinted in *Oeuvres complètes de Guy de Maupassant*, 1919, pp. 257-63.

Maupassant, Guy de (1891) 'Notes sur Algernon Charles Swinburne', introduction to Gabriel Mourey's translation of *Poèmes et Ballades de A.C. Swinburne*, pp. v-xxvi.

Meibom, Johann Heinrich (1643) *Ioan. Henrici Meibomi, De Flagrorum Usu in re Veneria, & lumborum renumque officio, Epistola ad V.C. Christianum Cassium, Episcopi Lubecensis & Holfatiae Ducis Consiliarium*, Lugd. Batavorum (Leyden).

Meibom, Johann Heinrich (1718) *A Treatise of the Use of Flogging in Venereal Affairs: Also of the Office of the Loins and Reins*, etc., E. Curll.

Meibom, Johann Heinrich (ca. 1870) *De l'Utilité de la Flagellation dans les Plaisirs de l'amour et du mariage. Ouvrage singulier traduit du latin de J.H. Meibomius avec les additions de Thomas Bartholin et de H. Meibomius fils. Nouvelle edition, enrichie de notes historiques, littéraires et bibliographiques, d'une Introduction et d'un index des auteurs cités*. London. Published for George Peacock, Drury-lane, in the year, 1000, 800, 2. Printed by John Harris, 39, New Bond Street. The imprint and publisher's name are false.

Mélinand, Camille (1893) 'Pourquoi rougit-on? Étude sur la cause psychologique de la rougeur', *Revue des Deux Mondes*, CXIX, pp. 631-46.

Mérat, François-Victor (1821) 'Urtication', *Dictionnaire des sciences médicales*, LVI, pp. 348-50.

Michelet, Jules (1870) *Nos Fils.*

Millingen, J.G. (1837) *Curiosities of Medical Experience*, 2 vols.

Milnes, Richard Monckton, Lord Houghton (1840-1865) 16 MS commonplace books, in the library of Trinity College, Cambridge.

Milnes, Richard Monckton (1871), see Coleman, George.

Minssen, J.-F. (1866) *Etude sur l'Instruction secondaire et supérieure en Allemagne.*

Mitford, Algernon Bertram, see Redesdale.

Modigliani, A. (1968) 'Embarrassment and Embarrassability', *Sociometry*, XXXI, pp. 313-26.

Modigliani, A. (1971) 'Embarrassment, Facework, and Eye Contact: Testing a Theory of Embarrassment', *Journal of Personality and Social Psychology*, XVII, pp. 15-24.

Moll, Albert (1891) *Die konträre Sexualempfindung*, Berlin.

Moll, Albert (1898) *Untersuchungen über die Libido Sexualis*, Berlin.

Moll, Albert (1909) *Das Sexualleben des Kindes*, Berlin.

Moll, Albert (1912) *The Sexual Life of the Child*, translated by Dr M. Eden Paul.

Monroe, Paul (ed.) (1911-1913) *A Cyclopedia of Education*, 5 vols., New York.

Montgomery, H.J.B. (1906) 'Flogging in Gaol', *The Humane Review*, VII, pp. 89-94.

Montucci, H. *see* Demogeot, J.

Moreau, Paul (1887) *Des Aberrations du sens génésique.*

Morris, Desmond (1969) *The Naked Ape*, Corgi Books. First published 1967.

Morten, Honnor (1901) 'Inhumanity in Schools', *The Humane Review*, I, pp. 16-27.

Muir, Surgeon Rear-Admiral (1938) '[Flogging as Punishment]', letter to the *Daily Telegraph and Morning Post*, 5 March 1938, p.11.

Mussen, Paul Henry, Conger, John Janeway and Kagan, Jerome (1974) *Child Development and Personality*, New York, Harper and Row, 4th edition.

National Foundation for Educational Research (NFER), see Highfield.

Neill, A.S. (1975) *Summerhill*, Harmondsworth, Penguin Books. First published 1962.

Nesterus, Johann Matthias (1672) Letter, dated 24 February 1672, to Christian Friedrich Garmann, published in *L. Christiani Friderici Garmanni a Alior Viror. Clarissimor. Epistolarum Centuria*, etc., 1714, *Epistola* 88, pp. 363-68.

Nevill, Ralph (1911) *Floreat Etona. Anecdotes and Memories of Eton College.*

Newell, Peter (ed.) (1972) *A Last Resort? Corporal Punishment in Schools*, Harmondsworth, Penguin.

'Newsom Report, The' *see Report of the Public Schools Commission.*

Nicolson, Harold (1926) *Swinburne.*

Niven, David (1975) *The Moon's a Balloon*, Coronet Books.

Nunberg, Hermann (1932) 'Psychoanalyse des Schamgefühls', *Psychoanalytische Bewegung*, IV, pp. 505-7.

'One Who Has Experienced It, By' (1905) 'Flogging in the Navy', *The Humanitarian*, March 1905, pp. 114-15.

Orwell, George (1971) 'Such, Such were the Joys', in *The Collected Essays, Journalism and Letters of George Orwell*, Harmondsworth, Penguin Books, vol. 4, pp. 379-422. First published 1952.

Parent-Duchâtelet, A.J.B. (1836) *La Prostitution dans la ville de Paris*.

Partridge, G.E. (1897) 'Blushing', *Pedagogical Seminary*, pp. 387-94.

Paullini, Christian Franz (1698) *Flagellum Salutis, das ist: Kurieuse Erzählung wie mit Schlägen*, etc., Frankfurt am Main.

Pearsall, Ronald (1972) *The Worm in the Bud: The World of Victorian Sexuality*, Harmondsworth, Penguin Books. First published 1969.

Pearsall, Ronald (1975) *Night's Black Angels: The Forms and Faces of Victorian Cruelty*, Hodder and Stoughton.

Pekin, L.B. (1932) *Public Schools: Their Failure and their Reform*. Published by Leonard and Virginia Woolf at the Hogarth Press, London.

Péladan, Josephin Aimé (ca. 1896) 'Le Vice anglais', chs. XX and XXXVII of *La Vertu suprême*, no. XIV of *La Décadence latine*.

Perls, Frederick S. (1972) *In and Out the Garbage Pail*, New York and London, Bantam Books.

Petronius Arbiter (1963) *The Satyricon*, translated, with an introduction, by William Arrowsmith, New York, Mentor Books.

Pfeiffer, Prof. (1899) *Allgemeine Einführung zur soziopsychologischen Geschichte des Begriffes des Körperstrafens*, Leipzig. Not seen: source d'Olbert (1967), p.138.

Pico Della Mirandola, Giovanni (1502) *Joannis pici mirandule disputationum adversus astrologos*, Davĕtrie.

Pico Della Mirandola, Giovanni (1946) *Disputationes Adversus Astrologiam Divinatricem*, ed. by Eugenio Garin, Florence, Vallecchi Editore.

Piers, Gerhart and Singer, Milton B. (1971) *Shame and Guilt: A Psychoanalytic and a Cultural Study*, New York, W.W. Norton.

Pisanus Fraxi, see Fraxi, Pisanus.

'Plowden Report, The', see *Children and their Primary Schools*.

Pope-Hennessy, James (1949) *Monckton Milnes: The Years of Promise, 1809-1851*, Constable.

Pope-Hennessy, James (1951) *Monckton Milnes. The Flight of Youth, 1851-1885*, Constable.

Powell, George (1866-1881) 12 MS letters to Swinburne in the Brotherton Library, University of Leeds.

Praz, Mario (1960) *The Romantic Agony*, translated by Angus Davidson, Collins, Fontana Books. Italian title: *La carne, la morte e il diavolo, nella letteratura romantica*, Florence, 1930. Davidson's English translation was first published in 1933.

Prescott, E. Livingston *pseud.* [Miss Spicer Jay] (1897) *Flogging NOT abolished in the British Army. A Reasonable Inquiry into the Present Abuse of the CAT and BIRCH in our Military Prisons*.

Priestley, J.B. (1974) *Victoria's Heyday*, Harmondsworth, Penguin Books.

Puissant, Vital, see Viest' Lainopts.

Reade, Rolf S., see Rose, Albert.

Redesdale, Algernon Bertram Mitford, Lord (1915) *Memories*, 2 vols.

Reich, Wilhelm (1973) 'The Masochistic Character', in *Character Analysis*, translated by Vincent R. Carfagno, Vision Press, pp. 225-69. First published (in German) 1933.

Reik, Theodor (1962) *Masochism in Sex and Society*, New York, Grove Press, 'Black Cat Books'. First published 1941.

Reik, Theodor (1975) *Of Love and Lust*, Souvenir Press, 'Condor Books'.

Report of the Commissioners appointed by Her Majesty to inquire into the Education given in England, not comprised within her Majesty's two recent Commissions on Popular Education and on Public Schools ['The Schools Inquiry Commission Report'], 21 vols., 1868-1869.

Report of the Departmental Committee on Corporal Punishment ['The Cadogan Report'], Command 5684, 1938.

Report of Her Majesty's Commissioners appointed to Inquire into the Revenues and Management of Certain Colleges and Schools, and the Studies Pursued and Instruction given therein; with an Appendix and Evidence ['The Clarendon Report'], 4 vols., 1864.

Report of the Public Schools Commission ['The Newsom Report'], H.M. Stationery Office, 1968.

Report to the Secretary of State for the Home Department of the Departmental Committee on Reformatory and Industrial Schools, 2 vols., 1896.

Reports of the Commissioners of Prisons and the Directors of Convict Prisons, 1937-1967.

Reyntiens, N. (1864) *L'Enseignement primaire et professional en Angleterre et en Irlande*.

Rhodiginus (or Richerius), Ludovicus Coelius (1562) *Lectionum Antiquarum*, Leyden.

Richards, James Brinsley (1883) *Seven Years at Eton*.

Ricks, Christopher (1974) *Keats and Embarrassment*, Oxford.

Riezler, Kurt (1943) 'Comment on the Social Psycology of Shame', *American Journal of Sociology*, XLVIII (1942-1943), pp. 457-65.

Roberts, W.J. (1908) 'The Flogging Outbreak in Cardiff', *The Humane Review*, IX, pp. 65-75.

Rose, Alfred (1965) *Register of Erotic Books*, New York, Jack Brussel, 2 vols. First published as *Registrum Librorum Eroticorum*, etc. 1936, under the anagram of Rolf S. Reade.

Rousseau, Jean-Jacques (1783) *The Confessions of J.J. Rousseau with The Reveries of the Solitary Walker, translated from the French*.

Rousseau, Jean-Jacques (1954) *The Confessions*, translated by J.M. Cohen, Harmondsworth, Penguin Books. First published 1782.

Rousseau, Jean-Jacques (1966) *Emile, ou l'éducation*, chronologie et introduction par Michel Launay, Garnier-Flammarion. *Emile* was first published in 1762.

Rousseau, Jean-Jacques (1973) *Les Confessions*, préface de J.-B. Pontalis, texte établi par Bernard Gagnebin et Marcel Raymond, notes de Catherine Kolnig, Gallimard, Folio, 2 vols.

Ryan, Michael (1839) *Prostitution in London, with a Comparative View of that of Paris and New York*, etc.

Rycroft, Charles (1971) *Anxiety and Neurosis*, Harmondsworth, Penguin Books. First published 1968.

Sacher-Masoch, Leopold Von (1965) *Venus in Furs*, Luxor Press. *Venus im Pelz* was first published *c*.1870.

Sade, Donatien-Alphonse-François, Marquis de (1968) *Les Infortunes de la vertu*, Union Générale d'Editions, '1018'. The first draft of *Justine*.

Sade, Donatien-Alphonse-François, Marquis de (1972) *Les 120 Journées de Sodome*, Pauvert. First published 1904.

Sade, Donatien-Alphonse-François, Marquis de (1974) *Justine, ou Les Malheurs de la vertu*. Edition établie sur les textes originaux presentée et commentée par Béatrice Didier, Livre de Poche, no.3714. *Justine* was first published in 1791.

Sade, Donatien-Alphonse-François, Marquis de (1976) *La Philosophie dans le boudoir, ou Les Instituteurs immoraux*, Gallimard, 'Folio'. First published 1795.

Sadger, J. (1913) 'Über Gesässerotik', *Int. Zeitschrift für Psychoanalyse*, I, pp. 351-58.

Salt, Henry S. (1906) 'The Ethics of Corporal Punishment', *The Humane Review*, VII, pp. 14-26.

[Salt, Henry S.] (1910) *Eton under Hornby: Some Reminiscences and Reflections. By O.E.*

Salt, Henry S. (1916) *The Flogging Craze. A Statement of the Case Against Corporal Punishment*, published for the Humanitarian League, George Allen and Unwin.

Salt, Henry S. (1928) *Memories of Bygone Eton.*

Sandwith, Humphry (1871) 'Earl Russell, the Commune, and Christianity', *The Fortnightly Review*, X, New Series, no.55, 1 July 1871.

Schertel, Ernst (1957) *Der Flagellantismus in Literatur und Bildnerei*, Stuttgart, 12 vols.

Schools Inquiry Commission, see *Report of the Commissioners* ...

Schmideberg, Melitta (1948) 'On Fantasies of Being Beaten', *Psychoanalytic Review*, XXV, pp. 303-8.

Schurig, Martin (1720) *Spermatologia*, etc., Frankfurt.

Serrurier, Jean-Baptiste (1820) 'Pollution', *Dictionnaire des sciences médicales*, XLIV, pp. 92-141.

Shadwell, Thomas (1966) *The Virtuoso*, ed. by Majorie Hope Nicolson and David Stuart Rodes, Edward Arnold. The play was first published in 1676.

Shaw, George Bernard (1897) Letters to *The Saturday Review* on flogging in the Navy, 28 August, 18 September, 2 October, 13 and 27 November 1897.

Shaw, George Bernard (1898) 'Flagellomania', a summary of Shaw's lecture of 24 March 1898, *Humanity*, April 1898, pp. 26-7.

Shaw, George Bernard (1904) Letters to *The Times* on flogging in the Navy, 14 June, 2 and 14 September, 11 October 1904.

Shaw, George Bernard (1912) 'The Roots of the White Slave Traffic', *The 'Awakener'*, 16 November 1912, pp. 7-8.

Shaw, George Bernard (1914) 'Under the whip', in preface to *Misalliance. The Bodley Head Bernard Shaw. Collected Plays with their Prefaces*, IV, 1972, pp. 76-80.

Shenstone, William (1764) *The School-Mistress. In Imitation of Spenser*, in *The Works in Verse and Prose of William Shenstone, Esq.*, I, pp. 333-45.

Simon, Brian and Bradley, Ian (ed.) *The Victorian Public School: Studies in the Development of an Educational Institution*, Gill and Macmillan.

Sims, George R. (1917) *My Life: Sixty Years' Recollections of Bohemian London*.

Sinibaldi, Giovanni (1642) *Geneanthropeiae*, etc., Rome.

Souffrin, Eileen (1951) 'Swinburne et sa légende en France (avec inédits)', *Revue de Littérature comparée*, XXV, pp. 311-37.

Spanker, Colonel, see Cinglant, Le Colonel.

Speculator Morum *pseud.* (1885) [according to Craig (1962) p.236 this is the pseudonym of Rev. John M. McClellan 'who appears to have written Preface. Compiled by Sir William Laird Clowes'] *Bibliotheca Arcana seu Catalogus Librorum Pentralium*, George Redway. Reprinted by the Piscean Press in facsimile in 1971.

Stables, William (1868) *Medical Life in the Navy*.

Stansky, Peter and Abrahams, William (1974) *The Unknown Orwell*, Paladin Books. First published 1972.

[Stead, W.T.] (1885) 'The Maiden Tribute of Modern Babylon', *Pall Mall Gazette*, July 6, 7, 8, 10, 1885.

[Stead, W.T.] (1885) *Les Scandales de Londres, dévoilés par le Pall Mall Gazette*. Traduction littérale des articles de ce journal, Dentu.

Steele, Richard (1711) articles against corporal punishment in *The Spectator*, 30 August and 12 September 1711, nos. 157 and 168.

STOPP *see* Newell, Peter.

Storr, Anthony (1965) *Sexual Deviation*, Harmondsworth, Penguin Books. First published 1964.

Storr, Anthony (1972) *The Dynamics of Creation*, Secker & Warburg.

Storr, Anthony (1973) 'The Man' in *Churchill: Four Faces and the Man* [essays by A.J.P. Taylor, Robert Rhodes James, J.H. Plumb, Basil Liddell Hart and Anthony Storr], Harmondsworth, Penguin Books. First published 1969.

Stowe, Harriet Beecher (1972) *Uncle Tom's Cabin*, Dent, Everyman's Library. First published 1857.

SWINBURNE, Algernon Charles
Since several of the MSS are undated, this section is arranged alphabetically.

'Arthur's Flogging' (1888), *The Whippingham Papers*.

Atalanta (1865), in *The Poems of Algernon Charles Swinburne*, Chatto and Windus, IV, 1911.

'A Boy's First Flogging at Birchminster', *The Whippingham Papers*.

'Charlie Collingwood's flogging', by 'Etoniensis' (1879), *The Pearl*, no.3, September 1879.

Chastelard: A Tragedy (1865).

'Cuckoo Weir: An Ode. (By Arthur Clement Swinfield)' British Library, Ashley 5271.

'Eton: An Ode' (1892), *Astrophel and Other Poems, The Poems of Algernon Charles Swinburne*, Chatto and Windus, VI, 1911, pp. 191-93.

'Eton: Another Ode', British Library, Ashley 5271.

The Flogging-Block. An Heroic Poem. By Rufus Rodworthy, Esq. (Algernon Clavering) With Annotations by Barebum Birchmore, Esq. (Bertram Bellingham) London: 1777. British Library, Ashley 5256.

'Frank Fane: A Ballad of the Birch', British Library, Ashley 5751.

'Frank Fane – A Ballad' (1880), *The Pearl*, no.11, May 1880.

'Hints on flogging, shewing how to enjoy it in perfection, in a letter to a lady from Allan Bummingham' (1888), *The Whippingham Papers*.

'Laugh and Lie Down. A Comedy', British Library, Ashley 4356.

Lesbia Brandon, edited with a commentary and notes by Randolph Hughes, Falcon Press, 1952.

Lucretia Borgia: The Chronicle of Tebaldo Tebaldei – Renaissance Period – by Algernon Charles Swinburne. Commentary and Notes by Randolph Hughes. Engraving by Reynolds Stone. Printed and published for the first time by the Golden Cockerell Press, 1942.

Poems and Ballads. First Series, in *The Poems of Algernon Charles Swinburne*, Chatto and Windus, I, 1911. First published 1866.

The Queen-Mother and Rosamond (1868), John Camden Hotten, 2nd edition.

'Reginald's Flogging' by 'Etonensis' (1888), *The Whippingham Papers*.

'Simeon Solomon: Notes on his "Vision of Love" and Other Studies' (1871), *The Dark Blue*, Oxford, July 1871, pp. 568-77.

The Sisters: A Tragedy (1892).

The Swinburne Letters, edited by Cecil Y. Lang, Yale and Oxford, 6 vols., 1960-2.

A Year's Letters, edited by F.J. Sylpher, Peter Owen. 1976. First published 1877.

William Blake: A Critical Essay (1868), John Camden Hotten.

Tarnowsky, B. (1886) *Die krankhaften Erscheinungen des Geschlechtssinnes*, Berlin.

Tarnowksy, B. (1898) *The Sexual Instinct and its Morbid Manifestations, from the Double Standpoint of Jurisprudence and Psychiatry*, etc. Translated by W.C. Costello and Alfred Allison, Paris, Charles Carrington.

Tartivel, A. (1877) 'Flagellation', *Dictionnaire Encyclopédique des sciences médicales*, II (4 série), pp. 354-58.

Taxil, Leo *pseud*. [i.e. Gabriel Antoine Jogand-Pagès] (1884) *La Prostitution contemporaine. Etude d'une question sociale.*

Thiers, Jean-Baptiste (1703) *Critique de l'Histoire des Flagellans, et Justification de l'Usage des Disciplines Volontaires.*

Thoinot, L. (1898) *Attentats aux moeurs et perversions du sens génital.* Leçons professées a la Faculté de médecine, etc.

Trevor-Roper, Hugh (1976) *A Hidden Life: the Enigma of Sir Edmund Backhouse*, Macmillan.

Trudgill, Eric (1976) *Madonnas and Magdalens: The Origins and Development of Victorian Sexual Attitudes*, Heinemann.

[Tucker, W.H.] (1892) *Eton of Old or Eighty Years Since, by An Old Colleger, 1811-1822*.

Uffer (?) (1902) *Über Knabenbestrafung*, Gottingen. Not seen: source d'Olbert (1967), p.138.

Ullo, Dr (1901) *Die Flagellomanie*, etc., Dresden.

Viest' Lainopts *le Bibliophile, pseud.* [i.e. Vital Puissant] (1875) *Essais bibliographiques sur deux ouvrages intitulés: De l'Utilité de la flagellation, par J.H. Meibomius, et Traité du Fouet de F.A. Doppet*, etc.

Villiers de l'Isle Adam, Auguste, Comte de (1885) 'Le sadisme anglais', *Le Succès*, 18 September 1885. Reprinted in *Histoires insolites* (1888), pp. 145-61.

Virey, Jules (1816) 'Flagellation', *Dictionnaire des sciences médicales*, XVI, pp. 6-15.

Virey, Jules (1816) 'Frigidité', *Dictionnaire des sciences médicales*, XVII, pp. 11-28.

Voltaire (1819) 'Verge. Baguette divinatoire', *Dictionnaire philosophique*, VI, p.464. The dictionary was first published in 1769.

'Vox in Solitudine Clamantis' (1893) 'Our Public Schools: their Methods and Morals', *New Review*, IX, July 1893, pp. 34-44.

Walker, Roger M. (1977) 'A Possible Source for the "Afrenta de Corpes" Episode in the "Poema de Myo Cid" ', *Modern Language Review*, Cambridge, LXXII, pp. 335-47.

Weiss, Eduardo (1933) 'A Recovery from the Fear of Blushing', *Psychoanalytic Quarterly*, II, pp. 309-14.

Welldon, J.E.C. (1893) 'Our Public Schools: a Defence of their Methods and Morals', *New Review*, pp. 248-65.

Wilson, Edmund (1966) 'Swinburne's Letters and Novels', *The Bit Between my Teeth: A Literary Chronicle of 1950-1965*, W.H. Allen, pp. 228-69.

Wilson, Erasmus (1846) 'Punishment by flogging', three letters to the *Lancet*, 1846 i, pp. 570-2; ii, pp. 488-89, 540-2.

Wilkinson, Rev. C. Allix (1888) *Reminiscences of Eton (Keate's Time)*.

Wilkinson, Rupert (1964) *The Prefects: British Leadership and the Public School Tradition*, Oxford.

Winnicot, D.W. (1975) *The Child, the Family and the Outside World*, Harmondsworth, Penguin Books. First published 1964.

Wise, Thomas James (1925) *The Ashley Library. A Catalogue of Printed Books, Manuscripts and Autograph Letters Collected by Thomas James Wise*, VI.

Woolf, Virginia (1940) *Roger Fry: A Biography*, Hogarth Press.

Wulffen, E. (1913) *Das Kind. Sein Wesen und seine Entartung*, Berlin.

'Y' (1975) *The Autobiography of an Englishman*, Paul Elek.

Young, Wayland (1959) 'Sitting on a Fortune: The Prostitute in London', *Encounter*, 19 May 1959.

Young, Wayland (1965) *Eros Denied*, Weidenfeld and Nicolson.

Index

'A., Mrs', flagellant 'governess' known to Swinburne, 256

abolition of corporal punishment of school children in other countries, 318-19

Acton, William, venereologist, 28, 34, 44, 45; *The Functions and Disorders of the Reproductive Organs*, 30-2; warns of the dangers of beating children, 32, 136

Adam, Corinna, journalist, on beating in Britain; 62, 86, 91, 94

Adam and Eve, naked and ashamed, 301

Adams, Ms Gene, founder of STOPP, 86, 88

Admiralty, on naval flogging, 171 n.56, 173, 175, 176

advertisements, flagellant, 58-60, 230, 257-8, 263, Plates 7, 8, 24 and 25

Advisory Council on the Treatment of Offenders, see *Corporal Punishment: Report of the Advisory Council on the Treatment of Offenders* ['The 'Barry Report']

Ainger, A.C., on Swinburne and Joynes, 129 n.31

Albert, Dr, on flagellation in German schools, 44

Alington, Dr, headmaster of Eton, restores birch, 138

Alison, Michael, M.P., favours birch, 191

Allen, David, *The Fear of Looking*, 287 n.5, 301 n.13

America, beating in, see United States of America

anal eroticism and flagellation, 288-94

Angeli, Helen Rossetti, *Pre-Raphaelite Tragedy: The Story of Charles Augustus Howell*, 131

Anglican clerics and beating, 64-6, 68-9, 71-3, 75-7, 100, 188, 190

Annual Register, or A View of the History and Politics of the Year 1860, 70n.

Anxiety Makers, The (Comfort), 30

Aphrodisiaque externe, ou Traité du fouet (Doppet), 22-4

Approved Schools, beating in, 89-91; Lord Goddard on, 183n

Army Act (1867), abolishes flogging in peace time, 168

Army Act (1881), abolishes flogging except in prisons, 168

Army Act (1955), abolishes prison flogging in Navy, 178

Army, flogging in the, 168-9

Army prisons, flogging in, 176-7

Arnold, Matthew, poet and schools inspector, disapproves of flogging, 65

Arnold, Dr Thomas, headmaster of Rugby and apologist for corporal punishment of children, 64-6, 115

Ashbee, C.R., architect, son of H.S. Ashbee, 234, 241 n.16

Ashbee, Henry Spencer, see Fraxi, Pisanus

Ashton-under-Lyne workhouse, flogging at, 79

Asquith, Lord, of Bishopstone, favours judicial birch, 183

Asquith, Mr, M.P., anti-flogger, 158

Australia, corporal punishment in schools today, 318

Austria, corporal punishment abolished in schools, 318

Autobiography of an Englishman ('Y'), 95-7, 311-12

Backhouse, Sir Edmund, pupil at St George's, Ascot, 69

Bagnall, Colin, secretary of STOPP, 87

Baker, Edward, of Portia Trust, on beating in schools today, 88 n.25

Balston, Dr, headmaster of Eton, 113

Barbados, corporal punishment in schools today, 319

Baring, Maurice, pupil at St George's, Ascot, 69

Barker, Rev. Arundel C., on virtues of corporal punishment, 190

Barrett, Vicki, flagellant prostitute in Ward case, 261-2

'Barry Report', i.e. *Corporal Punishment: Report of the Advisory Council on the Treatment of Offenders*, 187-8

Bartholinus, Dr Thomas, his additions to Meibom, 1, 7, 9, 11

Barville, Mr, flagellant in *Fanny Hill*, 13-16, 26, 237, 270, Plate 4

Bath, alleged flogging in girls' school, 212-13

Bath Grammar School, beating at, 71
Beano, children's comic, beating in, 83
Beecher, Henry Ward, believes buttocks made for beating, 201n
Beeton, Samuel, founder of the *Englishwoman's Domestic Magazine*, 218
Belgium, corporal punishment abolished in schools, 318
Bellamy, E., friend of Burton and Milnes, 242, 250
Bending of a Twig, The (Coke), 82 n.20
Benedek, Therese, psychoanalyst, on biting and blushing, 287 n.5
Benedictus, David, *The Fourth of June*, 139-40
Benson, A.C., on Swinburne's tutor at Eton, 123, 129 nn. 31 and 32
Benson, George, M.P., anti-flogger, 182
Bergler, Edmund, psychoanalyst, on flagellation and blushing, 285, 286-8, 302
Berkley, Theresa, flagellant 'governess', 237-9, 246-7, 260, 263
'Berkley Horse, The', 238-9, Plate 26
Bertram, James G., see Cooper, Rev. Wm. M.
Besford House Council Home, Shrewsbury, beating at, 91
Betuliad, The (Milnes), 240
Beuttler, Captain, superintendent of Heswell Reformatory School, Liverpool, a flogger, 77-8
Bible, The, and beating, 7, 8, 48-9, 51-2, 53, 60; Proverbs, 48-9, 50, 111; Solomon, 48-9, 50, 51, 53, 60, 100
Bibliotheca Arcana (Speculator Morum), 10 n.12
Binet, Alfred, psychologist, 22 n. 23, 33, 35
Binns, Alfred, on physical consequences of judicial birching of children, 148-9
'Birch, The: A Poem. Written by a Youth of Thirteen', 216
Bird, John, book on Percy Grainger, 263
Bloch, Iwan, German sexologist, on flagellation, 16, 196, 231-2, 238, 260n, 297, 298, 305
Bloom, Leopold, desires whipping in Joyce's *Ulysses*, 270
blushing and flagellation (see also shame), 286-8, 297, 300, 302-8; and castration, 303; and exhibitionism, 286-7; as 'hysterical upwards conversion', 303-4; and oral aggression, 286-8; and voyeurism, 286-7
Boileau, Abbé, on ecclesiastical flagellation, 6-10
Boileau Despréaux, Nicolas, poet, on 'lower discipline', 9
Bon Ton Magazine, flagellant insertions, 195, 196-8, 203, 268, 280
Borrassá, Luis, Catalan painter, 6,

Plate 3
Bourneville, Dr, regrets British censorship of French medical books, 46n
Bowyer, James, flogging headmaster of Christ's Hospital, 116n
boys' fiction, beating in, 82-4
Boy's Own Annual, beating scenes in, 82
'Boys' Weeklies' (Orwell), 83
breasts and flagellant fantasy, 279, 285-6
Bresler, Fenton, on Lord Goddard, 182 n.82, 185
Briggs, Asa, reviews Gladstone diaries, 143n
British Library: Ashbee bequest, 234; editions of Meibom, 1; Private Case, 1, 61n, 234-5
British Medical Journal, 148
Broadhurst, Mr, M.P., opposed to flogging, 147
Brodie, Fawn, biographer of Richard Burton, 245 n.27
Brooks, Lt-Col John, spanking adventures on the Thames, 262
Browning, Oscar, Etonian tutor, 113, 123
Brownrigg, Elizabeth, flogs apprentice to death, 224
Bruce, Sir Charles, recalls beatings at Harrow, 71
Brunfels, Dr Otto, on flogging and impotence, 2
Brutalitarian, The: A Journal for the Sane and the Strong, 174 n.67
Buckbury, James, brutally birched at Ilkeston, 148
Bullus, Wing Commander Eric, M.P., his flogging Bill (1953), 184-7
Bunter, Billy, of Greyfriars School, 83
Burden, Freddie, M.P., favours the birch for 'thugs', 189
Burgess, Betsy, flagellant 'governess', 237
Burgess, Dr Thomas, on blushing, 300, 304
Burn, Colonel, M.P., pro-flogger, 161
Burnett, T.A.J., on Swinburne and Mary Gordon, 134 n.40
Burton, Sir Richard, explorer and scholar: appears as 'Dr Bartsh' in Goncourt diaries, 244; describes his meeting with Hankey, 240; his liking for Hankey, 242; on Hankey's odd sexual tastes, 242-3; offers to procure a human skin for Hankey, 243; enquires after Gen. Studholme Hodgson, 242, 250; reads Milnes's *Betuliad* in Paris, 240; his letters to Milnes, 250; enquires after Sarah Potter, flagellant 'governess', 250; meets Swinburne, 245; Swinburne calls him 'my tempter and favourite audience', 253

Busby, Dr, flogging headmaster of Westminster School, 13, 70, 299

Butler, Samuel, *Hudibras*, 49, 50, 53, 87, 98, 138n

buttocks: in flagellant fantasy, fixation on, 5, 39, 120, 265-8; beating of 'ordained by nature', 200; and blushing, 302-3; identification of with maternal breasts, 285-7; movements of during flagellation, 288, 298; reddening of in flagellation, 196, 197, 268, 288, 297-8; part played by in rump-presentation theory of flagellation, 296-8

Byles, Sir William, M.P., anti-flogger, 171 n.56, 176

Byrd, William, headmaster of Cholderton College, 91

Cadogan, Hon. Edward, M.P. (see also *Report of the Departmental Committee on Corporal Punishment* ['The Cadogan Report']), 144, 178

'Cadogan Report', see *Report of the Departmental Committee on Corporal Punishment*

Camberwell workhouse, flogging at, 79

Camden Square School, Seaham, Co. Durham, beating at, 89

Cameron, Mrs, beating superintendent of Maryhill Girls' School, Glasgow, 80-1

Campbell, Mrs L.J., manager of Toxtell Park Reformatory, Liverpool, on beating, 81

Canada, corporal punishment in schools today, 319

Canavan, Denis, M.P., abortive anti-beating Bill (1976), 97-8

Cancellor, Reginald, beaten to death in Eastbourne school, 70n

Cannon, George, pornography publisher, 236, 237, 247

Capucins, abandon 'upper' for 'lower' discipline, 7

Cardiff, flogging sentences passed in by Judge Lawrence, 160

Carne, La, la morte e il diavolo nella letteratura romantica (Praz), ix

Carrington, Parisian publisher of sex books, 46

Carrington, Earl, on birching at Eton, 146-7

Carter, Rev. W.A., birching Lower Master at Eton, 100n, 101-2, 106

Cassius, Christianus, incredulous friend of Meibom, 2

castration and flagellation, 294-5, 302-3

ceremony, the flagellant, 15, 205-6, 269-76, 294-302

Cervantes, Miguel de, Ashbee's collection of, 234

Chakravarti, Hiralal, on whipping in India, 154

Chalmers, Mrs, flagellant 'governess', 237

Channel Islands, beating legislation in, 165

Chanson de Florence de Rome, mediaeval epic, sadism in, 6

Chaps of Harton, The (Coke), 82 n.20

Chaumière Dolmancé, Powell's retreat at Etretat, 253

Cheetham, Anthony (ed.), *Eton Microcosm*, 141

'A Child is Being Beaten', see Freud

Child, The, The Family and The Outside World (Winnicott), 285-6

Children's Act (1908), whipping provisions, 147

Children and their Primary Schools ['The Plowden Report'], 86

Children's Petition, The; Or, A Modest Remonstrance, etc., 64, Plate 5

Chiswick, alleged flagellant school at, 203-4

Cholderton College, beating at, 91

Christ: castigation of money lenders, 48; gentleness with children, 48, 50; flagellation, 6, 8, 51, Plate 3; Swinburne's dislike of, 308

Christ's Hospital School, flogging at, 73-4

Chums, beating scenes in, 82-3

Churchill, Randolph, on Winston Churchill at St George's prep school, Ascot, 68

Churchill, Winston: unhappiness at St George's preparatory school, Ascot, 68, 78, 167; as Home Secretary disapproves of excessive beating in Reformatory Schools, 78; confirms prison flogging sentences, 167; as First Lord of the Admiralty modifies corporal punishment of cadets, 176; flogging debate while Prime Minister in 1952, 182

Church Times, insertion of flagellant advertisements in, 57, 58

circumcision and flagellation, 294

'Clarendon Report', see *Report of Her Majesty's Commissioners appointed to inquire*, etc.

Cleland, John, author of *Fanny Hill*, 13-16

Coffignon, A., French writer on prostitution, 40

Coke, Desmond, author of school stories, 82 n.20

Coleridge, Arthur Duke, on beating at Eton, 114, 115-16

Coleridge, Gilbert, on beating at Eton, 118-19

Coleridge, Samuel, man of letters, pupil at Christ's Hospital, 116n.

Collett, Mrs, flagellant 'governess', 246

Collins, Lord, on legal right of teachers to beat *in loco parentis*, 64

Collinson, Joseph, leading opponent of flogging, secretary of The Humanitarian League, 46, 79, 157 n.25, 173, 177 n.72

Colman, George, the Younger, poet, alleged author of *The Rodiad*, 240-1

Comfort, Dr Alex, human biologist, on flagellation, 5, 30, 297 n.9

comics, boys', beating scenes in, 82-4

Commissioners on the Criminal Law, declare themselves against judicial flogging (1843), 153

Committee against Corporal Punishment in Schools, 85

Confessions, Les (Rousseau), 17-22, 26, 27, 29, 32, 40-1, 42, 45, 47, 142, 273, 279, 288, 316-17

'Confidential Paper on Swinburne's Moral Irregularities' (Gosse), 127, 254, 255

Congreve, William, playwright, on shame, 298

Connolly, Cyril, writer and critic, on beating at prep school, 69; at Eton, 137-9, 141

Cook, Ivor, denounces irregular beating at Court Lees, 89, 90, 91, 94

Cookesley, Rev. William, of Eton, free with the cane, 114

Cooper, Rev. Wm. M. [pseudonym of James G. Bertram], *A History of the Rod*, 168 nn. 49 and 52, 171 n.57

Cormack, Patrick, M.P., favours corporal punishment, 98, 310

Corporal Punishment Bill (1889), 155-7

Corporal Punishment Bill (1900), 158-9

Corporal Punishment Bill (1977), 190-1

Corporal Punishment Restriction Bill (1908), 160

Corporal Punishment: Report of the Advisory Council on the Treatment of Offenders ['The Barry Report'], 187-8

Corpun Educational Organisation, cane suppliers, 61

correspondence columns, flagellant, 194-232; *Bon Ton Magazine*, 196-8; *Crim Con Gazette*, 198; *Englishwoman's Domestic Magazine*, 218-27; *Family Herald*, 198-209; *Forum*, 232; *Gentleman's Magazine*, 194, 196; *Notes and Queries*, 215-18; *Penthouse*, 232; *Public Opinion*, 227-9; *Queen*, 209-15; *Rambler's*, 195-6; *Society*, 230-2; *Town Talk*, 230-1

Corset and the Crinoline, The, 218-19

Cotton, Sir Henry, on flogging in India, 154

'Count, The', flagellant client of Sarah Potter, 248, 250

Court Lees Approved School, flogging scandal at, 89-91, 94

Coutumes théâtrales ou Scènes secrètes des foyers, 16-17

Coventry Herald and Observer, 107, 110

Covey-Crump, A., naval author, 177 n.74

Crauford, Charles, naval advocate of flogging, 172 n.64

Crim Con Gazette, flagellant insertions, 198

Criminal Justice Act (1948), incorporates recommendations of the Cadogan committee, 181, 187, 188

Criminal Justice Act, 1948 (Adaptation of Naval Discipline Act), Order, 1949, finally abolishes 'cat' in Navy, 177

Criminal Justice Act (1967), abolishes prison flogging, 167

Criminal Justice Bill (1938), incorporates recommendations of Cadogan committee, 181

Criminal Justice (Amendment) Bill (1953), flogging provisions, 184-7

Criminal Law Amendment Act (1885), flogging provisions, 146, 155, 161

Criminal Law Amendment Act (1912) ['White Slave Act'], 151, 160-4

Cripps, Sir Stafford, M.P., opposed to flogging, 181

Critique de l'Histoire des Flagellans (Thiers), 8-10

Cross, Sir Richard, M.P., advocates flogging, 155

Croydon Paper on Corporal Punishment (STOPP), 89

Cupid, alleged birching of by Venus, 216-17

Curiosities of Medical Experience (Millingen), 29

Curtis-Bennett, Mr, cross-examines in Marylebone 'massage' case (1898), 260

Curzon, Lord, recalls his monstruous Nanny, 52-3

Cyclopedia of Education (ed. Monroe), 44n

Cyprus, corporal punishment abolished in schools, 318

Daily Express, approves of corporal punishment, 87, 189, 190

Daily Mail, 89, 188, 310

Daily News, 162, 169

Daily Post, Liverpool, 58

Daily Telegraph, 54, 87, 88, 91, 98n, 137, 164, 189, 223, 259-60, 262, 264, 310

Dandy, children's comic, beating in, 83

Darwin, Charles, 53; on shame and blushing, 300, 304

Davies, Francis Byam, perhaps Swinburne's fag at Eton, 128

Davies, Sir John, Elizabethan poet, flagellant epigram, 12

Day, Mr, Etonian tutor involved in

Morgan Thomas case, 107, 109
De Flagrorum Usu in Re Venerea, etc., see Meibom
De Freitas, Geoffrey, M.P., opposed to flogging, 185
De Jongh, Nicholas, reviews Gladstone diaries, 143n
De la Cour, Michael, on beating in schools today, 89
De l'Enseignement secondaire en Angleterre et en Ecosse (Demogeot and Montucci), 65-6
Delolme, John Lois, *The History of the Flagellants*, etc., 10
Demogeot, J., and Montucci, H., on beating in Victorian public schools, 65-6
Denham, Mr, sadistic tutor in Swinburne's *Lesbia Brandon*, 133-4, 306-7
Denmark, corporal punishment abolished in schools, 318
De Quincey, Thomas, man of letters, deprecates corporal punishment, 208
Devon, Lord, on Clarendon Commission, 101
Dictionary of National Biography, 142
Dictionnaire alphabétique et analogique de la langue française (Robert), 35 n.38
Dictionnaire de l'Académie française, 35 n.38
Dictionnaire de la langue française (Littré), 35 n.38
Dictionnaire encyclopédique des sciences médicales, 28
Dictionnaire étymologique de la langue française, 35 n.38
Dictionnaire philosophique (Voltaire), 17
Dictionnaire des sciences médicales, 27-8
Dillon, Mr, M.P., opposed to flogging, 158
Diplomatic Privileges Act (1708), flogging provisions, 153
Disputationes Adversus Astrologiam Divinatricem (Pico della Mirandola), 3-4
D'Olbert, Gervas, writer on flagellation, 44n, 61n, 82 n.20
domestic beating, Victorian, 48-58; more recent, 60-4
Doppet, François-Amédée, on flagellation, 22-4, 26, 45
Dynamics of Creation, The (Storr), 310

East Chapelton Reformatory for Girls, beating at, 81
'Economic Problem of Masochism, The', see Freud
ecclesiastical flagellation ('upper' and 'lower' discipline), 6-10, 51, 201-2
Ecuador, corporal punishment abolished in schools, 318
Ede, Rt. Hon. J.C., M.P., opposed to flogging, 185-6

Edinburgh Review, against school beating, 106-7, 117, 313
Education Act (1944), no changes as regards corporal punishment in schools, 85
Edwards, Anne, journalist, approves of corporal punishment, 189
Edwards, Jimmy, star of 'Whacko!', 94
Edwards, Maud, flagellant 'governess', 259-60
Ego and the Id, The, see Freud
Egypt, corporal punishment abolished in schools, 318
Ellis, Havelock, sexologist, 5-6, 45n, 297, 300n
Emile, ou l'éducation (Rousseau), 21, 23
enemas and flagellation, 290-3
Enemies of Promise (Connolly), 69, 138-9
English, beating words in, 84-5
Englishwoman's Domestic Magazine, 50, 200 n.5, 218-27, 229, 231
Erikson, Eric, psychoanalyst, on shame, 300
Ernst, Max, his painting *The Blessed Virgin Chastising the Infant Jesus*, 217
erythrophobia, see blushing
Eton, sanctus sanctorum of English flagellomania, 71, 74, 96, 99-143, 147, 171, 196, 215, 221, 253, 269-70, 271, 298, 307; Alington reinstates the birch, 138; bullying, 117-19; Cyril Connolly at, 137-9, 141; fagging system, 114-19, 141-2; Lyttelton abolishes the birch in Upper School, 136-7; George Orwell at, 137-9; Swinburne at, 119-35; the Morgan Thomas case, 107-12; tutorial system, 112-14
'Etonian, An', recalls Eton birchings, 104-5
Eton in the Forties (Arthur Coleridge), 114, 115-16
Eton in the Seventies (Gilbert Coleridge), 118-19
Eton Microcosm (ed. Cheetham and Parfit), 141
Eton Register, The, 100n, 101 n.3, 112n, 122 nn.17 and 19, 128 n.30, 134 n.41
Eulenburg, Dr Albert, German psychiatrist, on beating, 33, 238
European Commission of Human Rights, Strasbourg, and Isle of Man birching, 190, 191, 192
Evening Standard, 80n, 262
Eversley, Lord, opposed to flogging, 162-3
Eye workhouse, flogging at, 79
excretion and flagellation, see anal eroticism
exhibitionism and flagellation, 302-3; and blushing, 287
Exhibition of Female Flagellants, The, 266, 273n, 275, 280

Exploring English Character (Gorer), 61-2, 84-5

Expression of the Emotions in Man and Animals, The (Darwin), 300, 304

Eyre, A.M., on St John's Wood, 252n, 254 n.42

Eyre, Governor, orders brutal repression of Morant Bay rioters, Jamaica, 168-9

Facts about Flogging (Collinson), 46

Family Herald, 51-2, 99n; flagellant correspondence column, 198-209, 212, 213-14, 215, 217-22, 226, 231

Fanny Hill , see *Memoirs of A Woman of Pleasure*

fantasy, the flagellant: analysed, 265-83; originates early, 284, 314; identity of characters in, 276-83

Faragher, Ms Millicent, Manx anti-birching campaigner, 191-2

Farm School, Redhill, flogging at, 76-7

Farquharson, Dr, M.P., opposed to flogging, 158

Fashionable Lectures, 266, 273n, 279, 280

father figure in flagellant fantasy, 281, 295

Father and Son (Gosse), 53, 96

Faustin, La (Goncourt), 253 n.40

Fear of Looking, The (Allen), 287 n.5, 301 n.13

Feldman, Sandor, psychoanalyst, on blushing, 292, 300n, 302-3, 304-5, 308

Fenichel, Otto, psychoanalyst, 287 n.5, 290, 291

Fenwick, Rev. Collingwood Forster, tutors Swinburne for Eton, 119, 133-4

Fenwick, Robert Orde, Etonian, brother of Collingwood Fenwick, 134

Féré, Charles, French psychologist, 46

fiction, beating in boys', 82

Fighiera, F.C.C., approves of flogging, 78-9

Finland, corporal punishment abolished in schools, 318

Finmore, Eton birch-maker, 101

Fitzgerald, Vice-Admiral Penrose, naval pro-flogger, 50, 173-4

flagellants, itinerant religious, 6

Flaybum, Lady Termagant, character in *The Sublime of Flagellation*, 280, Plate 27

Flogging-Block, The, see Swinburne

Flood, Rev. Frederick, approves of birch for vandals, 189

Floreat Etona (Nevill), 101, 104n

'Florence', flagellant 'governess' known to Swinburne, 256

Fly, Spanish, aphrodisiac, 16

Foot, M.R.D., edits Gladstone diaries, 143n

Forbidden Books of the Victorians (ed. Fryer), 235 n.5

Forsyte Saga, The (Galsworthy), 252n

Fortnightly Review, 229

Forum, flagellant communications in, 232

Foster, Sir Walter, M.P., opposed to flogging, 147, 148, 150

Fourier, Charles, French philosopher and sociologist, 200

Fourth of June, The (Benedictus), 139-40

France: alleged beating in convents, 201-2; alleged beating in schools, 204-5; beating outlawed in schools, 24, 66, 318; flogging abolished in Army and Navy, 168; French disapproval of flogging in English schools, 65-6

France, Hector, on flogging in England, 59n, 231

'Frank Fane – A Ballad', see Swinburne

Fraxi, Pisanus [pseudonym of Henry Spencer Ashbee]', Victorian collector and bibliographer of erotica: asserts that women enjoy beating, 277-8; bequeaths Cervantes and erotica collections to British Museum, 234; bibliographies, importance of, x, 265; on *The Rodiad*, 240-1; meets Fred Hankey, 246; friendship with Richard Monckton Milnes, 241; on erotic sculpture by Pradier, 245; *Index Librorum Prohibitorum*, 227n, 235, 236-7, 238, 246, 251, 277, 278, 281; *Centuria Librorum Absconditorum*, 12, 196, 235, 239, 278; *Catena Librorum Tacendorum*, 16, 196, 235, 239, 245, 278

Freeman, Gillian, on prevalence of English Vice, 266

Freke-Palmer, Mr, cross-examines in Marylebone 'massage' case, 259-60

Freud, Sigmund, 21, 32, 33n, 38, 109, 233, 281, 299, 304; on Rousseau, 21, 288; 'A Child is Being Beaten', 284, 285, 288, 295, 299; *The Ego and the Id*, 285 n.2; 'Female Sexuality', 292; 'The Economic Problem of Masochism', 288, 290; *Three Essays on Sexual Theory*, 21 n.22, 31, 288, 288-9, 303 n.17

Fry, Roger, art critic, on flogging at St George's, Ascot, 68-9, 175

Fryer, Peter, 30 n.35, 276-7; on British Library's Private Case, 61n, 235 n.4, 236 n.7

Fryston, Milnes's library of erotica at, 239-40

Fulcher, Misses, run alleged flogging school for girls at Chiswick, 203-4

Fuller, Jean, biographer of Swinburne, 119, 128-9, 130n, 134 n.40, 242 n.19, 253

Functions and Disorders of the Reproductive Organs, etc. (Acton), 30-2

Fyfe, Sir David Maxwell, Conservative Home Secretary, opposed to flogging, 185

Galsworthy, John, on St John's Wood, 252n

Garbett, Dr, Archbishop of York, approves of flogging, 184

Garmann, Christian Friedrich, receives letter about flogging, 5-6

Garnier, Jules, French psychologist, 33

'Garrotters Act' (1863), flogging provisions, 153-4, 156, 160

Gathorne-Hardy, Jonathan, on British Nanny, x-xi, 52-3, 67-8, 290-1, 293

Gem, comic, beating in, 82-3

Geneanthropeiae (Sinibaldi), 5

Genesis, on shame, 301

genitals, avoidance of, and flagellation (see also castration), 268-9

Gentleman's Magazine, flagellant communications in, 10-12, 194, 196, 267

George IV, alleged visitor to flagellant brothel, 246

Gerald, Queenie, flagellant prostitute, 261

Germany: beating of children in, 40, 44; Havelock Ellis on prevalence of sexual flagellation in, 45n; Krafft-Ebing on flagellant advertisements in, 45n; Albert Moll on same, 59-60; Meibom on sexual flagellation in, 2

Gibbens, Edward Brian, on Court Lees beatings, 90-1

Gibbs, Vicary, M.P., favours birching, 147

Gibbs, William, commits suicide at Christ's Hospital, 73-4

Giggleswick School, cane for smoking, 183-4

girls, beating of, 79-82; not in Victorian private schools, 79-80; at Royal Patriotic Asylum, 80; in Reformatory and Industrial Schools, 80-2; in contemporary State schools, 86-9

Gladstone, Herbert, M.P., confirms prison flogging sentences, 167

Gladstone, William: beaten at Eton, 143; self-flagellant activities, 142-3; press reviews of edited diaries, 143n

Gladstone Diaries (ed. Foot and Matthews), 143n

Glasgow, tawse in primary school, 88

Globe, pro-flogging newspaper, 173 n.65

God, see Bible

Goddard, Pamela, spanked by Lord Goddard, 182 n.82

Goddard, Raynor, Lord Chief Justice of England, favours the birch, 182, 183, 185, 299

Goncourt, Edmond de, *La Faustin*, 253 n.40

Goncourt, Jules and Edmond, meet Hankey, 243-5

Goodford, Dr, headmaster, later Provost, of Eton, 99, 101, 108-9, 110, 121

Good Words, 229

Gordon, Mary, Swinburne's cousin, see Leith, Mrs Mary C.J.

Gorer, Geoffrey, on parental beating, 61-2, 84-5

Gorst, Sir John, on British predilection for corporal punishment, 177

Gosse, Edmund, writer and friend of Swinburne: *Father and Son*, 53, 96; *Life of Swinburne*, 119, 128, 133; 'Confidential Paper on Swinburne's Moral Irregularities', 127, 254, 255

graffiti, flagellant, 263

Grainger, Percy, flagellant tastes, 263

'*Grannie: A Victorian Cameo*' (C.R. Ashbee), 241 n.16

Greenwood, George, M.P., eloquent opponent of flogging, 161, 162

Grenadier Guards, clandestine beating in, 177

Greyfriars School (of Billy Bunter fame), 83

Griffith-Jones, Mr, cross-examines in Stephen Ward case, 261-2

Guardian (newspaper), 63, 89, 97, 141-2, 143n, 189, 191, 192, 262

Guardian (religious weekly), 59, 257, Plate 8

Guide to Eton (anon.), 105-6, 117

guilt and flagellation, 292, 295

Hall, Bradley, on flogging at Manchester Grammar School, 74n

Hammond, Dr, American psychiatrist, 33

Hankey, Frederick, eccentric collector of erotica: meets Richard Burton, 240; on flagellant establishment 'in Regent's Park', 247, 252, 255; described by the Goncourts, 243-4; as Milnes's agent in Paris, 239-40; physical appearance, 239; sends account of flagellant brothels in London to Ashbee, 246-7, 252, 255; acquaintance with Swinburne, 244-5, 253

Hankey, General Sir Frederick, father of the above, 239

Hansard, *Parliamentary Reports*, flogging debates: *Commons*, 61, 78, 80, 97-8, 147, 150, 155-6, 156-7, 158-9, 160, 161, 163, 181, 182, 185, 186, 310; *Lords*, 146-7, 162-3, 182, 299

Hansen, D., German writer on flagellation, 238, 260n

'hardening process' in flagellation, 106-7

Harewood, Reginald, character in Swinburne's *A Year's Letters*, 127

Harrow School, beating excesses at, 71, 147

Hatherton, Lord, flogging magistrate, 159

Hawtrey, Dr, headmaster, and later Provost, of Eton, 101, 103-4, 108, 114, 121-2, 142, 143, 270, 271

Haydon, Denis, headmaster of Court Lees Approved School, 90

Heaton Comprehensive School, Newcastle upon Tyne, moves to introduce tawse for girls, 88

Hemphill, Serjeant, M.P., opposed to flogging, 147, 158-9

Henderson, Philip, biographer of Swinburne, 119

Hendrick, Ives, psychoanalyst, on identification of breasts and buttocks, 286

Henriques, Fernando, sociologist, 218, 232, 259

Hereford, Lord James of, his Youthful Offenders Bill (1900), 146-7

Heswell Reformatory School, Liverpool, flogging scandal at, 77-8

Hill, Lady Anne, recalls her unpleasant Nanny, 52

Hillingdon LEA, beating regulations, 89

'Hints on Flogging ...' see Swinburne

Histoire d'O (Réage), 94

Historia Flagellantium, etc. (Boileau), 6-8, 10

Historia Flagellantium Vindicata (Boileau), 9

History of the Flagellants (Delolme), 10

Hitschmann, Edward, psychoanalyst, on blushing, 287 n.5

Hodgson, Gen. Studholme, friend of Burton and Milnes, 239, 250

Hogarth, William, aware of sexual flagellation, 233, Plate 21

Holland, corporal punishment abolished in schools, 318

Holt, John, child psychologist, 319 n.4

Holy Trinity Church, Stratford on Avon, flagellant misericord, 218

Holywell Street, centre of pornography trade in nineteenth-century London, 266

Home Chat: flagellant article, 59; Plates 6 and 10

homosexual pornography, scarcity of in nineteenth century, 282

Hopley, Mr, brutal headmaster at Eastbourne, 70n

Hopwood, Mr, Q.C., anti-flogging Recorder of Liverpool, 157 n.25

Hornby, Dr, flogging headmaster of Eton, 105, 135

Horsbrugh, Florence, Conservative Minister of Education in 1952, 86

Hothouse Society, The (Lambert), 92-3

Hotten, John Camden, publisher of flagellant erotica, 131, 240-1

Houghton, Lord, see Milnes, Richard Monckton

Houghton Papers, in Trinity College Library, Cambridge, 118n, 124 n.23, 240 n.12, 241 n.16

House Prefect, The (Coke), 82 n.20

Housman, A.E., poet, uninformed on Eton birchings, 127

Howard, Philip, reviews Gladstone diaries, 143n

Howell, Charles Augustus, art dealer, friend of Swinburne and recipient of his flagellant letters, 126, 131

Howson, Rev. J.S. of Liverpool College, misgivings about flogging, 75-6

Hudibras (Butler), 49, 53, 87, 98, 138n

Hughes, Randolph, editor of Swinburne's *Lesbia Brandon*, x, 131

Humane Review, The, 82 n.19, 136

Humanitarian, The, opposed to flogging, 79, 105, 148, 151, 152, 159, 162, 164 n.41, 165, 167, 171-8, 310

Humanitarian League, 46, 60, 79, 137, 151, 157, 159, 162, 173, 174 n.67, 176

Humanity, 157-8, 172 n.62, 174 n.68

Hunter, Miss C., superintendent of East Chapelton Reformatory for Girls, approves of corporal punishment, 81

Huntingdon, Eric, cane-supplier, 62-3

Iceland, corporal punishment abolished in schools, 318

ILEA, see Inner London Education Authority

Ilkeston birching case, 148

impotence and flagellation, 2-5, 12-27, 40, 42-3, 45, 142, 233, 237, 262, 298-308

In and Out the Garbage Pail (Perls), 304

India, judicial whipping in, 154-5, 313

injections, gluteal, and flagellation, 291

Inner London Education Authority (ILEA), 86-7

Ireland, Republic of, corporal punishment in schools today, 319

Irish Times, 319 n.3

Isle of Man, judicial birching on, x, 188, 190, 191-3

Israel, corporal punishment abolished in schools, 318

Italy, no corporal punishment in schools, 318

Jamaica, flogging of women during Morant Bay reprisals, 168-9

James, Mrs, flagellant 'governess', 246

Janus, flagellant magazine, 186 n.83, 266, 289, 299

Jeffreys, Arthur, M.P., favours the judicial birch, 147

Jeffries, Mrs, flagellant 'governess', 258-9

Jenkins, Mrs, flagellant 'governess', 243-4, 250

Jesuits, alleged beating excesses among, 201

Jocelyn, Percy, bishop of Clogher, alleged sodomite, 239 and n.11

John, Brynmor, Minister of State at Home Office, disapproves of judicial birching, 191

Johnson, Hugh, writer, alludes to beatings at Rugby, 94

Jones, Mrs, flagellant 'governess', 237

Jordan, corporal punishment abolished in schools, 318

Joyce, James, aware of sexual flagellation, 270, 280n

Joynes, Rev. James Leigh, Swinburne's tutor at Eton, 122-7, 128-9

judicial flogging: of juveniles, 144-52, 178-9, 181-2, 187-8; of adults, 152-65, 178-9, 187-8; prison flogging, 165-8

Juliette (Sade), 124, 125

Justices of the Peace, see Magistrates

Justine (Sade), 24-7, 123-5, 239, 243, 245

Juvenile Male Offenders Act (1862), 146

Kalton, Graham, on beating in public schools recently, 92

Keate, Dr, flogging headmaster of Eton, 70, 105-6, 111, 141, 143, 183, 214, 299

Keats and Embarrassment (Ricks), 305

Kennedy, Catherine, flogged in Sarah Potter's brothel, 248-9, 250

King-Hamilton, Judge Alan, Q.C., approves of corporal punishment, 188-9

Kingsley, Charles, *Westward Ho!*, 107

Knacker's Act (1786), flogging provisions, 153

Knight, Prof. Wilson, on authorship of *The Rodiad*, 242 n.19

Koss, Stephen, reviews Gladstone diaries, 143n

Krafft-Ebing, Richard von: *Psychopathia Sexualis*, 3, 20, 22, 28, 32-46, 127, 273, 278, 284, 299, 315; on congenital origins of the deviations, 33-4; on fantasy and erection, 42-3; coins word 'masochism', 22, 35; analysis of masochism, 36, 38-43; horror of masturbation, 28, 34; analysis of sadism, 35-8; warnings about beating children, 43-5, 136

Labouchere, Henry, editor of *Truth*, 54

Lafourcade, Georges, Swinburne scholar, 119n, 128, 245 n.28, 255, 256

Lamb, Charles, man of letters, pupil at Christ's Hospital, 116n

Lambercier, Mlle, unwittingly provokes Rousseau's flagellant fixation, 18-21

Lambert, Dr Royston, *The Hothouse Society*, 92-3

Lancet, The, 153-4, 168 n.51, 224-5

Lang, Cecil A., editor of Swinburne *Letters*, 58n, 123 n.22, 130n, 252n, 254

Larceny Act (1861), flogging provisions, 145-6

Last Resort, A? Corporal Punishment in Schools (ed. Newell), 64, 86, 87, 91, 314

Lawrence, A.T., K.C., flogging judge, 160

Lawrence, T.E., of Arabia, passive flagellant, 251

Law Times, opposed to flogging, 159, 166-7

Layng, Henry, *The Rod*, 215-16

Leader and Saturday Analyst, 169-70

LEAs, see Local Education Authorities

Lectionum Antiquarum (Richerius), 3-4

Lee, Arthur, M.P., advocates flogging, 160

Leeds Mercury, correspondence on flogging girls, 164

Lefevre, Shaw, M.P., opposed to flogging, 156

legislation and Bills mentioned (page references given under separate entries): Army Acts (1867, 1881, 1955); Children's Act (1908); Corporal Punishment Bills (1889, 1900, 1977); Corporal Punishment Restriction Bill (1908); Criminal Justice Acts (1948, 1967); Criminal Justice Act, 1948 (Adaptation of Naval Discipline Act) Order, 1949; Criminal Justice Bill (1938); Criminal Justice (Amendment) Bill (1953); Criminal Law Amendment Act (1885); Criminal Law Amendment Act ['White Slave Act'] (1912); Diplomatic Privileges Act (1708); Education Act (1944); Juvenile Male Offenders Act (1862); Knacker's Act (1786); Larceny Act (1861); Malicious Damage Act (1861); Naval Discipline Act (1957); Security from Violence Act ['Garrotters Act'] (1863); Summary Jurisdiction Acts (1879, 1889); Vagrancy Acts (1824, 1898); Youthful Offenders Bill (1900)

Legman, Gershon, on *My Secret Life*, 269n

Leith, Mrs Mary C.J. (née Gordon), Swinburne's cousin, 126, 132, 133, 134

Lenzer, Gertrud, sociologist, on Sacher-Masoch, 279

Lesbia Brandon, see Swinburne

L'Estrange, Rev. A.G., on birching at Eton, 103-4, 269-70, 271

Lewis, John Delaware, on birching at Eton, 103

Life of Algernon Charles Swinburne, The (Gosse), 119, 128, 133

Linton, Ralph, on Marquesans, 301 n.13

Local Education Authorities (LEAs), beating regulations, 85, 86, 89

Lockwood, Colonel, M.P., advocates

flogging, 161

Lombroso, Cesare, criminologist, 33

Lord Byron's Daughter (Knight), 242 n.19

'lower discipline', 6-10, 201-2

Luxembourg, corporal punishment abolished in schools, 318

Lynd, Helen Merrell, *On Shame and the Search for Identity*, 300-1, 302, 305, 308, 312

Lyttelton, Rev. Edward, headmaster of Eton: abolishes birch in Upper School, 136-7, 138; book on sex education, 136

McAllister, Bryan, satirical cartoon on Gladstone bag, 143n

McCrum, Michael, current headmaster of Eton, on beating at the school, xii, 143

Maccurdy, John T., psychologist, on shame, 300n

Mack, John E., biographer of T.E. Lawrence, 251 n.36

McKenna, Reginald, Home Secretary and First Lord of the Admiralty, approves of flogging, 160-1, 171 n.56, 175, 176

MacNeill, Swift, M.P., opposed to flogging, 173

Madame Birchini's Dance, 280

Magistrates as floggers, 150-2, 155, 159, 160, 182, 184, 185

Magnan, Dr J., French psychologist, 33

Magnet, comic, beating in, 82, 83

Maiden Tribute, The (Terrot), 258-9

'Maiden Tribute of Modern Babylon, The' (Stead), ix, 149, 155, 258

Malcolm, Ian, M.P., regrets abolition of Etonian birch, 137

Malicious Damage Act (1861), flogging provisions, 145-6

Manchester Cathedral, flagellant misericord, 218

Manchester Grammar School, flogging at, 74

Man of Property, A (Galsworthy), 252n

Mantegazza, P., psychologist, 33

Marcus, Steven, *The Other Victorians*, x, 30, 233-4, 235, 276, 278-82 *passim*

Marks, Claire, journalist, interviews cane-supplier Huntingdon, 63

Marlborough School, attended by Lord Goddard, 183n

Marlowe, Christopher, poet, to whom flagellant epigram wrongly attributed, 12

Marquesans, of Pacific, and shame, 301 n.13

Martinet, flagellant magazine, 266

Maryhill School for Girls, Glasgow, beating at, 80-1

'Marylebone massage scandal', 259-60

masochism: Krafft-Ebing coins word,

35; his analysis of, 38-43

Mason, C.P., headmaster of Denmark Hill School, Camberwell, on disadvantages of birching, 75

masturbation: Acton on alleged effects of, 31, 136; Acton on masturbation and flagellation, 32; Krafft-Ebing on, 28, 34; Lyttelton on, 136

Matthews, Mr, M.P., makes unexpected point about judicial corporal punishment, 157

Maupassant, Guy de, on Powell and Swinburne at Etretat, 253 n.40

Mauritius, corporal punishment abolished in schools, 318

Medical Life in the Navy (Stables), 170-1

Meibom, Dr Heinrich, correspondence with Bartholinus, 1

Meibom (or Meibomius), Dr Johann Heinrich, *De Flagrorum Usu in Re Venerea*, etc., 1-5, 7-8, 22, 23, 27, 29, 32, 39, 45, 111, 142, 168 n.51, 194, 195, 201, 224, 233, 265, 284, 289, 315

Mélinand, Camille, French writer, on blushing, 300n

Memoirs of a Woman of Pleasure ('*Fanny Hill*') (Cleland), 13-16, 26, 237, 274-5, Plate 4

Memories (Lord Redesdale), 106n, 134 n.41, 142

Memories and Friends (Benson), 123, 129 n.31

Memories of Eton Sixty Years Ago (Ainger), 129 n.31

Memories of Sixty Years (Browning), 113, 123

Mercier, French translator of Meibom, 1

Midhurst, Lady, in Swinburne's *Lesbia Brandon*, 307

Miller, Dr H.C., advocates birch for drunkards, 164

Millingen, Dr John Gideon, on flagellation, 29, 30

Milnes, Richard Monckton, Lord Houghton: arranges meeting between Burton and Hankey, 240; meets Ashbee, 241; author of *The Betuliad*, 240; commonplace books, 118, 125, 126, 134 n.41, 239, 240 n.14, 242 n.20; on excesses of fagging system, 118; figures in Goncourt diaries as flagellant, 243-4, 250; sends flagellant advertisement to Swinburne, 58; relationship with Hankey, 239-40; on Gen. Studholme Hodgson, 239; lends *Justine* to Swinburne, 27, 123; disagrees with Swinburne about the intelligence of *Justine*, 124 n.25; probable authorship of *The Rodiad*, 124, 149, 240-2, 250; first meeting with Swinburne, 245; Swinburne's letters to, 99, 126, 130, 150-1, 253, 323 n.4; possible client of Sarah

Potter, flagellant 'governess', 250

Milton, John, poet, reference to in Swinburne letter, 124

Milvain, A.T., M.P., advocates judicial flogging, 156

Misalliance (Shaw), 107, 143, 164 n.40

misericords, flagellant, 217-18

Miss Coote's Confession, 267, 268

Mitchell, Mrs, flagellant 'governess', 246

Mitford, Algernon Bertram, Swinburne's cousin, see Redesdale

Modern Sexuality (Henriques), 218, 232, 259

Moll, Dr Albert, German psychiatrist, 33; on flagellation, 44n, 46, 59, 289-90

Montucci, H., see Demogeot, J.

'Monty Python's Flying Circus', flagellant allusion in, 262-3

Moon's a Balloon, The (Niven), 95

Moore, Sir T., M.P., advocates corporal punishment, 60

Morant Bay, Jamaica, riots and reprisals, 168-9

Morgan, J. Lloyd, K.C., M.P., abortive anti-flogging Bill, 160

Morning Post, pro-flogging newspaper, 111-12, 152, 173 n.65, 177

Morocco, prison flogging in, 166

Morris, Desmond, zoologist: on breasts as imitation buttocks, 286; rump-presentation theory of sexual flagellation, 296-8, 305

Morton, Honnor, opposed to flogging, 82

Moss, Rev. H.W., flogging headmaster of Shrewsbury School, 72-3

mother figure in flagellant fantasy, 281, 295

My Early Life (Churchill), 68

My Life: Sixty Years' Recollections of Bohemian London (Sims), 254

My Secret Life, 269

Mysteries of Flagellation or, a History of the Secret Ceremonies of the Society of Flagellants, etc., 250-1

Naked Ape, The (Morris), 286, 296-8

Napoleon III, commissions reports on foreign education, 65

National Association of Headmasters, statement on beating, 88

National Association of Schoolmasters (London Branch), opposed to abolition of corporal punishment in primary schools, 87

National Committee to Abolish Corporal Punishment in Schools (U.S.A.), 319 n.4

National Foundation for Educational Research (N.F.E.R.), 85-6, 88

National Society for Prevention of Cruelty to Children, favours judicial birching in 1900, 147 n.6

National Society for the Retention of

Corporal Punishment (see also Wildman, Eric), 60-1, 187

Nature and Human Nature (Comfort), 297 n.9

Naval and Military Record, opposed to flogging, 174

Naval Discipline Act (1957), no flogging provisions, 178

Naval Historical Library, Earl's Court, London, 177 n.74

Naval Information (Covey-Crump), 177 n.74

Naval Prisons, flogging in, 177-8

Navy, flogging in, 50-1, 74, 169-76, 177-8, 298

Nears, Colin, reviews book on Percy Grainger, 263

Nesterus, Johann Matthias, letter on flagellation, 5-6

Nevill, Ralph, on birching at Eton, 101, 104n

Newell, Peter, editor of *A Last Resort?*, 64, 85, 87, 91, 314

News of the World, 263

New Statesman, 62, 189, 310

'Newsom Report' (*Report of the Public Schools Commission*, 1968), opposed to school beating, 93-4

New Zealand, corporal punishment in schools today, 319

N.F.E.R. (National Foundation for Educational Research), 85-6, 88

Nichol, John, friend of Swinburne, 256

Nicolson, Harold, on Swinburne, 308

Niven, David, on beating at Stowe, 95

Norway, corporal punishment abolished in schools, 318

Notes and Queries, flagellant communications, 10, 22, 50, 59, 80n, 215-18, 240

Nouvelle Justine, La, ou les Malheurs de la vertu, 123 n.22

Noyeau, Mrs, flagellant 'governess', 237

Nunberg, Hermann, psychoanalyst, on blushing and castration, 303 n.16

Observer, The, 88, 94-5, 293

O'Connor, T.P., M.P., opposed to flogging, 147

Offences Against the Person Act (1861), flogging provisions, 145-6

Olivier, Sir Laurence, on sadistic component in flogging, epigraph, 94-5

Onomastikon Medicinae (Brunfels), 2

On Shame and the Search for Identity (Lynd), 300-1, 302, 305, 308, 312

oral aggression: and flagellation, 285-8; and blushing, 286-8

Orwell, George: on comics, 83; at Eton, 137-9; humiliated at prep school, 69-70, 94

Other Victorians, The (Marcus), x, 30, 233-

4, 235, 276, 278-82

Oxford English Dictionary, 4, 35

Oxfordshire County Council, recommends restoration of caning (1975), 87, 189

Page, Graham, M.P., advocates return to judicial birching (1977), 190-1

Pall Mall Budget, 149

Pall Mall Gazette, 148, 149, 150, 258

Paradise Lost (Milton), 124

parental beating, Victorian, 48-58; more recent, 60-4

Paris, Le, quotes English flagellant advertisements, 59n

Parfit, Derek (ed.), *Eton Microcosm*, 141

Parker, Derek, reviews Gladstone diaries, 143n

Partridge, G.S., of Giggleswick School, approves of corporal punishment, 183-4

Pathologie des émotions, La (Féré), 46

Paton, Mr, flogging headmaster of Manchester Grammar School, 74

Pearl, The, Victorian pornographic magazine, 255 n.46, 265, 268, 306, 321

Pearsall, Ronald, social historian, x, 52, 54, 71, 72, 112, 142, 224, 267, 320

Pearse, Sophia, flagellant 'governess', 260

Péladan, Josephin Aimé, on the English Vice, ix

Penthouse, flagellant communications, 232

Perls, Fritz, Gestalt psychotherapist, on blushing, erection and shame, 304

Petronius Arbiter, on urtication, 2

Pfeiffer, Prof., German writer on flagellation, 44n

Philippines, the, corporal punishment abolished in schools, 318

Pickersgill, Mr, M.P., opposed to flogging, 156-7

Pico della Mirandola, on flagellation, 2-3, 5, 7, 23

Picture Post, flogging debate in, 183-4

Piers and Singer, American psychiatrists, on etymology of word *shame*, 301

Pinches, C.H., headmaster of Clarendon House College, on disadvantages of birching, 76

'Plowden Report' (*Children and their Primary Schools*), 86

Poema de Myo Cid, mediaeval Spanish epic, beating scene in, 6

Poems and Ballads, see Swinburne

Poland, corporal punishment abolished in schools, 318

Pollard, R.S.W., anti-flogging letter to *Picture Post*, 184

Pope-Hennessy, James, biography of Richard Monckton Milnes, 241, 245

pornography, flagellant, 233-6, 265-83

Portia Trust, 88 n.25

Portland, Duke of, advocates flogging, 152

Portugal, corporal punishment abolished in schools, 318

Post Office Directory, 254, 255

Potter, Sarah, alias Stewart or Stuart, flagellant 'governess', 238, 241, 247-51

Powell, George, Old Etonian friend of Swinburne: at Chaumière Dolmancé, 253; fails to procure large photograph of Eton block for Swinburne, 131; procures birch and photo of block for Swinburne, 130; Swinburne's letters to him about birching and Eton block, etc., 122, 130, 245, 253, 254, 256

Pradier, James, his erotic sculpture owned by Hankey, 245

Praz, Mario, *The Romantic Agony*, ix, x, 244, 253 n.40

Preparatory Schools, beating in, in nineteenth century, 67-70; more recently, 91-2, 96-7

Pre-Raphaelite Tragedy: The Story of Charles Augustus Howell (Angeli), 131

Prescott, E. Livingston, on flogging in Navy, 176-7

Price, Bonamy, on monitorial system at Rugby, 115

Priestley, J.B., *Victoria's Heyday*, 218

Prince of our Disorders, A: The Life of T.E. Lawrence (Mack), 251 n.36

Pringle, H., Jamaican stipendiary magistrate, on Morant Bay floggings, 169

prisons, flogging in, 165-8

Prison Offences Act (1898), flogging provisions, 166

Private Case (of British Library), 1, 61n, 234-5, 235 n.4

Private Case – Public Scandal (Fryer), 30 n.35, 61n, 235 n.4, 236 n.7, 276-7

Progrès médical, Le, regrets British censorship of French medical books, 46n

prostitution, flagellant, 2-3, 12-17, 23, 29, 32, 45n, 143n, 158, 163-4, 233-64

Prostitution in London, with a Comparative View of that of Paris and New York (Ryan), 29, 30, 45, 238-9, 266

Proverbs, see Bible

Prussia: beating of schoolchildren in, 44n; laws on beating, 44n

Pryce, Mrs, flagellant 'governess', 237

psychoanalysts, British, on disadvantages of flogging, 180

Psychopathia Sexualis, see Krafft-Ebing

Public Opinion, flagellant letters, 227-9

Public and Preparatory Schools Year Book, 67 n.9

Public Schools, beating at, in nineteenth century, 70-4; more recently, 74, 91-7
Public Schools, The: A Factual Survey of Headmasters' Conference Schools (Kalton), 92
Pudique Albion, La: Les Nuits de Londres (France), 231
Punch, 58, 105, 224, Plate 7

Quatar, corporal punishment abolished in schools, 318
Queen, The, flagellant correspondence column, 50, 209-15, 217

Rambler's, The, flagellant contributions, 195-6, 203
Rare Verities: The Cabinet of Venus Unlocked, 5
Raymond, John, reviews Gladstone diaries, 143n
Reade, Rolf S. [pseudonym of Alfred Rose], *Registrum Librorum Eroticorum*, 234 n.3
Recollections of Eton ('An Etonian'), 104-5
Reddie, James Campbell, collector and writer of erotica, 241 n.17
Redesdale, Lord (Algernon Bertram Mitford), Swinburne's cousin, 106n, 134-5 and notes, 142
Reformatory and Industrial Schools, beating at: in boys', 76-9; in girls', 80-2
Registrum Librorum Eroticorum (Rose), 234 n.3
Rehoboam, Solomon's son, not improved by rod, 50
Reik, Theodor, psychoanalyst, on masochism, 14, 272n, 285 n.2
Reminiscences of Eton (Keate's Time) (Wilkinson), 105n
Report of the Commissioners Appointed by Her Majesty to inquire into the Education given in England, etc. ['The Schools Inquiry Commission Report'] (1868-9), 67, 74-6, 79-80, 203
Report of the Departmental Committee on Corporal Punishment ['The Cadogan Report'] (1938), 144, 153, 157, 178-81, 182-7, 191
Report of Her Majesty's Commissioners appointed to inquire into the Revenues and Management of Certain Colleges, etc. ['The Clarendon Report'] (1864), 67, 74; on Eton, 99-101, 113-15, 135
Report of the Public Schools Commission ['The Newsom Report'] (1968), opposed to school beating, 93-4
Report ... on Reformatory and Industrial Schools (1896), 67, 76-9, 80-2
Reports of the Commissioners of Prisons, 166-8
Réveil, Le, quotes flagellant letters from *Town Talk*, 231

Reynold's Newspaper, 158, 177 n.72, 249n, 261
Rhodiginus, see Richerius
Richards, Judge Bertrand, on nature's purposes for the buttocks, 189, 310
Richards, Frank, author of school stories, 83
Richards, James Brinsley, on birching at Eton, 101-2, 106, 107, 313
Richards, T.F., M.P., opposed to flogging, 175
Richerius or Rhodiginus, Ludovicus Coelius, on flagellation, 3-4, 5, 23
Ricketts, Major, Parisian acquaintance of Ashbee, 241 n.16
Ricks, Christopher, on blushing in nineteenth century, 305
Ridding, Dr, flogging headmaster of Winchester, 72
Ridley, Sir Matthew White, M.P., swings to anti-flogging view, 159
Riezler, Kurt, sociologist, on shame, 298-9
Rise and Fall of the British Nanny, The (Gathorne-Hardy), x-xi, 52-3, 290-1, 293
ritual, the flagellant, see ceremony
Robert, Paul, *Dictionnaire alphabétique et analogique de la langue française*, 35 n.38
Robertson, Col. P.F., believes in flogging children, 60
Rock, The, religious journal, 174 n.67
rod, as symbol of phallus, 296-7
Rod, The (Layng), 215-16
Rodiad, The (ascribed to Monckton Milnes), 124, 149, 240-2, 250
Rodin, sadistic surgeon in Sade's *Justine*, 26, 123, 124, 269
Roger Fry: A Biography (Woolf), 68-9, 175
Romance of Chastisement, The, 267, 279-80
Romance of Lust, The, 273-4, 279, 280
Romantic Agony, The (Praz), ix, x, 244, 253 n.40
Rombeau, Rodin's assistant in *Justine*, 242 n.18
Rose, Alfred, *Registrum Librorum Eroticorum*, 234 n.3
Rossetti, William, letter from Swinburne, 126
Rousseau, Jean-Jacques: *Confessions*, 17-22, 26, 27, 29, 32, 40-1, 42, 45, 47, 142, 273, 279, 288, 316-17; *Emile, ou l'Education*, 21, 23
Royal Patriotic Asylum, Wandsworth, girls beaten at, 80
Rugby School, beating at, 65, 94, 115, 253
rump-presentation of primates and flagellation, 296-8
Russia: corporal punishment abolished in schools, 318; judicial flogging abolished, 156; prison flogging, 166
Ryan, Dr Michael, warns against

flagellation, 29, 30, 45, 238-9, 266

Sacher-Masoch, Leopold von: breast fixation, 279; gives name to 'masochism', 35
Sade, Donatien Alphonse, Marquis de, 22, 36, 239, 245, 253; *Justine*, 24-7, 123-5, 239, 243, 245; *Juliette*, 124, 125
Sadger, J., psychoanalyst, on flogging in *Uncle Tom's Cabin*, 38n; on identification of breasts and buttocks, 286, 291
sadism: history of word, 35; Krafft-Ebing's analysis of, 35-8
Sadismus und Masochismus (Eulenburg), 238
St Cyprian's preparatory school, Eastbourne, Orwell and Connolly attend, 69-70
St George's preparatory school, Ascot, birching at, 68-9
St John, Rev. E., flogging warden of Working Boys Home, Greyfriars Road, 77
St John's Wood, flagellant brothels, 252-5, 257, 260, 276
Saint John's Wood (Eyre), 252n, 254 n.42
Salt, Henry, Old Etonian writer, leading opponent of flogging, 49, 64, 105, 129 n.31, 135, 137, 138n, 149, 166, 168 n.53, 173, 174 n.67, 177 n.71, 313
Sandwith, Humphrey, on Morant Bay reprisals, 168 n.54
Satyricon (Petronius), on urtication, 2
Saturday Review, 72, 157 n.25, 172 nn.63 and 64, 223-4
schizoid component in flagellant fantasy, 310-11
Schmideberg, Melitta, psychoanalyst, on anal elements in sexual flagellation, 292, 293
Schools Inquiry Commission, see *Report of the Commissioners Appointed by Her Majesty to inquire into the Education given in England*, etc.
Schrenck-Notzing, German psychiatrist, 33, 35
Schurig, Martin, on sexual flagellation, 9-10
Scotland, judicial flogging of adults abolished (1862), 153, 157, 166
'Sealskin', flagellant client of Sarah Potter, 248, 250
Security from Violence Act ['The Garrotters Act'] (1863), 153-4, 156, 160, 182
Selected Letters of James Joyce, 280n
Selwin-Ibbetson, Sir H., M.P., advocates flogging, 155
Serrurier, Dr Jean-Baptiste, on flagellation, 28
Seven Years at Eton (Richards), 101-2, 106, 107, 313

Sexual Deviation (Storr), 278, 289
Sexual Life of the Child (Moll), 46
Seyton, Herbert, much flogged character in Swinburne's *Lesbia Brandon*, 125, 306-7
Shadwell, Thomas, *The Virtuoso*, 12-13, 14, 233, 262
shame and flagellation (see also blushing), 298-309
Sharpe, Montagu, flogging magistrate and ornithologist, 159-60
Shaw, George Bernard: on British flagellomania in general, 107, 143, 157-8, 163-4, 178, 259; on naval flogging in particular, 50-1, 172, 173
Sheffield Blue-Coat Charity School, 78
Sherborne Abbey, flagellant misericord, 218
Shrewsbury School, flogging at, 72-3
Sim, Robert, dies after Army flogging, 168
Simcox, Howard, Manx supporter of judicial birching, 192
Simpson, Prof., on Court Lees photographs, 91
Sims, George R., on John Thomson, 254
Sinibaldi, Giovanni, on sexual flagellation, 5
Sisters, The, see Swinburne
Skeffington, Owen Sheehy, Irish senator, opposed to corporal punishment, 319 n.3
Sleigh, Mr, prosecutes in Sarah Potter case, 249
Smith, Alice, engaged at Sarah Potter's brothel, 249, 250
Smith, Mrs Walter, the girl-flogger of Clifton, 54-8, 59n, 63, 204, 205, 260, 267, 273
Sneyd-Kynnersley, Rev. Herbert, sadistic headmaster of St George's prep school, Ascot, 68-9, 78, 175
Society, flagellant communications, 230-2, 259, 260, 268
Society for the Suppression of Juvenile Prostitution (London), 239
Society of Teachers Opposed to Physical Punishment (STOPP), address 86, 86-9, 91, 311, 314, 329
Solomon, his beating injunctions, 48-9, 50, 51, 53, 60, 100
Solomon, Simeon, painter, friend of Swinburne, 130-1
South Africa, corporal punishment in schools today, 319
South Wales Daily News, 151
Spain, alleged use of enemas as punishment, 292
Spank, flagellant magazine, 266
Spanking, flagellant magazine, 266
'Spare the rod and spoil the child' (*Hudibras*), 49, 53, 87, 98

Speculator Morum, _Bibliotheca Arcana_, 10 n.12
Spencer, Herbert, philosopher, moves to St John's Wood, 252n
Spermatologia (Schurig), 9-10
Stables, William, on naval flogging, 170-1
Standard, The, 59n, 118
Star, The, correspondent suggests Universal Whipping Bill, 164-5
Stead, W.T., editor of _Pall Mall Gazette_, ix, 149, 155, 258
Stewart, Gershom, M.P., advocates flogging, 161
Stewart, Sarah, see Potter
Sting, flagellant magazine, 266, 268
Stock und Peitsche in XIX Jahrhundert (Hansen), 238
STOPP, see Society of Teachers Opposed to Physical Punishment
Storr, Dr Anthony, psychoanalyst, 68, 278, 289, 310
Stowe, Harriet Beecher, _Uncle Tom's Cabin_, 38, 57
Student's Reading List (published by STOPP), 329
Studies in the Psychology of Sex (Ellis), 5-6
Sublime of Flagellation, The, 280
'Such, Such were the Joys' (Orwell), 70
Summary Jurisdiction Act (1879), flogging provisions, 146
Summary Jurisdiction Act (1889), flogging provisions, 146
Sunday Express, 189
Sunday Times, 94, 143n, 263
suppositories and flagellation (see also anal eroticism), 291
Survey of Rewards and Punishments in Schools (National Foundation for Educational Research), 85-6
Swaziland, corporal punishment in schools today, 319
Sweden, corporal punishment abolished in schools, 318
Swetenham, Mr, M.P., advocates flogging, 155
Swinburne (Nicolson), 308
Swinburne: A Critical Biography (Fuller), 119, 128-9, 130n, 134 n.40, 242 n.19, 253
Swinburne: The Portrait of a Poet (Henderson), 119, 245 n.27
Swinburne, Algernon Charles: on look out for flagellant advertisements, 58; meets Richard Burton, 245; hatred of Christianity, 308-9; at Eton, 99, 100, 102, 114, 119-35; disgust with Gen. Eyre, 169; his pre-Eton tutor, Rev. Fenwick, 119, 133-4; relationship with his cousin Mary Gordon, 126, 132, 134; meets Fred Hankey, 244-5, 246; Joynes, his tutor at Eton, 122-9; reads _Justine_, 27, 123-4; first meeting

with Monckton Milnes, 245; Mitford, Algernon Bertram, Lord Redesdale, his cousin, 134-5, 134 n.41; stays with Powell at Etretat, 253; at Putney, 255; frequents flagellant brothel in St John's Wood, 252-5; use of word 'sadique', 35; describes experience of shame in relation to flagellation, 305-9; enjoys Wilberforce birching scandal, 126, 150-1. _Individual works_: 'Anactoria', 256; _Atalanta_, 308-9; 'Charlie Collingwood's Flogging', 320-4; 'Eton: An Ode', 132; 'Eton: Another Ode', 132; _The Flogging-Block_, 119-22, 125 n.26, 129, 270n, 271, 306, 320 n.2; 'Frank Fane – A Ballad', 324-8, 324n; 'Hints on Flogging ...', 275-6, 279; _Lesbia Brandon_, x, 125, 133, 135, 306-7; _Letters_ (edited by Lang), 58n, 122, 123, 126, 127, 130, 131, 169, 242, 245, 253, 254, 256; _Poems and Ballads_, 308-9; _The Sisters_, 125; _The Whippingham Papers_, 121, 271, 272, 275, 275-6; _A Year's Letters_, 127, 133, 135, 256
Swinburne, Admiral Charles Henry, the poet's father, 133
Switzerland, corporal punishment abolished in schools, 318

Talboys, Mrs Mervyn, flagellant aristocrat in Joyce's _Ulysses_, 270n
Tarnowsky, B., psychologist, 33
Tartivel, Dr A., on flagellation, 28, 39
Taylor, Peter, M.P., opposed to flogging, 155
Taxil, Leo, French writer on prostitution, 33, 40
teachers, in favour of corporal punishment today, 85-8
Teare, Dr, on Court Lees photographs, 91
Templewood, Lord, opposed to flogging, 182, 183
Thiers, Jean-Baptiste, on ecclesiastical flagellation, 8-10, 201
Thomas, Morgan, protests against Eton birching, 107-12
Thompson, Agnes, engaged in Sarah Potter's flagellant brothel, 247-8, 250
Thomson, D.C. and Co., publishers of children's comics, 83
Thomson, John, friend of Swinburne and perhaps involved in flagellant brothel, 254, 255
Thorne, Rev. G.E., advocates birch for Mormons, 164
Three Essays on the Theory of Sexuality, see Freud
tight-lacing, 218-19
Times, The, 50, 54, 58, 59n, 71, 72, 73-4, 88 n.24, 95, 107, 110, 111, 115, 143n, 144, 171 n.58, 173-4, 184, 185, 187,

190, 190-1, 192, 212, 247-9, 260, 261-2, 310
Times Literary Supplement, 143n
toilet training and flagellation, see anal eroticism
Tom Brown's Schooldays (Hughes), 65
Topper, children's comic, spanking in, 83
Town Talk, flagellant communications in, 230-1, 252n, 257-8, 260, 268, 299
Toxtell Park Reformatory for Girls, Liverpool, beating at, 81
Training of the Young in the Laws of Sex (Lyttelton), 136
Traité du fouet, see *Aphrodisiaque externe*, etc. (Doppet)
Treason Act (1842), flogging provisions, 153, 208
Trevor-Roper, Hugh, historian, 69
Trimmer, Mrs, flagellant in *Madam Birchini's Dance*, 280
Trinidad and Tobago, corporal punishment in schools today, 319
Trounce, Alderman W.J., magistrate, 151
Trusty in Fight; or, The Vicar's Boys (Leith), 134 n.40
Truth, Labouchere's journal, 54-8
Tullibardine, Marquess of, approves of flogging, 78, 161
Turkey, prison flogging in, 166
Turner, E.J., Visiting Justice, approves of flogging, 152
Tweedie, Jill, journalist, disapproves of beating, 97
Tynwald, Manx Parliament, see Isle of Man

'Ubi stimulus ibi affluxus' explanation of sexual flagellation, 4, 9-10, 27
Ulysses (Joyce), flagellant allusion in, 270
Uncle Tom's Cabin (Stowe), 38, 57, 58
Undergrowth of Literature, The (Freeman), 266
United States of America: Havelock Ellis on prevalence of flagellant pornography, 45n; current flagellant pornography, 268; 'indecent whipping' in Massachusetts, 80n; corporal punishment in schools today, 319
urtication, alleged medical virtues of, 2
U.S.S.R.: corporal punishment abolished in schools, 318; judicial flogging abolished, 156; prison flogging, 166

Vagrancy Act (1824), flogging clauses, 153, 157, 159, 178
Vagrancy Act (1898), flogging provisions, 157, 159, 160, 259
Vanity Fair, 123, 136, Plate 14
Vaughan, Dr Charles, headmaster of Harrow School, 71, 72

Vence, bawdy misericord at, 218
Venus School Mistress; or, Birchin Sports, 236-9
Vert de Vert's Eton Days (L'Estrange), 103-4, 269-70, 271
Vertu suprême, La (Péladan), ix
Vibak, Mrs Betteena, flagellant madame, 263
Victoria, Queen, 198, 208
Victoria's Heyday (Priestley), 218n
Vine, Rev. M.G., flogging headmaster of the Farm School, Redhill, 76-7
Virey, Dr Jules, on flagellation, 27, 28, 29, 39
Virtuoso, The (Shadwell), 12-13, 14, 233, 262
Vizetelly, Ernest, advocates birch for suffragettes, 164
Voltaire, disapproves of beating children, 17
voyeurism, flagellation and blushing, 120-1, 270-1, 287, 295, 302-3

Walker, Dr Roger, on sadism in mediaeval epic, 6
Ward, Dr Stephen, flagellant revelation during trial of, x, 261-2
Warre, Rev. Edmond, headmaster of Eton, 128, 135-6
Waterhouse, Captain, M.P., makes novel flogging suggestion, 186
Watts-Dunton, Theodore, Swinburne's friend and protector, 255
Way of the World, The (Congreve), on shame, 298
Wellcome Medical Library, London, editions of Meibom, 1n
Westminster Abbey, flagellant misericord, 218
Westminster School, flogging at, 12, 13
Westward Ho! (Kingsley), 107
Whalley Church, Lancs., flagellant misericord, 218
Wharton, Lloyd, M.P., abortive flogging Bill, 158-9
Whipping Act (1862), 153
Whippingham, Isle of Wight, 121n, 326n
Whippingham Papers, The, see Swinburne
White, John Frederick, dies after Army flogging, 168
'White Slave Act' (1912), 151, 160-4, 261
Wilberforce, R.G., magistrate, administers illegal birching, 126, 150-1
Wildman, Eric, caning campaign (see also National Society for Retention of Corporal Punishment), 60-1, 90, 187
Wilkes, Mr and Mrs Vaughan, proprietors of St Cyprians preparatory school, Eastbourne, 70
Wilkinson, Rev. C. Allix, on Dr Keate of Eton, 105n
Williams, Carvell, M.P., opposed to

flogging, 147

Williams, Llewellyn, M.P. and magistrate, opposed to flogging, 163

Wilmot, Emma, engaged in Sarah Potter's flagellant brothel, 249n

Wilson, Erasmus, surgeon, on Army flogging, 168 n.50

Wilson, F.A.C., on Swinburne and Mary Gordon, 134 n.40

Wilson, H.W., naval advocate of flogging, 173 n.64

Wilson, Mary, reputed flagellant 'governess' and writer, 236 n.7

Wimbledon, petitions to restore judicial flogging, 185

Winchester School, flogging at, 12, 72, 116

Winnicott, D.W., psychoanalyst, on child's aggression at the breast, 285-6

Winston S. Churchill: Youth 1874-1900 (Randolph Churchill), 68 n.10

Winterton, Earl, regrets abolition of Etonian birch, 137

Winterton, Nicholas, M.P., expresses belief in benefits of caning, 190

Wood, Edward, M.P., deterred from misbehaviour by beating, 310

Woolf, Virginia, *Roger Fry: A Biography*, 68-9, 175

Wordsworth, Bishop, on flogging at Winchester, 72

workhouses, flogging in, 79

World, The, on cruelty of clergymen, 72-3

Worm in the Bud, The (Pearsall), x, 52, 54, 71, 72, 112, 142, 224, 267

Worst House at Sherborough, The (Coke), 82 n.20

Wright, Mr, involved in irregular beating at Court Lees Approved School, 90

'Y', on beating at prep and public school, 95-7, 311-12

Year's Letters, A, see Swinburne

York, Duke of, reduces severity of Army flogging, 168

Youthful Offenders Bill (1900), 146-7

Zamora Cathedral, misericords, 218